MW01169592

# SCHOOL

# Sucks!

Educational
PSYCHOLOGY

Critical Pedagogical Perspectives

Greg S. Goodman, *General Editor*

Vol. 20

The Educational Psychology series is part of the Peter Lang Education list.
Every volume is peer reviewed and meets
the highest quality standards for content and production.

PETER LANG
New York • Washington, D.C./Baltimore • Bern
Frankfurt • Berlin • Brussels • Vienna • Oxford

# SCHOOL

# SUCKS!

## Arguments for Alternative Education

EDITED BY
ROCHELLE BROCK & GREG S. GOODMAN

PETER LANG
New York • Washington, D.C./Baltimore • Bern
Frankfurt • Berlin • Brussels • Vienna • Oxford

**Library of Congress Cataloging-in-Publication Data**

Brock, Rochelle.
School sucks!: arguments for alternative education / Rochelle Brock, Greg Goodman.
p. cm. — (Educational psychology; vol. 20)
Includes bibliographical references and index.
1. Education, Urban—United States. I. Goodman, Greg S. II. Title.
LC5131.B75 370.9173'2—dc23 2012042556
ISBN 978-1-4331-1704-6 (hardcover)
ISBN 978-1-4331-1705-3 (paperback)
ISBN 978-1-4539-0969-0 (e-book)
ISSN 1943-8109

Bibliographic information published by **Die Deutsche Nationalbibliothek.**
**Die Deutsche Nationalbibliothek** lists this publication in the "Deutsche Nationalbibliografie"; detailed bibliographic data is available on the Internet at http://dnb.d-nb.de/.

The paper in this book meets the guidelines for permanence and durability of the Committee on Production Guidelines for Book Longevity of the Council of Library Resources.


29 Broadway, 18th floor, New York, NY 10006
www.peterlang.com



Printed in the United States of America

I dedicate this work to my close friend and mentor,
Karen T. Carey. Karen's heartfelt generosity is an example to all
that giving of one's self is the quintessence of being human.
I cannot overstate my appreciation for all that she has taught me.
— Greg S. Goodman

This book is dedicated to my students in the
Urban Teachers Education Program.
You are the hope for students and for the change
we need to see in schools!
— Rochelle Brock

"When I think back on all the crap I learned in high school,
it's a wonder I can think at all!"
— Paul Simon

# CONTENTS

# Poetry

by Howard P. Hanson

# Acknowledgments

This book was created from an amalgam of social justice literature that has comprised two of Peter Lang Publishing's educational series: Educational Psychology: Critical Pedagogical Perspectives and Black Studies and Critical Thinking. *School Sucks!* showcases the contributions of a few of the many talented and polymath contributors to these two series. These writers dare to challenge the neo-liberal commodification discourse that dominates public education. We also thank the teachers who resist selling out to the myth of value-added education and who love the work and cherish the chance to keep hope alive.

We also thank our colleagues and friends who have supported our work. They have given us the chance to continue our sedulous pursuit of critical pedagogy and its promise of a socially just world. Peter Lang Publishing's managing editor, Chris Myers and this book's production editor, Bernadette Shade have been supportive throughout the book's process. Our mentor, Shirley Steinberg, has provided us with a vision of what collaborative projects can accomplish: a whole greater than the individual pieces. Finally, our models of social justice: Frederick Douglass, Paulo Freire, and Mary McLeod Bethune, have taught us that courage and conviction can never be set aside in our endless fight for the rights and dignity of all of our children.

In order of their appearance, we would like to thank Peter Lang Publishing for permission to reprint the following chapters:

Chapters one, two and three were previously published in Knaus, Christopher. (2011). *Shut up and Listen.* New York: Peter Lang Publishing.

Chapter four was previously published in Goodman, Greg S. (2007). *Reducing Hate Crimes and Violence Among American Youth*. New York: Peter Lang Publishing.

Chapter five was previously published as Alfred W. DeFreece Jr Where Do We Go from…Where? Identifying the Ideological Bases of Low-Income, Urban Black Adolescents' Views on Racism in *Reading African American Experiences in the Obama Era: Theory Advocacy Activism,* (eds.) Ebony Elizabeth Thomas & Shanesha R.F. Brooks-Tatum. New York: Peter Lang Publishing.

Chapter six was previously published in Lewis, Chance W., Chambers, Terah V., & Butler, Bettie R. *African American Students in Urban Schools.* (2011). New York: Peter Lang Publishing.

Chapters seven and eight were previously published in Beachum, F. D. & McCray, C. R. (2011). *Cultural Collision and Collusion: Reflections on Hip-Hop, Culture, and Schools*. New York: Peter Lang Publishing.

Chapter nine was previously published by Mirón, Luis F. How Do We Locate Resistance in Urban Schools? in Steinberg, S. R. (ed.) (2010) *19 Urban Questions: Teaching in the City*. New York: Peter Lang Publishing

Chapter ten was previously published by Greg S. Goodman & Adriel A. Hilton titled Urban Dropouts: Why Persist? in Steinberg, S. R. (ed.) (2010) *19 Urban Questions: Teaching in the City*. New York: Peter Lang Publishing.

Chapter eleven was previously published by Fuhrman, Susan. Urban Education Challenges: Is Reform the Answer? in Diana T. Slaughter-Defoe. (ed.) (2011). *Messages for Educational Leadership.* New York: Peter Lang Publishing.

Chapter twelve was previously published by Rochelle Brock. What Does Good Urban Teaching Look Like? in Steinberg, S. R. (ed.) (2010) *19 Urban Questions: Teaching in the City.* New York: Peter Lang Publishing.

Chapter thirteen was previously published in Sleeter, Christine. *Professional Development for Culturally Responsive and Relationship-Based Pedagogy* (2011). New York: Peter Lang Publishing.

Chapter fourteen was previously published by Thomas, Ebony Elizabeth. The Next Chapter of Our Story: Rethinking African American Metanarratives in Schooling and Society in Ebony Elizabeth Thomas & Shanesha R.F. Brooks-Tatum (eds.) *Reading African American Experiences in the Obama Era: Theory Advocacy Activism* (2012). New York: Peter Lang Publishing.

Chapter fifteen was previously published by Julia Ellis, Susan Fitzsimmons, and Jan Small-McGinley. Encouraging the Discouraged: Student's Views for Elementary Classrooms in Goodman, G.S. (ed.) (2010). *Educational Psychology Reader: The Art and Science of How People Learn.* New York: Peter Lang Publishing.

Chapter sixteen was previously published by Jane Bean-Folkes. Schools of Hope: Teaching Literacy in the Obama Era in Ebony Elizabeth Thomas & Shanesha R.F. Brooks-Tatum (eds.) *Reading African American Experiences in the Obama Era: Theory Advocacy Activism* (2012). New York: Peter Lang Publishing.

Chapter seventeen was previously published by Brock, Rochelle. A Pedagogy of Wholeness, *Sista Talk: The Personal and the Pedagogical* (2005). New York: Peter Lang Publishing.

Chapter eighteen was previously published by Larry F. Forthun, Jeffrey W. McCombie, & Caroline Payne. A Comprehensive Evaluation of Life Space Crisis Intervention (LSCI) in Goodman, G.S. (ed.) (2010). *Educational Psychology Reader: The Art and Science of How People Learn.* New York: Peter Lang Publishing.

Chapter nineteen was previously published by Shanesha R.F. Brooks-Tatum. Transformative Educational Spaces: Black Youth and Education in the Twenty-First Century" in Ebony Elizabeth Thomas & Shanesha R.F. Brooks-Tatum (eds.) *Reading African American Experiences in the Obama Era: Theory Advocacy Activism* (2012). New York: Peter Lang Publishing.

Chapter twenty was previously published by Mary Hollowell & Donna Moye. Therapeutic Art, Poetry, and Personal Essay: Old and New Prescriptions in Goodman, G.S. (ed.) (2010). *Educational Psychology Reader: The Art and Science of How People Learn.* New York: Peter Lang Publishing.

We also express our profound gratitude to artist Mark Franchino for his contribution of the cover art. Mark captures the quintessence of a perfidious public school.

# Within My Reach

Between windows forever blinded to the sun
Between fights, kicks, curses and the gauntlets they must run
Live the children I teach
Between doors like blackened teeth in decaying gums
Between pushers, pimps and punks
Let's not forget the ever swaying drunks
Live the children I must somehow reach
Amid scattered, shattered shards of glass
Swimming among predatory sexual sharks
Like listed ships upon the ocean bleak and dark
Are the twisted, broken dreams of the children
I must tend
Piled high like the garbage on these tattered sidewalks
Are the frigid, frozen wills
Of children who have learned to survive without hope,
Without friends
I pray that at least one in ten
Is still within my reach

# School Sucks!

## *Arguments for Change in Urban Education*

Greg S. Goodman & Rochelle Brock

School sucks! This ubiquitous claim is the bane of every teacher's existence. A bold refutation of our existence, essence, and teacher identity, the words cut at our very core. After years of our own schooling, and believing that we can be the harbingers of all the good education can bring, we become teachers. The hope and idealized dreams that we had about education and schools are shattered when we first hear this scorn from our students. Sadly, few of us can deny that these words challenge our teacher identity and leave us to ask ourselves: how valid are these critiques? We wonder: what are our students really saying? What does 'sucks' mean for them?

In today's schools, teacher self-efficacy can be both constructed and shattered within the same day. Period to period and hour to hour, we face a sea of hope, possibility, despair, and apathy. Maintaining our sense of direction and staying on course are ever-present challenges. Every day we need to reinvent ourselves, and each day is different from the last. One of the great values of the job, its diversity of experience, is also one of the biggest challenges. Our energy gets drained with each class. The best teachers know that teaching is a lead's performance, and the show is totally dependent upon our active presence. We are the captains of our classrooms, and most of the leadership must come from within ourselves.

Yet, still, school sucks. Not for everyone, but for far too many. With drop-out rates reaching the high 60-70% in our most challenged communities (Spring, 2008), we cannot ignore that for vast numbers of our students, the disconnection between their lives and the realities of schooling make 'school sucks' the truth. They say this by being late, sleeping in class, ignoring our lectures, retreating to the bathroom, ignoring our invitations to participate, skipping class or school, failing to perform even the simplest tasks, and finally, by leaving. Many students consciously decide they will not learn from us and school is not for them. Fifty ways to escape the classroom. Herbert Kohl (1994) called this phenomenon "refusal to learn." He took this concept from Dr. Martin Luther King, Jr's "creative maladjustment." The system is wrong; therefore, I will adjust to protect myself from a bad situation. Too many teachers compromise the intelligence, creativity, and enthusiasm of their students with pedagogies of standardization and impersonalization.

New? No, this negative assessment of school is not a new phenomenon. Many notable geniuses gave school thumbs down and left for their own, personalized reasons. For example, Nobel Prize winner Rabindranath Tagore (Literature: 1913) wrote that [School] "forcibly snatches children away from a world full of mystery of God's own handiwork, full of the suggestiveness of personality" (learninfreedom.org/Nobel_hates_school.html). He goes on to state that schools depersonalize the individual child and instead attempt to assimilate children into one preconceived identity. Albert Einstein also saw the ways in which schooling attempts to strangle "the holy curiosity of inquiry; for this delicate little plant, aside from stimulation, stands mainly in need of freedom; without this it goes to wreck and ruin without fail" (learninfreedom.org/Nobel_hates_school.html). And finally, Literature laureate (1925) George Bernard Shaw compares schooling to the dehumanization of prisons. He states that

> …there is, on the whole, nothing on earth intended for innocent people so horrible as school. To begin with, it is a prison. But it is in some respects more cruel than a prison. In a prison, for instance, you are not forced to read books written by the wardens, and beaten and otherwise tormented if you cannot remember their utterly unmemorable contents. In prison you are not forced to sit listening to the turnkeys discoursing without charm or interest on subjects that they don't understand and don't care about, and are therefore incapable of making you understand or care about. (learninfreedom.org/Nobel_hates_school.html)

Of course the various quotes from Nobel winners were crafted in the early 1900s, and skeptics may say, "Well, it is different today!" Unfortunately that is not the case. In speaking of their contempt for school, one recent student made the following statement,

> I hate school. I don't mean it's a pain in the ass. I don't mean it's annoying. I mean that if you told me today that if I drove a red-hot nail through my hand and in exchange for that I could have my degree and wouldn't have to go to class anymore, in two seconds that nail would be through my hand. I'm not joking. I'm not being hyperbolic, either. Week in and week out of having to drag myself to an experience I loathe so deeply and so passionately has been one of the biggest psychic drains on me of the last two and a half years. (school-survival.net/articles/school/Man_I_Hate_School.php)

As schoolteachers have been stripped of their creativity and autonomy through draconian policies of standardization and zero tolerance, it is not surprising that some children are equating today's classroom with the institutions such as prison or of slavery. A Frederick Douglass inspired analysis of this parallel by thirteen year old Jada Williams was recently reported by Liz Dwyer (2012):

> In a bold comparative analysis of *The Narrative of the Life of Frederick Douglass*, Jada Williams, a 13-year old eighth grader at School #3 in Rochester, New York, asserted that in her experience, today's education system is a modern-day version of slavery. According to the Frederick Douglass Foundation of New York, the schools' teachers and administrators were so offended by Williams' essay that they began a campaign of harassment—kicking her out of class and trying to suspend her—that ultimately forced her parents to withdraw her from the school. In her essay, which was written for a contest, Williams reflected on what Douglass heard his slave master, Mr. Auld, telling his wife after catching her teaching Douglass how to read. "If you teach that nigger (speaking of myself) how to read, there will be no keeping him," Auld says. "It will forever unfit him to be a slave. He would at once become unmanageable, and of no value to his master."
>
> Williams wrote that overcrowded, poorly managed classrooms prevent real learning from happening and thus produces the same results as Mr. Auld's outright ban. She wrote that her white teachers—the vast majority of Rochester students are black and Hispanic, but very few teachers are people of color—are in a "position of power to dictate what I can, cannot, and will learn, only desiring that I may get bored because of the inconsistency and the mismanagement of the classroom." (Dwyer, p. 4)

According to psychologist Sarah Fitz-Claridge students who experience this complete and unabashed hatred of school should not feel alone. Instead they need to know that their feelings are valid and that although others experience similar reactions "they don't feel entitled to say so, and many can't bear to think about it so they hardly even know how they feel. You are not mad—you don't have a Deep Psychological Problem; and you are not bad for wanting to live your life the way you choose, doing what you think right—that is what everyone should be doing. You are not the problem: coercion is the problem. Being forced to go to school is the problem. (school-survival.net/articles/school/Who_wouldn't_be school_phobic.php).

As powerful as this critique can be, these words too often face thick walls of denial. The defenses of the school machine can be unyielding. The dissenter's voices are discounted as singular, rude, uninformed, and inaccurate. When students are constructed as the "trouble" and they leave or are forced out of the door, what's left to be done? Are the administrators truly happy to see these failures go away and leave the ranks of our schools? Do our teachers and administrators just shrug off our teenagers' rejection of school as reductive, adolescent assessments? Do educators simply fall victim to the immaturity inherent within the adolescent's argument that 'school sucks' and respond as did Nick Nolte in the movie *Teachers*: "Yeah, but what we got (meaning the students) sucks!" Is our only defense denial or a repression of the truth behind this all too common slur of the disaffected? Or could it be true? Should we take this seriously?

We believe our students, both the brightest and the disaffected, are telling their truth when they say 'school sucks.' Students are honestly reporting on their reality and their feelings; the alienation and the pain they experience within their schools and the twenty-first century, business-centered educational system. Clearly, the consequences of these students' conclusions are having a disastrous affect upon their school outcomes, their families' lives, and the communities they inhabit. Our chapter Urban Dropouts—Why Persist? elaborates on the toll in one community, Bridgeport, CT. This city has experienced dropout rates exceeding 50% in its public high schools! Despite interventions proposed by several prominent educational consultants, Bridgeport's culturally mismatched educational praxis still fails to dramatically change the course of its dropout dilemma.

This phenomenon of gross failure is not unusual; it is ubiquitous within historically subordinated and marginalized groups (Beachum & McCray, 2011). The effects are so widespread and schools are so seemingly complicit in the promotion of failure that this process has been given the name: the school to prison pipeline!

Beachum and McCray articulate the issues attending school failure in their brilliant critique of school and culture: *Cultural Collision and Collusion: Reflections on Hip-Hop, Culture, Values, and Schools* (2011). In districts rife with poverty, crime, drug use, and gangs, it is too easy to lay the blame on the victims of this breakdown: the children. "The situation in far too many schools is one of despair, poverty, isolation, and distress" (Obiakor & Beachum, 2005, p. 20). When the teachers and administrators give up and abdicate their agency over the attendant issues of the distressed community, the collapse of the school can be hope's demise. "When the school culture is characterized by value disagreement, lack of communication, and little collegiality among teachers and students, many students view themselves as incapable, incompetent, and worthless" (Beachum & McCray, 2011, p. 38).

Of course, there are very successful districts, too. The Clovis Unified School District in Clovis, CA, touts multiple Blue Ribbon Schools and numerous scholastic and athletic accolades attributing to its stellar reputation. But with NCLB and other state and national bell curve assessments, schooling has become a zero sum game, and with every winner, 'someone has to fail' (Labaree, 2010). For every Clovis, there is a Newark, a Bridgeport, and a Compton to balance the equation. Our point: there are too many losers. Since writing *Alternatives in Education* (Goodman, 1999), 2,000,000 more students have left public school for home schooling. This triples the number from 1999 to include a total of 3,000,000 students removed from public education's ranks. Parents and students who can choose are voting with their feet and walking away from the public schools. The less fortunate, those without parental support to create a home school, have no choice; they are simply out.

Our purpose in these pages is to present a compendium of critical pedagogical writings that analyze the current issues in urban education and demonstrate alternatives to the failing schools that abound. These alternatives include changing the current structures and philosophy of existing schools. They suggest the development of new charter, alternative, or other educational delivery systems.

Whatever the choices, we are weary of test-driven, bureaucratic, policy-polluted, and violence-wracked public schools. Learning must be engaging, meaning-making, and exciting. Shy of this, school is all of the bad things our non-learning, school haters have reported. For far too many, 'school sucks' is an understatement!

As the editors of Peter Lang Publishing's Educational Psychology and Black Studies and Critical Thinking Series, we have collected a selection of writings representative of our series' pedagogy and praxis. This collection's purpose is to introduce our readers to the pretext of urban educational problems and the praxis of urban educational reform. The book is divided into three parts. The first section, Tales from the Field, contains several gripping anecdotes of student, teacher, and administrative perspectives on the school experience.

Section two, Urban Education, examines the pretext of urban educational failure and the current dilemmas urban educators are facing. Drawing chapters from Floyd Beachum and Carlos McCray's (2011) excellent volume, *Cultural Collision and Collusion*, the stage is set for understanding the undergirding issues facing today's urban educators.

Section three presents praxis for urban educational reform. Using one example of best practice in educational psychology, the empirically demonstrated Life Space Crisis Intervention model is suggested as a model of school reform. This section is rich in specific suggestions for creating successful school communities.

Like our mentors Mary McLeod Bethune and Paulo Freire, we are filled with hope for positive changes within our schools and the communities they serve. For this to become reality, we need to develop teachers and administrators who are knowledgeable, courageous, and motivated to challenge the old paradigms so that we can create models for success. *School Sucks* challenges you to engage in this fight for the future of our students.

## References

Beachum, F. & McCray, C. (2011). *Cultural collision and collusion: Reflections on hip-hop culture, values, and schools.* New York: Peter Lang Publishing.

Dwyer, L. (2012). A 13-year-old's slavery analogy raises some uncomfortable truths in school. Retrieved from: http://www.good.is/post/a-13-year-old-s-slavery-raises-some-uncomfortable-truths-in-school/

Goodman, G. (1999). *Alternatives in education: Critical pedagogy for disaffected youth.* New York: Peter Lang Publishing.

Kohl, H. (1994). *"I won't learn from you" And other thoughts on creative maladjustment.* New York: The New Press.

Obiakor, F.E. & Beachum, F.D. (2005). Developing self-empowerment in African American students using the comprehensive support model. *The Journal of Negro Education, 74*(1), 18-29.

Spring, J. (2008). *American school: From the Puritans to No Child Left Behind 7th Edition.* New York: McGraw Hill.

PART ONE

# Tales from the Field

# If You Could Only See

**See**
While you're playing your X-Box Kinnect and your WII
While you're hooked on so called Reality—TV
While you're facedown, facing off on facebook
A book never gets a second look
While your future gets.... took
**See...**
They're stealing your education
Your future's a hostage
To the Castle Doctrine and gun nuts on the right
'Cuz if you can't read or write
And since might makes right
They damn sure know you'll fight
For whatever cause and carnage
They feed you.
**See....**
While you're terminally distracted
With the relative quality of your toilet paper
And Charlie Sheen's latest caper
They're steady stacking paper
Papering over your health care
And the only paper you'll hold
Is your... walking papers
**See......**
Soon they'll be selling you your air
Once they're done privatizing medicare
They're fracturing a fractured earth
'Cause there's no residual income in the Sun
Once it's all said and done...

**You'll see.....**
That there's no true democracy
That you're a slave to your vanity
That you're hooked on Redbox and mindless TV
That education is your last hold on the dream of meritocracy
**See...**
Won't you......
Just take a moment to see....
**©H²11**

ONE

# Developing Urban Youth Voice

## *A Framework for Culturally Responsive Classrooms*

Christopher Knaus

> Urban schools are not broken; they are doing exactly what they are designed to do. (Duncan-Andrade & Morrell, 2008, p. 1)

On a cold, rainy Monday morning, I noticed Juan, a student who had all but dropped out of East Bay High, slip over the fence. Through our classroom window, I watched him toss his journal over the 7-foot-tall chain link fence, and then scale, pivot, and in one smooth motion, his feet hit the ground, he scooped up the journal, and within seconds was at our classroom door. He slid into an open desk as I glanced at the clock: 10 minutes left. He immediately began free-writing (the topic from the beginning of the class was still written on the board), and did not move again until after the bell rang. A few students greeted him as they left our room, and as I was packing up our class, putting our stack of journals into the box I used to carry our supplies, he finished his writing and asked me if we could talk. As students began to fill into the classroom (which would be used by its fifth teacher of the day), Juan and I settled onto a bench relatively hidden from others. As soon as his body touched the bench, Juan began:

> Chris, I'm so sorry I've been missing class. My brother was involved in a gang fight and our family has been forced out of our house. I aint got nowhere to go and I know I'll be kicked out of this school for missing so much class. I know I wasn't a good student before all this. But I want to ask if you will let me keep on writing, even if I am kicked out. I have been writing; I lost this journal a few times, but I keep finding it again, so I know I'm supposed to keep at it.

We talked for an hour, with Juan clarifying the continual threat of violence and homelessness, wondering what he could do to escape juvenile hall for missing so much school. As we strategized approaches to engage with his probation officer, I realized what Juan was actually asking. He wanted my permission to keep writing, to keep journaling, and he wanted my affirming feedback. Despite not caring about the rest of his education, Juan was learning how to write for himself, and was developing a practice of using reflective writing to help make sense of his impossibly complicated, violent world.

Such intimacy and trust with a teacher has largely been lacking throughout urban student experiences, and yet such closeness is a precondition for instructors learning to respond to their students; if we do not know our students, how can we respond to them? If we do not create conditions for students like Juan to reach out, then we will not engage them. The purpose of this chapter is to clarify how developing voice can lead to classroom communities where students like Juan deepen their approaches to life. I demonstrate how I integrate the process of developing voice into classroom practice, and capture my attempts to model student-centered culturally responsive instructional approaches.

This chapter specifically focuses on how schools can create instructional loops with students, wherein students learn to speak aloud their experiences, listen to their peers, give feedback on each other's work, and begin to educate others about the struggles they live within. As an educator, my role is to co-create the conditions through which students can develop and refine voice, then step back and allow students the space to express themselves as needed. In the classroom, this entails, at a minimum, structures that allow students the space to be themselves, but that are rigid enough to keep students moving forward, with concrete assignments and routines. I use personal at-home and in-class journals, punctuation-free papers, daily freewrites, cycles of editing to workshop writings, and a continual stream of exciting, passionate, relevant intellectual sparks, including poetry, music, novels, short stories, films, documentaries, but also live voice-filled poets, musicians, and artists to incite students to write.

## Self-Recognition and Examination

Maricella was a student in a high school class that I was co-teaching with an English teacher. Maricella had not turned in the first few assignments, and this troubled my co-teacher, who had thought she would do really well in the class because of her prior academic performance in the school. I met with Maricella a month into the course, and she was shaking with nervousness as we sat down to chat. After a few minutes of small talk, Maricella burst out: "I just don't know who I am. Everything in this class asks me to write about who I am, but I don't know." I remained silent as I listened to Maricella express her frustrations with being seen as a "good" student, but she had always felt she did not know what to say. "I know how to say things, that's what those A's mean. But teachers don't ask me what I think 'cause I'm the good, quiet kid." She continued, her voice trembling: "I never know what to think because I've never been allowed to talk about me." Maricella clarified why she did not want to be seen as talking: "The students who talk—they talk about their problems. And see, they got in trouble. Every time. So why talk? Plus, who is going to listen to a little *Mexicana Negrita*?"

Because she had always done well in school, Maricella told me she never had anyone ask about how she was doing. She never felt like she developed opinions because she just kept quiet and did the assignments she was given. Yet Maricella had witnessed complicated, violent circumstances, like when her cousin was being beat by her uncle. When he said something to a school counselor, he was placed into a group home; she hadn't seen him in the two years since. Her older sister was also arrested as an accomplice to murder when she was trying to explain to her teacher and counselor that she was forced into a gang. Her point was that she had lived through a lot and was only seen as successful because she had been able to hide these experiences from her teachers.

But now, in our class, she struggled because she really wanted to talk about her family, about how teachers silence her, and how few choices she has. "My parents don't have papers, and I have to go to college to get a job and pay for them. I think I've never had a chance to stop and just think about what I want to be." Our class became a chance for Maricella to learn how to speak aloud and develop her thoughts. But she needed support in overcoming her intense reluctance to write or speak. She did not think she had a voice, and she thought the role of school was to reinforce her silence. Maricella reminded us that we had to do a better job of setting the tone, of helping students be honest with themselves and their peers. A focus on self-recognition and self-examination requires students to be comfortable being uncomfortable, as they are being asked to confront personal fears (not just about speaking in public, but about being who they are). This means creating the conditions for students to be themselves, and we then set up space for one-on-one, outside-the-classroom discussions where students like Maricella could open up and talk about fears and frustrations.

> *My Voice*
> *(a freewrite by Maricela)*
> I wish my voice was as
> loud as it is in my
> head. I want to explode
> and let my voice go. I'd
> talk until my throat got
> dry and my voice went hoarse.
> Since I don't speak, no
> one hears my voice and
> I'm left to sink, real
> deep. I have no choice. My
> voice is unheard. You never
> hear me say a word.

Developing voice begins with a thorough examination and critical self-reflection on who the writer is as a person. Such centering on who we are requires, at a personal level, recognition of the pain that shapes how we navigate the world. This requires not only creating a classroom community of trust and respect, but also modeling how, as educators, we live with purpose and grace while also being transparent about the tremendous burdens we carry. Key to developing such trust is developing what bell hooks (1994) argues is a commitment to "insist that everyone's presence is acknowledged" (p. 8). In my classrooms, I try to create an environment where all students are valued for who they are, and that means that students have a responsibility to express their languages, cultures, and insights. Such expression is particularly important in an anti-immigrant, anti-ethnic studies political environment, where students of color face a barrage of English-only laws, and mandatory reporting that limits capacity to trust educators with intimate details. Such a context of oppressing children of color led me to encourage Maricella, and it was precisely my insistence on recognizing her that led to her realization that because societal pressures wanted her silent, she had a responsibility to speak. She soon wanted other students to develop voice, and reached out to reluctant peers helping, as she told them, "to free yourselves from the racism we are taught." A few weeks after our chat, she read her paper to our class and invited three additional students into our class, all of whom were identified by Maricella as "silenced."

While I create opportunities for students to write about how they experience the world, the point is to also get students to write with passion, to undo the damage from previous educators who have silenced through White, English-Only educational notions. That means letting students free in their words, and encouraging them to capture pieces of who they are that have often been silenced. In addition, educators must help undo the damage previous English teachers might have enforced, such as a focus on structures without ensuring students develop something to say; students of color often internalize their failure rather than question that the way they are being taught might be the problem (DeMeulenaere, 2009; Fordham & Ogbu, 1986; Gibson & Ogbu, 1991; Steele & Aronson, 1995). A central aspect of developing voice is affirming in students that what they actually think is valid, and our role is to help them say what they think more clearly, and to push on depth of thought. Because this work is intensely personal, I do not require students to share aloud everything they write, but I do require all students to write, and all students are expected to share their voices at some point. I also set the tone for students, modeling that while writing about our pain is difficult, speaking aloud this pain in public is even more difficult. I am clear to students: speaking voice aloud is partially what enables us to learn how to feel and walk with more dignity in the world.

## Setting the Context: Instructor Modeling

All of this framing requires that I be present to what has shaped me, to the very things that have silenced my own voice. I cannot do this work without developing trust throughout the modeling process, and this includes showing students how I examine my own context, edit my work, and learn to express myself. I am intentionally transparent about my personal work to learn about who I am and where I teach. I begin classes by sharing my own critical voice and what led me to teach that particular course, in that particular school, and in that particular community. I continually process my upbringing, my educational experiences, my pain, and the details from my life that have taught me to be an educator. And this very personal work is exactly what teacher education programs do not teach, is exactly what brings me closest to my students; this is what educators are taught to not share with our students. Without having the support of educational institutions, educators have to learn to process who we are and how we have come to be with others. And we have to demonstrate to students that we have developed a sustained community of people around us. This is difficult work, not seen as relevant to teaching, and yet is exactly what fuels my capacity to teach in student-centered ways. In short, if I do not know myself, I cannot help students learn to develop voice.

I thus come into the classroom with a developed sense of self, in which I try to be both pro-student and deeply anti-oppressive. I write about my experiences as a student, teacher, and faculty member, but also as a violently abused child. I show my students my writings, which they critique and challenge so they can see me as also trying to learn, also trying to shape the realities I live in. Being known is a precursor to knowing students; I cannot expect them to share details of their lives if I do not share who I am. And I do not try to compare my wounds. Instead, I share who I am, what has impacted me, and what I do with my lessons (and subsequent issues). In this way, I do work prior to the class that informs how I think about my life, and this continual work informs what I do in classrooms.

*Shared in-class freewrite*
Last week we talked of rape and
molestation in academic settings
not meant to be meaningful After
class my office filled with women
raped molested beat down always
by men and now I think of my
father the only male influence in
my life beating down my mother
16 stitches across her chin beating
down my brother our baseball
football and soccer coaches public
humiliation nothing compared
to his fists splattering against my
chest my face my arms these are
the 7 fingers he broke 7 different
times the only thing saving me
most days are the very words you
listen to now and the hope that
speaking out up and on will move
each of us to live how we need

Who I am also frames how much work I need to do to learn about my students *before* planning out a course. Because I am male, I know that I need to build up working knowledge about sexism and how my own male privilege affords me opportunity to speak. Because I am White, I know that I need to build up working knowledge about urban communities, especially the community in which the students I will be teaching live (Howard, 1999; McIntyre, 1997). Before the class begins, I research the community, gaining a general idea of wealth, employment status, and the educational background of local adults. I look into incarceration rates and examine how prisons might impact students growing up. I look at incidents of police brutality and violence rates against residents in that community. I do background work on local community advocates and try to identify historical figures that played a role in civil rights struggles. Most of this is available online, and all of this I do prior to reaching into local resources.

Armed with basic demographic knowledge of the community, I reach out to local community leaders. I call or stop by local churches and service providers (including social workers, probation officers, HIV counselors), and stop by a local food bank to have an idea of who is being served and what kinds of food they are being served. While some of these interactions lay a foundation for me to later invite experts into the classroom, many simply provide a deeper understanding of the context in which my students live. Such community voices shape content areas that I might prioritize in class, such as a lack of local grocery stores, abnormally high HIV infection rates, and a lack of mental health services. Knowing about communities before teaching builds bridges to local resources that might not be connected to school, all while highlighting community voice for students.

Then I dive into the school itself, chatting with counselors, teachers, custodial staff, parents, and district personnel, trying to understand what people think of the school, the staff, and the students. Such conversations directly inform my understanding of previous curricula, histories, and recent local politics. This is particularly enlightening in underfunded, low-performing, and/or alternative schools that are designed to serve low-income students of color so that I can identify potential curricular gaps that limit student knowledge and writing preparation (Duncan-Andrade & Morrell, 2008; Knaus, 2007). In short, I invest significant time and energy prior to teaching to prepare myself for the specific school. I research the context of the school in which I am to teach as a way of setting the stage for my curriculum and teaching approaches. This is especially important, as I will be pushing students to document their realities, and they will know if I am unprepared to deal with these realities: thus, I tap into the resources

*Excerpt from Shantel's letter to me*

... This, Chris, is my point: My previous teachers have molded me into quietness have smashed my mind to where everything I think I know is wrong and everything you told me makes sense but I didn't want to hear you and was able to shut you out until three weeks ago when you came to my house and met my grandmother and brought that social worker you hafta know that the 12 before her were wack mean punked my grandmother disrespect you showed me was colonial and you taught me learning is the best respect we can give you taught me that there are more out there like me like you like the speakers in our class like the poets like the guitarista there are always people learning and I want to be one of them one of us the ones who know who we are that can support me and students, but also gain an understanding of what living in the community feels like prior to urging students to capture what they feel like.

With a basic understanding of the local neighborhood and resident resources, I tap into a larger community of experts to inform and expand the curriculum. I reach out to other area educators, artists, poets, musicians, comedians, playwrights, and chefs, looking to see who might be available to come and speak to the class during the term. I plan ahead to identify experts I can call on to potentially bring them into my larger framed curriculum. This previous work positions me as a practitioner instructor; when I come into class knowing about the context these students struggle in and the resources they may benefit from, students see how I have prepared. This shows that I am humble enough to still want to learn, that I use what I learn to inform what I do, and that I know a bit about the context within which they live. This is essential; urban students often complain about not having educators who know them, who know their realities and understand some of what they live through (Delpit, 2006; Goldstein, 2007; Wyngaard, 2007). This drive to learn is precisely what I am trying to teach and model for students and precisely what is key to developing voice: being humble is required to continually frame ourselves as learners who reach out because we simply cannot know everything we need to.

The key to setting up classrooms that center students, student voice, and student realities is transparent educators who practice what we preach (Duncan-Andrade & Morrell, 2008; Freire, 1973; hooks, 1994; Krishnamurti, 1953). This means listening to students so that we know enough about them to shift our curriculum and teaching to reflect their needs. My goal is to help students make sense of the power of their voice, and that means I must demonstrate such power. If the goal is to help students tap into their own experiences, to help arm them with personal tools to transform their experiences into power that informs their efforts to shape the world, then educators have to model how to do that. That means making sense of the oppression we have lived (and take part in). In essence, I set up outside-the-classroom structures to help me reflect on how I have grown up on my own, navigating through less-than-stellar K–12 schools, through college, and through emotional trauma and structural silencing. All of this directly informs how I set up my classroom, and informs my work prior to stepping into class on the first day. This is an important clarification: caring, responsive curriculum and teaching approaches are still limited by my own capacity to reflect on and address race, gender, and class-based privileges that shape everything I do within (and outside of) a classroom (hooks, 1994). This is particularly important as a straight White man; I cannot know what life is like as a young person of color, as a queer youth, or even growing up poor in today's world, but I can learn as much as I can, and develop a team to support me.

## The First Day of Class at East Bay High School

Prior to students arriving for their first class at East Bay High School, I write "Who Are You?" on the board. I sit in a desk, watch students settle into the same desks as far away from me as possible. A few minutes after the bell rings, students look around a bit bewildered: who is this teacher and why is he not in front of the class? After a few minutes of letting students talk to each other, discomfort begins to show as they glance nervously towards me, waiting for me to begin class. Just as students start to get up and walk around, I stand up. The class becomes quiet, and I ask students if they think I know more than they do about everything. They laugh dismissively. I keep asking until a dialogue begins: some note that I am the teacher and that they have to listen to me in order to pass the class; others say I probably do know more than they. I ask if they think I know more about race and racism than they do, and students emphatically reply "no." "Then why," I counter, "Are you waiting for me to start a writing class in an urban school? And deeper, why are you all sitting in rows of desks facing the front of the class, as if I have all the answers?" A discussion erupts as students talk about their frustrations with school. They talk about how they have to learn to be quiet. One student, Sherise, notes that students are graded by how well they "shut up and listen to the teacher." I tell students that this class will be different if, and only if, students in this class are different. I tell students that if they take themselves and this class seriously, then we can shift the dynamics by designing the class as they wish. I stop the discussion and tell everyone to move desks how they want to be arranged.

At this point, I bring the now-sitting-in-a-circle class' attention to the board, pass out new journals, and lay out freewriting ground rules: continual writing, no worries about grammar, spelling, or getting it "right." I state multiple times that the point is to continually write, so the pen or pencil is always moving. I tell students to push beyond their names, urging them to show us how they think of themselves. "Set a context for how you want this class to be," I urge, before joining students to write for five minutes about the question on the board ("Who are you?"). I continually remind students to write and not talk, not text, not do anything other than write. After five minutes, we share what we wrote as an introduction to the class, and despite initial hesitations and discomfort, everyone shares. Below are three introductions shared aloud that day:

Enrique Intro:

*Yo Soy Enrique and I am in este clase porque I hafta be*

Jasmine Intro:

*Alive today I am Jasmine and*

*I am here to tell you I matter*

*I am from Moms and Pops*
*but Pops passed and Moms is*
*hardly here and I have two younger*
*sisters I take care of them and*
*I think you'll all know me soon enough*
*because I am here to say*
*something.*

Marco Intro:

*I been rappin with style*
*when others lay tile*
*I am the ghost of my pahtnas*
*layin low they been taken*
*and I still fakin tryin to stay alive*
*when my body be shakin*
*gots lots ta say just be listenen*
*cause I drop truths like home runs to babe ruths*

As we shared introductions, the above examples stood out because of their vibrancy, rhythmic flow, and language. While students clapped loudly after Marco's poetic introduction, his content did not tell the class much about who he is, though we can assume he's known friends that were killed. Enrique, though brief, demonstrated that he speaks English and Spanish and was not particularly excited about being in the class. Jasmine, in contrast, got several quieter claps, despite that she shared several details about her life. But it was only the first day, and students were not yet focused on purpose, meaning, or voice: instead the default purpose is either to make other students laugh or to sound "smooth." Thus, students on the first day save their reactions for peers who read their words with the most energy. Meanwhile, I take notes during student read alouds, recording students who read powerfully, have sharp words, are nervous, are trying to say something meaningful, or are trying to avoid sharing much, and those who are generating laughter.

Because I work in urban schools with huge ranges in abilities to read and write, there are also corresponding disparities between comfort levels in public speaking. I often work with students who have only a rudimentary foundation of writing, and I strongly encourage them to read aloud to help come to terms with why they have not been taught to read or write very well. Some students have refused to read, and I work one-on-one with them until they are comfortable sharing in front of the class. Most students, at least at the outset, share relatively boring introductions, with several class poets and clowns serving as obvious exceptions. A more typical intro is one by James, written in a juvenile facility in 2008: "I am James, still loct up." In the class at East Bay High, perhaps a third of the students introduced themselves with something similar, stating their name and sharing one additional, not-very-revealing line.

The dynamic of the classroom, shifted slightly by the alteration of the classroom chairs, our discussion of school issues, and students sharing with each other, moves even further when I share my writing last. Students do not expect me to share, but particularly nothing engaging or powerful. While I freewrite a new version for each course, here is the intro I wrote and shared for Jasmine, Marco, and Enrique's class:

Chris' Intro:

*Christopher Bodenheimer Knaus I*
*born into dad's punches*
*welfare lunches and teacher hunches*
*everyone assumed I cheated on tests*
*couldn't be smart this poor white kid*
*no one knew my grandmother was*
*a social worker in watts*
*fled nazi germany at 17*
*or that my mom was kicked out of*
*8th grade, 4 kids by 21, divorced and on*
*her own by 24 and I*
*told I'd fail every day I*
*flunked 7th grade*
*never gave up even as my rage*
*burned bridges at every turn*
*and still burning I*
*fighting so that each of you*
*stand on your own words*
*powerful, alone and exactly*
*what and who and how you and I need to be:*
*Christopher Bodenheimer Knaus I*
*honored to be with you all*
*ready to learn and grow and push and move*
*and move*
*and move*
*and be moved.*

As soon as I finish reading, students erupt into excited hoots and hollers, likely exacerbated by their surprise. Students call out: "Teacher can kick!" "Step back, Chris is about to flow" and "Whooo, teacher's a poet!" I ask students how they feel about this process of starting off the year. "I feel like we could be a family," one student remarks, while another argues that "we already shared more in this class than we have all last year in all of our classes." A few students are notably quiet and have muted responses, and I jot down their names so I can follow up later if they are not more engaged within the next few days. I let the class out on a high note; students are generally excited at the notion of building up a community around sharing their own voices.

On the second day, I lay out the course syllabus. When I first began teaching, I used ground rules from June Jordan's Poetry for the People, but I have since learned to guide students in the development of their rules. I provide ground rules only for our freewriting process, and then ask the students to develop additional ground rules for ensuring students will feel comfortable reading aloud their work, and will honor what each student says. Students develop a list, write it up creatively on posterboard, and I post these laminated ground rules in front of the class. I remind students that while I will hold each student accountable for the agreed-to rules, it is their responsibility to maintain these rules, and I will also hold them accountable for holding each other accountable. Within a few weeks, students generally begin to take charge of the classroom, stopping someone mid-sentence when they challenge a peer too harshly, or dismiss someone's attempt at writing.

Ground Rules
(adapted from June Jordan's Poetry for the People)

1 We consciously respect each other
2 We foster in ourselves and each other an ability to craft our messages for others to contemplate
3 Expression is an art of telling the truth
4 We are the community
5 Writing is how we connect
6 We are responsible for what we say and how we say it just as we are responsible for helping others craft writings through critical feedback

## Writing Assignments: Self-Recognition and Examination

As we begin the second week, I frame the rest of the major assignments, and focus on the first paper. This paper extends the class intro read aloud. Sample extended prompts have included: "This is how I live Racism," "Capture what your voice sounds like," and "Here I Am, Listen." At East Bay High, the class completed a draft of a "What You Need to Know About Me" paper at the end of the second week. A complete draft was due the following week, and students had to read the three-page paper aloud and turn in at least three sets of peer feedback. I demonstrate how we begin the feedback process later in this chapter, and more extensively in Chapter Four, but these first few weeks focus more on writing than providing feedback. "You have to learn to write before you can learn to edit," I tell my students.

> **What You Need to Know About Me**
>
> This assignment has three purposes:
>
> 1 Introduce yourself to the class in a way that dramatically extends beyond your intro read aloud
> 2 Help develop your capacity to clarify, in public, who you are in a voice that reflects who you are
> 3 Push beyond your notion of standardized writing to see that you can write powerfully
>
> Thus, there are two rules:
>
> 1 This paper is to be written and spoken in your voice
> 2 No punctuation or standardized writing structures of any kind are allowed
>
> This paper is expected to be the equivalent of approximately 3 pages, and should be well edited to capture your points in vibrant language. Avoid any vague terms (it, good, nice, interesting, etc.), and speak with purpose and passion. As with all assignments in this class, the more effort and energy you put in, the more you will get out. This paper will be read aloud in class. This paper is non-graded; there will be no credit given unless the paper is read aloud, is free from punctuation, and includes three edited drafts from peers.

To help scaffold the "What You Need to Know About Me" assignment, I asked several students to share aloud "Where I Am From" poems (Lyon, 1999), which they had written the previous year in their English class. While students appreciated their flow, there was general consensus that the poems were vague and did not tell nearly as much as did the introductory read alouds. Students were ready to push beyond what is typically written for other courses, but many expressed that they did not know how to do that in creative ways that demonstrated their voice. We continued freewriting with prompts to help stimulate ideas to write about, and I provided a different poem each day that demonstrated voice.

In addition, I played several hiphop and reggae songs, and printed out lyrics so students knew what exactly was being said. The class would respond or engage in found poetry, a process where students listen to a poem or song, and write down any words, phrases, or ideas that come to them as they listen. From there, the class wrote, edited and eventually read aloud their papers, continuing the practice of getting students comfortable sharing their voice in front of the class.

Self-recognition Writing Assignments

1 Where I Am From A popular assignment used widely in schools, these short poems or essays typically capture a student's personal history and family context.
2 Describe a Scar on My Body Adapted from an assignment by John Malloy, an educator and community leader, this assignment encourages students to capture, with concrete detail, what a scar on their body looks like, where it came from, and what it might represent.
3 Letter to Your 10-Year-Old Self This assignment teaches students how to write personal letters, using traditional letter-writing structures, but encourages critical writing as students talk to themselves when they were 10 years old. These letters include self-affirmation, but also require students to use knowledge they know now to ensure mistakes they made are addressed.

Examination Writing Assignments

4 How You See Me/How I See Myself This comparative assignment asks students to capture a portrait of themselves as others see them, and then contrast that often-stereotypical image to how they see themselves. This assignment encourages students to challenge assumptions about themselves, and requires students to show how they are different from how others see them.
5 This Is How I Am Beautiful This paper encourages students to develop a list of how they see themselves as beautiful, and then turn that list into a creative writing. Beginning with a list of 20 examples of how the writer is beautiful, the paper requires challenging stereotypes of beauty, but also requires students to convince the audience of their beauty, focusing on persuasive skill sets.
6 Snap Shot of Grade-Level Navigational Strategies This more advanced-level paper encourages students to identify personal strategies they developed to navigate schooling at each level, and requires evaluation of each strategy's success. Examples include tuning out, becoming a class clown, drugs, alcohol, and violence.

## Reflection on Context

After setting ground rules on the second day, we review the syllabus and lay out a bare-bones curriculum. I typically begin a high school class with a no-more-than-two-page syllabus with course expectations, an overview of key assignments, and due dates. This syllabus clarifies two key course goals that can be integrated into other content areas: (1) Students will develop their voice as a tool to capture and make sense of racism and urban life, and (2) Students will express their voice in forums that make sense to them. The point, to which I return throughout the rest of the class, is that students are living reporters: most mainstream news perpetuates urban stereotypes of violence, drugs, gangs, and low test scores, and students know the community better than mass-media reporters, and often their teachers.

Their role, as framed by the syllabus, is to become the types of reporters we need, the sort that stay alive because they have to report on what is happening through their unique voices and insights. Thus, students expect that we will shift readings, assignments, and strategies to respond to what comes out of their writings.

> **Introduction to the Syllabus**
>
> 1 Course Overview This course is designed to develop your intellectual and personal voice. Using critical writing, film, and creative expression, we will analyze identity, oppression, and the use of voice as a way of working toward our definitions of social justice. As high school students, our role is to develop our voice, our understanding of who we are, how we fit within society, and our tools of expression, so that we become more articulate about the social issues we care most about. Two core questions that we will return to throughout the course will guide us: What do I, personally, have to say? And How do I say it?
>
> 2 Course Expectations Every member of our course community is expected to deeply engage, participate, challenge our self and others, learn, critique, express, and ultimately develop our voices. We each come as experts in our own experience, with our own voices, insight, and unique perspectives. Our entire classroom community is expected to be open, supportive, and critical of how we express ourselves and how we assist our peers in expressing themselves.

After spending the first third of the class helping students wrestle with and document the pieces of their identity that make them who they are, I shift focus to examine personal context. I remind students of the point they already made: very little of their schooling is framed on urban realities, and I tell students that in speaking their realities, in the everyday voices they speak and listen to, they honor their communities and begin to document their communities. Capturing and preserving local, cultural, and linguistic knowledge is a skill, I state over and over again, and we are going to practice that skill until we become adept at sharing who we are and where we come from and what moves us with whatever audiences we think need to hear us. This entails guiding student assignments and thoughts around the immediate world in which they live, encouraging them to capture the social conditions that shape their lives, including what literally surrounds them on a daily level (including family, community, school, but also violence, racism, sexism, abuse, drug use, food, housing conditions). When done well, students capture their everyday realities, and with support, learn to see writing as a tool to capture the ugly and beauty of their world, but also as a means of demonstrating who they are, and what they survive. This is how students reclaim their identities and begin to see school as useful. For when students see a purpose in writing, they can tap into what they need to say, and ensure words reflect their lives.

Depending on the course length, I select two to five core texts, which I use as a foundation for discussions around voice, language, and reporting about our personal realities. I have used Sapphire's (1996) *Push*, LeAlan Jones and Lloyd Newman's (1996) *Our America*, James Baldwin's (1962) *The Fire Next Time*, June Jordan's (2000) *Soldier*, and Jamaica Kincaid's (1988) *A Small Place*, among dozens of others. I purposefully choose nonfiction and fiction that offers direct insight into the author while demonstrating voice that reflects the authors' language and personal cultural context. *Our America*, for example, reflects two young African American students talking about what living in low-income urban Chicago looks like. The authors, who spoke their text through voice recorders, capture their daily life, narrating what they see in their neighborhood, complete with interviews of family members, educators, and neighbors. Photos that provide concrete imagery accompany the book. Such texts also show students that people just like them write and publish books.

*Our America* contrasts with *A Small Place*, which students appreciated because Kincaid's writing, as Jasmine argued: "helps me see that I can write using standards and still show how fucked up those standards are." Rather than narrated from a personal perspective, Kincaid shows colonization from a national perspective, and uses details often known by those who live in the context of the colonized. Many urban students, quick to dismiss formal writing structures, often find Kincaid's work useful to see that the issue they have is not with formal writing structures. Instead, her work helps students see the racism that shapes how educators uphold formal writing structures. After reading *A Small Place*, Jasmine argued that there should not be "one true correct way to write that just so happens to be the way White people talk." I thus use a combination of books to show that there are multiple types of reporting and reporters, and all can be engaging and well written, while showing how racism works.

My America by Shantel
LeAlan and Lloyd tell me what they see on the bus
so listen to my never seems to end bus ride because
I too have a voice and I too have something that no
one seems to want to hear Mr. Bus Driver pats my
ass as I squeeze past He never seems to care that
the 75c I pay mean I am younger than his daughter
I sit down next to an old man with drool on his chin
Clutch my bag and hope I get off this bus But my
stop aint for 25 minutes 35 if cars litter Oakland
streets or if these girls act like the bitches the
rappers behind me be rappin about I don't like that
the words they say about me come out of my mouth
These girls telling the bus driver this stop this stop
even though they never get off Those open doors
just hang empty in the west Oakland wind Bringing
the same cancer my mom died from I see men my
age hangin on the corner with 40's in their hands
Brown sacks don't hide them they should be with
me on the way to school Too cool they just wait for
some life to take hold Instead the police linger two
blocks down our bus flies passed Boarded up homes
Just like the one I live in with my 3 cousins 2 aunties
one uncle and way too many "friends" who like to
creep into our room or sell us the weed they sell to
the addicts on the corner that looks just like the one
we ride by almost every morning the police arrest
kids my age who should be in school But at 8 am
they head towards another day in jail I am on the
way to school And Mr. Bus Driver pats my ass as I
squeeze past.

The rest of the course is rooted in student perspectives, energy, and decisions. I continually affirm student effort in writing, and just as continually urge students to express themselves more deeply, more in the language they use daily, with friends, and at home. How we communicate about the things we care about becomes the focal point for both the curriculum and my instructional techniques. I center the ways in which students talk and communicate on a daily basis as a way to deepen their writing and to honor the ways they frame ideas (Gay, 2000; Lynch, 2006). I tell students I will hold them accountable, and that they need to hold each other accountable, for what their words literally mean. I then demonstrate how their words can mean something other than they intend, and that they must be responsible for their clarity. We examine offensive terms used to degrade people of color, women, people with disabilities, and dissect our daily language for the historical roots of oppression in words, and students attempt to shape the languages they have previously felt oppressed by. One particularly powerful exercise is a discussion to generate a list of everyday words with oppressive roots (such as "gyped" or "gipped," "red-handed," "ghetto," "peon," but also what many educators refer to as the "N-word," to name but a few). The sheer impact of filling up every whiteboard or chalkboard in the room within just a few minutes reminds students of the powerful negative impact our words have.

In reclaiming affirming language, students begin to take more responsibility for the words they use. But beyond being more purposeful about word choice and what we say, I expect students to shape daily agendas, writing assignments, and classroom dialogue (Knaus, 2009; Stovall, 2006). My role, which I make clear throughout the course, is to ensure students are continually writing, continually editing, always pushing deeper to communicate what they see and feel, and to ensure they respect each other and themselves in our shared space. In essence, my role becomes a drive to ensure students are getting what they say would bring them to school. Collectively, this means striving to say what we mean with as much passion as we can, and then critiquing to ensure our purpose is conveyed well. In this way, students begin to frame themselves as reporters capturing the reality they live but rarely see reflected in traditional school curriculum.

## Freewriting

Perhaps what most marks my voice-focused courses is the daily freewrites; much of our time throughout the year is spent freewriting about our daily context. Sherise talked about my classes like this: "Chris be havin' us writing every-dang-day!" Almost every time I run into a former writing student, the first thing they'll tell me about is how they still freewrite in journals. I recently ran into a former student who was relatively disengaged throughout our course. He had just walked down a block that I had taken his entire class through during a neighborhood freewrite four years earlier. With his memory spurred, he purchased a journal so that he could get back into freewriting. Our chance meeting just a few days later reminded him of the imperative to keep on writing, and reminded me how free-writing sticks with students years later. Even with the students who do not write daily during class.

> Neighborhood freewrite by Jacinda
> Graffiti, boarded up doors, liquor stores,
> nice new alternative school lock up,
> Mental health services, boarded up
> They serve them
> A field of dew green grass,
> Drugs, street named MLK Jr,
> Cars, more beat up cars,
> the majority of us students isn't white,
> no smoking but some flowers,
> the ones that smell good,
> some nice houses, some not
> stop BUSH signs, bikes,
> purple house that's where the Smoke spot used to be,
> graffiti, stop.

My typical writing courses begin each week by checking in about the previous week's work, and each day begins with 5–10 minutes of freewrite, followed by a chance for volunteers to read aloud what they just wrote. Within a few weeks, most students begin freewriting on their own, writing phrases or topics on the board as a prompt to guide their classmates' writings. I hold fast to my freewriting rules: continual writing about the topic or whereever your mind takes you. Once we begin, the pen is constantly moving and there is no self-editing, no worries about grammar, spelling, or punctuation, and no stopping to think about what you want to say (and what you will not say). I push hard on students who come into class not on task; I continually assert that the five or ten minutes are exclusively for writing. This is when I am most harsh on discipline: there is no talking, no sharing, and no texting; nothing except the quiet scratch of handwriting. The point is to write about what is on your mind, what you are struggling through, or what you need to get out of your system. And I restate this whenever students need reminders.

While there are dozens of examples of potential freewrite ideas available in writing resource books (Behn, 1992; Berdan et al., 2006; Goldberg, 1986; Muller et al., 1995; Tannenbaum & Bush, 2005), the vast majority of writing prompts come from listening to students, having them bring in ideas, and from feedback that sparked further writing. Some days we focus on close writing assignments, with students capturing feelings, items, and experiences in thick, descriptive details (Muller et al., 1995; Tannenbaum & Bush, 2005). Other days students write about a highly charged topic at the forefront of many students' minds (such as recent police brutality or a drug bust that resulted in a student being arrested). Some days I play a short film clip to spark ideas, other times, a song, and occasionally, I'd temporarily place snacks students were eating in the middle of the room to spark topics on texture, taste, and smell. If we had a guest speaker, the speaker might initiate the freewrite. Mostly, however, after the first few weeks, students initiate the bulk of the topics. By the end of the term, many students fill their in-class journals with daily writings, and I provide a new journal for each completed journal. As an additional incentive, I remind students to freewrite about papers they need to develop for other courses.

I occasionally use extended or linked freewrites to help students expand upon previous ideas. One particular musician-centered exercise helped deepen class notion of how to ensure the flow of writing enhances emotion. I played a song for students to freewrite with, capturing what they hear, feel, see directly in response to the song. This method is commonly known as "found poetry," where students write down words, phrases from a piece and then later edit their own notes into a poetic response to the original piece (Dunning & Stafford, 1992). The song the students wrote to was *Tozeza*, a soft yet upbeat tune typical of Oliver Mtukudzi and the Black Spirits (2004). The students wrote about how the music took them to the Caribbean, to the beach, and how the song seemed happy, yet was also building up importance as the song went on. They liked the rhythm of the call and response throughout the song. I told them the song was by Mtukudzi, from Zimbabwe, and we talked about how little we know of Africa, which might explain the guesses of Caribbean or how urban youth might correlate African music to being on holiday at the beach.

> Tuku Response by Marco
> Baby reggae this song takes me to beachez
> on a sunny day I could sit there watching wavez
> I think its from Jamaica I wonder what he sez
> I think he means something like:
> 'Live life free and resist these chains'
> the music is upbeat this is good roots music
> I like it

The next day, I played a video of the same song (Mtukudzi, 2006). In the video, we see a man hard at work chopping down huge trees. The backdrop is of Mtukudzi singing and dancing, yet somehow somber looking amidst a forest. Meanwhile, the man works tirelessly, his muscles bulging through his sweat soaked skin. The video shifts to a woman the man comes home to; she serves him food, but rejects him when he pulls her towards him. He beats her for rejecting his sexual advances; all the while we see a young child watching from under a table, hiding and afraid. The video transposes to trees being chopped down, and in the final scene, the boy is crying as he watches the woman we assume is his mother being pulled away from him: she is holding a finger in front of her lips, urging him into silence.

The class mirrors this silence and we freewrite for ten minutes. The students barely contain themselves, and when I tell them to stop writing, students burst out that while the song seemed upbeat, it really was not. They are conflicted about the meaning they previously attributed to the song and what they now recognize the song is about. We dive into a discussion about tempo and rhythm, and how to carry a message forward ensuring your words are conveying what you want them to. Several students note that the song seemed hopeful, that in hindsight, the upbeat tempo actually helped them think of the song as hope that the child will end the cycle of violence. Many students excitedly jot down notes about how they can read aloud their work more rhythmically, but also how they can write in ways that capture hope. The conversation about violence against women and children lingers. Students raise this just before the bell rings, and we pick up the conversation the following class when a student writes the words "parent abuse" on the board to kick start the day's freewrite. We spend the next two weeks focusing on family violence, child abuse, and domestic violence, all stemming from freewrites about a song and accompanying video.

Another example of the power of freewriting to engage students in conversation about what they live occurred during a class at Central High School. Several students heard that a fight was going on in front of the school, and word spread immediately to all students; the excitement in the room made editing peer papers impossible. As several students rushed out of the room to watch the fight, the rest of the students looked around confused. While most wanted to watch the fight, they did not want to leave our room, and we had already talked about avoiding violence by not rushing into it. A student stood up, marched up to the board, and wrote, "Capture what you feel right now." The student-initiated freewrite topic was relevant, and tapped directly into the heat of the moment; students began to write furiously. When the students who ran out of the room came back in, they already knew what to do, and despite their heaving breaths, began to write. Many of those freewrites became the foundation for poems that students later read at a district-wide student convening on youth violence.

This is the importance of continual, everyday writing; students develop their craft while engaging in conversation about the very issues they see around them, but often do not have a language to talk about. Providing numerous forums to reflect and then to share with peers allows students to frame a dialogue they have largely been kept from through standardized curriculum. Yet these are the very skills students need to develop if they are to arm themselves with skills to negotiate this increasingly violent world. Continual freewriting helps build up foundations for such conversations, but also helps prepare students for dialogue around issues that are risky to bring up without some sort of structure. Having students write prior to discussing potentially traumatic issues helps ensure students have the time and space to reflect *and then* speak. Freewriting thus becomes the backbone of a voice-centered class, bridging the academic structures that often limit voice with the need for students to make sense of the world around them. Freewriting becomes a tool through which students capture their daily reality, and students begin to freewrite in cafés, on the bus, at parks, on street corners, and in bathroom stalls as they hide away to record their thoughts and emotions.

## Writing Assignments: Reflection on Context

Depending on the length of the course, I usually assign two or three assignments to clarify personal experiences with racism, such as a paper based on interviews with local elders or a letter to a newspaper advocating for a local urban issue. Drafts are due in advance of deadlines, and students are required to provide critical feedback to each other (and to turn in feedback they have received and addressed in their final drafts). The course ends with student performances of the final paper and with letters to an adult of the student's choosing. Throughout the course, topics loosely follow themes from the readings, music, film, and guest speakers, adapting according to student writings. I focus on quick writing exercises, capturing details, eliminating passive voice from our vocabulary, and creating the maximum impact with a minimum of words.

In a class at East Bay High School, one assignment designed to encourage students to detail their context, and then reflect on what those details mean was a paper framed around an incident that happened during class. A student at the school was placed into a forced mental health facility because, as one student had said, "she just went ka-razy." Several students in the class were close with the student and asked for help in supporting her while she was detained in the mental health facility. The two-part assignment documented issues that make children "go crazy," including a bullet point list of up to 50 examples from the local neighborhood, and the second part was an up-close expansion of one of those issues. The lists of examples included police brutality, dismissive teachers and administrators, violence amongst peers, watching parents get beat, and watching parents beat other people, homelessness, lack of quality food, and addictions (to drugs, alcohol, violence, porn, and gambling).

Students were continually checking in with each other about how they experienced most of these painful circumstances firsthand, and then they shared the exact details they expanded upon to ensure others felt they captured enough to make the reader "go crazy." This was one of the students' favorite assignments because they were able to rely upon peers to identify issues, and, as Angela shared, "they got to talk about what hurt in a safe way, with a friend they could trust." She continued: "That was how we got to know each other, and our class was so tight after, cause we *felt* each other."

## Personal Responses to Our Context

After setting a foundation for student writing that vacillates between capturing who students are, and the world they live within, I urge students to begin writing

Assignments to Capture Student Reflection

1 Responsive freewrites:
   a Neighborhood walks. At least once per week, students walk around the local community, and at random stops, do 5–10 minutes of freewriting to capture local neighborhood details. These help students learn to capture concrete details, while documenting aspects of their communities they often do not notice.
   b On-spot writing about tense issues. Throughout the class, tense discussions emerge, often about racism, sexism, or other forms of oppression. In the beginning of the year, I often stop students in the midst of a heated conversation, and urge them to freewrite for 5–10 minutes on a perspective that is valid, but not being heard. Within a few weeks or months, students begin to stop conversations on their own for freewriting to help clarify complexities.
   c Textured Close Observations. Once per week, students freewrite a textured, close detail-filled capturing of a small object or area. Students might be asked to write an entire page about a broken yo-yo, an ice cream cone on the sidewalk, a crack along a wall, or someone's shoe. The point is to narrowly focus on detail to sharpen capturing skills.

2 Longer assignments:
   a Capture Your Block. This 4–5 page paper, which can also be read aloud in class, provides a comprehensive portrait of every building on the block that the student lives on. The focus remains on concrete details to show the condition of the buildings, the state of repairs, the depth of potholes and the amount and type of plants, trees, cars, and how trash is disposed of.
   b Where You Buy Food. This 4–5 page paper captures the 3–4 closest stores and marks the distance to the nearest full-service grocery store. Students are required to interview nearby shop owners, assess for fresh produce, and provide an overview of what is primarily sold at each store, including overviews of what sort of food is marketed in which ways to which customers.
   c Driving Through Your Community: What the Police See. This 5–6 page paper captures the neighborhood through the perspective of local police, and includes either a ride-along with an officer or a drive with a school security or resource officer. The assignment includes interviewing the officer, probing for specific details the officer is trained to notice and respond to, and then an analysis of what the officer was not noticing.

about concrete survival strategies. This is where students begin to merge the first two sets of exercises, expanding upon previous writings and thinking about who they are and what the world around them looks like. Here I shift writing exercises to guide students to reflect on how they respond to the world, literally prompting students: "Given the racism you already captured, what are your personal strategies for survival? And how is this working?" Writings include critical recognition of the ways individuals respond to their personal contexts, and include concrete capturing of what students do every day to survive. This is where I also focus on capturing emotional responses, including anger, pain, fear, love, and safety. But there is no guarantee that students writing about these issues will be rewarded by other educators.

> What I have learned is this: No matter how well I speak, my words will be used to show how I am not like my peers. White people will use me to show how I am not like these other niggas. And now I write to show that we are all the same: articulate, powerful, and young. We live in their racist world, so now I have to write because my life, because our lives, depend on my words. Even if they twist our words against us, we must still write.
> —Shantel

Shantel names the central problem with developing urban student voice: no matter how well students of color speak, they will often be disregarded because of their fashion, their styles, the tone of their diction, their race, gender, poverty, and youth. And even if Shantel is "heard," she will often be framed as being better than her peers, as an exception to the rule, as articulate despite her surroundings. And because of this reality, because urban students of color are simply not afforded the same opportunities that more privileged students are, I center curriculum around racism so that students of color develop an understanding of and language about the structures of racism that they know intimately. While students capture the intricacies of racism in their daily writings and in their papers, they share such work as a way of informing each other about the realities they live. Focusing on racism so intensely also allows students to detail what they do in response to the racism they capture.

A powerful example of students teaching each other about race and racism came from student assignments that directly capture how students live racism. At Central High, two students who had previously fought each other during what they had called a "race war" in their school came together in our class. I paired them up knowing they had been violent towards each other, and urged them to capture how they are seen individually and collectively by the world. David, a tattoo-covered Latino who had been in and out of juvenile hall for his gang-related activities, wrote about how everyone assumed he was stupid and violent, despite his love of playing the acoustic guitar and his desire to take care of his mother and father. Robert was also in and out of juvenile facilities, a young African American man who never got the chance to play basketball though his 6'4" frame and athleticism likely could have provided him with a college scholarship. He had intense rage at how he saw his family treated by White police and had a thick distrust of White people and teachers. After

Excerpt from You Judge Us by David and Robert

You Judge Us
The way you walk by
Cant look away
Afraid to stare
Eyes peeled
Will we rob you steal your purse your pride
But you the ones who stole from us
Our youth our manhood our identity
What you take you afraid we take
but you the ones who stole from us
setting black and latino against each other
we suppose to fight each other
but you the ones who stole from us

initial resistance to working together, David and Robert read each other's papers. I set up a meeting with the two of them to talk through feedback, concerned that they did not have the tools to listen to each other, despite what I perceived as similar growing up contexts. Getting them to start talking was difficult, but after they began to share, I became irrelevant, sitting back to take in the beauty of two young men of color who have been taught to hate each other bond over their shared stereotypical treatment. They wrote a powerful collaborative paper about how their White teachers were constantly afraid of them, and four years later, still reach out to me letting me know how they are friends, aligned in their commitment to addressing racism against young African American and Latino gang-affiliated men.

Centering racism in the curriculum encourages and allows for the dialogue that David and Robert needed to validate each other, to see each other as human and as being treated in similar ways. Students continually make connections to understanding racism as a system that silences critical challenge and that makes their voices ever so essential. My point in centering racism is to help students of color see that just as their White peers normalize racism, so too do students of color. We do this through our daily writing and sharing, but also through creative assignments: Students show how "normal" racism is through freewrites and, sometimes, through creating 4-minute documentaries or through interviews with elders about what today's racism looks like. Creating racism-focused assignments helps students dive into racism while still being able to maintain their own voice (and thoughts) around race. The focus also enables students to illuminate their own survival strategies, enabling them to talk through what they do to navigate racism, and how effective their strategies appear to be.

Students of color often find the purposeful centering of voices of color to be inclusive and empowering, yet White teachers often ask if I am excluding the few White students by doing such. One White student clarified the tension of focusing on racism, and on centering the experiences of people of color: "I always feel welcome in this class, even though I don't have much to say about racism. But it's good, I get to learn a lot, and I realize that [White] people like me are never quiet enough to hear what racism is." I encourage such dialogue in the class, and urge students to wrestle with why I chose which readings, and with my focus on prioritizing authors of color who speak clearly about racism. Most White students have had tremendous exposure to White authors; few students of color have been exposed to many authors of color, much less authors that speak directly to the pervasiveness of racism. For most students, this will be the only class they will ever take that has readings only by authors of color. Regardless of who is in the class, and what I might want to assign, the key for me is in acknowledging everyone's presence, being transparent about what sorts of authors I assign, and not allowing the conversation to shift away from racism. Even as I facilitate in such a way to center the racism we all live, I still strive to respond to student needs, no matter how well planned out a curriculum may be.

An opportunity to shift the curriculum and course focus came midway through a high school writing course in 2004, when school-wide rumors spread about several students who had been recently diagnosed with HIV. We were in the midst of creating documentary film shorts about local community leaders when the class erupted into a physical fight; one student had called a student with HIV a "fag." While I had known of this student's HIV status, he had not disclosed it to the class, and now everyone correctly assumed that this was one of the students with HIV through the context of another student's homophobia. The student who initiated the fight was immediately expelled from the district (he had numerous prior offenses), and the rest of the class had a week-long discussion about how we support students who are being marginalized, particularly when it is around something life-threatening like HIV. The class ultimately bonded over the incident, and wanted to increasingly understand both homophobia in the black community and the prevalence of HIV amongst people of color. I asked the class if we should shift our focus to these two issues or maintain our focus on our already-in-progress projects. The class unanimously decided to merge the focus and continued the interviews they had begun, but shifted the focus to homophobia and HIV within the black community. I reorganized the class, identified relevant readings, film clips, and guest speakers, and aligned additional assignments to focus on our new topics. The course concluded with a school-wide forum on HIV within the black community, whereby the students presented the findings from their interviews and brought in guest speakers to educate the school. Student papers documented how their collective response informed their individual strategies to address racism.

Even the student who was expelled was invited back to the classroom to offer an apology. Despite the fact that the student was not allowed back on campus, I was able to negotiate bringing him to campus (with his parole officer, two police officers, and the school principal) for one class period, during which the student broke down, asked for forgiveness, and disclosed that his mother died of AIDS-related complications (which he had not known at the time of the fight he initiated). The class wrote a collective letter to his parole officer, formally accepting his apology and testifying to his growth and humility in a powerful display of forgiveness and recognition of responsibility for peers. While that student has not yet attained his G.E.D., he regularly reaches out to several of the students from the class (they became friends after he was expelled from the school). Despite living as a young adult in poverty, he regularly volunteers at an HIV clinic, and speaks to the importance of a class he was kicked out of.

For me, the importance of that class was the lesson that no matter how invested I am as an instructor in course content, I must remain flexible so that I can support student needs. Student-generated topics should shape the class, and while I might begin with a curriculum framework, I build into the curriculum space for students to guide content, topics, readings, films, and writing assignments. No matter how essential a topic is to me, I do not own the curriculum. I am reminded, when I listen to students, that the purpose of a curriculum is to foster student thought, action, and voice development. So when students speak to a greater, more pressing need, I shift with them, integrating the lessons I was trying to teach with what they ask for. This is based entirely on my capacity to create the conditions for voice, and to step out of the way, facilitating based on what students say, write, or share so that they recognize their experiences are shaping what they learn, how they learn, and what role I take as the formal instructor. And this is precisely how I create the conditions for students to explain their responses to what they see as racism.

## Peer Feedback to Focus Voice

Throughout my shifting of the curriculum to reflect student need, I continually center racism through editing. I set a foundation from the first days of the course so that students recognize that part of racism in schools means their work is typically ignored by teachers. This is demonstrated through educators who pass students of color despite the fact that these students might not yet have developed the capacity to read and write (Howerton & Thomas, 2004; Jimerson & Kaufman, 2003). As a way of dealing with this institutional racism, I remind students that they have to help each other develop because schools are not often invested in their intellectual development outside of standardized tests. In addition, while students like Lupe, a multiracial Black, Latino, and White junior at Central High, might state that "I don't like school because it's racist," I use editing as an opportunity to push her to clarify vague terms like "racism." Most everyone, I argue, is against racism generally. But when students get detailed, capture the concrete feelings that racism creates, and highlight the ways in which racism manifests, they move beyond terms and metaphors to reality. So I push Lupe to clarify what she means by "racist" and she eventually, with help from peers, comes up with this: "My white teachers tell me what learning means. They tell me that to know means to speak like them. And to be successful means to act like them." Lupe continued: "But they don't act 'right,' they act white." Her observation is critical; Lupe sees that how her teachers teach requires her to be what she frames as "White" which would mean denying her Black and Latino heritages.

The importance of students clarifying what racism actually means, looks like, and feels like is essential in schools that do not acknowledge or teach about what critical race scholars term "racial microaggressions," the dozens of seemingly minor acts of racism that people of color face throughout the day (Allen, 2010;

Pierce, 1974; Solorzano, Ceja, & Yosso, 2000). The notion of racial microaggressions reflects critical race theory's assertion that racism occurs every day to people of color, and I urge students to identify the racism they face each and every day. Editing becomes the academic lever to help students clarify reality in more concrete terms, and so just after setting up the practice of in-and-outside the classroom freewriting, I set up the notion that writers need to continually refine our words to ensure our voices are heard in the ways we would like to be heard. One component of this clarity is to push beyond blanket terms (such as racism and oppression) that lead to White defensiveness. This requires intense, personal editing to ensure what is written actually reflects what the author intends, including aligning with the tone, language, and details that clarify personality and presence. Julia remarked that when she edits, she does so in order to ensure that "White people cannot tell me what I am saying didn't happen, and if I say it was racism, they get all denial-like. But when I break down racism, and don't even use the word, then they get all mad for me—instead of at me." Julia captures here the process of turning words on the page into "voice," what poets often call "workshopping poems." This editing is the bulk of the "academic" work in my classes, where students learn to spend time crafting their words, learn to ensure they are saying what they want to, in ways that reflect who they are but also maximize the potential to be heard by the intended audience.

Going back to Jasmine's, Marco's, and Enrique's introductory writings, I frame the second week to push beyond the excitement of voice. By then, as is typical, the class is back in rows, and I ask why students are waiting for me to tell them what they need to know again. Some students grumble, then move desks into a circle so that we are facing each other again. The culture of resistance to students taking over the class is something that I confront continually over the first few weeks. Even as students excitedly challenge how most of their schooling has silenced them, they slip back into their roles as subservient students. This becomes my continual push, arguing that students have to take space if they want to shape classrooms, schools, and communities. If students wish to develop their voices, I argue, then they have to claim our classroom dynamics. They have to make this space what they want it to be, despite not having formal training or experience being in classrooms that value their voices or perspectives.

I ask the class to freewrite for five minutes about the first week, and several volunteers read aloud their insights. A few students share their excitement and hope that the class will keep being this real. I make a point to stop the class after each student who describes the class as "interesting," "great," "okay" or even "freakin' fabulous." "These are very vague words," I press, "be clear what is 'interesting,' what specifically is 'great,' and what 'freakin fabulous' actually means to you. Do not assume we know what you feel—show us with your words." Students begin to express frustration at me jumping in, and I argue that clarity of our words about what we think and feel is our collective point, and vague words will not get us there. Vague words, I often say, will not shift society. Eventually, after everyone has read, several students speak up that they appreciate me challenging them because they agree, vague words are everywhere. The class falls into a discussion about how we are taught in English classes, and then reinforced in all other writing assignments, to write passively, to not say anything concretely for fear of being told we are wrong.

I tell students to bring out their introductions from the first day and reread them in pairs, with each partner asking clarifying questions or responding as appropriate. They do this for ten minutes, and then I ask for a brave volunteer to help deepen our class commitment to voice. Jasmine volunteers and writes her original introduction on the board. I ask her if she is ready to have her work dissected in public, and she reaffirms that she is. In just the second week of class, I begin to demonstrate how our words are often vague, and while a particular set of words might get applause, the words might not mean all that much. Jasmine reads aloud her poem twice; the first time I ask students to listen. The second time I urge Jasmine to slow down, to read in her "normal" voice, and to help us listen to her. I tell the other students to jot down any line that sticks out because it is fabulous or because the line is not working. After students complete their notes, I guide the class in collectively analyzing the poem, going word-by-word and line-by-line.

We start with Jasmine's first line: *Alive today I am Jasmine.* The class loves the line, notes the reference to being alive when so many young people they know are killed. I point out that Jasmine tells us who she is after telling us she's alive, and students reply that being alive is the most important thing given the daily violence they face. Several students appreciate how "today" tells them that she may not expect to be alive tomorrow. That leads perfectly, they argue, into the second line: *I am here to tell you I matter.* I agree with students but ask them to clarify how that line works, and for the first time in the class, there is total silence. One student notes the importance of stating why she is here, and students start talking about what it means to matter. I ask the class to whom Jasmine matters, and they all agree: while she sounded like she meant she mattered to herself, they also thought she meant they had to think she mattered, too. Students dissected this line into hearing Jasmine issue a directive, like Marco argued: "Jasmine told me straight up she matters. She didn't give me no option to think she don't."

At this point, the students are engaged in breaking down the meaning of each line, and eagerly shift to the third line without my prompting. *"I am from Moms and Pops"* immediately becomes a problem. The students do not like it and do not have a language to critique without stating that they do not like it. Juan captures the class sentiment: "It just don't do nothing." I push them to clarify why and one student retorts: "Duh, we all from moms and pops." I step us back and note that not all of us know our birth parents, and ask "how many of us were raised by aunts, uncles, and grandparents." A show of hands indicates two thirds of the students were raised by a range of relatives, neighbors, and adoptive parents. They conclude: the line is too vague. I ask them to think about what this line adds and where the line moves us from the previous forceful directive, and they agree that the line is not needed. We talk for a few minutes about the importance of having meaning in each word, in each line, and not wasting words. I remind them of June Jordan's (in Muller et al., 1995) notion of maximum impact with minimal words and then students start to resist, complaining that I am too focused on meaning and that I care too much about each word. I have gone too far, they

Jasmine Original Intro

*Alive today I am Jasmine and*
*I am here to tell you I matter*
*I am from Moms and Pops*
*but Pops passed and Moms is*
*hardly here and I have two younger*
*sisters I take care of them and*
*I think you'll all know me soon enough*
*because I am here to say*
*something*

Jasmine Revised Intro

Alive today I am Jasmine and
I am here to tell you I matter
I am from torn sheets and bullet riddled streets
too much sugar and ribs and 40's and Pops passed
too much wine and diabetes and tricks and Moms is hardly here
and though barely raised I raise two others
6 am I wake Bobbie and Senti, hurry them into the shower
Unfold the clothes I washed last night
pick their day's outfits
I rush quick oats into the microwave into their mouths
I put the homework I made them do last night into their packs
with quick-made sandwiches, apples, granola bars, and cheetos
because I am here to say even if I don't matter to you
I matter to me
I matter to Bobbie
I matter to Senti
and if I don't matter to you
I am here to say
I should because I am their future
I am you are we are in the same streets
and will only be beautiful together
Alive today I am Jasmine and
I am here to tell you I matter

argue, but then a few students jump in, clarifying that we are helping Jasmine's piece get even better. Jasmine agrees that this process is helpful, and urges the class to continue: "Ya'll have no idea! This is helping me think about where to go next. I can write a *whole* paper from all this stuff!" She continues, cautioning: "But can ya'll take it easy on me? Dang! I can't wait to tear your stuff up!" The class erupts into laughter.

We continue to examine the next few lines, pushing Jasmine for more detail. We stop again at "*I take care of them*" when students ask specifically what Jasmine does. After a few vague starts ("I clean up, I wash up, I make dinner") students guide Jasmine into creating a quick list, which, after some minor editing, ends up on her revision. The last line splits the class: half of the class likes how Jasmine tells us she is here to say something, but the other half is confused. "Why not just tell us what you want to say," they ask Jasmine. She ultimately agrees, and in her revision, tells more about who she is and how she lives. And that is the point in writing with voice: saying what you want to say in a voice so clearly, so powerfully that your intended audience can hear and feel your point. Jasmine's example is typical; most students revise their intros to say more about who they are, and excitedly share details about their lives that they do not share with most of their friends.

The second week ends with students presenting their revised intro read alouds, after spending a few days providing feedback to each other in pairs. When pairs get stuck, they come up to the front of the class, write the troublesome lines on the board and lead the class in soliciting feedback. The point is to get used to starting the class with freewrites, to provide and receive feedback, to ask for individual and collective help from peers, and to get into the practice of continually editing. This helps everyone become more comfortable expressing oneself in public. A shift begins at this point, when students start to share their work in public, and become responsible for honest feedback to each other. They've never done this before, and while it feels scary at first, within a few days, most students are eager to get feedback from peers. There are always exceptions; the impact of being silenced by peers, teachers, and other adults has shut down many students, and some need additional support to open up. I meet one-on-one with those who are most uncomfortable and resistant, and usually after a short discussion or my offer to provide feedback prior to sharing with the rest of the class, students dive in.

## Writing Assignments: Personal Responses to Student Context

There are countless examples of assignments that help students examine how they respond to the context of racism they live within. I often have students respond directly to a poem, song, or short video clip that demonstrates racism in a quick, concise way. I have used dozens of poets, including Audre Lorde, Ai, Chrystos, June Jordan, Sherman Alexie, Aurora Levins Morales and Rosario Morales, Patricia Spears Jones, Rita Dove, Assoto Saint, Ana Castillo, Jimmy Santiago Baca, Justin Chin, Haunani-Kay Trask, augmented by a dozen poetry compilations. I also use books and writing excerpts from James Baldwin, Richard Wright, June Jordan, Sherman Alexie, Derrick Bell, Jonathan Kozol, Sapphire, Jamaica Kincaid, Sara Lawrence-Lightfoot, Danzy Senna, Dorothy Allison, Wallace Shawn, Ngugi wa Thiong'o, Edwidge Danticat, and Junot Diaz, to name a few. In addition to writing texts, I use songs by Oliver Mtukudzi, Zap Mama, Thandiswa, Asa, Gigi, Gil Scott-Heron, Sade, Nneka, Roots, Ice Cube, Midnite, Damian Marley, Clinton Fearon, Annie Humphrey, Immortal Technique, Blue Scholars, Ise-Lyfe, and artists that students bring in to share. To stimulate using visual media, I encourage students to identify YouTube clips that offer particularly concrete or creative examples of racism, and augment these student-initiated sources with clips from films such as *Not One Less* (Guangxi Film Studio & Yimou, 1999), *Life and Debt*

Found Poetic Response to Chrystos' They're Always Telling Me I'm Too Angry by Christina

*For every person who is quiet*
*There are dozens of us dying*
*We bleed their racism*
*While they tell us This Is Not Blood*
*Angry that I cannot walk down the street without someone being afraid*
*Angry that I cannot speak in class without a white student saying I talked over them*
*Angry that I cannot feel human without some white man saying I am in their way*
*Angry that welfare line is as big as my hunger*
*Angry that when I say its always about racism some white person makes me tell him what "it" means when "it" means EVERYTHING!*
*Angry that health care is a battle because white people don't seem to mind war with me*
*Angry that my dad is in prison for what white people do on Saturdays, Mondays, and Wednesdays*
*Angry that everywhere and everyhow and all the time there is racism*
*Seeping into my pores so that I sometimes think*
*I should be afraid of Samoans or Laotians or Croatians*
*So Damn Angry that I sometimes say bitch or ho or whore when I'm referring to my people*
*So So So So impossibly angry that I sometimes am exactly the problem*
*Angry that I sometimes believe what they say about me so that I say*
*What they say about me*
*Angry Angry Angry but thankfully*
*I can breathe on Tuesdays, Wednesdays, Thursdays, and Fridays because we have this class*
*the one place where racism is Not Okay*
*The one place where I am*
*The one place where my sisters and brothers*
*Are allowed to be as angry as me.*

(Black & Kincaid, 2001), *The Business of Fancydancing* (Alexie, Bond, & Benear, 2003), *The Matrix* (Silver, Wachowski & Wachowski, 1999), and other films that are popular at the moment. These sources challenge, critique, and raise awareness of the extensive nature of racism, highlight personal responses, and remind students that racism, and voices highlighting it, is everywhere.

One poem that I have used for years is Chrystos' (1995) "They're Always Telling Me I'm Too Angry." In this passionate poem, Chrystos clarifies the many things that make her angry, justifying both why anger is a natural reaction to oppression, and that voice should be used to identify what these examples of oppression are. The power in the poem is that Chrystos captures racism, sexism, classism, and heterosexism, but also the negative reaction to calling out such oppression from peers, colleagues, and random others. Students read the poem aloud several times, and then respond to one of her final lines: "If you're furious

Assignments to Capture Student Responses

1 Creative freewrites:

a Senses of Racism. In this introductory writing, students freewrite responses to my intermittent prompts of "Racism sounds like…, Racism tastes like…, Racism looks like…, Racism smells like…, Racism feels like…."

b Another word for Racism is….In this freewrite, I encourage students to come up with a list of words that explain what racism is without using the words "race" or "racism." The key is that this list has to be compelling and clear to someone who lives in the distant future.

c Race is What? In this recurring freewrite, students define race as it looks in the room they are currently in. We begin this freewrite in our class, but move to different locations throughout the course, including a grocery store, a homeless shelter, and walking through the neighborhood.

2 Longer assignments:

a Capturing Racism. This paper explores what racism looks like from the author's perspective, and encourages the writer to capture, using descriptive analysis, what racism feels like without using the word. Given your capturing, what do you do to not internalize racism?

b Racism in the Media. In this paper, students compare and contrast two different sources of media, including, for example, one corporate media source such as CNN, Fox News, MTV, and BET, and one independent media source or locally produced musician or radio broadcast. The purpose is to explore what each media source is saying about racism and what the author does to inform herself about the nature of racism.

c Interviewing Racism. This paper combines research with analysis of racism, and is based on students interviewing elders within the community about how they have seen racism changing over the years. Students then compile the interviews into a paper, analyzing themes and providing a comparative perspective of racism today.

with me because I haven't mentioned something you're angry about get busy & write it yourself" (p. 49).

My intent is to teach writing and expression as a developing skill set that can help students survive the daily violence, racism, and trauma that often reflects urban realities. If students need self-defense, then my role as a writing instructor is to help them develop their words as a way out of dangerous situations. If students need anger management, then I encourage them to develop writing as a way of releasing anger. But I also provide curriculum around how schooling teaches us to silence and deny our anger and emotion. I teach students to write about their addictions, to capture what addictions feel like, in the hopes that they will begin to reflect on their reliance upon drugs. And I provide curriculum around the history of drug use, around plantation labor that provides the drugs so many are addicted to. I provide students forums to capture how those they love may be disrespected by society, and then juxtapose that with historical analyses of legal disrespect of low-income communities of color. In essence, I blend what they tell me they need with curriculum content that deepens their understanding of the issues they write about and ways they can respond to increase their chances at meaningful survival.

## Conclusion

This chapter provides a framework for educators to develop, strengthen, and reflect on their own approaches to teaching voice to urban youth. Through capturing stories, experiences, and background context to my personal approaches, I attempt to clarify flexible, responsive, and transparent instructional approaches that encourage students to be themselves, to understand racism and oppression, and begin to develop and find strength in using their voice to challenge what they see as injustice. Because teaching for voice means modeling our voices, demonstrating others who use voice as a profession, and setting up continual writing about the world we live in, assignments allow students the space to write what they need to. Educator techniques that center on freewriting and providing intense feedback and that align classroom management to the purpose of developing voice provide needed structure. The purpose of voice-centered courses is to develop voice through examining personal identity and the larger social context, and then through examining responses to the larger context of racism. This examination is based upon capturing student reality and moving audiences with critical expression. Thus, I try to center student realities, to tap into what motivates students, and to help students express what they would like to change about their immediate world. And in the end, the effectiveness is based entirely upon educator passion; the extent to which students blossom is largely a reflection of the extent to which educators decenter silencing factors that are the norm in most classrooms and schools.

Final Assignment: Letter to my Professor by Shay

Dear Chris:

I feel that this class has helped me express myself better with my words. I've learned how to speak what's on my mind, instead of bottling me all inside. I once thought I used to give too much detail when I spoke. But I've learned that the more I speak with detail others can feel what I feel. This class has helped me get ready for the world's criticism. It has also helped me get a better mindset on how others feel and what they go through. That I'm not the only one struggling in this cold-hearted world.

Chris – Thank you for pushing me when I wanted to just sit back and be lazy. You've seen the words that are stuck in my mind and left on the tip of my tongue. You kept pushing when I couldn't push myself any more, when I wanted class and this school and this world to just be gone. Thanks for helping me express myself. I've always had trouble with that but I feel very confident now that I've been in this class. It was your helping hand that helped me get on that stage to read my poem to all these unknown people. As I clung to the paper and my voice got shaky I remember the love and support from our class and kept on reading. Your voice kept me reading. Thanks for helping me speak out instead of speaking in.

## References


Alexie, S. (Writer/Director), Bond, B. C. (Producer), & Benear, J. (Producer). (2003). *The Business of Fancydancing* [Motion picture]. New York: Wellspring Media.

Allen, Q. (2010). Racial Microaggressions: The Schooling Experiences of Black Middle-Class Males in Arizona's Secondary Schools. *Journal of African American Males in Education, 1*(2), 125–143.

Baldwin, J. (1962). *The Fire Next Time.* New York: Vintage.

Behn, R. (1992). *The Practice of Poetry: Writing Exercises from Poets Who Teach.* New York: Harper Paperbacks.

Berdan, K., Boulton, I., Eidman-Aadahl, E., Fleming, J., Gardner, L., Rogers, I., & Solomon, A. (2006). *Writing for a Change: Boosting Literacy and Learning through Social Action.* National Writing Project. San Francisco, CA: Jossey-Bass.

Black, S. (Director/Producer), & Kincaid, J. (Writer). (2001). *Life and Debt.* New York: Tuff Gong Pictures.

Delpit, L. (2006). *Other People's Children: Cultural Conflict in the Classroom.* New York: New Press.

DeMeulenaere, E. (2009). Fluid Identities: Black Students Negotiating the Transformation of Their Academic Identities and School Performances. *International Journal of Critical Pedagogy, 2*(1), 30–48.

Duncan-Andrade, J. M. R., & Morrell, E. (2008). *The Art of Critical Pedagogy: Possibilities for Moving from Theory to Practice in Urban Schools.* New York: Peter Lang.

Dunning, S., & Stafford, W. (1992). *Found and Headline Poems. Getting the Knack: 20 Poetry Writing Exercises.* Urbana, IL: NCTE.

Fordham, S., & Ogbu, J. (1986). Black Students' School Success: Coping with the Burden of "Acting White." *Urban Review, 18*, 176–206.

Freire, P. (1973). *Education for Critical Consciousness.* New York: Continuum.

Gay, G. (2000). *Culturally Responsive Teaching: Theory, Research, and Practice.* New York: Teachers College Press.

Gibson, M. A., & Ogbu, J. U. (1991). *Minority Status and Schooling: A Comparative Study of Immigrant and Involuntary Minorities.* New York: Garland.

Goldberg, N. (1986). *Writing Down the Bones: Freeing the Writer Within.* Boston, MA: Shambhala.

Goldstein, R. A. (2007). Who You Think I Am Is Not Necessarily Who I Think I Am: The Multiple Positionalities of Urban Student Identities. In J. L. Kincheloe & K. Hayes (Eds.), *Teaching City Kids: Understanding and Appreciating Them,* 97–107. New York: Peter Lang.
Guangxi Film Studio (Producer) & Yimou, Z. (Director/Producer). (1999). *Not One Less* [Motion picture]. China: China Film Group Corporation.
hooks, b. (1994). *Teaching to Transgress.* New York: Routledge.
Howard, G. R. (1999). *We Can't Teach What We Don't Know: White Teachers, Multiracial Schools.* New York: Teachers College Press.
Howerton D., & Thomas, C. (2004). Help for High School Students Who Still Can't Read. *English Journal, 93*(5), 77–82.
Jimerson, S. R., & Kaufman, A. M. (2003). Reading, Writing, and Retention: A Primer on Grade Retention Research. *The Reading Teacher, 56* (7), 622–635.
Jones, L., & Newman, L. (1996). *Our America: Life and Death on the South Side of Chicago.* New York: Pocket Books.
Jordan, J. (2000). *Soldier: A Poet's Childhood.* New York: Basic Books
Kincaid, J. (1988). *A Small Place.* New York: Farrar, Straus, and Giroux.
Knaus, C. B. (2006). *Race, Racism, and Multiraciality in American Education.* Bethesda, MD: Academica Press.
Knaus, C. B. (2007). Still Segregated, Still Unequal: Analyzing the Impact of No Child Left Behind on African American Students. In *The State of Black America: Portrait of the Black Male,* 105-121. Washington, DC: National Urban League.
Knaus, C. B. (2009). Shut Up and Listen: Applied Critical Race Theory in the Classroom. *Race, Ethnicity, and Education, 12*(2), 133–154.
Krishnamurti, J. (1953). *Education and the Significance of Life.* Ojai, CA: Krishnamurti Foundation.
Lynch, M. (2006). *Closing the Racial Academic Achievement Gap.* Chicago, IL: African American Images.
Lyon, G. E. (1999). *Where I Am From: Where Poems Come From. Young Writers Series #2.* Spring, TX: Absey & Co.
McIntyre, A. (1997). *Making Meaning of Whiteness: Exploring Racial Identity with White Teachers.* New York: SUNY Press.
Mtukudzi, O. (2004). *Tozeza. Nhava.* Tuku Music/Sheer Sound: Zimbabwe.
Mtukudzi, O. (2006). *Tozeza. Wonai.* Tuku Music/Sheer Sound: Zimbabwe.
Muller, L., Bright., S., Changler, G., Esteva, A., Lewis, S., Rose, S., Smith, S., Teves, S., Villalobos, R. A., & Wilson, P. (1995). *June Jordan's Poetry for the People: A Revolutionary Blueprint.* New York: Routledge.
Pierce, C. (1974). Psychiatric Problems of the Black Minority. In S. Arieti (Ed.), *American Handbook of Psychiatry,* 512–523. New York: Basic Books.
Sapphire. (1996). *Push.* New York: Vintage.
Silver, J. (Producer), Wachowski, A. (Writer/Director), & Wachowski, L. (Writer/Director). (1999). *The Matrix* [Motion picture]. Burbank, CA: Warner Bros.
Solorzano, D., Ceja, M., & Yosso, T. (2000). Critical Race Theory, Racial Microaggressions, and Campus Racial Climate. *Journal of Negro Education, 69*(1), 60–73.
Steele, C. M., & Aronson, J. (1995). Stereotype Threat and the Intellectual Test Performance of African Americans. *Journal of Personality and Social Psychology, 69*(5), 797–811.
Stovall, D. (2006). From Hunger Strike to High School: Youth Development, Social Justice, and School Formation. In S. Ginwright, P. Noguera, & J. Cammarota (Eds.), *Beyond Resistance! Youth Activism and Community Change,* 97–109. New York: Routledge.
Tannenbaum, J., & Bush, V. C. (2005). *Jump Write In! Creative Writing Exercises for Diverse Communities, Grades 6–12.* San Francisco: Jossey-Bass.
Wyngaard, M. V. (2007). Culturally Responsive Pedagogies: African American High School Students' Perspectives. In J. L. Kincheloe & K. Hayes (Eds.), *Teaching City Kids: Understanding and Appreciating Them,* 121–129. New York: Peter Lang.

# In Search of Peace

I have tethered my soul with boulders
I have reforged my will in the cauldron of suffering
And now, I enact my ultimate choice....
I step back from the circle of life.

I will give sustenance to the corn
As I stare sightlessly at the sky
Striving to behold the glory of God
I will prove a bounty for the field mice
And on my silent lips, flies shall sing
Of their newfound home

The cloying fragrance of my putrefaction
Will lead you to my intended state
Perhaps then, you'll have a glimpse
Of my personal hell

To those of you I leave behind
Know that I loved you all too well
But of the pain that swam behind my eyes
I could not tell
On my demise, please, do not dwell

I have anchored my soul with boulders
And I chose to step outside the circle
In search of peace.

||TWO

# Students' Stories: Bear & Antoine

Greg S. Goodman

The short vignettes in this chapter are stories from students about their experiences in traditional and alternative schools. Our goal in the interviews was to hear the stories of the affects of schooling from those involved. Importantly, we wanted to know what we as educators could do to ameliorate the problems with schooling. The first interview, Bear's story, was one of approximately forty interviews conducted in conjunction with a research project funded by the University of California Educational Research Center. Bear's story stood out because we hear his voice speaking from a position of tremendous personal agency. Bear, a Native American, grew up in a gang driven, chaotic culture of violence, drugs, and hate. This young man's tale is the quintessential story of transformation. Bear turns a life of hate and violence into a love-linked story of his recovery.

This research and analysis follows the advice of Giroux (1992) to take seriously the voices of the students on the border. Before the voices turn to screams of gunfire, we need to hear when these students ask us to listen. We can no longer wait for the words to explode in symbolic manifestations of rage against the real or imagined perpetrators of exclusion. Exclusion is not solely the externalizing bailiwick of cliques such as preps, jocks, stoners, skaters, or an "other." Exclusion is internalized as the victim feels the isolation from multiple separations: familial disintegration; personally meaningless curriculum; large, alienating school/institutions; addiction's malaise; and linguistic/cultural disconnections (Bourdieu, 1993). Giroux (1992) appeals to all critical educators to "not only hear the voices of those students who have been traditionally silenced, they must take seriously what all students say by engaging the implications of their discourse in broader historic and relational terms" (p. 33).

Bear is both Native American and a border youth, and his story is inspirational. Refined through the experience of multiple telling at Alcoholics Anonymous (AA) and Narcotics (Users) Anonymous (NA) meetings, Bear's tale takes the reader on a trip into the horrors of alcohol and other drug abuses like a travel log. Bear is a modern Jean Valjean. A convict transformed, Victor Hugo's character Valjean is able to overcome a life of tremendous adversity to inspire *Les Misérables* as he reaffirms the possibility that good can prevail despite the powerful and ubiquitous press of evil. This, too, is Bear's work. He rises from jail to join his community and exemplify positive change. As Bear tells his story in Alcoholics Anonymous meetings or less formalized groups, the impact of his suffering and the pain he imposed reflect the reality that border youth experience.

## Bear's Story

> The natural education of the Indian boys and girls was a simple method of teaching the young how to live successfully and well, just as their fathers and mothers had done it. Indian boys and girls went to the school of life and in it learned from the taskmaster of Experience how to live. (Parker, 1954, p. 112)

**Bear:** OK. When I was around the age of five, I was introduced to alcohol and my family was a really dysfunctional family. My father was never around for me. My mother was an alcoholic. My father was a drug addict/drug dealer. Ah, so I was around an environment from day one, you know. My mother, from what I've heard, she was drinking when I was in her, while she was pregnant. So I already had the feel of what alcohol was. Ah, as I grew up, around the age of eight years old, I was introduced to marijuana because my brother was out there doing drugs, you know, ah, and so I got on to drugs. My brother and his friends used to come to the house, get high. I remember a time when I'd get high I'd be so stupid, I'd end up going to a friend's house, a good friend, I'd tell him to come over and I'd fight him. You know, I was high; I didn't know what I was doing. You know the drug controlled me. And as I got a little older, I started hanging around the wrong crowd, which was a tagging crowd. You know writing on walls and things like that. I started getting into stealing cars a lot. And doing more drugs, more alcohol, hurting people more. I was around the age of eleven years old, or twelve years old. And I was already out there into gangs, writing on walls, taking people's cars, like on a daily basis. I got caught a couple times stealing cars.

*Bear starts to discuss the low self-esteem that burdened his entire existence. It was his lack of self-esteem that allowed him to succumb to the negative influences that were all around. Between his mother's alcoholism and his father selling drugs the two most important adult figures in his life were not and could not be there for him in a positive way. Bear began to steal at the age of 12 to support his drug habit. As his drug and alcoholic habit became more intense, so did he begin to steal larger, items eventually ending up in juvenile hall for Grand Theft Auto.*

*By the age of 14 Bear was stealing cars and committing home invasions making it so he was in and out of several detention centers in his area. After a stint of three months in a detention center, Bear entered his sophomore year at Hoover High. Because of his newfound sobriety, Bear began to get good grades. Unfortunately his sobriety lasted only eight months when he began hanging out with old friends and doing old things.*

*After he started drinking again, Bear became involved in gangs. His grades began to drop. Ah, my grades were dropping a little bit. Bear stated that even though he went to school noticeably high "the teacher wouldn't tell me to go to the office, or nothing." You know, it's just, everything, is like a repeating cycle. Everything just does the same thing over and over and you can't get out of it. And everything progresses. You start off tagging and it leads to hardcore gang banging and things like that.*

**Goodman:** How did you get out of that lifestyle?

**Bear:** Well, I got out of it, actually, I'll tell you how it all happened. The last time I got locked up, ah, I was real drunk. I was drinking at five o'clock that day until, like, two o'clock in the morning. And I was off acid, off like a whole bunch of alcohol and weed. And I blacked out. I stole a car, went out, and I tried to kill someone. I don't remember doin' it, but I tried to kill someone. So they caught me. They locked me up. And I went to court and I found out that I had attempted murder, assault with a deadly weapon, vehicle theft, and all these hard charges. So I was already facing fifteen to life. So it scared me to death right there. And I was locked up for the first two months and I was still gang banging because I couldn't let go of it. I was scared 'cause I was afraid I was going to get killed from the gang that I was in. Like if I was going to get out, they were going to kill me. So the first two months I was still gang banging, getting into fights with people in Juvenile Hall. And then one day, my sister sent me a letter, and it had her picture in it. And, ah, I started to cry and I started to pray to God that I don't want to live this life no more. I'm tired of this life. Get me out of this life, please, Lord. And, ah, so, ah, one of the counselors heard me praying and everything, crying and everything, like that, and he comes in there and goes, you know what, have faith. Have faith, God will get you through this. God will get you through this. You'll be all right. He started reading the Bible to me and everything. So finally, every day after that, I started thinking about the Lord all day and things just started changing for me.

It's just a miracle because I didn't do it on my own. It was like a higher power and God. You know God is a higher power. And, ah, he started changing me inside out. I mean I started having feelings for people. I didn't want the life I was living. And, ah, I just started worshipping God. I started getting into the Lord. And I started doing ministry in there to keep me focused on the Lord. I talked to kids in there. When people in the Hall would start having problems, the counselors would change me from the room I'm in and put me in their room. And I would calm everything down. You know, I'd help people out. You know, so, ah, I was in there for eight months. For six months I was doing that right there, doing like peer counseling. And doing God's work.

So, after eight months, ah, I finally get out. You know, I get put in a recovery home. I'm in a recovery home for five months. And, ah, the recovery home was really, really good. They helped me to get to know my inner self. Which now I feel comfortable with myself, because I had a lot of past emotions which I've explained, like my dysfunctional family and things like that. And I had to let these things out. I had a lot of anger towards my father and things like that, because he was never around. So, ah, the recovery home really helped me out. And it helped me to live life on my terms, how it is today. And to try to take one day at a time. And that's what I do; take one day at a time until the day is over. And anyway, that's basically what made me want to change. I was going to get fifteen-to-life, and that the hurt I put my family through. And I had to do it. After being sober for a while, it was my time. I had to surrender.

**Goodman:** I'd like to turn this now toward school and ask you about your school experiences

**Bear:** OK. Elementary I got in a few fights. But seventh grade, junior high, that's when it all started. That's with the taggin' stuff, you know. I would get into fights. I got into a good seven, eight fights at that school. And I got put in Opportunity (Alternative Education). I was there in seventh grade for 'bout two months, three months the most. And they put me in the Opportunity class. And I stayed in the Opportunity class, still getting in fights with people. And then, my eighth grade year, I did the same thing. I was able to go back to the regular school, regular hours, and I was getting in fights all the time. And it's crazy, man. Filled with anger, lots of anger. It was like the family. I didn't have anyone there to really help me. I mean my mother was there, but, my father, I never had that male role model in my life. So I never had no guidance, no direction. There was always a person to comfort me, my mother. But I never had that man in my life telling me, "No, you can't do that."

You know, so in my eighth grade year, I'm still fighting and they put me back in Opportunity school. Opportunity, it was good. It was all right. But, ah, I still didn't like school. I didn't come to school. I didn't come to school because I was busy out there drinkin' and smokin' weed. I didn't like school. I hated school. From eighth grade, I got kicked out of school. I had to go to Juvenile Hall School now. Now, I'm at the Juvenile Hall school, I'm still doin' drugs. Basically, my life is all based on doin' drugs and alcohol. They put me this way and put me that way, you know.

Ninth grade I got some credits, ah, in ah, in ah, community school, Juvenile Hall school. And then from being locked up, I was able to catch up on a lot of work, though I got out in Wakefield. I got put in C K Wakefield, so I was able to catch up on a lot of work. So, I'm actually happy that I got locked up to catch up on the work. Today, I'm caught up with all my credits. Ah, it, it, it's been hard. It really has.

And then I went to my sophomore year. My sophomore year I had no problems at school. Everybody loved me because I'm really an outgoing person. I'm really outspoken. And I don't really like hurting people's feelings. You know, that's when I'm sober.

I'm at Quality now. I started there at the beginning of this school year I've been doin' great there. I mean, I haven't gotten in no trouble at all. It's like my life turned completely around. I'm a better human being. It's all because I do meditation to God. I cannot do anything on my own. You know, I'm hopeless without God. That's something I had to have. And, ah, so today, I'm doin' great in school. I'm graduating this year. I'm involved in peer counseling, talkin' to kids. Like I go to schools and I do speeches based on my past history like I did today. I talk to families and things like that about what grade level to watch your kid at. When things start changing, when their hormones start kickin' in. Everything starts changin' for them.

I've been involved with recovery for six or seven months. And it's great, you know, it's good because when you go to meetings you can let everything out. I mean, you go to meetings, AA meetings, NA meetings, whatever, and you can just let everything out. And nobody will not say anything to you like all right, because we all been there. We all know how it is to be addicted to the alcohol and drugs. We also do that here.

In fact we'll be doin' that today. We have AA meetings and NA meetings at school. You know I thought that was a great thing to have because, I mean, at the beginning, when we first started the Alcohol Anonymous program and the Narcotics Anonymous program at our school, people were not talking. So, I was more, having to talk, get 'em through it, and so they would feel comfortable and trust you, you know. Because one thing that's really important is confidentiality. That's something that's really important. We don't talk about nothin'; after that meeting, you don't talk about nothin'. Not to anyone. You know, that was that. If you want to talk to that person one on one, after the meeting, that's all right. But you can't let no one else's information out. Unless, it's a school environment, unless they're havin' sexual problems, and things like that, you know, normal things that have to be reported. I thought it was a really great thing because kids are able to come to school, go to these meetings, and let all the frustration and anger out.

And you know, they're doin' it now. They had to get used to it. They had to start getting that trust. And we gave 'em that trust. They're opening up. And they're letting their feelings out about things. And some people, they want to quit doin' the drugs. It's just so hard. I know how it is and how hard it is because I had to get locked up just to quit doin' drugs. Them out here, they're not locked up and they're hangin' around with the same people. And it's really hard. You know, it's just, what I'm trying to get into them is, you know, your life is more important. You've got to think about yourself first, right now. And not worry about the other people. Your self comes first right now. When you get your self, when you get your roles fixed, then you can go out and help other people.

**Goodman:** One more question for you concerning racism and your experiences with racism both within the traditional public school and in the alternative school you now attend.

**Bear:** As a matter of fact it was, it was racism. You can say it. But it was more of a racism on the gangs. But it was also racism on Hmongs. I could not stand Hmongs because they killed some of my friends, so, ah; I had that racism in me. You know, but now, it's over, you know. I talk to Asians; I talk to every ethnic group. But, yeah, that was a problem.

**Goodman:** At Quality High School?

**Bear** No. Not a problem. At Quality High School right now, is really goin' great. I mean, I try my best to keep everything calm. And which, I'm glad it's working, you know. God gave me the gift to talk to people, and I've been keeping things calm. I mean, not too long ago, a kid was gonna fight someone, but I calmed it down, and I talked to them for a little while. I let 'em know it's not worth it. Right now you're in school. Let this be on the streets or whatever. You know, handle your business in school.

So I think, if you have a really good role model in the school, especially in a small environment like this, it makes a big difference.

Bear's story first came to me in a training session for peer mediators at an intermediate school where I worked. Bear had come to help train seventh and eighth grade students in the processes of peer mediation. As Bear stood before these students and told them his story, everyone in the room was deeply moved. His message was, "I was the kid no one wanted to associate with. I was trouble for everyone who knew me." The message that Bear shared needed to be heard, as all students need to be listened to and respected. Short of that, those students end up raging and on a mission to destroy.

After hearing Bear's talk at my school, I knew I wanted to interview him to find out more about how his personal transformation occurred. Although Bear credits God with his salvation, the experience of violence and the pain of sober reflection on the past ravages of his life must also be factored in to Bear's change.

A follow-up with him one year after this interview located him in attendance at the local community college and continuing his sobriety. Whatever the motivation for his recovery and redirection, Bear's story is one of hope for those who work with disaffected youth.

Lessons and conclusions from Bear's story are multiple. First, we must listen to the voices from the border if we are ever to begin to connect to the people who need help the most. Listening is the first step in the process of validation and the development of personal agency (Rogers, 1969). As Bear's story is heard, he is transformed, and he develops a meaningful identity. Bear, in his new role as a positive model, is winning the recognition and respect necessary for the development of a positive self-esteem and the maintenance of successful relationships.

## Antoine's Story

> What are we gonna do when all we seen is fuckin' drugs, alcohol, fighting, this and that, no one going to school? (MacLeod, 1995, p. 117)

Not all students benefit from alternative school experiences. Some alternative schools are unable to break from the heavy rule sets that make them strikingly similar to the schools from which the students were removed (Goodman, 1999). Antoine's case is instructive because his school is really not an alternative, it is a court school within a detention facility. Like the "Hallway Hangers" in Jay MacLeod's (1995) *Ain't No Makin' It*, Antoine is enrolled in a program designed for "fuck-ups" (pp. 116–117).

Antoine is working to make good decisions and to overcome the racism and alienating social factors that confront him. Sadly, he is still schooled in an environment that demeans his culture and doubts his integrity. This is the total opposite of Antoine's need for emancipatory education (Murrell, 1997).

**Goodman:** Tell me about your family, friends, and yourself.

**Antoine:** To start off with my life, I am a young 15-year-old Black male. I come from Los Angeles, California. I moved to Las Vegas when I was 10 years old. I moved to Las Vegas with my mother. She wanted me to get away from Los Angeles because it seemed that every Black male we knew was getting killed or locked up. I understand why my mother moved, but at times I wish we hadn't because that doesn't mean it would've happened to me. We also knew a lot of people who survived living in Los Angeles. It seems the same things in Los Angeles are in Las Vegas, but not as bad.

When I got to Las Vegas I got into more trouble since day one. I miss it in Los Angeles. It seems I never did fit in with people here in Vegas. I guess different people from different habitats don't mix. I say that because the things people do in Vegas are backwards from the things people do in Los Angeles. A lot of people from

California or other places feel the same. I had some friends and a lot of them turned on me or we just stopped talking. That's why I trust no one anyway but some of my family. I stay with my mother. She's single; its just her, my sister and niece, and me. My other family is in California or dead or in other states. I often think about them, especially the dead ones. My grandfather and uncle are dead, my grandmother and aunt are still alive. My other aunties and uncles are in Los Angeles. They're all right I guess; I haven't heard from them in awhile. I come from a family where Jesus is important in your life, that's why I stay strong with the Lord.

I stay in an all right neighborhood. It's not made for me though. It has racism over here especially because more Blacks are moving over here. It used to be mostly Whites. You can tell by the way the people talk to you or look at you. They get as far away from you as possible, and call the police on you just for standing outside. The school police are racist, too. When I used to sit across the street from my friends' school waiting for them, the school police said I couldn't wait. But I saw White kids and parents waiting for their kids and they didn't tell them anything. Then another day after school the Metro Police pulled over all the Black kids, saying they're looking for drugs and weapons but didn't say anything to the White kids that carry weapons and do all sorts of drugs. They found nothing on me and my friends, but that's just the way it is in life. I hang around a couple of people. They're cool I guess. I used to hang around a lot of people but they were shady. They would turn on me, say false things about me, and be phony. The people I hang around with now we've known each other for a while. They're cool. One of them likes to get in trouble by just doing stupid stuff. That's why I limit myself away from him now. I also got another friend who is older. He's cool. He's about doing positive things which is cool, because I get tired of getting in trouble all the time. He laces me up and plays a peep game out of me. I guess it's because he's been there and through it and don't want me to. He could be fake like everybody else. But I just want to make it in life and get through things in this generation. It's hard for this generation to make it because the world wasn't right since the U.S.A. was established. But I know I can't change the world so I just have to cope with things the way they are, even if it ain't right. That's why I don't let things hold me down in life. If I did, I wouldn't get anywhere in life, because the world is too full of drama. Out of all the things I have done and experienced, I hope I'll make it in life, but I think I will. I made it this far. I just don't want to be like some people I know trying to get their lives together and change, and then life just catches up with them worse than before. That's why it all comes back on you when you least expect it. It ain't right, but its payback for something you did way back.

**Goodman:** Tell me about your traditional school experiences.

**Antoine:** In my elementary I went to Purche Elementary School in Gardenia, California. It was a cool little school. I knew everyone there because I stayed in the same neighborhood as everybody else who went to the school. I walked to school in the morning with my friends who stayed across the street from me. We always stopped at the wash in the morning and wasted all our money on video games, and when we got to school we got somebody for their money or lunch ticket. Other kids used to try to talk about me because I was bigger than the kids in my grade, so I had to let them know what was happening.

My first grade teacher was cool. She was always on my case, and when I messed up she would be the first to tell my mamma what I did. I remember when I spit on this kid at school and she told my grandpa when he picked me up from school. I used to get into fights every other week in school. Kids would try to test me. I got into trouble but not like the trouble I get into in Vegas. I was getting cool grades in school. I used to score good on tests at the end of the year. I had friends. Everyone knew me and my reputation because I was there so long. I remember one school year we had a new rookie teacher. He didn't know what he was doing or what to do with us, so we took advantage and did what we wanted to. It was fun until they gave us another teacher.

The memories I had in school are good and bad; the good ones are the field trips and friends. I got into more trouble when I came to Vegas in elementary than in Los Angeles. I got into a fight my first day in school. I started high school in Opportunity School. I should be going to regular high school next year. The traditional school for me was fun when you could wear your own clothes, go to lunch, and have fun.

Drugs weren't really a problem because if kids did it, they did it after school.

There kind of was racism in regular school. You could tell the White kids were the favorites.

**Goodman:** Tell me about your alternative school experience.

**Antoine:** I got into Opportunity School after I had just got out for fighting. I got into a fight with some dude. A teacher got in the way and she fell. She got back up, then I hit her by accident. My opinion on Alternative School is it's stupid because of the stupid rules. They treat you more like you're in jail instead of helping us. Rules like "tuck your shirt in," "wear a belt," some regular, but more complicated rules. There was this one teacher I didn't like. She was some woman who would say you were sagging when you wasn't. One time she said I was tagging on the board when I was erasing it. There was some cool ones who would help you get out. The only thing I like about this school is the time you got out; we go from 7:30 to 11:15 a.m. I miss the freedom and fun of going to regular school and it was bigger. I also miss the education. You learn more and better. I think it tells you how the system will treat you.

I think the problems that are going on are because people don't understand other people. If someone gets angry in their head and no one understands, it's going to make a person more mad, especially kids today. They come from messed-up families, don't fit in, do crack and heroin, and face a lot of problems people in the world face but worse.

The school I'm in now does not have racism because we have all done something to be in here. They have no drug problem because the school is right inside of juvenile detention, but some have tried to bring in the weed, minor things and got caught because they told everybody.

Well that sums it all up for what I have to say about Alternative School and how I feel about it. I hope you can use my information about my life experiences that I have gone through and dealt with while being in this isolated schooling.

*Antoine is in jail school. He is not enrolled in an alternative school. Alternative schools are spaces of liberation and transformation, not isolation and discrimination! Ironically, Antoine has a greater awareness and knowledge of his needs than the educators charged and paid to provide for him.*

*As Antoine begins his story, the singular issue of race portends to tell it all. Antoine knows of African Americans' disproportional experience of death by homicide and suicide, and his immediate family has experienced violence and death. As Antoine says, "She [his mother] wanted me to get away from Los Angeles because it seemed that every Black male we knew was getting killed or locked up." Antoine feels betrayed by America: "The world wasn't right since the USA was established." Sending Antoine to an alternative placement within a jail reinforces negative stereotypes of African Americans and does little, if anything, to instill feelings of personal agency. Continuing to isolate African Americans from the world is reinforcing of institutional racism and should be strongly refuted by educators and contested by community advocates.*

*It is through critical process that we must work to build schools of support for all alienated students. Peter Murrell (1997) cites Cornel West: "The collapse of the meaning in life—the eclipse of hope and absence of love of self and others, the breakdown of family and neighborhood bonds—leads to the social deracination and cultural denudement of urban dwellers, especially children. We have created rootless, dangling people with little link to the supportive networks—family friends, school—that sustain some sense of purpose in life" (p. 26).*

*Antoine's story is too common. His experience speaks to the continuing immensity of racism's stranglehold on African American youth. Our responsibility is to feel the urgency and to confront this war on youth with positive alternatives for all students within each of our communities.*

## References

Bourdieu, Pierre. (1993). *The field of cultural reproduction*. New York: Columbia University Press.
Giroux, Henry. (1992). *Border crossing: Cultural workers and the politics of education*. New York: Routledge.

Goodman, Greg S. (1999). *Alternatives in education: Critical pedagogy for disaffected youth*. New York: Peter Lang Publishing.
MacLeod, Jay. (1995). *Ain't no makin' it.* Boulder, CO: Westview Press.
Murrell, Peter C. (1997). Digging again the family wells. In *Mentoring the mentor: A critical dialogue with Paulo Freire,* edited by Paulo Freire. New York: Peter Lang Publishing.
Parker, Arthur C. (1954). *The Indian how book.* New York: Dover Publications.
Rogers, Carl. (1969). *Freedom to learn.* Columbus, OH: Charles E. Merrill Publishing Co.

# Poetry

I feed the anger
Caress it gently like an old lover
I feel the hunger rise, an insatiable vortex
An eater of words
I consume galaxies and constellations
Re-forging truths from the dawn of eternity
I spit them back... jewels in a hurricane
Tears disguised as rain.

# THREE

# Interlude II

## *So, I Never Speak. I Write.*

Rasheedah S. Woodard

I was born with fluid-filled lungs; coughing, choking, no tears, no screams, no voice…silent. I filled notebooks with stories about little girls with no voices, little girls who could make themselves disappear, pretty skinny girls with light skin long hair and light skin boyfriends. My mama bought me my first diary at 10. I wrote that I wanted to be pretty to be light to disappear. At times, I wrote that I wanted to die. I wrote songs of pain and desperation. Black, Brown, white, men, women, and children slashed my tongue each time they told me "you ugly too Black too dark stupid too smart a girl poor too skinny too fat too tall not girly enough too angry too sensitive too quiet talk ghetto talk white dyke faggot homo." I swallowed and absorbed these racist, sexist, classist, and homophobic shards of glass until I was blood stained with self-hatred that kept me quiet and wanting to die. So I never speak. I write.

Surrounded by people who hated me crushed my spirit but made me a fighter. Like a sheep amongst wolves, I walked into my cracked dingy dirty apartment building infested by gangs, guns, drugs, drunks, attackers, abusers, perverts, and murderers; I was always vulnerable, exposed. Hoping and wishing no one offered me drugs, fought me, grabbed me. My mama tried to protect me by never allowing me to play outside until middle school, teaching me how to fist fight, how to use a switchblade, never to talk to strangers, to stay away from parked cars, keep my legs closed, stay away from boys, men, and she forced me to confront anyone who messed with me. Like daggers, "ugly" "Black" "burnt" "ho" stabbed me by vicious tongues of *brothers*, *aunties*, *sisters*, and *friends*. Constantly having to fight venomous tongues, ferocious girls trying to jump me, seeing if I was a "punk," friends talking behind my back, touchy, grabby, boys trying to see if I would fuck, bloods trying to fight me for wearing blue, kept me ready to throw punches and quick to pull out my switchblade. My mama always told me "if anybody ever put they hands on you, fuck 'em up," "don't trip off what people say; only trip if they put they hands on you," "always speak yo' mind," and "be an independent strong Black woman." I fought to prove I wasn't a punk, I said no to prove I wasn't a ho, I acted like nothing bothered me to prove I was a strong independent Black woman but was I ugly? My mama always said I was beautiful but every one else said I was ugly. I wrote that I was unwanted, dirty, dark.

I never felt safe at home. Men's and women's assaults carved me with self-hatred so deep I hid under hoody's, baggy sweats, baggy uniforms, and x-large jackets. I figured if everyone said I was ugly, then what's the use of trying to be anything more? I stayed to myself. Grinning men called me ugly while grabbing my butt, trying to put their slobbering mouths on me, trapping me in corners and trying to steal my innocence. Light skin men who, when no one was around, pinned my fighting arms down, shoved their tongues in my mouth, and rammed their hands between my legs. The same light skin men who, in public, called me "ugly" "Black" and "burnt." I never asked to be assaulted. Light skin boyfriends told me I was cute, pretended to be my friend, and didn't accept *no*. My ovaries were torn from my womb and breasts ripped off each time a Black man grabbed my wrists, dug their nails into my skin, clasped their hand over my mouth, forced me down, fought my fists and kicks, and rammed their penis inside me because I was a dark Black girl *asking for it*. I wrote: Maybe I *was* ugly? Maybe I *was* stupid? Maybe I *was* trash? Maybe it *was* my fault men kept assaulting me?

My mama's words and hugs weren't enough to fight against everyone else's words and touches. I started to believe I was ugly, *Black*, stupid, too smart, too dark, too fat, not worthy of living. I stayed in my room with my bad thoughts, my music, and my writing.

IAMblackuglystupiddarkfatunworthy

IAMblackuglystupiddarkfatunworthy

IAMblackuglystupiddarkfatunworthy. I force-fed myself the hatred spewed at me. I never smiled because I knew I was ugly. I suffered in silence; a mixture of hating myself, fearing men, and denying being molested, raped, and abused that imprinted me with an internal sadness and volatile anger never acknowledged but increasingly building. I erupted with each punch thrown, each slice of my wrists, each carve of my thighs, each pill swallowed, and each time I shoved my face in the toilet vomiting out my hate, pain, and insides.

size 13

size 10

size 6

Spitting up blood, I watched my soul swirl away and my curves drop. So I wrote.

School was the only place I felt relatively safe. Mostly Black, much Brown, a few Pacific Islanders and 3 white boys, my inner city school lacked books, adequate teachers, and financial resources, which created low API scores and most of us never graduating. Surrounded by barbed-wire fences and subject to lockdowns, school was an incarcerating assimilatory process of memorizing rich white heterosexual men, chemical equations, mathematical proofs, grammar, a celebration of murderers and regurgitation of information meant to get me into the *best* schools, obtain the *best* careers, and obtain the *best* house, car, and family. But school is where teachers said, "you're smart advanced gifted intelligent." I worked hard to be a great scientist, a critical thinker, an excellent writer. School is the only thing I succeeded in; the only place life was kinda ok. Graduating top 1% of my class, I focused on my education to deny life at home. I wrote that I was accepted into the University of California, Berkeley.

At Cal, I was repeatedly reminded of my background being around white, Asian, Latino, and Black students who grew up in one family inhabited houses, with parents who were business owners, professors, doctors, and lawyers. Private school students who drove Mercedes and BMW's, and made me feel small for being the poor lil' Black girl who had to work, that went to *that* type of school, grew up in *that* type of neighborhood, and had *that* type of family. UC Berkeley is a microcosm of corporate America where Black folks represent less than 3%, white Americans 32.8%, Asian Americans 39.9%, Latinos 13%, and Indigenous Americans less than 1% and is just as divisive (Office of Student Research and Campus Surveys, 2010). White and Asian students constantly assumed I was an idiot athlete incompetent affirmative action charity case. White and Asian students calling me a "nigger affirmative action case" to my face, touching my hair like they were buying me off an auction block, staring at me, the only Black student, to speak for the entire Black community, and always asking if I was an athlete made me cut deeper lacerations into my thighs. I was a diversity token to enhance white students' *well-rounded* college experience. I walked around campus with purses clutched at the sight of me, rolled up windows and locked doors from fear of me. I wrote that I cut my arms and legs.

I want to be an OB/Gyn so I was pre-med. General Chemistry had 6 Black students out of over 500 and in Calculus there were 9 of us out of a different 500 students. I was constantly faced with entitled glaring Chinese and white students with stares of rejection "*you're* in this class?" "why would I study with *you*?" "I'd rather study with *anyone else.*" Advisors told me I should think about something *other* than medicine. I focused on my stoichiometry and writing to forget the constant attacks. I just wanted to stay under the covers, but sleep was night terrors, lost hair, stomach pains, migraines. I was dying in the sciences. I wrote that I *was* a stupid, unworthy, charity case.

Writing has always been my escape, my outlet, my solace. When I couldn't speak, I wrote. When there was no one to talk to, I wrote. I wrote to bury my thoughts and emotions. I was alone. I couldn't breathe. I needed a space to write. Freshmen year, I forced my way into an African American Studies R1A writing class entitled Social Justice and the Written Word: Developing Personal and Critical Expression because I was in pieces, disconnected, numb, and dying. I was screaming inside. I needed to write to get away. In this class, I sat in a circle, waitlisted. I listened to a white man thank students for sharing this space, ask us how we were doing, and critique his whiteness and privilege as a professor in African American Studies. He asked us to freewrite for 1 min and share. I heard him and fellow students read freewrites on child abuse, violence against women, 1st generation students with undocumented parents, racism at Cal, and so much more. Listening to my colleagues share that much on the first day of class forced me to sit with myself and write, rewrite, and begin to share my truth. My professor pushed me to write seriously and profusely; not to write blindly, vaguely, or passively but with purpose. I started to write about white slave owners raping Black women, Black male headed organizations pushing Black women into kitchens, Black women fighting to be seen as Black AND female, rich white males leaving crumbs for everyone else to share, and a legacy of discriminatory poverty-stricken second-class citizenship stemming from genocide of Indigenous Americans and Western slavery to this day.

Through this class, I began to listen and acknowledge experiences long silenced. This meant admitting that I endured a horrific past and was hurting myself in the present. I beat myself down more and more as I tried to put myself back together. I was numb, detached, and in fragments. Through writing and reflecting, I confronted the internalized hatred and distorted image I had become. I took walks, sat alone in my room, cried, and fought myself to write my thoughts. My classmates listened, snapped, and said "you're such a powerful writer, I'm soooo glad you said that, I wish I could be as brave as you, write like you." Sitting in a circle, facing each other, raw and uncompromised, we listened to each person share their voice. We wrote together, sat in silence together, read Pumla Gobodo-Madikizela, bell hooks, June Jordan, Edwidge Danticat and gave feedback on each other's papers. With my skin inside out, I read my poems and papers aloud to the class. Repeatedly, my classmates and professor critiqued my writings. My professor's voice screamed in my head "Stop being vague!" "Show ME, don't tell me!" "here is where your voice comes in…PUSH on that!" I fought the feedback tooth and nail. How could someone critique my experiences? Critical feedback forced me to reflect on my delivery, thought process, expanded my consciousness and strengthened my voice. By writing, sharing my thoughts, feelings, and experiences, I acknowledged and validated myself. Through my process, I realized how broken I had become. Now, I write to heal my mind, body, and soul.

I write because Black women are dying. I was dying. I am still not completely whole but my process helped me to write, speak, and act. Once I acknowledged and voiced my past and pain, I cut myself less and less, vomited less and less, beat myself less and less; until I stopped. Instead of hurting myself, I mentor women and girls with similar backgrounds as mine; I tell them my story to help them write theirs. I write with them. Constantly sitting with myself, thinking and writing forced me to realize I dropped everything to listen, console, and heal a woman who revealed being raped by a man because I was molested and raped by men. I work with girls and women suffering from suicidal thoughts, eating disorders, depression, low self-esteem, mental disorders, colorism, and any other "isms" plaguing her existence because our community, collective reflection, writing, and sharing helps me face my own depression, suicidal tendencies, eating disorders, low self-esteem, and internalized isms. I continue to heal myself while I empower and validate the voices of other lil' Black and Brown girls thinking death is a better option, that her curves are disgusting, that food is the enemy, eating a battle, and that vomit has to be a daily part of life. Collective healing, reflecting, and writing are how I transform my silence into action. So I continue to write.

Silence won't help you, save you, or benefit you. I struggled writing this piece because I still struggle with believing my voice is valid. That anybody cares. I can't believe I've revealed so much to you, the reader; but acknowledging, vocalizing and writing, my internalized racism, classism, colorism, and homophobia marked the transformation of my silence into liberation of my mind, body, and spirit through voice. Everything I fought not to say, I fought to keep hidden, I fought to relinquish and/or deny only festered and became the poison that contaminated my mind, body, and spirit. So I write to release and heal other women of color. I write because 1 in 6 women will be sexually assaulted/raped (Tjaden & Thoennes, 1998). I write because 65% of Black women living with AIDS will die. I write that 77% of new HIV/AIDS diagnoses are Black women (Centers for Disease Control and Prevention [CDCP], 2010). I write that over 40,000 women die of breast cancer (CDCP, 2010). I write that only 50% of Brown and Black students graduate from high school (NAACP, 2006; Orfield, Losen, Wald, Swanson, 2004; Stillwell, 2010). I write that 65% of prisoners are Black and Brown men and women (Human Rights Watch Backgrounder, 2003). I write that 52% & 35% of homicides are Black males and females (Bureau of Justice Statistics, 2007). I write because women of color are dying. I write to live.

## References

Bureau of Justice Statistics. (2007). Black Victims of Violent Crimes. Available online at: <bjs.ojp.usdoj.gov/content/pub/pdf/bvvc.pdf>

Centers for Disease Control and Prevention. (2010). U.S. Cancer Statistics Working Group. *United States Cancer Statistics: 1999–2007 Incidence and Mortality Web-based Report.* Atlanta, GA: Department of Health and Human Services, Centers for Disease Control and Prevention, and National Cancer Institute; 2010. Available at: http://www.cdc.gov/uscs

Human Rights Watch Backgrounder. (2003). Incarcerated America. Available online at: <http://www.hrw.org/legacy/backgrounder/usa/incarceration/>

National Association for the Advancement of Colored People. (2006). *Equity Matters: Ensuring Access to Quality Education for Minority Students.* Baltimore, MD: Author.

Office of Student Research and Campus Surveys. (2010). Undergraduate Statistics. Available online at: <osr2.berkeley.edu/twiki/bin/view/Main/UgStatF2010#table%205>

Orfield, G., Losen, D., Wald, J., & Swanson, C. (2004). *Losing Our Future: How Minority Youth Are Being Left Behind by the Graduation Rate Crisis.* Cambridge, MA: The Civil Rights Project at Harvard University. Contributors: Urban Institute, Advocates for Children of New York and The Civil Society Institute.

Stillwell, R. (2010). *Public School Graduates and Dropouts from the Common Core of Data: School Year 2007–08.* National Council on Education Statistics, NCES 2010341. Washington, DC: Department of Education.

Tjaden, P., & Thoennes, N. (1998). *Prevalence, Incidence and Consequences of Violence Against Women Survey.* Washington DC: National Institute of Justice & Centers for Disease Control & Prevention.

# Lives Forever Changed

Pow, pow, pow

Shots ring out on a spring afternoon
Don't look now
As lifeblood flows to the gutter
Don't look now
As a heart slows to a feeble flutter
Tears flow from a child
Striving to be a man-child in the Promised Land
Willing to get rich or die trying……
Buying the dream the media's been selling
Caught up in the storytelling
Can't tell bling lies from reality
Totally twisted, unable to see
The bars that will never set you free

Pow, pow pow

Don't look now
As we strive to pick up the pieces
Gunshot wounds scarring our nieces
Lives forever changed
A spring afternoon filled with the stench of cordite
As blood red lilies blossom from the young man
Lying inert on the unyielding concrete
Of the jungle we've created

Pow, pow, pow

Shots ring out on a Monday afternoon filled with spring rain
And I don't recognize your pain filled voice
Ten years gone by and my heart echoes your pain
For the life lessons never learned and your firstborn's choice
To be in the wrong place at the wrong time
Unwilling, unwitting accessory to a homicide
Yet another casualty in the black genocide
A statistic, a number, an inmate
After you sold your soul in order
To make him graduate
This was not to be his fate

Pow, pow, pow

Echoes from the chambers of your heart
As three days later
I hold you close
Your eyes filled with unshed tears
I Feel you gather will and resolve
Watch you harness the forces that
Allowed us to survive the black holocaust
That allowed us to move forward remembering the cost
Unmarked graves and stranger fruit
Litter the highway to the 21st century
As we, children of a lesser god,
Now ventilate each other in pursuit
Of a glittering, intrusive, elusive dream

Pow, pow, pow

A twenty-first century overture

Pow, pow, pow

A jarring reminder that many
Of our so-called gains have largely
Been in vain

Now, Now, Now

Let us stop the reign of lead
Let us heal the pain.

|| FOUR

# You Are the Ones Who Need to Hear Us

## *The Role of Urban Youth Voice in a Democracy*

Christopher Knaus

*The purpose of schools is to shut us up. —Pedro (11th Grader)*

Much of my professional life is spent convincing White educators that the depth of racism shaping the lives of African American, Latino, and indigenous American students is real. I speak to disbelieving suburban and urban educators, to teachers, principals, district staff, and university faculty around the country, and in almost every conversation where there are more than a few White people, eyebrows roll, my words are dismissed, and the reality of racism is denied. And yet almost every single high school dropout I have talked with, almost every young African American and Latino man who has been locked up in juvenile hall or in prison can clarify powerfully what that racism looks like. How can so many people who have been failed by schools go on and on about the details of racism while the vast majority of White educators who have successfully navigated K–12 schools and college are unable to explain how racism operates on a daily basis? The same is also true for a number of educators of color. Tyrone Howard (2008) clarifies that this is partially because, "as a country, and as a community of researchers we have yet to engage one another in an authentic, honest, and sustained dialogue about race and racism" (p. 954). Yet our children learn from our collective avoidance of these real issues, and while educators read books about how to have "courageous conversations," few efforts entail systemic analysis of the historical roots of racism, how those roots inform schools today, and how our students live through the racism many of the adults paid to educate them collectively deny (Singleton & Linton, 2005).

Yet if educators and scholars cannot have authentic conversations about the racial realities we live, that we force upon our children, then how can we expect younger generations to learn to transform our segregated society into the integrated, multilingual, multi-social democracy that schools prematurely celebrate? I am less concerned with questions of fault, because most young African American students already know the skin tones of the educators who limit their capacity to be themselves. Instead, I am concerned with action; how do educators recognize the silencing, colonial purpose of schools so that we can teach students to be themselves, to become what Paulo Freire (1973) called "authentic human beings" (p. 20). Such authenticity, where children learn to maintain the languages of their grandparents, but also learn to speak in the dominant language, learn to navigate socially, learn to advocate for resources, all while learning to be themselves, is a requirement for a socially diverse democracy. But transforming into such an affirming purpose of education requires understanding what schools have intended to do, and have successfully achieved, in communities of color.

In what follows, I provide a foundation for how the United States has continued to benefit off of the free and low-wage labor of African Americans, and how education has been structured to maintain such dramatic—and purposeful—inequalities. I argue that schools have justified the usage of African American labor through segregated schools that have been contradictorily written into law through *Brown vs. Board of Education.* After framing the colonial mission of schools, I capture the importance of voice in transforming what we could do in schools to empower multicultural, multilingual communities. I caution that the purpose of schooling has to shift so as to not require Black youth to choose between identity and academic success, and demonstrate how developing voice is key to shifting this false choice. I share stories that show the impact of developing voice on students and educators alike, and clarify two components of voice that emanate from my work with students and from the work of poet educators. I argue that voice cannot be easily defined and in an era of accountability and school efficiency, likely should not be. I conclude by laying out a process to develop urban youth voice, which leads directly into the following chapters, in which I clarify how I develop voice through instructional strategies that create relevant, supportive school structures.

## Education and the Silencing of Black Children

While conversation about Black exclusion from the fabric of society is silenced in mainstream representations of the struggles for schooling, racial educational inequalities intentionally abound. On almost every single indicator of educational success, urban students of color lag significantly behind White, Asian, and suburban students (Aud, Hussar, et al., 2010; Jacobson, Olsen, Rice, Sweetland, &

Ralph, 2001; Rampey, Dion, & Donohue, 2009). The foundation of education in the U.S. is deeply conflicted; on one hand, many Native Americans were abducted and forced to attend violent schools with one purpose in mind: assimilation into White norms (Archuleta, Child, & Lomawaima, 2000; Trafzer & Keller, 2006). On the other hand, most enslaved Africans were violently punished for attempts to learn anything not seen as immediately productive for their White imperialistic owners (Williams, 2005; Woodson, 2004). This contradictory educational philosophy resulted in dramatic inequalities that are often referred to as achievement gaps, but these gaps simply reflect mono-cultural White supremacist frameworks of schooling that deny the experiences, languages, cultures, and oppressions facing urban families of color (Apple, 1993; Banks, 1996; Ladson-Billings, 1999). Schools, in effect, have been designed to do different things with different students, and to misrepresent this oppressive purpose as an "achievement gap" denies the role of education in purposefully maintaining a poverty-stricken workforce (Giroux, 2001; Macedo & Bartolomé, 1999). Yet federal policy efforts center almost entirely on the "achievement gap."

The foundations of U.S. schooling remain: White slave owners and many White abolitionists were adamantly against Black people learning to read, write, add, or subtract. Such acts were severely punished by cutting off tongues, whipping, and hanging (Webber, 1978; Woodson, 2004). This is the foundation of anti-educating Black children and adults in the U.S.; many White people wanted Black bodies for labor, and this was directly supported by policy that legislated fear of Black people who were educated (Davis, 1966; Goodell, 2009). And even after emancipation, even after the literal chains were taken off of Black necks, the education of Black children and adults was resisted, by legal policy and the continual threat of White violence (Anderson, 1988; Watkins, 2001; Williams, 2005). The fear of Black people who could communicate to wide masses, who could count, who could develop community, and think on their own ran deep in the minds of many White people. Of course Black people could already think on their own, had been teachers and healers and farmers and leaders before, during, and after they were enslaved, but White America did what it could to convince themselves and the Black people they relied upon that anything Black people already knew was irrelevant. Throughout the history of the U.S., through policies and *de facto* segregation, Black people, as a group, have not been allowed to learn in well-funded schools, and even when individual Black students have been allowed in, the scope of education is framed around navigating White society (Allen, 1990; Ladson-Billings, 1999; Ture & Hamilton, 1967). Thus ethnic studies and multicultural education are still relegated to the sidelines of academia, under constant threat of closure, and continually underfunded (Ethnic Studies Now, 2007; Forbes, 2008; McCombs, 2007; Santa Cruz, 2010). While ethnic-framed educational approaches are minimalized, and students of color and poor whites are pushed out of schools in high numbers to ensure an uneducated workforce.

James Baldwin (Baldwin, 1985b) clarifies the impact of this fear of Black thought in his Talk to Teachers:

> The point of all this is that black men were brought here as a source of cheap labor. They were indispensable to the economy. In order to justify the fact that men were treated as though they were animals, the white republic had to brainwash itself into believing that they were, indeed, animals and deserved to be treated like animals. Therefore it is almost impossible for any Negro child to discover anything about his actual history. The reason is that this "animal," once he suspects his own worth, once he starts believing that he is a man, has begun to attack the entire power structure. This is why America has spent such a long time keeping the Negro in his place. What I am trying to suggest to you is that it was not an accident, it was not an act of God, it was not done by well-meaning people muddling into something which they didn't understand. It was a deliberate policy hammered into place in order to make money from black flesh. And now, in 1963, because we have never faced this fact, we are in intolerable trouble. (pp. 328–329)

At East Bay High School, I played a song by Antibalas (2004) to one of my high school writing courses, made up entirely of African American and Latino students. Antibalas' message of anti-imperialism is clear in just about every song, and their Afro-beat rhythms are based on the music of Fela Kuti, a Nigerian musician (Coker, 2004). Antibalas, in a lyric from the song "Big Man," captured the corporate nature of employment in the U.S.:

> *What can I do for you?*
> *I beg o, give me job now*
> *Let me work eighty hours a week to make money*
> *So I can give the same money back to you, big man*
> *When I buy your beautiful products.*

After playing the song, students wrote responses that connected the lyrics to their personal experiences. One student, Jasmine, asked, "what's the point of getting a job when all our money has to go back to the people who keep us poor?" The students resonated with Antibalas' framing of "the system," and wanted to learn more about similar artists. These students also wanted to know where they could read about the historical connections to why, as Jasmine questioned, "shit got this way," and she continued that "my teachers aint never taught me about this, either in history or economics." The class continued, with students expressing frustration with Pedro's quote that opened the chapter: "The purpose of schools is to shut us up." And the students knew *why* they were being made to shut up, demonstrated in Jacinda's argument: "We supposed to work at Taco Bell or Jamba

Juice or Target or as day-laborers. We aint supposed to go to college, learn to question so they have to deal with us."

Despite many popular musicians with similar anti-colonial messages,[1] many educators do not teach (and have not been trained to teach) about the historical purpose of enslaving Africans to create a free labor pool, nor the continued reliance upon low-income labor in maintaining a middle-class standard of living. And yet students feel this purpose every day, when they sit in classrooms that ignore and deny Robert Allen's clear statement about Black power: "In these cities we do not control our resources. We do not control the land, the houses or the stores. These are owned by whites who live outside the community" (Allen, 1990, p. 7). These disparities in power and wealth reflect a larger struggle: the United States has always had a purpose for Black people. This purpose has ensured the continued benefit of middle-class White communities at the expense of impoverished African American communities. As sung in "Big Man," immigrant and low-income families often work upwards of two full-time jobs, only to give the money they earn back to White-run corporations that contribute to the very low-wage labor that forces them to work multiple jobs in the first place. This is in exchange for products meant to convey wealth and status (think iPods, cell phones, nice clothes, shoes, and fancy cars). The issue Antibalas and Jacinda raise is that low-wage labor continues a cycle of poverty, ensuring communities of color remain poor and in the hands of the corporations upon whom they rely for employment.

Education is often framed as the one way out of this cycle. Yet despite being lured by the promise of success that the world equates with American education, being successful in American schools does not guarantee economic stability. There is no denying the economic benefit that *can* come with educational success, including enhanced income, access to social capital, higher-quality food, produce, health care, and schools that promise (but do not always deliver) continued access for future generations. Increased income *can* allow poor families to move from unhealthy communities, avoiding medical incinerators, toxic ground water, cancerous air quality, and some forms of violence. Thus, education is framed as a gateway towards the safety, security, happiness, and white picket fences that wealth can provide.

Yet almost 50 years after James Baldwin delivered his talk, educators have still not faced the historical or continued colonial nature of the education of Black children, and still have not addressed the stark disparities in health, wealth, and livelihood. In many schools, students are taught about passive slaves, taught that *Plessy vs. Ferguson* was wrong, that separate but equal was well intentioned but did not result in the diverse, equal democracy that we currently live. In short, complicated historical realities are often left out of instruction, perhaps as much a result of standardized assessments guiding curriculum as unintentional racism limiting knowledge of historical reality (Banks, 1995; Barone, 2006; Loewen, 1996). And so *Brown vs. Board of Education* is often taught as the easily remedied solution to America's racism. There is little connection to why the civil rights struggle erupted into riots some 10–15 years after *Brown vs. Board of Education.* Little is taught about the intense struggles and continual threats of violence that led to *Brown vs. Board of Education.* The immediate fierce resistance to implementing anything remotely resembling desegregation, or any other complicated racially historical incident, is also silenced in American curriculum (Apple, 1993; Loewen, 1996; Martinez, 1995). Instead, stories of the Little Rock Nine are highlighted, Rosa Parks is framed as a tired Black woman and not a community advocate, Dr. King and Malcolm X are positioned in opposition to each other, and the reasons why the U.S. decided to legally desegregate are framed as America addressing past wrongs (Bell, 2004; Bigelow, 1995).

Reality is often more complicated than what schools teach. Immediately after *Brown vs. Board of Education*, incarceration rates for African Americans skyrocketed, and this trend has continued (Mauer & King, 2004). This can be directly traced to the closing of woefully under-resourced Black southern community schools that had been educating Black children to successfully navigate White society while maintaining the cultural values and linguistic traditions of the local (and historical) community (Morgan, 1995; Walker, 1996). Most of the Black-organized, -led, and -focused K–12 community schools were closed so that their students would "integrate" White schools. And immediately, these Black students, used to culturally responsive pedagogy, caring teachers, and educators who were active in their neighborhoods, were tracked into segregated classrooms. In addition, some tens of thousands of Black educators were forced out of jobs when these Black community schools were shut down (Futrell, 2004; Morgan, 1995). So while America celebrated its newfound integrationist schools, within those schools, Black children sat with other Black children, had their Black teachers replaced by White ones, and were no longer embraced as equal members of the community. In addition, as Black children enrolled, en masse, in White schools, White students increasingly fled farther away, attended newly created, almost entirely White schools (Clark, 1987; Kruse, 2005). This left Black families with minimal choices. Their schools were being shut down; they had no option but to send their children to schools that were legally forced to educate their children, but not legally required to educate in ways that reflected Black culture, community context, or White racism.

Derrick Bell (2004) argued that *Brown vs. Board of Education* became law in part because the interests of Black families to be more adequately educated coincided with White interests to address growing fear of the communist threat. In addition to global critiques of America's Jim Crow system, quite a number of Black soldiers who had helped liberate Europe from Nazi Germany had returned empowered by fighting for justice. But fighting to free European White people only to return home to be considered second-class citizens did not sit well with many of these men, the majority of whom were excluded from the college expansion that followed WWII and from meaningful job opportunities. In part to quell potential unrest, and in part to address the growing criticism from communist countries that the U.S. was itself a two-tiered society, desegregation became a quick solution to multiple growing problems (Bell, 2004).

While the tangible benefits to adhering to and adopting White values are clear, the benefits to the larger community are more suspect. A debate has continued to filter throughout Black educator circles as to whether or not to embrace the values of White mainstream society, and whether or not to attend, prioritize, and support predominantly White institutions. From an individual perspective, it is hard to argue that access to Harvard, Princeton, and elite public institutions like the University of Michigan, UCLA, and UC Berkeley is not beneficial; the doors of opportunity do open for elite graduates. Examination of some forty years of Affirmative Action programs in college admissions shows that the numbers of Black graduates from elite colleges significantly increased (Bowen & Bok, 1998). But these graduates were far too few to decrease segregation, poverty, violence, or the long list of indicators that reflect the dire state of Black America. Indeed, an argument could be made that these educated elite have been taught precisely that the issues facing Black communities are due to individual lack of drive; those who succeed in school are told they are "different" because they work harder and are smarter than other Black students, just as many Black students, particularly males, have been socialized to not be seen as academically successful (DeMeulenaere, 2009; Ferguson, 2001; Fordham & Ogbu, 1986; Ogbu, 1991).

As the number of elite graduates of color increased, the number of Black families living in poverty also increased, just as did the number of incarcerated Black men. Not surprisingly, and despite increased access to elite education, school inequality largely looks the same as it did 50 years ago, and the achievement gap still correlates directly with a wage and wealth gap (Western & Pettit, 2005). While *Brown vs. Board of Education* can be seen as the legal justification for sending Black children to White schools, this argument works only when focused on the individual. Sending children to elite schools has resulted in a larger middle class, but has not diminished racism against Black people, nor begun to address racial inequalities.

*Brown vs. Board of Education* ultimately cemented in the public imagination that excellent education is White education. Thus, meritorious students are the students who explicitly embrace the values of whiteness and who can demonstrate such on standardized tests. Ensuring Black students are educated by White teachers in White-run schools also contributed to the silencing of cultural norms, the conflicted reality of Black children who are taught to act "White," and a conflating of mainstream White thinking with academic excellence. Desegregation resulted in Black children attending schools taught and organized by White educators uncomfortable with Blackness, with Black children, and with any obvious reminders of the cultural distance Black people might be from whiteness. Thus students operating on a communal basis, concerned about their peers or siblings, socialized to value voice and storytelling, particularly from elders, were (and are) taught to ignore these values, to focus on individual grades and individual notions of success. But this silencing occurred (and occurs) in the curriculum, too, with White European biased curriculum, standardized English only, and "proper" behavior encouraged while "improper" behavior is punished. This leads Black students to adopt survival strategies; those who are quiet are rewarded with success, and those who resist the stereotype often required for Black academic success are punished. Thus desegregation, without meaningful integration to shift White schooling into multicultural, multilingual educational approaches, has led to the purposeful silencing of Blackness.

This silencing creates a tremendous social cost that has been documented by scholars throughout the world (Fordham & Ogbu, 1986; Gibson & Ogbu, 1991; Woodson, 1933; Wright, 1957). In short, children are told to give up who they are in order to become successful in schools, and for Black children, this equates to giving up a lot more of themselves than must White children. And not surprising, many do not wish to give themselves up for a pathway towards the promise of wealth. And many recognize that there are other pathways (that have been illegalized), and that the promise of wealth is nothing more than a fleeting potential. Many youth of color do not graduate high school, and even fewer go on to graduate college, and even fewer of those become economically stable (Aud, Fox, & KewalRamani, 2010; Children's Defense Fund, 2006; Holzman, 2006). In essence, Black wealth is neither permanent nor promised, and the pathways towards education and prestige are purposefully limited. Black children recognize this.

But just as making something taboo encourages its popularity, the very traits Black children have been punished for exhibiting become stereotypical outlets for behavior. Black children have continually been punished for being too loud, too violent, too disregarding of authority, too late, too anything that broke the established norms of whiteness. And just like when alcohol was outlawed and subsequent drinking increased, so too do punishments lead some Black children to adopt stereotypical behaviors, reinforcing societal myths and fears. Black children who are told they are not smart because they choose to adhere to values their families and communities embrace, because they speak languages or colloquiums that reflect those they love or how they grew up often begin to act out. And what other choice are such students given? Consider a six-year-old Black student continually punished for trying to help a peer student on math problems when they are supposed to be working on their own. Or what about a twelve-year-old Black child whose teachers tremble in fear of him? One can imagine such children rejecting the values of their teachers, and such rejection should be seen as responsible choices. But instead, children are encouraged to survive as quietly as possible, to not support their peers, to ignore the fear in their teachers' eyes. There is little middle ground here.

Perhaps the most insidious impact of the legal commitment to require Black children be educated by White society is the internalizing of oppression by many Black children, who are rewarded for embracing societal values that deny their individuality, culture, community, and history. Educators could not have planned this better; Black children learn to prioritize White values above their own, and this has been exemplified year after year in studies documenting Black children preferring White dolls to Black dolls (Clark & Clark, 1947; Davis, 2007; Fegley, Spencer, Gross, Harpalani & Charles, 2008). But this is also demonstrated when Black children really do believe that White children are smarter than they are when they score higher on tests designed for White children to score higher on (Steele & Aronson, 1995). When Black families move out of urban areas, following White flight, fleeing to the suburbs, they do so in part to send their children to better resourced schools. That these schools are also predominantly White is not coincidental, the hope is that such schools will provide more access to wealth and stability for Black children. The issue, though, is that there is little legal requirement for such schools to teach Black children, which is why dropout rates for Black and Latino students are significantly higher than for White students regardless of attendance at suburban or urban schools (Hauser, Simmons, & Pager, 2004; Rumberger & Thomas, 2000).

Schools directly teach Black children to embrace the values that directly oppose their physical, emotional, spiritual, and economic well-being. An obvious example of this can be seen in the teaching of history from a White European perspective, wherein enslaved Africans are often taught as docile and passive, rather than as a forced collective of community-driven people living under intense, purposeful violence. The complexity of being taught to be like the very people who colonized one's historical family is clarified by James Baldwin (1962) in a letter to his nephew: "There is no reason for you to try to become like White people and there is no basis whatever for their impertinent assumption that they must accept you" (p. 8). And yet there are tangible reasons to become like White people, tangible rewards in the form of access and wealth. The very purpose of education is to force Black children to become like White people, even though, as Richard Wright (1957) argued, the "chances of resembling [White people] are remote, slight" (p. 7). Baldwin (1985a) further clarified that "to be poor and Black in a country so rich and White is to judge oneself very harshly and it means that one has nothing to lose" (p. 64). Having nothing to lose is hardly justification for applying oneself in school, particularly when schools intend to colonize young Black minds. The impact of imperialism and colonization are magnified when those colonized begin to take on the values of the colonizers, begin to embrace the values that directly deny Blackness.

In all of this, Wright (1957) reminds us that "we are here dealing with values evoked by social systems or colonial regimes which make men feel that they are dominated by powers stronger than they are" (p. 7). His point is that we can shift the internalized oppression we teach our children. Educators can begin to undo the trauma schools impart in students, can begin to arm children with culturally relevant knowledge. But this means refocusing our efforts, becoming student centered to help students see the power of their voices and perspectives. This cannot happen without authentic conversations about the purpose of school, the historical roots of oppression that shape what we do in schools today, and the reality that the United States has yet to meaningfully include Black communities in shaping democracy.

## Standards, the Achievement Gap, and Racism

Recognizing that the purpose of schools is to silence Blackness, to ensure young Black people silence their cultural strengths, values, insights, ways of thinking, knowledge, and language in favor of standardized notions of whiteness is key. Because otherwise, educators cannot get our minds around the ever-present and intellectually irrelevant achievement gap, which, as Kitty Kelly Epstein has stated repeatedly, is "nothing more than a wealth or opportunity gap" (Epstein, 2006; Epstein, personal communication, November, 2010). The achievement gap was created by standardized tests that were designed specifically to segregate society; this is well documented (Epstein, 2006; Garrison, 2009; *Larry P. and Lucille P. v. Riles*, 1979; Rees, 2003). And after years of struggle against standardized assessments, the battle has been lost. In schools, districts, and communities across the country, Black educators, parents, and community advocates assess schools in terms of their standardized test scores, despite that these tests have much more to do with family income than intelligence, academic engagement, or student effort.

What the focus on the achievement gap has done is shift meaningful conversation away from the silencing mission of schools. Rather than discuss school reform in terms of transforming the mission of schools, national conversations focus on more efficiently educating children. In practice, this means more efficiently silencing Black children. Reform efforts focus on opening and closing schools, research-based best practices to increase test scores, and hiring new, highly qualified teachers. But none of this addresses what schools intend to teach, that the teaching force is still mostly White, or that to become a classroom teacher, educators have to successfully navigate exclusive schools that rarely challenge such racist views. In urban communities, that means we have not changed the dynamic of sending Black children into the arms of White educators, who are taught to defend their colonial mission. Many of these White educators do not intend to colonize; they are often disengaged from this conversation because they, too, have never been forced to challenge their own notions of knowledge, academic success, and what it means to develop a multicultural, multilingual democracy.

The achievement gap will continue to exist until educators reframe the purpose of schooling to reflect multiple perspectives and uses. In English Only schools and classes, students are taught that "correct" ways of communicating mirrors Western thinking. Regardless of whether or not funding in schools is equalized, gaps will always remain when students are forced to learn and respond in languages that were not designed to encompass their experiences. Standardized notions of English exclude the vast majority of students who come from homes that might communicate in ways that conflict with how they are taught at school (Gay, 2000; Ladson-Billings, 1994; Valdes, 1996). This disjoint is enhanced by schools that completely deny the existence and value of indigenous knowledge. Linda Tuhiwai Smith (1999) clarifies: "Having been immersed in the Western academy which claims theory as thoroughly Western, which has constructed all the rules by which the indigenous world has been theorized, indigenous voices have been overwhelmingly silenced" (p. 29). The focus on standardizing language has been increasing with the onslaught of standards-based high-stakes testing, and No Child Left Behind and Race to the Top federal reform efforts only exacerbate such alienating approaches that deny indigenous knowledge and the languages designed to communicate such knowledge. Rochelle Brock (2005) asks the question educators and scholars should be concerned with: "How can I use a language that is more meaningful, but less academically accepted?" (p. 3).

This narrow focus on assessing for standardized adherence to White values creates a double bind for urban educators attempting to empower students of color. Even if educators respond in culturally relevant ways to their students, their effectiveness is still measured by student test scores that measure their facility at expressing White values and White-normed language. Silvera (1983) argued that "the traditional methodological instruments of the academic are inadequate to handle the complexities of recognizing the extent of powerlessness and engaging in the task of empowerment" (p. ix). The tools we use for measuring and defining academic merit are simply not complex enough to capture the nuance of how oppression shapes student thought. Effective teachers, then, often try to develop the capacity for urban students to code-shift, i.e., to be able to express themselves in their cultural tongue and still excel at the White-framed language of school (De Fina, 2007; Perry & Delpit, 1998; Wheeler & Swords, 2006). While this multilingual approach should be taught, the problem is that multiple languages are not valued, and many of the cultural nuances of urban students are not classified as language systems anyhow. So, as happened in Oakland, California, in the mid-nineties, when urban educators tried to teach students to communicate in

Ebonics and standardized English, their efforts became a debate over whether or not Ebonics is a *real* language (Epstein, 2006; Perry & Delpit, 1998). The notion of code-switching is relegated to the backburner because of intense White racism to efforts that actually validate cultural forms of communication.

And this is what it means to standardize writing: ultimately, as a society, we decide which forms of communication are valid and which are invalid. Gloria Ladson-Billings (1999) clarifies the use of critical race theory in capturing "the official school curriculum as a culturally specific artifact designed to maintain a White supremacist master script" (p. 21). If the purpose of school curriculum is to maintain White supremacy, then it should be no wonder that urban students of color often argue that they must devalue who they are in order to do well academically; that is precisely what the formal school curriculum asks students of color to do. The problem with the way standards have been defined and framed is that they simply are not adequate in framing an understanding of what is happening with students of color in schools, because they are only designed to assess adherence to a *White supremacist master script*. While many have advocated for multiple measures in assessing high school graduation readiness, individual schools, and increasingly individual educators, are being assessed not in terms of multiple measures, but their students' test scores in just a few standardized tests (Darling-Hammond, Rustique-Forrester & Pecheone, 2005). But even multiple measures will not address gaps in knowledge unless the entire way knowledge is seen is democratized (and not uniformly standardized along notions of whiteness). Instead, what is often measured is capacity to express oneself in a passive language that is more readily heard by the largely White mainstream academics who design the tests based on their own cultural values and norms. The processes through which urban students are taught to write in dispassionate, emotionless ways that often directly contradict the cultural context of urban youth of color are demonstrated throughout studies on schools (Delpit, 2006; Fine, 1991; Gay, 2000; hooks, 1994; Macedo & Bartolomé, 1999; Oakes, 1985; Valdes, 1996).

Standardizing language is not a new phenomenon; dictionaries offer historical timelines of the status quo of language in America. Taught to school-aged children as the source to go to for "real" definitions of words, dictionaries provide limiting definitions of words that reflect societal racism, sexism, and oppression (Carr, 1997). When students are taught that the source for "accurate" meaning in words is the biased definitions developed by corporate publishing houses with a vested interest in sustaining their roles as knowledge producers, students are taught that their own cultural context around such words is irrelevant. In a similar vein, much reading, writing, and comprehension is taught with only a White, European-background cultural context behind words (Gay, 2000; Ladson-Billings, 1994). Thus as children of color begin to develop language and vocabulary in schools, they learn to speak words that deny their very existence. Urban students of color are, in many ways, made to forget what is important about who they are when they enter the classroom, but also learn to speak in ways that deny who they are as well.

Standards are the formal way of measuring this process, but instead of framing the process as colonization and racism, standards are framed as a way of measuring intelligence. Adherence to whiteness, then, is a direct equation to the capacity to be defined by our schools as "intelligent," "smart," and "well-qualified" for admissions into college. My point is not that urban educators should not be evaluating our work, but instead that we need accurate measurement tools that assess culturally relevant knowledge forms as well as a range of academic skill sets. As Duncan-Andrade and Morrell (2008) clarified, "We, as educators and researchers, need to be ready to show how the students are learning everything they need to in the context of undertaking meaningful, life-affirming work. All of this could be accomplished, we believe, without the use of most of the standardized-tests that currently occupy so much of our thinking" (p. 170).

## The Importance of Developing Voice in Schools

James Baldwin (1972) clarified the importance of voice as a foundation for the role of educators in a democracy. "If one really wishes to know how justice is administered in a country," Baldwin argued, "one does not question the policemen, the lawyers, the judges, or the protected members of the middle class. One goes to the unprotected—those, precisely, who need the law's protection most!—and listens to their testimony" (p. 149). Black youth have answers to how our nation's schools contribute to societal segregation, poverty, and racial animosity, and it is in the interests of schools to prepare youth to express such voices. Schools should be in the business of developing the skills in youth to identify problems that shape their inequalities, and then to testify about such inequalities. Transforming schools into such proactive roles requires doing something dramatically different—something that we, as a society, have yet to try: empowering and affirming children of color to express themselves, providing forums for such expression, then shutting up and listening. And isn't that exactly what we want from children—active, critical thinkers?

I am certainly not the first to advocate for developing youth voice, nor for student-centered education (Dewey, 1916; Freire, 2004; Krishnamurti, 1953; Power, Higgins & Kohlberg, 1989). Many educators, activists, civil rights leaders, artists, writers, and musicians have advocated for, through multicultural education, Afrocentrism, and culturally relevant and responsive approaches, an arts-integrated, culturally rich curriculum (Asante, 1998; Banks, 1996; Gay, 2000; Greene, 2001; Ladson-Billings, 1994). But these efforts have been decreasing in direct relation to the standards movement, pushed outside a narrowing curriculum (Knaus, 2007). Public expression has continued on, despite how Black voices have been made illegal throughout historical policy and practice. Yet expression cannot be silenced: despite intense racism, the Harlem Renaissance demonstrated the potential impact of aligning education, youth development, and the arts world with local businesses, churches, and civic organizations. Such periods of vibrant Black communities were built up in in urban cities across the U.S., always on the foundation of artistic expression, always reflecting the soul of the community, with songs clarifying racism, oppression, and resistance (Campbell, 1994; Martin, 1983; McKay, 1930). Pulling on such work, individual schools have maintained a strong focus on the arts, music, dance, or poetry throughout history. The core problem, however, is that most of this work, and certainly the development of skills related to expression, is outside the scope of everyday public education, as exceptions to the rule. My push is to transform schools to center on developing such critical, culturally rooted voice, and help foster student voice so they can express exactly what they see as wrong in the world.

Such testimony is already spray painted on walls throughout urban environments. Urban youth speak their voices, claim what space they can, and do so despite their schools, in part because there is no room for their voice in schools. So urban youth are forced to break laws, to sneak their points in between railroad cars, on delivery trucks, abandoned billboards, and through YouTube videos, blogs, and Tweets. Graffiti is a powerful example of an expression of voice that is systemically silenced and literally painted over. Many urban communities stand out because of graffiti, which to those less familiar, may simply look like random scratches and spray painted names on buildings across a cityscape. But many graffiti artists spend time crafting messages of hope and anti-police brutality, recording the names of young children killed in urban violence. Impromptu and commissioned murals pop up all over urban cities, often only to be silenced by poorly paid maintenance workers, who are made to paint over youthful artwork. While not all graffiti is meaningful or tells a story of resistance to violence, racism, or negativity, most graffiti is an attempt to claim space, to honor the community or the individual artist in culturally responsive ways (Alonso, 1998; Brewer, 1992; Feiner & Klein, 1982). June Jordan, in talking about poetry, argued that she "would hope that folks throughout the U.S.A. would consider the creation of poems as a foundation for true community: a fearless democratic society" (in Muller et al., 1995, p. 3). Graffiti, in many ways, reflects such a democratic society, with freedom of expression taking on a plea for recognition, as young people attempt to tell community stories on the concrete walls that block their view of the world.

Because most schools have not historically taught content that reflects multicultural histories, languages, and resistance to oppression, nor linked such content to contemporary community struggles, much work is needed to reframe schools to provide a foundation for developing such voice. Pihama (1985) argued that:

"Maori people struggle to gain a voice, struggle to be heard from the margins, to have our stories heard, to have our descriptions of ourselves validated, to have access to the domain within which we can control and define those images which are held up as reflections of our realities" (p. 241). A voice-centered curriculum cannot operate in isolation from the reality that oppressed voices are silenced systematically throughout the educational system, but also in mainstream mass media. Yet forums for voice, which exist outside the realms of schools, cannot be integrated into education without developing student voice. The two must occur at the same time, as core functions of public schooling.

Thus schools must provide relevant curriculum, encourage students to develop their voices as part of what it means to "be educated," and create forums for youth expression. In the process of coming to see schools as reflecting the inequalities of society, students can begin to create their own ways of expressing themselves based on who they are, what they see, live, and feel in the world around them, and begin to merge the social distance between school and their personal lives. The focus on voice helps prepare urban students to interrogate still-in-place racist, colonial educational structures in ways that will not ultimately lead them to turn away from school. This is entirely the point of teaching for voice; in my courses, students are reminded that they should be themselves, should use their own experiences as ways of informing what they say and write, and should recognize the cultural knowledge they live by so that they can challenge the oppression they live. Centering the cultural context of students in the classroom is needed in order to help students recognize that academic knowledge must include their perspectives and can be useful in helping understand how distinct communities fit within larger social struggles (Banks, 1993; Gordon, 1995).

Multicultural education has long argued for approaches to help students find their voice through inclusive curriculum content (Banks & Banks, 2009; Gay, 2000; Nieto, 1996). Recent efforts have highlighted the need for students to develop their own stories; this allows for comparative analysis of student stories with historical narratives (Duncan-Andrade & Morrell, 2008; Fisher, 2008; Morrell, 2004). Shields, Bishop, and Mazawi (2005) clarify that "A narrative approach argues that we story our lives, and repositioning requires new stories" (p. 147). Multicultural education efforts that lead to more inclusive curriculum lays a foundation for repositioning schooling, but in order to transform the silencing impact of schools, student culture has to be centered in more meaningful ways than adding curriculum content that might mirror student life (Banks, 1995). Developing personal stories empowers youth to begin to document their own history while building a student-generated curriculum that interacts with cultural histories. Such an ongoing process of students generating curriculum also helps ensure educators do not co-opt student ideas and water down student passion into a removed, academic discussion about the main point.

Geneva Gay (2000) argues that "because of the dialectic relationship between knowledge and the knower, interest and motivation, relevance and mastery, Native Americans, Latinos, African Americans, and Asian Americans must be seen as co-originators, co-designers, and co-directors (along with professional educators) of their education" (p. 111). As students become more centrally involved in shaping what they do in the classroom, they tend to become more invested in their education (Ginwright, Noguera, Cammarota, 2006). Unfortunately, most efforts at instituting cultural responsiveness in the classroom fall short of also empowering students to develop curriculum content, much less to analyze the content they are provided (Gay, 2007; Knaus, 2007; Weis & Fine, 2005). While Gay (2000) asserts that inclusive curriculum has to include a wide array of knowledge bases (including mass media, literature, music, personal experience, and research), she ultimately argues that "ethnically diverse students and their cultural heritages must be the sources and centers of educational programs" (p. 111).

Gil Conchas (2006) argues that "one pillar of a strong self-identity for African American students is pride of heritage" (p. 52). What this ultimately means is that schools have to be in the business of building up student consciousness about heritages (theirs and those of their peers). Centering students in the classroom ultimately entails centering the cultural contexts students bring; developing voice allows other students (and teachers) to learn how culture operates on a daily basis in students' lives. The more focused a curriculum and teaching approaches are on developing student voice, the easier centering the cultures of the students will be. Centering students does not always have to be teaching about presumed monolithic identity groups (such as African American or Latino). Indeed, centering culture may mean letting students clarify what growing up as a multiracial African American and Latino person feels like. This is the purpose of voice: to clarify exactly what life is like from the perspective of the speaker, author, poet, playwright, actor, musician, artist, and student. And when developing voice becomes the central purpose of schools, intricate complications such as living multiple realities as a multilingual, multiracial African American and Latino young woman become part of the curriculum, and part of how people learn about the boundaries of race, class, gender, sexuality, ability, and identity.

The issue with expressing voice, however, lies in expectation. After reading a poem that took her seven months to craft, edit, and finalize, and after months of tearful work spent trying to work through the trauma captured in the poem, Shantel gave an intense on-stage reading. The audience loved the performance; she brought them to tears, received a standing ovation, and after walking off the stage, was immediately surrounded with affirming hugs. But the next day, Shantel asked to meet with me. As we walked around the neighborhood after school, she expressed her frustration: "So what do I do now? I still need a job, still need to help my mom with rent, and still wake up in fear." Developing voice helps prepare urban students to be more present to their realities, more able to concisely capture the complications that shape their lives, but does not alter those realities.

Linda Tuhiwai Smith (1999) cautioned:

> Taking apart the story, revealing underlying texts, and giving voice to things that are often known intuitively does not help people to improve their current conditions. It provides words, perhaps, an insight that explains certain experiences—but it does not prevent someone from dying. (p. 4)

Shantel and Smith remind educators that teaching for voice does not actually remove young people from the oppression they navigate. And while the purpose is to arm urban youth with the tools to navigate and live more healthfully, the reality is that without also eradicating the oppressions they live, teaching for voice is ultimately not going to change society. Developing urban youth voice only prepares students to live more authentically, to develop a facility with language and words that enables and empowers them to speak more forcefully about the world they envision. But voice, as Dave, a Filipino and African American high school junior who had taken two writing classes with me, argued, is also about concrete solutions; voice clarifies what can be done about systemic inequities. "Let us write our own histories, study our own cultures, and examine what happens in our communities." History has to be more than pilgrims and Indians sitting down peacefully to a Thanksgiving dinner, but also has to be more than just victims and perpetrators of genocide; developing voice helps students begin to see themselves in a historical light, with responsibility in what happens around them. Developing voice requires educators to take responsibility for incorporating student knowledge in the curriculum. Students should be empowered to facilitate their own research studies, and educators can support and challenge urban youth to examine what has happened in local communities and what they can do to address local issues. This is what Dave argued is the responsibility of urban youth: "We can figure out solutions, but you gotta let us understand the problems and not keep testing us on White versions, because that doesn't help us with reality."[2]

Dave also pushed against notions of students as disengaged from their schools and communities. Urban students are often depicted as uncaring, and voice directly contradicts this false stereotype. An Oakland teacher who implemented a youth participatory action research process for her students as part of a requirement for an educational leadership course I taught had urban students focus on community trash, particularly in the streets. The neighborhood was dirty; heaps of trash sat on every street corner, and student lunches, bags of Cheetos and Doritos, empty beer bottles, used condoms, and never-attempted homework packets spiraled across lawns, front porches, and every sidewalk. The teacher's assumptions were that these African American and Latino students simply did not care enough about their communities to not litter. After spending time in the community, literally walking the streets with her students, the teacher realized that her assumptions were wrong. Students cared deeply about their communities, but had few trash cans. Overflowing trash cans rarely offer an enticing place to dispose of trash, and nearby apartment dumpsters were equally overfull. Midway through the project, students clarified that the people outside their community, who might have access to lobbying for better trash service, particularly in public areas, did not seem to care about their community. They were also increasingly frustrated by efforts to beautify their community, because those seemed like wasted attempts; they did get several trash cans placed on dirtier street corners, but the city did not regularly empty these (like they did in more affluent areas just a few blocks away).

Angela, a high school senior, expressed this frustration after her teacher lashed out at the class, thinking students were not taking their research projects seriously. "It's not that I don't care, I just don't know what to do. Everything I do is pointless because all my efforts are shot down by other teachers or the city." Angela's point was that efforts to care, to clean up a community, to fix broken realities eventually stop when each effort is met with resistance. "I went to the district office to ask for recycle bins," she continued, "and was told that 'niggas like us won't use them anyways.'" She continued, "And where were my teachers? They told me this was my job to fix this, saying it was 'student advocacy research.' But in order to change this, I need teachers to advocate with me." Angela's experience is not uncommon, and the point is that students cannot be told to fix their problems, but instead must be guided and supported to name problems; to identify causes; and then, in coalition with adults, educators, and others, move to action. Students do care, and yet often grow frustrated, because in most cases, students cannot transform schools or their communities unless they are actively supported well beyond what educators typically do.

> Voice (a freewrite by Jacinda)
>
> *Voice. My voice is so loud it can be heard, everywhere. My voice makes your body hot, N they stand up, every hair. My voice rips through the paper, every tear. But in jail, I never have a voice when im there. N at school, you hearin my voice is Very rare. N when I voice, sometimes I don't even think what im sayn, sprayn, I don't know when I stopped prayn. That's the big voice, but is he really there? She? Or maybe my god is me. But I rarely hear the voice that is said to be. Rarely hear the voice that come from me. Or the voice that rules the U.S.A. A collection of people, picking us off like prey. But the voice comes back and it's all just a stage. But it your voice that keeps everyone, their own individual, calm, everyday. N it's funny cuz it's your voice that let's you do fucked up shit, N with the help of other people's voices you know what it is.*

Many democratic theorists argue that young people are the foundation of building and sustaining democracy (Barber, 1992; Gutmann, 1999; Steiner, 1999).

Yet in the U.S., with few exceptions, students have very little role in structuring schools, shaping curriculum, or determining what matters in their educational processes (Duncan-Andrade & Morrell, 2008; Ginwright, Noguera, Cammarota, 2006). If urban students are continually limited in their local forms of expression, told to not clean up their neighborhoods, to not write on walls, to not claim local space, and are not allowed to shape any of their school day, what public opportunities do they have to express voice in sanctioned ways that help them sharpen their messages? Instead of promoting the development of and sharpening the impact of voice, educators continually silence expression of voice in urban students, the opposite of what is needed to prepare students for democratic participation. Indeed, as Geneva Gay (2000) argued, "the freedom to be ethnically expressive removes the psychological stress associated with and psychic energy deployed in 'covering up' or 'containing' one's cultural inclinations" (p. 36). Centering voice as the purpose of schooling sets a foundation for youth of color to wrestle with and make sense of the oppression they face while giving them space to be their authentic selves.

## The Impact of Voice on Students and Teachers

I tell the following story to demonstrate the impact my focus on developing voice had on one disengaged student and to show the impact students can have on educators. In particular, I share this story to capture how I came to deepen my teaching and how I dedicated myself to teaching for voice because I began to listen to my students. The student, Tony, also provided me with the space to reflect on my purpose as an educator, and reminds teachers of the humility required to continually learn from our students.

"Is there anyway," Tony asked me, "I can get into your class? I know I don't have good grades and can't write and got some issues an' stuff. But I really wanna get into your class." I asked him to write a one-paragraph justification for why I should let him in the class, given that he had been in fights and passed only two courses in the past two years (both in PE). He told me he had never before written a full paragraph, and after clarifying to him that a paragraph is essentially a complete idea in a small set of connected sentences, he left with a grin spread across his scarred, 18-year-old, stubbled face. He did not show up to school or my class the following day, confirming my concern that while he wanted in the class, he would not do the work it would take for him to fully engage. Indeed, I thought he had wanted to be in our class because we took fieldtrips, had cool guest visitors (poets, civil rights activists, filmmakers, graffiti artists), and because I was laid back (and he probably thought that meant I was an easy grader). Two days of my assumptions later, however, he gave me a crumpled up note, his scrawny chicken scratch scribbled in diagonal lines tilting downward towards the right; the last line started horizontal midway through the wrinkled sheet and ended exactly perpendicular, landing 2 inches from the bottom right hand corner of the page: what was clear was that he had never written that much in his life.

> *Drear Doc Kris:*
>
> *I wunt to b in ur class. YOU du thang diffrent. I c student b Peeple in ur class. u an them stan taller. N cuz 4 realz kidz in ur class be speakin trufh trufh I aint heard 4. I cant write I cant spell I cant I I cant. I mis class I clean KFC they git me hilth cure an I got baby sis and baby bruh and I don need gwramma I need to learnt to speak me mindz. Will u help Doc Kris? I wanna write I wanna speak.*
> *Uno—Toney*

Tony had been continually in and out of juvenile hall; teachers warned me prior to interacting with him that he was "violent," "crazy," "erratic," and "disrespectful." But he had always been very polite with me prior to asking to be in my class. The class was designed for students who excelled at writing; students had to be recommended by another teacher in order to get in. Tony certainly did not meet the stated requirements. "He spelled his own name wrong!" I thought to myself incredulously, as I read over his letter. And yet something was compelling me to push my own practice deeper: could I teach someone with very limited writing skills? Here was Tony, a young multiracial African American and Latino man telling me that he was frustrated by grammar and traditional writing instruction; this was his senior year after all, and his writing suggested that at least he be tested for a learning disability. I wondered if he might have been better served in special education classes, yet I knew that, as a senior, the school would be very reluctant to test him, just as he'd be reluctant to get tested. What would the point be for him? He already hated school.

I kept reading Tony's letter. The clarity he wrote with reminded me that what I was teaching was more about how to express oneself than English, more about how to live in this world than to pass writing tests or develop five-paragraph essays (though all of that, I would eventually learn, improves when students want to write). Tony was more to-the-point than I was: he just wanted into a class that let students be people, where he could be affirmed, and maybe, finally, learn how to write in a way that he wanted to write. Tony's voice showed that while he had not effectively learned how to express himself in standardized English, he could express himself well, and in minimal words. He was concise! Tony's letter captured that he cleaned Kentucky Fried Chicken restaurants so he could have health care to take care of his siblings; that meant he worked full-time while going to high school. Tony's vulnerability clarified precisely what voice is: the capacity to express one's reality, capturing the way we speak as a reflection of the world around us. How could I not let him into the course? Indeed, how could I not let him transform our course to focus entirely on developing voice instead of grammar, punctuation, or the nuances of writing form?

Yet I still feared that I would fail these urban students if I did not teach them basics; and being measured by test scores, I would fail as an educator. Tony's letter haunted me, implored me to rethink my practice. I had taught writing classes in prisons and juvenile halls at this point, but those students knew they would not be tested on Standard English; I was teaching them poetry as a way to release rage. My school-based teaching, in contrast, featured poetry and creative writing within a framework of academic skill sets. I had been using two completely different teaching approaches for two different student populations. When I taught in prison, I dove in deeply, urging incarcerated young men to find their voices. Something was holding me back in schools, though, and Tony made that clear. Shouldn't I be pushing all students to develop their voice, to speak to their realities, to capture what they see and live? Shouldn't I try to engage students before they drop out and end up in the prison classes I see them in later? Wouldn't all students do better if they developed a greater purpose for speaking, for sharing their thoughts on how they navigate and are seen by the world?

I had been thinking about voice for years, but Tony's letter made me realize I had no overarching framework from which to conceive of voice. I had been teaching based on my own experiences, and while I was a popular teacher, I was not nearly as effective as I could be. In hindsight, I was trying to bridge my own development as a writer with the academic success I never had; I had taught myself to write well, and was trying to teach that process to incarcerated youth. But since I did not know how to teach, I tried to do what I saw being done, despite the fact that those efforts did not work with me. And I was perpetuating a false notion that teaching for voice is separate from high-quality teaching, and should just be taught to those already deemed as academic failures. I justified my approaches to myself, but Tony helped me see that I needed to learn how to teach based on who I was, and needed to make school more meaningful for students who had not yet dropped out.

From my first effort to teach others, I had seen the purpose of my teaching as raising awareness about oppression. My first intentional public speaking was as an undergraduate student at a Women Take Back the Night rally, and from there, I began teaching about race and racism, hosting dialogues for high school and college students. Those experiences led me into the high school classroom, and I began teaching week-long seminars on civil rights history and poetry workshops. When I began teaching in my own classroom, I tried to combine my focus on civil rights with poetry, exposing students to stories and poems that expanded notions of privilege and oppression. My classrooms were always dialogue-based, and I rarely lectured. Instead, I posed questions based on the readings and urged students to make connections to their own lives. In these urban schools, my teaching was fairly effective; students were engaged, and students who were typically disengaged from school tended to be much more present in my classes. Because I did not have behavioral issues in my classes, I was never given feedback from a principal or another educator; they instead focused on the teachers who sent children out of their classroom regularly or who struggled with classroom management. So I thought I was doing well, my students appeared to appreciate me, and most continued to write poetry well after our class ended.

Around the same time, I was invited to teach poetry workshops for incarcerated young men. We talked about the purpose, and agreed that I would try to use poetry as a way of helping the young men make sense of and release their rage. I co-taught with an African American woman psychologist, and while she would help frame the writing process, I would push students on poetry and capturing details. From the first day we stepped into the barren concrete-walled room with bolted-down desks, barred windows, and prison guards observing each and every move (students or ours), my teaching began to develop in a parallel but distinct route. In that space, she and I collaborated across race and gender. We urged those young men to release their rage, to capture when they were most frustrated, angry, and emotional, and then to share aloud with the class. Despite the presence of the guards, the men exploded, cursing with angry voices, and afterwards, they'd slump into their desks, spent. After a few weeks, the men started asking for extra journals, and encouraged each other to keep writing, until ultimately, they asked for several journals a month. The guards also began to shift, as they would tell us the young men's behavior began to change; they got in fewer fights and some of them began breaking up fights.

We kept teaching to similar populations, and I began collaborating with a science teacher who was also in my doctoral program. We began combining our classroom-based approaches with community-based readings, local poets and artists to develop voice, and right about that time, I received Tony's letter. As my educational stars aligned, I began to question my methods of teaching. In my classroom-based efforts, was I preparing students to shape the curriculum, to shape what was happening in their classes? Was I ensuring that all students developed and expressed their voice, in the ways that they wanted to be heard? Was I helping the incarcerated young men develop skill sets to address violence as it happened around them? Was releasing rage enough? Was reading a range of poets writing about civil rights enough? While I did not have immediate answers, I knew that I needed to develop my own skill sets, and most importantly, knew I needed to develop a framework for teaching that blended these arenas.

Tony reminded me that as an educator I must learn from my students; even students not part of our classroom communities can dramatically reshape our purpose. My students were already telling me that they were learning how to navigate their world more effectively, that they were writing daily in journals about how demeaning people in their community were, how offensive television images were, and how difficult growing up in a racist society was. But they were not tapping into the same emotion that the incarcerated men were. They were not capturing concrete details that demonstrated what the racism they survived felt like, looked like, and tasted of. As I began to talk with my students more, I began to develop a more conscious philosophy of teaching. I considered the lessons I was learning from multicultural education experts, considered my multiple student populations, wrestled with my own voice, and rethought the purpose of schooling.

Tony is an example of how essential teaching for voice is for students and educators. Prior to my class, Tony had no reason for being in school. He had been repeatedly labeled by schools and his probation officer as illiterate, yet no one had reached out to him and taught him to write nor recognized how powerfully articulate he was. No one had seen Tony from a lens other than his academic failure, and in response, he rejected school. In our class, Tony began writing and developed a foundation to learn how to read well. I was impressed with his capacity to care, to be vulnerable when he had failed almost every class over the past two years. I was and am impressed by his purpose: he did not want to learn to write, he wanted to learn to express himself. As unprepared and unsupported as I was, I helped him learn how to be himself, and in the process, learned how to teach. He ended our class with a note to me:

> And I wanna say this so you stand me. school does evry thing wrong. I don need to learnt sentenences and pawragrafs. I don. I do need to learn to speak my mind. I do need to learn to speak my hart. And I need to speak how I talk, how I am. These are not schools. They are hear to train us to slave us. And I am no slave. I can say dat now.—Tony

While Tony eventually navigated through to college, his experience and relative success are not the norm. When urban student dropout rates hover around 50%, the urgency to engage students cannot be greater (Alliance for Excellent Education, 2009; Swanson, 2006). Teaching for voice in schools that are organized around invalidating such voice, however, sets up students to be punished for not adhering to academic norms. Tony was able to say what he felt he needed to, but also realized that he could only do that in our classroom; he continued to be standoffish with the rest of his teachers, who did not take the time to know him. Many urban schools also engage in urban poetry movements that have validated, in small subsets of populations, multiple forms of expression and have helped keep students like Tony engaged, at least in one class. But this expression is rarely connected to the standards these schools are measured against, leading many teachers to limit their creative approaches. In addition, critical expression can get these students in trouble. In essence, such efforts are limited because student-centered educators who focus on student voice are not the norm, and students have to learn to navigate the rest of their schooling without a focus on who they are. Julia, a 12th grader at the time, clarified teacher expectations. "They teach me what to say, how to repeat what the teacher wants." The problem, she argued, is that she is punished for developing her own ways of communicating that she sees as valid: "Pero no puedo speak in my native language. I cant say what I want to say, just what the teachers think I need to know. So they penalize me for writing in Español, for speaking en mi language." Julia and Tony both highlight the importance of centering voice as a school-wide strategy, and point out the need to develop voice, to clearly define what voice is, and ultimately require educational structures to be built to support their development.

## Defining Voice

The purpose of education, in my mind, is to provide space for students like Tony and Julia to learn to speak their own minds, to understand what society does to urban African American and Latino students, and to feel comfortable hearing their voices challenge such realities. Yet voice is not just documenting personal realities or challenging the purpose of schooling. Voice depends entirely upon the authors' experiences, ways of speaking and thinking, and reflects a complicated, multilingual, multicultural, multiracial, multiethnic world. I often tell my students that "voice is difficult to define concretely, but you know voice when you hear it." June Jordan, who wrote extensively about voice and the purpose of speaking out throughout her career as a writer, poet, and professor, argued that "poetry means taking control of the language of your life" (in Muller et al., 1995, p. 3). Poetry is one of the ways to express voice, but there are infinite ways to take control of our personal language (drawing, cooking, watercolors, building, song, dance, knitting, novels, journals). My focus here is on writing, but I argue that schools should be in the business of promoting all kinds of artistic expression that captures voice, with writing as a foundation.

In what has become a seminal article in defining critical race theory as a framework for educational transformation, Gloria Ladson-Billings (1999) clarifies that "the 'voice' component of CRT provides a way to communicate the experiences and realities of the oppressed, a first step in understanding the complexities of racism…" (p. 16). Voice, seen through the lens of critical race theory, is about "naming one's own reality with stories" and doing so in a way that clarifies oppression (Ladson-Billings, 1999, p. 16). In the poem below, Christina, a first-generation college student who took my classes in high school and again in college, provides her take on voice as a capturing of the details that make up the fabric of her life.

> *My voice is the sing song lullabies de mi tía screaming from prison walls Mi voz es the fist rising inside of me, breaking walls I did not know surround me*

*My voice might stab you with the sharpness of rape from mi molesting tíos*
*Mi voz might remind you that I sleep hungry and wake with medical bed sores*
*My voice should make you cry in shame at how little public assistance I survive on*
*Mi voz es the one thing I have left and yet my teachers teach me silence*
*I write to figure out what I have to say*
*And I speak to tell you who listen (which is not enough of you) how wrong the world is*
*I speak so that you who listen know how I bleed, what causes my pain*
*So that those of you who care will join me, join us*
*In speaking listening learning and then shaping a healing world where we can all be*
*Full of our languages, aware of our histories, writing survival manuals*
*Teaching others, through our voices, how to keep on when on might get us killed*
*Mi voz is the air that keeps me mi hermanas y perhaps you también alive*
*—Christina*

As Christina began to document her life through writing, she began to recognize the oppression that plagues her family, severely limiting her family's opportunity. Only through writing was she able to see her own role, as she came to recognize that the violence she grew up in is what gave her insight into the world. "When I started writing, started finding my voice, I realized that I was not alone, that I was just like the authors we read," Christina argued. Writing became a way to create her own living history, and she began to consider ways of disrupting what she saw as "the way things are because we all just tolerate this." For her, the key was in editing her work until her words reflected what she felt: "I realized, in our class, that saying what I want en mi voz es muy dificíl." She continued, "pero, I've been taught to never ever speak my voice, much less learn to speak how I actually talk about the things that make me me." Such work is difficult; Christina had spent years working on developing her writing, on learning to tell stories, and on learning to value writing in *Spanglish*, the conglomerated language she grew up speaking. Yet the importance of voice is that such writing creates stories that contradict mainstream U.S. avoidance of critical voices of people of color and oppressed people in general, but also helps individuals make sense of their own survival (Yosso, 2005).

The key to such voice is in developing a language to express stories that reflect what we live, how we live, and how students feel about both. Rochelle Brock (2005) argues that "language is personal and needs to bring forth the personal stories it is trying to relate to the reader. Words should be shaped and molded to your needs" (p. 3). Voice is a personal attempt to develop a language that makes sense to the author, and captures our stories in our own languages, in our own multicultural rhythms and multilingual words. Without voice, the language of the colonizer is used to explain the experience of being colonized, and those that live racism use the dominant language to try to explain that racism (Smith, 1999; Thiong'o, 1986; Wright, 1957). But the words don't match: such "formal" language frames the experience of the people who develop that language. When students begin to recognize that the English language really does define "black" as negative and dangerous and "White" as positive and beautiful, something happens to their voices. They begin to search for meaning, to develop new words and recognize that they are the ones who must recreate and reclaim language to reflect who they are.

But in the meantime, this language disjoint leaves women searching for language in a world dominated by men, people of color in search of words in languages imposed by White systems of colonization, and people with disabilities striving to recreate a way of speaking, talking, and writing that reflects disabled realities in a presumed able-bodied world. But our language doesn't work: "disabled" lives in opposition to "able-bodied," "Black" in juxtaposition to "White," "woman" in relation to "man." Our binary colonial languages struggle to find words to clarify the continuing marginalization of people who are multiracial, transgendered, multilingual, and multicultural. Thus, voice is resistance to systematic oppression kept firmly in place by our daily language, by academic language, by the very dictionaries that teach us, as we grow up, what words mean, and what part of which people matters more, as if there can be a universal definition of language, oppression, or experience.

Dorothy Allison (2002) speaks to the role of voice in daily survival: "Once in a while, I can make the world I know real on the page…Writing these stories is the only way I know to make sure of my ongoing decision to live, to set moment to moment a small piece of stubbornness against an ocean of ignorance and obliteration" (p. 7). Developing voice is a process of thinking through and documenting both what and how we survive; it is these realities that shape opportunity, awareness, and consciousness. Beth Brant (1994) clarified the responsibility of voice: "As an Indigenous writer, I feel that the gift of writing and the privilege of writing holds a responsibility to be witness to my people…to be witness to the sometimes unbearable circumstances of our lives" (p. 70). Voice is captured through writing that demonstrates exactly what is unbearable in our lives; these are the details that are systemically silenced through mainstream academics, literature, corporate mass media, and schools.

## Components of Voice

To capture the nuances of our lives, voice is full of concrete details that show the complexities of our lives and how we fit within oppression and privilege. Jordan clarifies the need for concrete details: "Good poetry requires precision: if you do not attempt to say, accurately, truthfully, what you feel or see or need, then how will you achieve precision?" (in Muller et al., 1995, p. 3). *Jordan here names the first component of voice: a concise capturing of the author's reality, responding to the author's culture(s), language(s), race(s), gender(s), sexuality(ies), ability(ies), religion(s), spirituality(ies), and class-based experiences.* Voice is who we are, all of the silenced parts that make up our identity, the very pieces of us that we have been told to hide. This means, like most artistic endeavors, practice is essential to ensuring our words convey truth that others can feel as we would have them feel. Jordan argued for maximum impact with minimal words, and I teach students and educators alike to repeatedly draft and edit to ensure clarity and purpose. Writing for voice requires continual editing to concisely capture personal context. Stories and experiences come out naturally, but through our schooling we are taught to write in ways that contradict our languages and cultures. Thus continual editing is required to ensure our words and personal contexts blend into our voice, full of our emotion and experience.

After one of my courses culminated in a public poetry reading, several of my students excitedly bounced with energy when they left the stage. Their words shook many in the audience, and they were reflecting the energy from the performance. Two students, Shay and Loni, could not contain themselves; they were shaking with nervous energy and excitement. I asked them how they felt, and they couldn't hold back: "I've never felt like anyone really listened to me before because I never really said anything." Loni said, "But now, I made people cry! CRY! Not because I hurt them but because I showed them how I have been hurt." Shay clarified the impact of expressing her voice: "I moved the audience. I did that. I didn't think I could. I didn't think they would care about what I had to say. But they were feeling me!" Loni and Shay were capturing *the second component: voice captures and exudes passion, moving audiences to feel a depth of emotion that reflects the speaker's life.* Musician Oliver Mtukudzi (personal communication, October, 2007), in visiting my voice-centered high school writing class several years ago, clarified that, culturally, in Zimbabwe, "if you are going to speak in public, you have to have something to say." Voice is used to convey something meaningful, and I argue in my classes that if what you have to say is not worth saying, then you do not say it. The very point is that voice reflects the passions of the author; thus teaching for voice means helping students see how they can share their passions. The end result is often shock as students express the beauty of finally having something to say, and at being validated when they say it (instead of being chastised for "incorrect" grammar or spelling). Voice moves people, and voice does this through honest representations of how we see, how we are seen, and how we attempt to be sane in a deeply conflicted, insane world.

Dorothy Allison (2002) clarifies the importance of clarifying her life through writing, arguing that the process is connected to the purpose of living: "I put on the page a third look at what I've seen in life—the condensed and reinvented experience of a cross-eyed, working-class lesbian, addicted to violence, language, and hope, who has made the decision to live, is determined to live, on the page and on the street, for me and mine" (p. 7). Voice is that decision to live, to be more conscious of our daily surroundings, and how the world we live in silences our reactions so effectively we are left searching for words to describe how growing up in violence, poverty, and systematized oppression *feels*. The point of voice is to capture clearly, powerfully, what exactly living as a "cross-eyed, working-class lesbian, addicted to violence, language, and hope" means. Whoever you are, whatever you live, the point is to help develop voice that captures what your own survival means, looks like, and feels like. I often use this example with high school students: "I grew up in a fucked up environment" simply does not clarify the depth of what precisely was fucked up. The reality is that one has to search for words that can clarify, in depth, what about us and what about those around us is "fucked up." Developing voice is the process of finding the right words, of learning how to speak those words in a way that conveys to your intended audience exactly what you feel and why you feel this way.

June Jordan taught poetry as a way of helping students make sense of their own lives. Her approach was powerful specifically because she saw the world around us as being committed to what Donaldo Macedo (2006) terms "stupidification," where people see the world around us through the silencing lenses of mass corporate media. Jordan clarified that:

> Because poetry is the medium for telling the truth, and because a poem is antithetical to lies/evasions and superficiality, anyone who becomes a practicing poet has an excellent chance of becoming somebody real, somebody known, self-defined, and attuned to and listening and hungering for kindred real voices utterly/articulately different from his or her own voice. (in Muller et al., 1995, p. 8)

Thus I see the role of education and the purpose of schools as to prepare students to navigate the structural and personal levels of oppression. Such navigation requires developing voice, and developing voice requires making sense of the oppression we live. Thus developing voice is a cycle of healing, where individuals make sense of themselves, make sense of the world around them, and learn to navigate, publically, through self-expression, to create the socially just world they believe in.

### *Process of Developing Voice*

The process I use to develop voice, in my courses, talks to educators, and in work with students and incarcerated men, is based upon five interrelated arenas:

1. *Self-recognition and Examination.* Developing voice begins with a thorough examination and critical self-reflection on who I am as a person. This includes an intense focus on learning to see myself as an individual, but also learning to center individual experiences (as I do in Chapter 1).

Writings center on what I literally look like, sound like, smell like, and feel, including multiple cultures, races, languages, families, geographies, and communities. This arena focuses entirely on the individual expressing what they see in themselves.

2. *Reflection on Context*. After beginning to wrestle with and document the individual, developing voice then requires an examination of and reflection on personal context. This entails examining social conditions that shape life, including what literally surrounds the author on a daily level (including family, community, school, but also violence, racism, sexism, abuse, drug use, weather, housing). Writings capture concrete details of the world around the author and ensure the author's perspectives are made clear.
3. *Personal Responses to Our Context.* After wrestling with who and where the author is, I urge those developing their voices to begin writing about how they are, given their context. In essence, how do I respond to how I see myself and how others see me? Writings include critical recognition of the ways individuals respond to their personal contexts, and include specific capturing of efforts made to ensure survival. Writings also include tapping into emotional responses, including rage, violence, and addictions, but also love, romantic relationships, and safety.
4. *Translation of Experience into Voice*. As students write about the first three components, they begin to transform these writings to capture emotional power. This requires extensive editing to ensure what is written actually reflects intended content, but also reflects the tone, language, and details that clarify personal nuance. This component is key to ensuring that voice actually develops; what poets often call "work-shopping poems," the focus is on connecting what is being said to the person saying it.
5. *Critical Expression*. After writings are work-shopped to capture the depth of the author, and drive home the intended message, the focus shifts to expressing that voice. With writing, this is most often through spoken word, poetry, or vocal storytelling, though creativity in expression is expected. Thus, many students create films, dance, drawings, photography, graffiti, and silkscreen t-shirts, and express their written voice in a range of artistic methods. The key is that the methods of expression fit with the purpose, tone, and overall feel the author is trying to capture and convey.

Each of these arenas, or areas of academic focus, is centered in the upcoming chapters. In Chapter Three, I capture how I frame classroom dynamics and academic courses, providing concrete examples of how I approach the first three arenas, in terms of assignments, structures, and feedback processes. In Chapter

Four, I center activities and processes I use to translate experience into voice, and focus on the role of trauma in shaping the importance of this work. This entails a critical need for educators to be responsive and not push students too quickly, too deeply, unless they have a solid foundation from which to engage. In Chapter Five, I frame school-wide approaches that can foster the first four curricular areas, and provide concrete examples of forums through which voice can be expressed. It is this fifth arena that I argue schools should be structured around, particularly in terms of shifting notions of academic success and measurement to community-based forums. These forums are key to validating student expression, and connect student voice to communities, families, and educators.

Shifting the purpose of schooling to preparing urban youth to shape their local communities begins to shift the historical treatment of urban communities. How schools develop urban student voice reflects how the U.S. prepares youth to lead communities in the future. In a similar vein to Paulo Freire's notion of critical consciousness (*conscientization*), students learn how to develop and express themselves through understanding their world, and then begin to take action about what they see as unequal in their world (Freire, 1973). Teaching critical literacy, which can be expressed through voice, is an essential condition of both a democratic society, and the schools that are the tools for transforming (or perpetuating) the social inequality that the U.S. is known for worldwide (Duncan-Andrade & Morrell, 2008; Shor, 1992). Ultimately, the greatest test of a democratic country is the expression of critical voice on an intimate, personal level; how schools help urban youth of color develop and then express who they are, how they live, and the structural limitations to both reflects a commitment (or not) to the work of creating and sustaining democracies. These five steps have become one way in which I have been able to deepen my efforts to develop such student voice, while ensuring an academic foundation that enables students to succeed in the rest of their courses as well.

## Conclusion

Shifting classroom practice to center on urban student voice is not enough to transform public schools into communities that culturally affirm student experience and worth. Adding voice as yet another responsibility or requirement for teachers will not shift the dramatic intentional inequities that are reflected in dropout rates and urban teacher turnover. As Ladson-Billings (1999) argued: "If we are serious about solving these [race, racism, and social injustice] problems in school and classrooms, we have to be serious about intense study and careful rethinking of race and education…we will have to expose racism in education *and* propose radical solutions for addressing it" (p. 27). Critical race theory and a focus on centering the development and expression of voice requires a deeper, sustained transformation of public schools to center on a social justice mission to prepare students to shape democracy. This means shifting the purpose of public schools to prepare students to express themselves on the social realities they live (and are shaped by).

This book is a culmination of attempts to develop urban student voice. This work is based on students I have had the honor and privilege of teaching, and includes direct quotes and writing excerpts from students over the past 12 years. These students have been my greatest teachers, and they have directly shaped how I teach, how I research, how I write, and how I move in the world as a White male educator. As I define how central their voices are in transforming schools to address structural racism and inequities, I argue that voice is the foundation for democracy: as schools prepare students and communities to express themselves, as students and communities listen to each other's clarifications of oppressed realities, our collective notion of reality deepens, as does our collective commitment to alter the oppression we perpetuate in schools. If we listen to these students, then we know the urgency cannot be more immediate. Schools cannot be allowed to train students to be silenced or, like Tony, to feel enslaved. Educators cannot allow more students of color to believe that they really are worth less than their White counterparts.

## References

Allen, R. L. (1990). *Black Awakening in Capitalistic America: An Analytic History*. Trenton, NJ: Africa World Press.

Alliance for Excellent Education (2009). *Understanding High School Graduation Rates in the United States.* Washington, DC: Alliance for Excellent Education.

Allison, D. (2002). Deciding to Live: Preface to the First Edition. In D. Allison, *Trash*. New York: Plume.

Alonso, A. (1998). Urban Graffiti on the City Landscape. Paper presented to the Western Geography Graduate Conference, San Diego State University. February 14, 1998.

Anderson, J. D. (1988). *The Education of Blacks in the South, 1860–1935*. Chapel Hill, NC: University of North Carolina Press.

Antibalas. (2004). *Big Man. Who is This America?* New York: Artemis Records.

Apple, M. W. (1993). *Official Knowledge: Democratic Education in a Conservative Age.* New York: Routledge.

Archuleta, M. L., Child, B. J., & Lomawaima, K. T. (2000). *Away from Home: American Indian Boarding School Experiences.* Heard Museum.

Asante, M. K. (1998). *The Afrocentric Idea*. Philadelphia, PA: Temple University Press.

Aud, S., Fox, M. A., & KewalRamani, A. (2010). *Status and Trends in the Education of Racial and Ethnic Groups*. Washington, DC: National Center for Educational Statistics (NCES 2010015).

Aud, S., Hussar, W., Planty, M., Snyder, T., Bianco, K., Fox, M. A., Frohlich, L., Kemp, J., & Drake, L. (2010). *The Condition of Education, 2010*. Washington, DC: National Center for Educational Statistics (NCES 2010028).

Baldwin, J. (1962). *The Fire Next Time.* New York: Vintage.

Baldwin, J. (1972). *No Name in the Street.* New York: Laurel.

Baldwin, J. (1985a) *The Evidence of Things Not Seen*. New York: Holt.

Baldwin, J. (1985b). A Talk to Teachers. In J. Baldwin. *The Price of the Ticket: Collected Nonfiction.* New York: St. Martin's Press.
Banks, J. A. (1993). The Canon Debate: Knowledge Construction and Multicultural Education. *Educational Researcher, 22*(5), 4–14.
Banks, J. A. (1995). Multicultural Education: Historical Development, Dimensions, and Practice. In J. A. Banks & C. A. M. Banks (Eds.), *Handbook of Research on Multicultural Education,* 3–24. New York: Macmillan.
Banks, J. A. (1996). *Multicultural Education, Transformative Knowledge, and Action: Historical and Contemporary Perspectives.* New York: Teachers College Press.
Banks, J. A., & McGee Banks, C. (2009). *Multicultural Education: Issues and Perspectives.* New York: Wiley.
Barber, B. R. (1992). *An Aristocracy of Everyone: The Politics of Education and the Future of America.* New York: Oxford University Press.
Barone, T. (2006). Making Educational History: Qualitative Inquiry, Artistry, and the Public Interest. In G. Ladson-Billings and W. F. Tate (Eds.), *Education Research in the Public Interest: Social Justice, Action, and Policy,* 213–230. New York: Teachers College Press.
Bell, D. (2004). *Silent Covenants: Brown v. Board of Education and the Unfulfilled Hopes for Racial Reform.* New York: Oxford University Press.
Bigelow, B. (1995). Discovering Columbus: Rereading the Past. In D. Levine, R. Lowe, B. Peterson, & R. Tenorio (Eds.), *Rethinking Schools: An Agenda for Change,* 61–68. New York: New Press.
Bowen, W. G., & Bok, D. (1998). *The Shape of the River: Long-Term Consequences of Considering Race in College and University Admissions.* Princeton, NJ: Princeton University Press.
Brant, B. (1994). *Writing as Witness: Essay and Talk.* Toronto: Women's Press.
Brewer, D. D. (1992). Hip Hop Writers' Evaluations of Strategies to Control Illegal Graffiti. *Human Organization, 51,* 188–196.
Brock, R. (2005). *Sista Talk: The Personal and the Pedagogical.* New York: Peter Lang.
Campbell, M. S. (1994). *Harlem Renaissance: Art of Black America.* New York: Abrams.
Carr, F. (1997). *Wicked Words: Poisoned Minds—Racism in the Dictionary.* Lakewood, CA: Scholar Technological.
Children's Defense Fund. (2006). *State of America's Children 2006.* Washington DC: Children's Defense Fund.
Clark, K. B., & Clark, M. (1947). Racial Identification and Preference in Negro Children. In T. M. Newcomb & E. L. Hartley (Eds.), *Readings in Social Psychology,* 169–178. New York: Holt.
Clark, W. A. V. (1987). School Desegregation and White Flight: A Reexamination and Case Study. *Social Science Research, 16*(3), 211–228.
Coker, N. (2004). *A Study of the Music and Social Criticism of African Musician Fela Anikulapo-Kuti.* New York: Edwin Mellon Press.
Conchas, G. Q. (2006). *The Color of Success: Race and High Achieving Urban Youth,* New York: Teachers College Press.
Darling-Hammond, L., Rustique-Forrester, E., & Pecheone, R. L. (2005). *Multiple Measures Approaches to High School Graduation.* Stanford, CA: Stanford University School Redesign Network.
Davis, D. B. (1966). *The Problem of Slavery in Western Culture.* Ithaca, NY: Cornell University Press.
Davis, K. (2007). *A Girl Like Me.* Reel Works Teen Filmmaking. Available at http://mediathatmatters.org
De Fina, A. (2007). Code Switching and the Construction of Ethnic Identity in a Community of Practice. *Language in Society, 36,* 371–392.
Delpit, L. (2006). *Other People's Children: Cultural Conflict in the Classroom.* New York: New Press.
DeMeulenaere, E. (2009). Fluid Identities: Black Students Negotiating the Transformation of Their Academic Identities and School Performances. *International Journal of Critical Pedagogy, 2*(1), 30–48.
Dewey, J. (1916). *Democracy and Education: An Introduction to the Philosophy of Education.* New York: Free Press.

Duncan-Andrade, J. M. R., & Morrell, E. (2008). *The Art of Critical Pedagogy: Possibilities for Moving from Theory to Practice in Urban Schools*. New York: Peter Lang.
Epstein, K. K. (2006). *A Different View of Urban Schools: Civil Rights, Critical Race Theory, and Unexplored Realities*. New York: Peter Lang.
Ethnic Studies Now. (2007). *A 2007 Student Report on the State of Ethnic Studies at Columbia University*. http://socialjustice.ccnmtl.columbia.edu/index.php/Ethnic_Studies
Fegley, S. G., Spencer, M. B., Gross, T. N., Harpalani, V., & Charles, N. (2008). Bodily Self-awareness: Skin Color and Psychosocial Well-being in Adolescence. In W. Overton & U. Mueller (Eds.), *Body in mind, mind in body: Developmental perspectives on embodiment and consciousness*, 281–312. Mahwah, NJ: LEA Inc.
Feiner, J., & Klein, S. (1982) Graffiti Talks. *Social Policy, 12*, 47–53.
Ferguson, A. A. (2001). *Bad Boys: Public Schools in the Making of Black Masculinity*. Ann Arbor: University of Michigan Press.
Fine, M. (1991). *Framing Dropouts: Notes on the Politics of an Urban Public High School*. Albany: SUNY Press.
Fisher, M. (2008). *Black Literate Lives: Historical and Contemporary Perspectives*. New York: Routledge.
Forbes, J. D. (2008). Ethnic or World Studies: A Historian's Path of Discovery. In T. P. Fong (Ed.), *Ethnic Studies Research: Approaches and Perspectives*, 58–91. Lanham, MD: Altamira Press.
Fordham, S., & Ogbu, J. (1986). Black Students' School Success: Coping with the Burden of "Acting White." *Urban Review, 18*, 176–206.
Freire, P. (1973). *Education for Critical Consciousness*. New York: Continuum.
Freire, P. (2004). *Pedagogy of Indignation*. Boulder, CO: Paradigm Publishers.
Futrell, M. H. (2004). The Impact of the Brown Decision on African American Educators. In J. Anderson, Byrne, D. N., & T. Smiley (Eds.), *The Unfinished Agenda of Brown v. Board of Education*, 79–96. New York: Wiley.
Garrison, M. J. (2009). *A Measure of Failure: The Political Origins of Standardized Testing*. New York: SUNY Press.
Gay, G. (2000). *Culturally Responsive Teaching: Theory, Research, and Practice*. New York: Teachers College Press.
Gay, G. (2007). The Rhetoric and Reality of NCLB. *Race Ethnicity and Education, 10*(3), 279–93.
Gibson, M. A., & Ogbu, J. U. (1991). *Minority Status and Schooling: A Comparative Study of Immigrant and Involuntary Minorities*. New York: Garland.
Ginwright, S., Noguera, P., & Cammarota, J. (2006). *Beyond Resistance! Youth Activism and Community Change*. New York: Routledge.
Giroux, H. A. (2001). *Theory and Resistance in Education: A Pedagogy for the Opposition*. Westport, CT: Praeger.
Goodell, W. (2009). *The American Slave Code in Theory and Practice: Its Distinctive Features Shown by Its Statutes*. N.P.: Bibliolife.
Gordon, B. M. (1995). Knowledge Construction: Competing Critical Theories and Education. In J.A. Banks & C. McGee Banks (Eds.), *Handbook of Research on Multicultural Education*, 184–199. New York: Macmillan.
Greene, M. (2001). *Variations on a Blue Guitar: The Lincoln Center Institute Lectures on Aesthetic Education*. New York: Teachers College Press.
Gutmann, A. (1999). *Democratic Education*. Princeton, NJ: Princeton University Press;
Hauser, R. M., Simmons, S. J., & Pager, D. I. (2004). High School Dropout, Race/Ethnicity, and Social Background from the 1970s to the 1990s. In G. Orfield (Ed.), *Dropouts in America: Confronting the Graduation Rate Crisis*, 85–106. Cambridge, MA: Harvard University Press.
Holzman, M. (2006). *Public Education and Black Male Students: The 2006 State Report Card*. Schott Educational Inequality Index, Cambridge, MA: The Schott Foundation for Public Education.
hooks, b. (1994). *Teaching to Transgress*. New York: Routledge.
Howard, T. C. (2008). Who Really Cares? The Disenfranchisement of African American Males in Pre K–12 Schools: A Critical Race Theory Perspective. *Teachers College Record, 110*(5), 954–985.

Jacobson, J., Olsen, C., Rice, J. K., Sweetland, S., & Ralph, J. (2001). *Educational Achievement and Black-White Inequality.* Washington, DC: National Center for Educational Statistics (NCES 2001061).

Knaus, C. B. (2007). Still Segregated, Still Unequal: Analyzing the Impact of No Child Left Behind on African American Students. In *The State of Black America: Portrait of the Black Male,* 105-121. Washington, DC: National Urban League.

Krishnamurti, J. (1953). *Education and the Significance of Life.* Ojai, CA: Krishnamurti Foundation.

Kruse, K. M. (2005). *White Flight: Atlanta and the Making of Modern Conservatism.* Princeton, NJ: Princeton University Press.

Ladson-Billings, G. (1994). *The Dreamkeepers: Successful Teachers of African American Children.* San Francisco: Jossey-Bass.

Ladson-Billings, G. (1999). Just What Is Critical Race Theory, and What's It Doing in a Nice Field Like Education? In L. Parker, D. Deyhele, S. Villenas (Eds.) *Race Is...Race Isn't: Critical Race Theory and Qualitative Studies in Education,* 7–30. Boulder, CO: Westview Press.

*Larry P. and Lucille P., v. Riles,* C-71-2270. 495 F. Supp. 926; 1979 U.S. Dist.

Loewen, J. (1996). *Lies My Teacher Told Me: Everything Your American History Textbook Got Wrong.* New York: Touchstone.

Macedo, D. (2006). *Literacies of Power: What Americans Are Not Allowed to Know.* Boston, MA: Westview Press.

Macedo, D., & Bartolomé, L. I. (1999). *Dancing with Bigotry: Beyond the Politics of Tolerance.* New York: Palgrave.

Martin, T. (1983). *Literary Garveyism: Garvey, Black Arts, and the Harlem Renaissance.* Dover, MA: Majority.

Martínez, E. (1995). Distorting Latino History: The California Textbook Controversy. In D. Levine, R. Lowe, B. Peterson, & R. Tenorio (Eds.), *Rethinking Schools: An Agenda for Change,* 100–108. New York: New Press.

Mauer, M., & King, R. S. (2004). *Schools and Prisons: Fifty Years after Brown v. Board of Education.* Washington, DC: The Sentencing Project.

McCombs, B. L. (2007). Balancing Accountability Demands with Research-Validated, Learner-Centered Teaching and Learning Practices. In C. E. Sleeter (Ed.), *Facing Accountability in Education: Democracy and Equity at Risk,* 41–60. New York: Teachers College Press.

McKay, C. (1930). *Harlem: Negro Metropolis.* New York: Dutton.

Morgan, H. (1995). *Historical Perspectives on the Education of Black Children.* Westport, CT: Praeger.

Morrell, E. (2004). *Becoming Critical Researchers: Literacy and Empowerment for Urban Youth.* New York: Peter Lang.

Muller, L., Bright., S., Changler, G., Esteva, A., Lewis, S., Rose, S., Smith, S., Teves, S., Villalobos, R. A., & Wilson, P. (1995). *June Jordan's Poetry for the People: A Revolutionary Blueprint.* New York: Routledge.

Nieto, S. (1996). *Affirming Diversity: The Sociopolitical Context of Multicultural Education,* 2nd Edition. White Plains, NY: Longman.

Oakes, J. (1985). *Keeping Track: How Schools Structure Inequality.* New Haven, CT: Yale University Press.

Ogbu, J. U. (1991). Low School Performance as an Adaptation: The Case of Blacks in Stockton, California. In M. A. Gibson & J. U. Ogbu (Eds.), *Minority Status and Schooling: A Comparative Study of Immigrant and Involuntary Minorities,* 249–285. New York: Garland Publishing.

Perry, T., & Delpit, L. (1998). *The Real Ebonics Debate: Power, Language, and the Education of African-American Children.* Boston, MA: Beacon Press.

Pihama, L. (1985). Are Films Dangerous? A Maori Woman's Perspective on *The Piano. Hecate, 20*(2), 239–242.

Power, F. C., Higgins, A., & Kohlberg, L. (1989). *Lawrence Kohlber's Approach to Moral Education.* New York: Columbia University Press.

Rampey, B. D., Dion, G. S., & Donahue, P. L. (2009). *The Nation's Report Card: Long-Term Trend 2008.* Washington, DC: National Center for Educational Statistics (NCES 2009479).

Rees, J. (2003). A Crisis Over Consensus: Standardized Testing in American History and Student Learning. *Radical Pedagogy, 5*(2). Available online at http://radicalpedagogy.icaap.org/content/issue5_2/03_rees.html

Rumberger, R. W., & Thomas, S. L. (2000). The distribution of dropouts and turnover rates among urban and suburban high schools. *Sociology of Education, 73*, 39–67.

Santa Cruz, N. (2010). Arizona Bill Targeting Ethnic Studies Signed into Law. *Los Angeles Times*, May 12.

Shields, C. M., Bishop, R., & Mazawi, A. E. (2005). *Pathologizing Practices: The Impact of Deficit Thinking on Education.* New York: Peter Lang.

Shor, I. (1992). *Culture Wars: School and Society in the Conservative Restoration.* Chicago: University of Chicago Press.

Silvera, M. (1983). *Silenced.* Toronto: Sister Vision.

Singleton, G. E., & Linton, C. W. (2005). *Courageous Conversations about Race: A Field Guide for Achieving Equity in Schools.* Thousand Oaks, CA: Corwin Press.

Smith, L. T. (1999). *Decolonizing Methodologies; Research and Indigenous Peoples.* New York: Zed.

Steele, C. M., & Aronson, J. (1995). Stereotype Threat and the Intellectual Test Performance of African Americans. *Journal of Personality and Social Psychology, 69*(5), 797–811.

Steiner, D. (1999). Searching for Educational Coherence in a Democratic State. In S. L. Elkin & K. E. Soltan (Eds.), *Citizen Competence and Democratic Institutions*, 225–257. University Park: Pennsylvania State University Press.

Swanson, C. B. (2006). Diplomas Count: An Essential Guide to Graduation Policy and Rates. *Education Week*, June 22.

Thiong'o, N. W. (1986). *Decolonising the Mind: The Politics of Language in African Literature.* Portsmouth, NH: Heinemann.

Trafzer, C. E., & Keller, J. A. (2006). *Boarding School Blues: Revisiting American Indian Educational Experiences.* Lincoln: University of Nebraska Press.

Ture, K., & Hamilton, C. V. (1967). *Black Power: The Politics of Liberation.* New York: Random House.

Valdes, G. (1996). *Con Respeto: Bridging the Distances Between Culturally Diverse Families and Schools.* New York: Teachers College Press.

Walker, V. S. (1996). *Their Highest Potential: An African American School Community in the Segregated South.* Chapel Hill: University of North Carolina Press.

Watkins, W. H. (2001). *The White Architects of Black Education: Ideology and Power in America, 1865–1954.* New York: Teachers College Press.

Webber, T. (1978). *Deep Like the Rivers: Education in the Slave Quarter Community, 1831–1865.* W.W. Norton.

Weis, L., & Fine, M. (2005). *Beyond Silenced Voices: Class, Race, and Gender in United States Schools.* New York: University of New York Press.

Western, B., & Pettit, B. (2005). Black-White Wage Inequality, Employment Rates, and Incarceration. *American Journal of Sociology, 111*(2), 553–578.

Wheeler, R., & Swords, R. (2006). Code-Switching: Teaching Standard English in Urban Classrooms. National Council of Teachers of English.

Williams, H. A. (2005). *Self-Taught: African American Education in Slavery and Freedom.* Chapel Hill, NC: University of North Carolina Press.

Woodson, C. G. (1933). *The Mis-education of the Negro.* Trenton: NJ: First Africa World Press.

Woodson, C. G. (2004). *The Education of the Negro Prior to 1861: A History of the Education of the Colored People of the United States from the Beginning of Slavery to the Civil War.* Whitefish, MT: Kessinger Publishing.

Wright, R. (1957). *White Man Listen.* New York: HarperCollins.

Yosso, T. (2005). *Critical Race Counterstories Along the Chicana/Chicano Educational Pipeline.* New York: Routledge.

# To Choose Ignorance

I'ma drop this plain
I'ma holla at you slow
So you can follow my flow
To choose ignorance
Is to hope that the light at the end of the tunnel is a train
Getting smashed is infinitely easier than using your brain
'Cause in a world of 'gimme that'
You ain't figured out that the world don't owe you squat!

You steady dreaming of fame
But you can't stay in frame
You done lost your focus
Caught up in the hocus pocus
You been hoodwinked and bamboozled
Into thinking a 6 X 4 with bars is beachfront property
And now, somehow
School is something that keeps you from living
Your great American Dream

But tell me how you living when
If it don't come in a box you can't cook it
Tell me how you living when
If it needs a needle you looking for a syringe
Tell me how you living when
Blunted is not a term for a knife that needs sharpening
Tell me how you living when
Dinner and a movie is Redbox and McDonald's
Tell me how you living when
You can't make change for a dollar without a calculator
Tell me how you living when
You gotta invite her back to your momma house?

I know that this might seem hollow
But… feed your mind
And the rest will surely follow.

|| FIVE

# Where Do We Go from . . . Where?

## *Identifying the Ideological Bases of Low-Income, Urban Black Adolescents' Views on Racism*

Alfred W. DeFreece, Jr.

*"Whether you know it or not, you're deep in politics —all inside of it. In fact you're the issue. Don't let this government dis' you."*—KRS-ONE, "The Mind," *The Sneak Attack*

*"To the real question, How does it feel to be a problem? I answer seldom a word."* —W. E. B. Du Bois, "Of Our Spiritual Strivings," *The Souls of Black Folk*

These passages remind us that dealing with the "Other" in our midst has always been a central preoccupation of all American institutions. The nation's colonial and imperialist roots have cemented this reality. Few would disagree with Michael Omi and Howard Winant's assertion that race is a preeminently political construct and one of the major axial divisions in the American polity (if *not the* major division) (1994). In recent decades, the plight of urban-based, low-income Black youth has garnered considerable attention from the media, policymakers, academicians spanning the disciplines, social service practitioners, and the lay public. All are concerned in some way with the presence of masses of socially disconnected youth across the nation's major metropolitan areas. No matter one's position on the political spectrum, there is no question that the failure to incorporate so many young people into mainstream America will continue to have far-reaching impacts on our racial-political dynamics, not just in cities, but also in varied communities across the country.

I conducted interviews with 24 graduating seniors attending a public charter academy in the city's university district.[1] Using a discourse analytic method inspired by the work of Michel Foucault (1982), I identify the discourses, or interpretative repertoires, underlying the ways in which the interview participants spoke about three areas of racial knowledge that emerged as significant during the interview process: economic stratification, the Black community, and racism. Through this analysis, I reveal a number of key interpretative repertoires reflecting both dominant and alternate modes of thought and featuring combinations of seemingly inconsistent symbols and interpretations.[2] The interview participants expressed views that defy straightforward grouping into traditional categories of Black ideological thought. This is true not only of the group, but also of individual youths. There are discernable patterns in the ways they talk about race, but these regularities exist at a supra-individual level. My findings suggest that ideological processes among Black youth are much more complex than has been made apparent through previous studies, and recommend the application of discourse analytic modes to future studies of this population.

At the heart of Foucaultian-inspired discourse analysis is the notion that what people say presupposes large-scale, sociohistorically grounded, and culturally specific forms of knowledge that guide their speech. There is an emphasis on the limiting and enabling aspects of these forms of knowledge. That is, the discursive formation, or the contesting ideas that govern what is possible to say on a given topic, is given preeminent status as a set of processes that delimit how people speak of and are able to orient themselves to social phenomena (Foucault, 1982). While the specific utterances made in the context of the interview situation surely reflect the subjective interpretations and personal biographies of the interviewees, the proper focus for sociological inquiry is the set of processes and practices that provide the conditions by which subjectivity and biography become meaningful (Keller, 2006). What the youth in this study have to say about race is not significant solely because it reflects their subjective understandings of social reality, but also because, collectively, their talk captures a range of possible ways that individuals sharing a similar social location can apprehend particular social phenomena.

In this study I apply a discourse analytic technique that takes the interpretative repertoire as the basic unit of analysis (Talja, 1999). That is, the goal of inquiry is not hermeneutical (to understand the subject's interpretative process given his or her understanding of broader cultural themes) or phenomenological (to explain how subjective meaning is constituted through and by lived experience); the individual's sensemaking and narrative construction is not the endpoint. For this reason, I follow Sanna Talja in utilizing a conception of interpretative repertoire that destabilizes the reliance on common concepts, objects, styles of speech, and narrative structures as indicative of discourses.

Rather, reasserting Foucault's formulation, discourses *determine* the selection of objects, the meaning of concepts, the styles of speech, and forms of narrative, on the basis of the starting points or basic assumptions conceptualized here as being interpretative repertoires. Interpretative repertoires or discourses are the starting points or basic assumptions that create a limited viewpoint through which objects are deemed relevant, meaning develops, terms are related, and articulations are made (Talja, 1999). Given the multiplicity of meanings that can be associated with any object and the context-dependence of those associations, discourse analysts interested in the generation, circulation, and transformation of knowledge are best served by being attentive to the basic assumptions that link concepts, circumscribe meaning, and create the conditions for emergent interpretations of social phenomena.

Between January and June of 2009, I interviewed 24 high school seniors, evenly split between males and females, who all self-identified as Black and/or African American. All of the students attended the same public charter academy and had been in attendance between three and four years. Admission was based on a statewide, first-come, first-served lottery, but the overwhelming majority of the student body, and 100% of my sample, lived within the city limits. All of the participants came from neighborhoods where the median household income was at least $4,000 less than the city median, placing them in the bottom two quintiles of all city households (Data Driven Detroit, 2010). I used theoretical sampling procedures (Glaser & Strauss, 2009) to identify interview participants who self-identified as Black, believed that being Black was a primary determinant of how they were perceived in society, and were from lower-income areas of the city.[3]

I developed a semistructured, in-depth interview protocol, with the intention of allowing considerable latitude in the participants' selections of accounts, descriptions, and arguments, while ensuring that a number of preselected topics were addressed in each interview. Further, my construction of this instrument was guided by two key tenets of the grounded theory approach to the collection and analysis of qualitative data: (1) the use of constant comparisons across data and between data and emergent concepts; and (2) the requirement that any theory used to explain relationships in the data are derived from the data itself (Glaser & Strauss, 2009). I adopted a funnel approach in structuring the protocol, such that participants would take the lead in carving out their positions on a given question, enabling relevant probes and elaborations and the orienting of theoretically significant concepts to the enunciated positions. In all of the interviews, an easy conversational tone was achieved, allowing me to unobtrusively probe apparent inconsistencies in participants' responses (Wiersma & Jurs, 2004). This ability to revisit "points of incompatibility" that emerge in the interview context proves essential to the identification of interpretative repertoires (Foucault, 1982, p. 66).

In the method introduced by Talja, three phases of interview text analysis are described (Talja, 1999). It begins with the careful examination of the interview text of one participant, in which the analyst looks for and records seemingly contradictory or inconsistent responses. In cases where interviewees do not attempt to resolve an inconsistency (whether brought to their attention or if they notice it themselves), this is taken as an indication that distinct interpretative repertoires are likely at play. That is, multiple, mutually contradictory repertoires can be operative in the construction of an object by an individual. This is possible because of the nature of discourses as systems of dispersions—as groupings of disparate and competing assumptions that can be used to develop versions of a given object (Foucault, 1982). Individuals are able to construct multiple versions of racism, of the Black community, or of economic stratification. Moreover, each version can be built upon mutually contradictory assumptions, depending upon the angle from which the object is being approached. Being attentive to internal inconsistencies and contradictory accounts across the sample is helpful for illuminating the building blocks of these various versions.

Next, the analyst identifies regularly occurring patterns across all of the accounts offered by the participants. Such regularities might include use of common terms, concepts, themes, or arguments, for example. These regularities point toward interpretive repertoires, but are not the repertoires themselves. Again, this is due to the nature of discourses as systems of dispersion. Within a field, and within language overall, there are only so many intelligible terms, relevant objects, and culturally recognizable concepts. In practice, the same term or concept or description of an object can be used to argue drastically different points, or their usage can be based upon widely divergent assumptions. Identifying the repertoires requires an additional step.

In this last step, an attempt is made to name the starting point from which an utterance or group of similar utterances may have been articulated. That is, the analyst asks these questions: What is a necessary condition for the validity of this utterance, description, argument, and so on? What limitation of perspective would yield these responses? The strength of the evidence for an identified interpretative repertoire lies in the data itself. The links between a response and its basic assumptions are made visible by considering the entire corpus of interview texts, rather than looking for or imposing a one-to-one correspondence between a response and a potential repertoire. Because repertoires are cultural regularities, publicly available forms of knowledge, their operation should be apparent across a number of responses and texts. Ultimately, by way of a grounded exploratory analysis of interview talk, I aim to provide an account of the interpretative repertoires that furnish the boundaries and possibilities of racial-political thought among one group of Black youth enmeshed in urban poverty.

## What We Need in Life: Money, Power, Respect Revisited

Across all three areas of racial knowledge that emerged as significant during the course of the interviews—economic stratification, the Black community, and racism—the participants' accounts, descriptions, and arguments displayed a stunning amount of ideological complexity.[4] This complexity was characteristic not just of the repertoires apparent within these areas of racial knowledge, but also in terms of the interrelations of repertoires across areas, and the combining of dominant and challenging strands of thought. That is, the interview talk evidences a great richness in the overall texture of racial thought among the interview participants. Taken together, a view of class as the central axis of social division in American society tends to exacerbate the existing tensions between collective identity and common oppression-based versions of the Black community (Shelby, 2002), which in turn reinforce views of racism as an individual pathology.

The prominence of the particular type of class-based analysis exhibited by these youth holds significant implications for their assessments of the Black community and their conceptualizations of racism. Though the three areas of racial knowledge appear to be mutually reinforcing, ideas about the labor market seem to drive articulations regarding the Black community and racism. The interviewees make numerous references to the economy/labor market; the transition from secondary education likely increases the relevance of this domain to their interpretations of a variety of social phenomena. Similarly, assessments of the Black community are likely to reinforce notions of racism as a monolithic individual-level phenomenon. Ultimately, any speculative causal relations among these ideas are less pertinent than the fact that, taken together, they provide an effective lens shaping what these youth see on the racial landscape and, therefore, how they are likely to navigate it going forward.

## Economic Stratification Processes

Knowledge concerning economic stratification—who has money, the processes by which one positions oneself to money, and the significance of money to who one is and can become in the United States—circumscribes many of the views expressed by these youth on a number of race-relevant topics. References to economic stratification processes and outcomes were made, even when the question being asked was not directly related to stratification. As soon-to-be high school graduates, their pending entry into the labor market surely increases the significance of this domain in their sensemaking. Also, given the recent economic collapse and what this can and does mean for their future prospects, it is not surprising that the state of the economy figures so prominently in their thinking on a range of subjects. Also, all of the participants were familiar with the media frenzy surrounding urban education and unemployment.[5] To a person, when asked what issue they considered to present the greatest challenge to African Americans, they responded "jobs" or "money."

Similar to prior research, the interviews reveal both support for and criticism of the traditional American achievement ideology. However, the discourse analytic approach reveals that these inconsistencies are not as paradoxical as they appear at first blush, but rather can be linked to interpretative repertoires cobbled together by the interviewees in creative ways. The first interpretative repertoire I label *meeting the standard*. In this repertoire, students acknowledge a firm belief in the validity of the performance standards deemed appropriate in mainstream American society. This stance was often visible in accounts of run-ins with Whites in authority. Eighteen-year-old female Autumn recounted an early experience with discrimination.

Well, I had a teacher in the first grade. Her name was Sister Margaret. She was supposed

> to be a nun, but she treated different students differently. So her White students she treated correctly, she didn't give 'em a hard time. And the Black students, they were like her target to always point out. So you had to always be on your game around her so that you wouldn't be a target for her all the time. And so it was like I learned to keep myself together when I talked to her—to hold my standards up.

To a follow up some time later that day, Autumn explained the nature of her teacher's targeting.

> If we're sitting in the classroom, she'll just do like a random check of homework to make sure and then it was like me and my two friends we would get picked to show our homework. And since I would have mine done, she really couldn't say anything to me. But then when she would start talking to her [the friend], it's "you people don't have y'all stuff done, y'all never do this and y'all always want excuses."

Finally, when clarifying the role of race in this incident, Autumn went on to say, "It was the way she would act like we all messed up if one of us wasn't ready. It wasn't a big deal to me 'cause I kept up. It wasn't that hard. But she just always would focus on us, like she was waiting for someone to slip."

Autumn responds to two aspects of this encounter: the performance goal or standard of achievement used to evaluate students and the differential application of these assessments by her teacher. In this account, the performance goals enforced by Whites in authority—the most frequent representatives of institutional power in the participants' accounts—are not deemed problematic; in some instances, they are even championed. What is problematic is the uneven way in which standards are applied, the overzealous application of the strictest standards to one set of students and not another. One might imagine that if Autumn were asked to rewrite that scenario, either all or none of the students would have been subjected to random homework checks, rather than just a few being singled out or targeted.

Further evidence for the *meeting the standard* repertoire was seen in accounts of run-ins with the law shared by several of the participants. Eighteen-year-old Cita described a time when a car she was riding in was pulled over. Though she seemed sure the stop was racially motivated (they were told they were stopped for speeding, while she was sure they were not), she expressed a sympathetic understanding of the police officer's rationale. My analysis suggests that her account, while not directly concerning knowledge of the economic mobility processes, reflects a logic similar to Autumn's, whereby actions of whites in authority are rationalized in terms of understood and unquestioned institutional imperatives. That these imperatives may excuse an abuse of power on the part of the power-holders does not appear to raise concerns with the students about the functioning of the institution itself. Cita's story went as follows:

> So we had went to the gas station to turn to go back and see if that was my cousin. So we was going slow, real slow. And the cop turned on the lights. I had been sitting back so he couldn't see me. It looked like he [the driver] was in there by himself. And that's what they do when a guy is alone in a nice car around there, you know. But as soon as I put my chair up, he seen me and he was like, "Oh, OK. Well y'all be careful," or whatever. Because a lot cars be getting stolen around there. So they do that just to the boys. It's messed up, but, you know, that's they job.

Another account addresses the same issue from another angle. In this passage we were talking about education and race. Here, 17-year-old Ronald discusses a friend who didn't get into the college of his choice after graduating high school the previous year, and as a result had to take remedial classes at a college that was a "backup" selection:

> They talking about "it's the man" [that made his friend not get into his school of choice]. I know that richer schools do better at getting they students into colleges, like ready. But there has to be some way to see who is, who should be doing what at what level. If you don't pull those grades, then....

The students' picture of the stratification system and its sorting processes was further complicated by the operation of another predominant repertoire present in the accounts of all interviewees. The repertoire of *Whites' investment in Black degradation* seemed to reinforce the validity of mainstream values and means, while attributing problematic racial relations within those institutions to a few Whites who either coveted the best positions or who, for unspecifiable reasons, maintained an innate desire to discredit and devalue Blacks. In the following passage, Autumn provides an account of an event that has impressed upon her the kind of discriminatory practices that held Blacks back in the past, and gave her ideas about ways in which she might be subjected to discrimination today.

In addition to centering discrimination as a workplace phenomenon, her story features a disgruntled White employee coping with the earned economic success and power of a Black colleague.

> My grandfather worked at Chrysler for 30 years. He was the only Black accountant in his department and he had to work for what he got. He got discriminated. He got to a point where his boss, a new representative, came in, and he didn't like him because he was Black. He knew he was qualified, but he couldn't take being on the same, equal footing to my grandfather. And he got to the point where well I'm gonna have to, you know, it's either him or me. I have a family to support. So he [the grandfather] had to make him provoke him. The guy put his hands on him and he [the White rep] got fired.

While it cannot at all be said that Black youth had unqualified support for mainstream American institutions, repertoires that suggested support appear to play a significant role in terms of the objects participants selected to speak on and the sheer number of responses that can be linked back to the *meeting the standard* and the *Whites' investment in Black degradation* repertoires. In concert, and taking into consideration the totality of the texts, it becomes clear that the participants are less concerned with critiquing the goals of our institutions than they are with questioning how their positions within them are assigned.

Two final interpretative repertoires round out the various discourses that delimit the parameters of the participants' talk on U.S. stratification and its processes. *Inclusion as the goal of struggle* was present in accounts across the sample. This repertoire not only helps us make sense of contemporary youths' connection to the legacy of racial justice, but also clarifies their overwhelming orientation to and acceptance into today's institutions. This sample of youth gravitates toward a loose version of multiculturalism, whereby they strive for incorporation into the mainstream institutional positions that confer success, but they want this incorporation carried out on their own terms. For participant after participant, this rang true as the endpoint of the Black struggle, as a form of progress that has, in the main, been achieved. Consider these words spoken by Devon, a 17-year-old male, commenting on the term "Uncle Tom," which he used to describe his uncle, who insists that "race does not matter":

> There is no other way to put it. He wants to be White. Everything he does has to be in a White fashion. He didn't want his daughter dating a Black guy or anything like that. He says, "Well race shouldn't matter. I'm a lawyer," and I did this and I did that. But I don't—when we look at him, he struggled all the way through school to get where he got. And he was thinking like well since I got into the circle, I'm fine. It was like at any moment plenty of lawyers have tried to get him kicked out of his job, tried to make him lose his job, but because he's so good at what he does, they can't get rid of him. But the same people that he's

trying to defend all the time and trying to lift up are the same people who are always trying to take his place.

In the context of a discussion about family members' experiences of discrimination, this excerpt does more than express disappointment with his uncle's behaviors and views. Earlier in the interview, Devon shared his pride in his uncle's accomplishments—a pride that is diminished by his uncle's subsequent distancing from his own cultural roots. While Devon is proud and considers following in his uncle's footsteps, he is dismayed at the types of sacrifice that so often seem part of the process of inclusion. His pride at his uncle's achievements is tempered by an awareness that our institutions are rife with Whites that play dirty—who do not wish to see Blacks advance up the socioeconomic ladder. While he is critical of such Whites, this criticism does not carry over into a more sweeping critique of the racial inequalities created by the normal functioning of American institutions. That is, his foci are individual "bad" actors and the potential compromise of cultural identity that comes along with institutional inclusion. The intersection of Devon's broad and localized knowledge ultimately rationalizes such abuses of power.

In a related passage, Ronald shared a story about advice he had received from his grandfather regarding fighting and its consequences. While this passage is packed with information, from it I glean a similar pattern of resolving that racial victories can be counted by an increase in Blacks' abilities to go where Whites have gone and do what they have done. In itself, this goal is not problematic. What is problematic, I suggest, is that the same limitation in perspective (the *inclusion as the goal of struggle* repertoire) that would support this interpretation of racial victory might also serve to delimit interpretations of historical racial struggle and cast future struggle in an unnecessarily narrow light. That is, the historical struggle for freedom might be reduced to a skirmish for better individual and collective standing in an unjust social system; and the necessity of struggles for social justice might be measured in terms of the numbers of highly paid, highly visible Black elites.

> Well my grandfather, he has a quote. It says, "Experience is the best key, but a fool will learn no other way." And so he'll talk about how, you know, him going to school, being the only Black boy, him and his brothers. Like living on a farm and they were the only Black people within like a forty-mile radius of their town. And them having to go to school and get into a lot of fights because they would be called nigga all the time. And he was at—he got to a point where it's like fighting is not gonna do anything but get me kicked out of school. It will keep happening, the cycle continues. And so when I got into school—my father, he fought a lot when he was in school and it didn't get him anywhere, got him messed up with a lot of his teachers. And when I got in school, it was like even though me being big I didn't fight. It was like no point of it. It was like break the

> cycle almost. Like, when you think about our history, what people had to do so we could be here today. We owe it almost to them to make it. To go places they weren't allowed.

Ronald, having spent some part of his schooling in largely White spaces, as well as having interracial exposure in other venues, had many opportunities to fight when confronted with racial epithets. In each case, he describes weighing the pros and cons and deciding consistently that playing into anything that might further his exclusion would be self-defeating, and an affront to his ancestors.

A final interpretative boundary present across the sample is the notion that class trumps race. This sentiment was often directly expressed and was related to a number of topics (for example, Blacks' social positioning, intragroup relations, White racial attitudes, and so forth). It expresses a general orientation to U.S. stratification that colors knowledge formation across a variety of related issues. Cita had this to say in response to a follow up regarding how the United States is "set up": "Far as the U.S. goes, it's not just about race. It's a big amount of middle-class people, but the U.S. is more so about money. They have their . . . people have their own opinions about racism, but it's like, well, whoever has the most money that's who I'm rolling with." When asked to clarify, she explained that race is often used to "break up" the middle class, but the really significant issues turn on the matter of one's economic position.

In explaining the position of Blacks in society compared to other racial groups, 17-year-old Shayla said bluntly, "We're on the bottom. We always on the bottom because we always working for someone else. We're never the bosses." Keith, 18, responded thus to a similar question, "They got the better schools, more money for good education, the better jobs making good money—so they have the best chances to stay on top." It is worth noting that these commonly made observations coexisted alongside the *meeting the standard* repertoire. That is, despite the sense that performance evaluations are skewed in the favor of non-Blacks, and an awareness that Blacks face conditions beyond their control that can hamper their achievement, they see social-class divisions and skirmishes as being at the heart of the storm.

These excerpts reveal the centrality of the stratification system and its processes, as references to it crosscut the students' discussions of educational inequity, the labor market, class formations, interracial contacts, racial pride, and racial justice. These youth display an array of perspectives on U.S. stratification, invoking multiple versions based on their perceptions of what is most relevant. As we analyze the common roots of these multiple versions, it also becomes apparent that their ability to talk about the intersection of race and stratification processes is severely limited by the interpretative repertoires identified in this chapter. That is, the basic assumptions upon which they fashion articulations of the intersection of race and U.S. stratification routinely ignore or rationalize abuses of power inherent in the dynamics of U.S. stratification. Such abuses are consistently attributed to individual Whites. Below we see how notions of economic stratification similarly drive the interviewees' discussions of Black American individual and collective identity. It is likely that the centrality of class to understandings of Black identity ultimately serves to reinforce class as the central prism through which these youth interpret racial phenomena.

## The Black Community

Time and time again, the interviewees' responses turned on some logic connected to notions of how Blacks as a group are constituted, what characterizes Blacks as individuals, what distinguishes Blacks from other groups, and what relationships amongst Blacks should look like. This arena of discourse features the greatest level of inconsistency. That is, statements ranged from praise to scorn, from presenting Blacks as homogeneous to being irreducibly diverse. Likewise, the interpretative repertoires underlying these statements reveal clearly distinct starting points and basic assumptions, which limit how the subject is approached.

The analysis revealed a strong tension between discourses on authentic Blackness and the vanishing community. The former rests on the notion of real racial differences based primarily in cultural performances and tastes (for example, style of dress, speech, or familial relations), as well as a rather surface recognition of Blacks' unique history of oppression. While all of these youth relied on the *authentic Blackness* repertoire, they also consistently commented on the lack of core values, interests, or identity linking Blacks—reflective of the *vanishing community* repertoire. That is, they longed for the type of unified Black community that they believe existed in some distant past. Most expressed serious reservations about the appropriateness of thinking of contemporary Blacks as in any way constituting a group ethnically, culturally, politically, or otherwise. Still, they upheld that the similarities among Blacks are more important than their differences—that the things that make Blacks Black do more to distinguish Blacks as a group among groups than the individual differences among Blacks do to distinguish Blacks from one another. Yet, at the same time, when asked directly they all balked at the idea that there were certain things one had to know, do, or believe in order to be deemed Black.

At first blush, the fact that contemporary Black youth maintain a sense of collective identity while demonstrating awareness that Blacks often have vast ideological and political differences does not appear problematic. In fact, to some it might signal a level of sophistication in the best case, or simply mirror a familiar social reality at the very least. However, based on my analysis, I suggest that this common and long-standing predicament foretells newly emergent and morphing obstacles to the realization of racial justice. The quest for a sense of individual and collective racial identity lies at the heart of this maelstrom. The deceptively benign expressions that reveal the authentic Blackness and the vanishing community repertoires are articulations of the problematic relationship between Black racial identity and notions of a unified Black community.

In his argument against what he describes as the "strong version" of a "thick" Black identity as a requirement for Black solidarity against racism and racial inequality, Shelby (2002) warns that the insistence on such an identity may do more harm than good.

> Thus, a prescribed black identity could actually reduce black unity, and it might even have the unintended consequence of inviting those who fail to identify with the prevailing conception of blackness to form alternative alliances, to become excessively individualistic, or to be simply complacent. (2002, p. 253)

Further, he suggests that Black solidarity can be achieved through identification based on the common experience of anti-Black racism, the adoption of anti-racist goals and values, the development of loyalty through resisting anti-Black racism, and the growth of trust through mutually beneficial efforts to proactively combat racism and racial inequalities (Shelby, 2002). I interpret the interview participants' descriptions and accounts of the Black community as reflecting a quest for that "strong," "thick conception" of Black identity—an identity that consciously preserves a distinctive cultural or ethnic heritage against the cultural hegemony of the White world. At the same time, these youth alternate between the celebration and condemnation of racialist, essentialist, ethnic, and cultural notions of Blackness. In defense of his argument for common oppression to be adopted as the basis for Black solidarity, Shelby asserts "the basis of blacks' commitment to equality is surely that this is what justice demands, not that such values are embedded in black cultural traditions" (2002, p. 247). My analysis suggests that justice has indeed been reduced to an attribute of a culture that has ceased to exist as a functioning community to most if not all of my interview participants.

My goal is not to suggest that one or the other side of this coin (common oppression versus collective identity as the "best" basis for Black solidarity) is correct, but to provide an empirical assessment of the extent to which these twin motivations are present in the articulated knowledge of these particular Black youths. Not only does this tension persist, but arguably it can be linked to the limiting perspectives on U.S. stratification discussed earlier, as well as to perspectives on racism yet to be discussed. A vast amount of conflicting racial imagery exists as part and parcel of the general stock of racial knowledge. These discursive formations provide the basis for the logical, if not competing, views of the Black community evidenced in the discussion of my interview participants.

Consider this next series of excerpts in which the participants affirm a sense of the unique qualities possessed by individual Blacks or by Blacks as a group; yet in subsequent sections of talk, they explicitly deny or pose strong challenges to the idea that Blacks can be thought of as a group. “Black people, we are the most inventive, creative people on the planet. Like this recession, this ain't really nothing new to us, because we've always had to make do” (Keith). And with regard to Blacks as a group, he continues, “I don't think, I know other, like races and ethnicities have been discriminated against, but nobody, like, we're natural survivors. We were forced here, on boats, and kept on, like, just living. Blacks are—no one else is like that really.” But when asked about what keeps Blacks together, he responded, “Blacks ain't really together. Like, we all, we come together for big things, like Obama, or Rodney King, but we mostly, we go back to our lives after that. We're not like, together like that.”

Autumn shared, “Struggle. Struggle, struggle, struggle. That keeps Blacks as a group. Our history, we all know what happened, and so, no matter where someone comes from, it's like, we're all Black. We know where we're coming from.” She also hit on another common theme regarding the ingenuity of individual Blacks. “My auntie, she always jokes about, but it's true, how Black people, we can all make a dollar out of two cents.” But on the subject of a shared Black identity, she goes on to say, “No, not really. There's a lot, I don't think there's like any one thing or ideas that we all have. There's too many, everyone does their own thing, so there can't be like a set of rules, like ‘you're in or you're out.”

Cita, speaking on Black culture, said,

> It's like everything we do. What we eat, the music we listen to, how we respect our parents. You not fittin to see too many Black kids falling out in the mall. Just those things we do that make us who we are. A lot of White people are not going to be into the same things like we are. Some do, there are some White rappers, and they're OK, but some of them, it's not their thing and it feels like they mocking us sometimes. You don't see us trying to rock out and jumping all around. They wouldn't like that.

Despite her sense of proper cultural boundaries, when asked directly about the kinds of values or beliefs Blacks have about things like freedom and equality, she quickly asserted, “When it comes to things like that, everybody has their own beliefs. Blacks don't agree, don't think about those things in the same way. I wouldn't say that there are any, I don't think we can agree. Like freedom to me, I feel very free. But the next person doesn't have to feel that way.”

There are several other instances where interviewees would affirm the distinctiveness of Blacks as a group, celebrate the strengths of Blacks as individuals, and still firmly suggest that Blacks have few or no common interests or bonds, or a shared identity. When they drew boundaries around Black versus White behaviors, the sketches were often quite murky, spoken half-heartedly or jokingly, and centered primarily on what academics would call the performative aspects of culture. A common theme running across the interviews was a learned disunity among Blacks, not as a feature of class skirmishes alone, but rather as a more deeply held distrust and disloyalty among Blacks in general. Many participants referred to the infamous Willie Lynch letter and associated it both with class cleavages and a general "crabs in a barrel syndrome" that was perceived as a key determinant in perpetuating racial inequalities and racism.[6]

The youth in this sample built versions of "Blackness" that articulated the tensions between (at least) two operative and opposing interpretative repertoires. The *vanishing community* is founded on a faltering knowledge of and commitment to Black historical struggles, combined with a tendency to emphasize the performative aspects of their cultural heritage. Simultaneously, their words reveal the difficulties encountered in constructing a healthy racial identity given their received and accepted critiques of Black failings. The *authentic blackness* repertoire points toward both the strategic necessity of differentiating Blacks from other American racial and ethnic groups, and the inability of these youth to convince themselves of any non-material basis of Black unity.

## Defining Racism

The discussion on racism displayed the most consistency and featured a set of interpretative repertoires that not only profoundly limit how the participants think about and discuss racism, but also set boundaries around the ways in which stratification is constructed, the Black community is imagined, and an end to racism is conceived. The overriding interpretative repertoire that pushed statements regarding racism is the racism as *individual pathology repertoire*.

All of the youth interviewed tended to conflate prejudice or individual discrimination with racism; that is, even when they were clearly speaking about institutionalized racism, their explanations of such phenomena did not rest on a sense of the historical and structural nature of racism, but turned on the (ill) will of a few well-positioned Whites. Below, Autumn discusses evidence that racism still exists.

> They are getting rid of Affirmative Action, the one thing that not just protected African Americans; it protected women also. And it's like people are ignorant because they're thinking well I got beat out by a Black person, which was not the case. And like the situation in Michigan when the lady, she was pushing this thing and she pushing to get rid of minorities. And I'm like, well, your granddaughter won't be able to get a job in a few years because, well, you got rid of Affirmative Action. So it's like it will—Affirmative Action was our protection. And I was like they have—I was reading something about the schools in California. Ever since they got rid of Affirmative Action, it's—the Black admissions

> have went down 35 percent. It's there. Now they can do something about it. Whenever they want to get rid of you. When they want one of their own. They can choose not to accept you. They can choose to fire you anytime.

When I asked her to elaborate upon who "they" were, she replied, "White people that want to keep their—that want to stay on top of Blacks."

Still, most instances of racism did not even allude to this surface-level recognition of institutions working in ways that systematically disadvantaged Blacks. Instead, they relied almost exclusively on accounts of individual Whites either learning to fear Blacks, or who, being aware of alternatives, simply choose to fear Blacks (again as an arbitrary means of justifying the maintenance of privilege or out of some fully irrational and inexplicable psychological need).

After he affirmed that racism still exists in the world, I asked Ronald what signs he saw that made him believe so.

> I see everybody is still segregated, like separated into different groups, in different races. And people are still being judged by who they are or whatever. Like it was certain people who not voting for Obama just cause of his skin color. Like it's still very serious. It's not just as serious, but it's serious. [ME: What's changed?] Just serious like back in the day when we couldn't go to certain restaurants, use certain things, do certain things. But we're still getting judged, so that's just as bad.

Interestingly, the fact of segregation, not the process by which it happens, became the target of Ronald's criticism. As he saw it, and many other participants used the same logic, segregation increases misunderstandings by not giving people of different races a chance to "get to know one another, for real." Despite this glint of optimism for racial reconciliation, when questioned as to the notion of racism going away, he staunchly replied, "No. Because it's always gon' be somebody that don't like somebody. I think it's impossible to get everybody to connect."

Next, Cita defined racism and explained why she believed it can't end. She said, "Racism is a lack of understanding of another race. You choose to be fearful of it without even trying to know it. People don't change overnight. People—it's a decision to be racist. Like it's a decision whether you're going to, you know, go to school or not. It's a decision and people choose to make that decision." When I asked why anyone would choose something like that, Cita responded,

> For some reason I think it's just in they heart, like they just look at us differently. Like I don't think they would expect to work with a Black person, even though in reality they may will. But I think it's just something in they heart that just say bad stuff like about us to think and feel bad stuff about Black people just because of their heritage and like where they come from and how they viewed us as. I mean they didn't view us no more than the dirt that laid on the ground or whatever, and I think it's just something in they heart.

Ronald was less pessimistic in his assessment of racism; although, or perhaps because, he utilized this same repertoire in a slightly altered way.

> I think if everybody just get to know each other or to see where everybody's coming from. Just because where they come from or where they live don't mean—that don't make them no different than you. Like I'm pretty sure if everybody got to meet each other or to mix, they will see a big difference between Blacks and Whites and how they really are.

Given the location of racism in the hearts and minds of Whites, it is not surprising that the main two perspectives that circumscribe articulations of how to solve the problem of racism were the *prove them wrong* and the *getting to know you* repertoires. They both assume that racist and prejudiced attitudes, rational or irrational, are justified by Black under-performance, be it in the academic realm, staying out of criminal mischief, or making poor moral choices in other domains. This final excerpt from Keith expresses this sentiment:

> Well, it started off as racism and it kind of changed into us just like provoking it on ourselves, bringing it on ourselves. 'Cause the education system would not be as bad as it is if parents stepped up and handled their business. If, you know, you made sure your student was in school instead of you having to find out after he gets kicked out. It's not just about racism. It's about you helping yourself also. So if you're hindering yourself because you're letting your son stay out 4:00 in the morning on a school day, there is nothing for him to do 4:00 in the morning on a school day except getting in trouble, you're contributing to the crime. You're contributing to the lack of education.

## Obama, Poor Black Youth, and the Promise of Postracial America

I began this analysis with the goal of revealing the interpretative repertoires or starting points and assumptions upon which Black urban youth in low-income areas articulate their understandings of society-wide racial dynamics. My goal was not to discover the sensemaking processes of individual Black youth, but to gain some insight into the cultural regularities that typify how poor, Black, urban youth construct racial knowledge. I employed a constructionist, discourse-analytic method using interview data gathered from graduating high school seniors hailing from various moderate- to high-poverty neighborhoods in the same economically challenged city. The results revealed a number of predominant, sometimes inconsistent and mutually contradictory bases upon which Black youth fashion their racial knowledge. I also observed how interpretative repertoires in one area of knowledge or discursive field could limit what is knowable (and speakable) in another.

Three areas of racial knowledge emerged as significant for the interview participants. Statements concerning stratification appeared most frequently. While the *meeting the standard* repertoire validated mainstream social expectations, the *White investment in Black degradation* repertoire located Blacks' inferior social standing with the covetousness of a few privileged Whites. The most problematic area of discourse was the Black community. The largely unreconciled tensions between the *authentic Blackness* and the *vanishing community* repertoires—the former emphasizing Black cultural distinctiveness while the latter denies an operative Black collectivity—also appear to be linked to the *racism as individual pathology* and the *prove ourselves* or *getting to know you* repertoires underlying the conversation on racism. These latter two repertoires emphasized racism as the manifestation of individual-level racial animosity and located the onus to eliminate racism with Blacks who need to follow the dictates of mainstream America in order to invalidate White fears.

In their 2001 article, Eduardo Bonilla-Silva and David Embrick (p. 48) pose an insightful and timely puzzle: they ask if Blacks "are colorblind too"—that is, if Blacks' discussions of race are articulations of colorblind frames. By and large, their answer is no. And while I agree that the interpretative repertoires and ideological functions of colorblind frames likely differ between Blacks and Whites, we would be remiss to ignore the ways in which the racial knowledge apparent in this analysis may be inextricably tied to the dominant American racial ideological lens. These youth may not be driven by a need to express the racial in nonracial terms, but the larger discursive arena in which Blacks do discuss race may impose limitations on how racial knowledge is constructed, in such a way that the functions of colorblind racial ideology—the naturalization and minimization of racism—are still accomplished.

Given the state of postracial discourse in the United States, it is not surprising that Obama, at least for the sample of urban Black youth who participated in this study, is not being read as an entity that is the result of any fundamental change to the status quo. That is, he is not being read as the end of racism (as they understand racism), or as the death of structural racism (though these interviewees show little understanding of the concept). Obama may reflect change given the sheer magnitude of his post, but the change he represents is fleeting, easily camouflaged in a new normal racial status quo.

Ideas about Obama's possibilities are circumscribed by the ways in which Black youth construct racism, its causes, and its remedies. Two discourses prevailed in relation to Obama: *he's the country's president* and *he's proof that Whites are wrong.* While the former supports awareness that we should have no expectations that Obama can or should "fix" Black America (despite the tendency to view Obama as "our guy"), the latter is mired in a truncated view of how racial inequalities are perpetuated. Together, both repertoires reinforce an avoidance of structural issues. That is, because of the overwhelming sense of pride in his accomplishment as an example of overcoming the racial odds, Obama's election is read primarily as proof that Black Americans are continuing to open doors that had been closed to them for so long. However, the doors that Obama has thrown open do not reveal institutional processes, but personal prejudices and anti-Black sentiments held by both Whites and Blacks. Both passages that follow were responses to a general inquiry regarding their feelings about the election of Barack Obama.

> And that was one thing that people say that Barack being elected was so, so, so spectacular and memorable, but I think that was the most memorable part about it, even though, that stereotype is still gonna exist, but now it gives . . . I think the thing was that, that was a, a stereotype, and Caucasian people and African Americans both believed that African Americans were always going to be under Caucasians. So I think with the election, that it just gave African Americans a little bit more boost of confidence to say, "OK, maybe we're not gonna always be under them." Maybe, now we see we do have a chance to do great things even though that's the way we've been looked at for so many hundred years. Now we're starting to come up, and things are starting to change. I think like, since him being elected, I think that after he's out of office, which will be in eight years 'cause he's gonna win again, I believe that more Blacks, are gonna like, run for president with him, since it's like, yea, we can have a Black president, the next person up will try to run and win also. So I believe by him doing that, he opened up a lot of things for Blacks to do, as far as like running for president. He's gotta get the economy right, since it's not just, it's like the whole country that's broke. But he'll show—he can make it better for all of us.

These excerpts, taken from Keith and Cita, respectively, are revealing not just for what they say about Obama, but also as examples of how multiple and conflicting assumptions about the nature of race in America can converge to limit the ideas and commentaries of these youth. Contemporary youth have their feet in two worlds—in two stories. On the one hand, they are stepping out of what many refer to as the victimization narrative, but their attempts to do so are hindered by a lack of critical engagement with America's ongoing racial struggles. On the other hand, they are stepping into a crude multiculturalist narrative, where there exists the potential for authentic crosscultural respect and collaboration, but this story has to contend with notions of Black authenticity and White malevolence. Another layer of complexity lies in the construction of racial identities that pull from a number of inconsistent culturally embedded ideals. The words of these interviewees reveal a new racial status quo, where mainstream goals are valued, but compete with perceptions that whites who evaluate progress towards those goals are often invested in Black failure; where surface essentialist notions of race mingle and compete with feelings that there is no extant Black community to speak of; where racism is primarily in the heads and hearts of whites, yet Blacks can and should alleviate racism through their own individual striving toward normative forms of success. Most striking, caught in this mid-step, there seems to be little sense of a new direction or goal for America that recognizes the victories of civil rights–era battles, but doesn't assume that the war has been won.

## Conclusion: Where Are We? Between "Parents (and Sundry Other Old Folks) Just Don't Understand" and "These Kids Just Don't Care"

Three years after the passage of the landmark Civil Rights Act of 1964, Martin Luther King, Jr., spoke these words as part of his famous "Beyond Vietnam: A Time to Break the Silence" speech, delivered at Riverside Church in New York City:

> I am convinced that if we are to get on the right side of the world revolution, we as a nation must undergo a radical revolution of values. We must rapidly begin the shift from a thing-oriented society to a person-oriented society. When machines and computers, profit motives and property rights, are considered more important than people, the giant triplets of racism, extreme materialism, and militarism are incapable of being conquered. (1967, para. 48)

King's hopes face their most steadfast opposition in the edifice of colorblind racial ideology. The continued "thingification" of American society can find no more comfortable a home than in the unwitting consciousness of abstract liberalism, with its focus on establishing equality of opportunity as an already-achieved aim of the civil rights era, the biologization of culture present in thoughts that encourage the view of Blacks as culturally deficient, the naturalization of racial issues that denies the constructed and politically plastic nature of race, and the minimization of racism inherent in its association with individual pathology. My analysis suggests that Black youths' views can be interpreted as being suffused with such ideological constraints, despite the obvious differences in the paths by which these dominant frames pervade the racial knowledge formed by Black, as compared to White, youth.

The seeds of King's hope exist in the minds of our youth, but they fight for light alongside the notion that racial struggle is a reality of the distant past and all that remains is for us, as Black individuals, to commit to personal mobility. To ensure that facile and individualist notions of race and culture do not smother our youth's imaginings of a just and equal society, activists, advocates, and academics must all engage in an intergenerational dialogue. We might begin with an open and honest discussion bent on revealing the different assumptions that we all have, with an eye toward understanding them all. Members of older generations need to appreciate how tensions related to participation in economic stratification processes, confusion over the significance and meaning of Black collective identity, ambivalence regarding the role of Whites in maintaining racism, and an overriding concern with individual White attitudes impinge on the imaginary of contemporary youth; youth need to appreciate that many of their issues are extensions and continuations of problems hundreds of years in the making. And still, the simple logic of "stuff is bad because there was slavery" will not be enough to wed ongoing experiences to a world-historical struggle for human development. My hope is that greater attention to those spaces where knowledge intersects to propel our stories might move us down that path.

## Notes

1. The findings in this chapter are based on an analysis of the interview texts of six students (three males and three females) who were all categorized as "mobile urban poor" based on family mobility (whether their families' economic stability had slid, increased, or stayed steady over their lifetimes), guardians' occupational status, subjective neighborhood safety, subjective neighborhood quality of life, and future prospects (self-reported class rank and post–high school plans). Even within this group of students marked as unique by being part of so large a graduating class, there was considerable variation in their experiences of urban poverty and their prospects for individual mobility following high school. All interviewee names are pseudonyms.
2. By "dominant" repertoires, I am referring to the work on colorblind racism, most notably as pioneered by Eduardo Bonilla-Silva. I consider his delineation of the colorblind interpretive repertoire (constituted by four central frames: abstract liberalism, biologization of culture, naturalization of racial matters, and minimization of racism) that underlies how Whites speak about race to be the standard statement regarding the pervasive racial ideology in the United States (Bonilla-Silva, 2001). Conversely, "alternate" or "challenging" repertoires can range from reflecting a relatively minor challenge to an outright oppositional stance toward the assumptions of colorblind frames.
3. The parameters of the sampling effort were limited to self-identification as Black and/or African and living in a neighborhood where the median income was in the lowest two quintiles of all households. Age, of course, was already built into the sampling method. Notable is the 100% graduation rate of the students in the sample. This is unique in a city that has been estimated to have a 58% graduation rate (State of Michigan, 2007). It may be argued, therefore, that the interpretative repertoires present may be unique to students with some sense of upward mobility, or at least the concrete experience of mobility. This critique does not negate the fact that this analysis can still account for a number of relevant discourses and reveal the inconsistencies between publicly available knowledge and the reworked local knowledge evidenced through the articulations of these youth. Findings of multiple and inconsistent repertoires among this group would suggest that similar variations are likely to exist in populations with more typical schooling experiences. Steps were taken to ensure the demographic comparability of these young people with high school–aged youth in the city.
4. The interview protocol included many items that could be grouped into similar categories (for example, personal experiences with discrimination, race socialization messages, media presentations of race, and so on). The categories here represent global topics to which participants tended to return, no matter what question was asked. With the exception of "economic stratification," which is my own shorthand, the selected labels were taken from the interview text. These categories, I argue, represent the grounded knowledge of the participants (Glaser & Strauss, 2009).
5. During the data collection period, the state in which this data was collected ranked number one in unemployment; the city had a 14.8% rate of unemployment, among the highest for metropolitan areas of its size (U.S. Census Bureau, 2010).
6. The controversial Willie Lynch Letter, purportedly a manual written in 1712 describing how to control the enslaved population by fomenting distrust and disloyalty through creating so-

cial divisions between Blacks (based variously on differential labor activities, proximity to the master's dwelling and family, and skin complexion, among other factors), has emerged as a staple piece of historical knowledge among contemporary youth, most if not all of whom are unaware of its potential fraudulent origins. Still, they are proud to wield this piece of history as evidence of a more sophisticated take on the current ills facing the Black community. It is most often referenced as an explanation for the lack of unity they believe to characterize the Black community today.

## References

Bonilla-Silva, Eduardo. (2001). *White supremacy and racism in the post–civil rights era.* Boulder, CO: Lynne Rienner.

Bonilla-Silva, Eduardo, & Embrick, David. (2001). Are blacks color blind too? An interview-based analysis of black Detroiters' racial views. *Race & Society*, 4(1), pp. 47–67.

Data Driven Detroit. (2010). Median household income, by census block group, 2008. Detroit, MI: Data Driven Detroit. Retrieved June 15, 2010 from http://datadrivendetroit.org/wp-content/uploads/2010/04/MedHHInc08BG.pdf

Foucault, Michel. (1982). *The archaeology of knowledge and the discourse on language.* New York: Pantheon.

King, Martin Luther, Jr. (1967). Beyond Vietnam: An address sponsored by the clergy and laymen concerned about Vietnam. Retrieved June 15, 2010 from http://www.americanrhetoric.com/speeches/mlkatimetobreaksilence.htm

Glaser, Barney, & Strauss, Anselm. (2009). *The discovery of grounded theory: Strategies for qualitative research.* Rutgers, NJ: Adline Transaction.

Omi, Michael, & Winant, Howard. (1994). *Racial formation in the United States from the 1960s to the 1990s* (2nd ed.). New York: Routledge.

Shelby, Tommie. (2002). Foundations of black solidarity: Collective identity or common oppression? *Ethics*, 112(2), pp. 231–66.

State of Michigan. (2007). 2007 cohort 4-year graduation and dropout rate report. Retrieved June 15, 2010 from http://www.michigan.gov/documents/cepi/2007_MI_Grad-Drop_Rate_246517_7.pdf

Talja, Sanna. (1999). Analyzing qualitative interview data: The discourse analytic method. *Library & Information Science Research*, 21(4), pp. 459–77.

U.S. Census Bureau. (2010). Table 1: Civilian labor force and unemployment by state and metropolitan area, 2010. Retrieved June 20, 2010 from http://www.bls.gov/news.release/metro.t01.htm

Wiersma, William, & Jurs, Stephen. (2004). *Research methods in education: An introduction* (8th ed.). Boston: Allyn & Bacon.

PART TWO

# The Pedagogy of Urban Education

# Free and Still Rising

In the kingdom of Freedom
There are twelve steps to recovery
And I'm always four steps away
From self discovery
An inner self that eludes me
A me that would set me free
Like the Colorado before Hoover
Free range chicken free… free
Like static electricity

In the kingdom of Freedom
I am George Jackson free
Eldridge Cleaver free,
Angela Davis free
Asada Shakur free
As long as I don't say a whit
About the Panther Party
Or jeopardize Homeland Security

Free,
Still rising
From the soporific stupor
Of mental slavery
Still rising
From the miasmic morass
Of social inequity

In the land of dreams
I am fifty acre lawn free
Gotta have a hummer free
Inner city drug free, thug free
Platinum grill free
Abandon my three baby momma free
Slave to my wick free
Respected pedophile free
(Forgive me father you have sinned)

In the land of Technicolor dreams
I am living on radioactive reservations free
Sweat-shop free economy Haitian-Laotian refugee
Migrant worker bent back tied to a basket
I will never eat from free (Oh the things NAFTA has done for me)
Oil robber barons who will never do time, free
Take back Iraq, fifty-first state
In the land of the free

Free
Still rising
Like the bile in my throat
Still rising
Trying hard not to choke
On the illusions of freedom
And equal opportunity

So…
In the kingdom of Freedom
I'm on the fourth step to recovery
And twelve steps away from my
Alternate reality
Where I can be free.

**©H²04**

|| SIX

# Urban Education in the 21st Century

## *An Overview of Selected Issues That Impact African American Student Outcomes*

Chance W. Lewis, Terah Venzant Chambers & Bettie Ray Butler

In the 21st century, K–12 schools in urban settings continue to face a variety of complex issues that have a direct impact on student outcomes (i.e., course grades, standardized test scores, discipline occurrences, high school graduation rates, etc.), particularly for African American students. Many of these complex issues have been clearly documented in the scholarly literature, but others are still yet to be adequately examined. These complex issues, in many cases, impact African American student outcomes even though they are beyond the control of these students. As a result, African American students, when compared to their counterparts in other ethnic groups, are at or near the bottom of every major academic barometer (Lewis, 2009). Even more disturbing is that many researchers and practitioners still do not view this as a crisis but as a normal level of achievement for African American students (Landsman & Lewis, 2006; Lewis, 2009; Lewis & Moore, 2008a, 2008b).

Based on the extant literature, we have come to learn that this level of performance by African American students does not happen solely according to their individual aptitude but according to a tangled web of issues that currently plague our urban schools. Many scholars have noted that issues in urban schools are not the same as issues in suburban and rural communities (Strizek, Pittsonberger, Riordan, Lyter, & Gruber, 2006). However, sometimes overlooked in this argument is that these current and future generations of African American students will not be prepared to be productive members in a society that demands that its citizens have the increasing levels of intellectual capacities and educational training needed to achieve financial prosperity. Given the multidimensional nature of this issue and the lack of appropriate attention in previous research to the implications of this situation, the overall goal of this chapter is to organize a set of core issues at the national, school district/community, and student levels that have an impact on African American student outcomes. We realize that one book chapter is inadequate to address every issue that exists; however, we provide an overview of selected issues that have an impact on African American student achievement in urban schools.

## National Issues

### *Teacher Stability*

In urban schools across the United States, one issue that all education stakeholders agree has an impact on African American achievement is teacher stability in urban schools and its impact on academic outcomes for African American students (Darling-Hammond & Bransford, 2005; Kunjufu, 2002). According to the scholarly literature, we still find an overwhelming percentage of teachers in all schools, particularly urban schools, who are White and female (Landsman & Lewis, 2006). The literature also informs us that larger percentages of teachers of color usually gravitate toward urban schools. As an example, "Black teachers comprise 15 percent of teachers in urban schools, which is twice their share of the entire public teaching force" (Frankenburg, 2009, p. 264). One trend that overwhelmingly impacts African American student outcomes is the instability of the teaching force in these same urban schools.

Teachers, particularly White teachers, in urban schools are more likely to transfer from schools with high percentages of African American and Hispanic students (Freeman, Scafidi, & Sjoquist, 2005; Hanushek, Kain, & Rivkin, 2004; Lankford, Loeb, & Wykoff, 2002; Loeb & Reininger, 2004). Thus, the challenge for urban schools is to keep a stable quality teaching force for all students, particularly African American students, from year to year to improve academic achievement. It is unfortunate that this is a rare occurrence, based on data from the most recent School and Staffing Survey (SASS; National Center for Education Statistics, 2009), which reports that urban schools have the highest percentage of novice teachers (who have been teaching from zero to three years): 18.3%. Given this trend, African American students in our nation's urban schools are exposed to many novice teachers, who, in many situations, are "trying to find their way" in negotiating the classroom (Milner, 2006). As a result of the instability of the teaching force in urban schools, African American student outcomes are, in most cases, compromised because of a very important variable they have no control over—the teacher in the classroom. The long-term ramification is that African American students are then placed at a severe disadvantage for the rest of their lives, because they have missed out on the quality instruction that scholars have documented to be a critical ingredient to the future success of this population (Kunjufu, 2002; Landsman, 2008; Thompson, 2004).

### *Dropout Rates*

Another issue that impacts student outcomes for African American students is the dropout rates of this population. Even though many constituents agree that this issue impacts student outcomes, finding reliable data on the impact for African American students is a major task, because of the lack of consistency of the term "dropout" and the trouble in defining it. The source of this obscurity stems from what many educational researchers and practitioners believe to be intentionally skewed dropout data from state education agencies, school districts, and schools (Fossey, 1996). In consequence, the research community cannot accurately determine if in fact there is decline or growth in the reported number of all students, particularly urban African American students, who exit school prior to completion. Another complexity in examining this issue is the fact that there is not a common definition or consistent reporting mechanism used across all states, districts, and schools. This type of inconsistency makes it difficult to accurately track the number of African American students that could be considered "dropouts" across these same states, districts, and schools.

In an attempt to inform this issue, the federal government utilizes multiple sources of data to determine the national dropout rate (Kaufman, 2004). One source is the Current Population Survey (CPS). This survey collects information on degree attainment and enrollment status for both the current year and prior year to identify dropouts. CPS data is collected by the U.S. Census Bureau and is recognized as the only source of national time series data on dropout rates (Laird, Cataldi, KewalRamani, & Chapman, 2008). Another source is the Common Core of Data (CCD). This national database reports public school dropout rates from 50 state-level education agencies, the District of Columbia, and other outlying areas (Kaufman, 2004).

The information reported by CCD is updated annually by the National Center for Education Statistics (NCES). The most common dropout statistics reported by CPS and CCD is the *annual,* or *event, dropout rate*, which measures the proportion of students who drop out within a single year without obtaining a high school credential (Thurlow, Sinclair, & Johnson, 2002). The Longitudinal Studies Program generally reports a very different dropout rate than those of CPS and CCD. This source reports the *cohort*, or *longitudinal, dropout rate*, which measures what happens to a single group of students (i.e., a cohort) over a specified length of time (Thurlow et al., 2002). Dropout data from these databases, High School and Beyond (HS&B) and the National Education Longitudinal Studies of 1988 (NELS: 88), are obtained by surveying students every year for an extended period of time (Planty, Hussar, Snyder, Kena, KewalRamani, Kemp, Bianco, & Dinkes, 2009). The most frequently used source of data within the most recent years is the U.S. Census Bureau's American Community Survey (ACS). Of all the data sources mentioned, this survey provides the most detailed comparison of *status dropout rates*—the percentage of 16- through 24-year-olds who are not enrolled in school and have not earned a high school credential—by race/ethnicity, nativity, and gender (Planty et al., 2009). The most current estimates by ACS reveal that, in general, African American dropout rates declined between 1980 and 2007 (Planty et al., 2009). Approximately 19% of all 16- through 24-year-old African Americans were reported to have dropped out of school and discontinued attempts to earn a high school diploma or the equivalent in 1980; in 2007, this rate dropped to 8%, contributing to a total decline of nearly 11 percentage points.

If taken at face value, this decrease in dropout rates suggests that today more African Americans are staying in school and earning their high school credential in comparison to two decades ago. Yet, because of the ambiguity in how dropout data is collected, no one can be entirely certain that this decline is as authentic as these statistics would allow one to believe. For this reason, it is necessary to conduct further assessments of this phenomenon for comparative purposes and in an effort to fully understand the magnitude of the national dropout rate.

### *Funding*

The issue of school funding is perhaps the most important one for schools in general, and urban schools in specific due to its direct impact on so many other issues with which schools contend. Although schools receive a significant portion of their funding from federal sources (approximately 10%), the majority of school funds are generated at the state (45%) and local (45%) levels through property taxes, although the proportions vary slightly in each state (Cohen & Johnson, 2004).

*Federal funding*. Because, under the U.S. Constitution, education has historically been the responsibility of the states, the federal government has largely played a supplemental role. The 1965 Elementary and Secondary Education Act (ESEA), reauthorized in 2001 as the No Child Left Behind Act (NCLB), is the federal government's first major contribution to education. Today, the federal government's contributions lie primarily in two programs: (a) Title I, which provides monetary assistance under ESEA to economically disadvantaged students, and (b) the Individuals with Disabilities Education Act (IDEA), which provides assistance to children with disabilities.

*State funding*. The most significant decisions about school operations lie at the state level. Not only do most states provide a large portion of the money for educational expenditures, they also retain the organizational and administrative power—through state departments of education, or similarly titled entities. However, although a significant amount of school funding comes from the state level, there remains a significant amount of variability *between* states with respect to the amount of money provided. For example, the average per-pupil spending across the nation in the 2006–2007 school year was close to $10,000, but New York spent almost $16,000 per student, whereas Idaho and Utah each spent less than $7,000 (U.S. Census Bureau, 2009). This also does not mean that those funds are distributed equally. According to a report by the Education Trust, a respected national education think tank, 26 states provide less money to the poorest school districts than to the richest (as much as $1,000 less per pupil in some states). Further, 28 states also provide more funding to the lowest minority districts than to the higher minority districts (Education Trust, 2006).

*Local funding.* Another significant source of funding for schools comes at the local level, primarily through the collection of property taxes. In accordance, communities with a higher tax base collect more funds and can do so with a lower tax rate. Many urban communities have a lower tax base and are therefore often unable to collect the same amount of money, even if they impose a much higher tax rate (which they often do). As a result, there continue to be disparities in the way funds at the district level are distributed, with high-poverty schools receiving fewer district dollars for teacher salaries and unrestricted funds (Education Trust, 2006).

The issue of school funding affects urban education in that schools in cities consistently get less money by every measure—their teachers are paid less and often live in areas with lower property tax bases, which give them less money to allocate to teaching; the states give urban schools less money than other wealthier districts in the same state; and the federal government does not adequately address or compensate for these disparities. Without urban schools having adequate funds to hire the best teachers, acquire high-quality instructional materials, and maintain good working order, how can we expect the African American children who attend them to fairly compete with students who attend more affluent schools?

### *Resegregation*

In gaining an understanding of the various variables that affect urban education in the 21st century, we see that resegregation is a major issue that has impacted African American student outcomes. This may be due to the fact that school segregation is widely thought to be something that was addressed many years ago and is believed to have very little connection to these current issues. Despite what many may imagine, issues of resegregation are now and have long been a pressing national concern, beginning with the 1954 *Brown v. Board of Education of Topeka* decision and continuing through the recent 2007 *Parents v. Seattle District* case. In large part as a response to diligent efforts by researchers at the UCLA Civil Rights Project (previously conducted at Harvard University), we have detailed comprehensive information about the legacy and implications of racial segregation in our schools today. The rapid resegregation now occurring throughout the United States is important to urban education because of the effect of desegregation on all students, particularly students of color. For these reasons, resegregation should be considered to be a critical issue affecting African American student outcomes, particularly in urban educational settings.

*Resegregation trends in the United States.* The 1954 *Brown* decision ended the era of schools that were legally segregated by race, but it was not until the 1960s that the enforcement power necessary to uphold that ruling was available through the 1964 Civil Rights Act, the 1965 Voting Rights Act, and the 1965 Elementary and Secondary Education Act (ESEA). Armed with the full enforcement power of the federal government, widespread desegregation was achieved throughout the nation, but particularly in the South. In fact, by 1981, there was not one school district in the nation that was more segregated than it was before desegregation orders were implemented (Frankenberg, Lee, & Orfield, 2003). Improvement in desegregation occurred through that decade until three separate Supreme Court decisions in the 1990s (e.g., *Board of Education of Oklahoma City v. Dowell* [1991], *Freeman v. Pitts* [1992], and *Missouri v. Jenkins* [1995]) reversed that progress almost overnight. At the current time, schools are more racially segregated in many areas than they were before the implementation of widespread desegregation reform in the 1960s and 1970s (Orfield, 2001; Frankenberg et al., 2003). The return to segregation continues to occur even as our current national student body is more diverse than any previous time in U.S. history (Orfield, 2001). The most recent Supreme Court case relating to desegregation was the 2007 *Seattle* case, where the Court found even the voluntary efforts that schools in cities like Seattle and Louisville were employing to achieve desegregation were unconstitutional (Orfield & Lee, 2007).

*Positive effects of desegregation.* Many positive benefits can be seen in students who attend integrated school environments. For example, those who attended integrated schools are more comfortable living and working among people with diverse backgrounds and are better prepared to work among diverse communities (Orfield & Lee, 2005). Evidence of the business community's support of employees with diverse school experience can be found in the many amicus curiae briefs filed by prominent corporations in the *Seattle* case supporting the continuation of voluntary desegregation plans. Other positive benefits of de-segregated environments include: (a) enhanced learning, (b) higher educational and occupational aspirations, (c) positive social interaction among members of different racial and ethnic backgrounds, (d) increased racial comfort, (e) increased minority high school graduation rates, (f) narrowed test score gaps, (g) increased college attendance rates, (h) higher rates of employment, and (i) the propensity to live in integrated settings as adults (Frankenberg et al., 2003; Orfield, 2001). In addition, a study of Black law students found that the majority had attended integrated college environments (Orfield, 2001).

*Negative effects of segregation.* Students attending segregated schools are often at a significant disadvantage in their learning, and they may experience positive benefits from desegregated school environments (Orfield & Lee, 2005). African American and Latino students are more likely to attend urban schools that are highly segregated. These schools have much higher numbers of dropouts, are more likely to be classified as "failing" under NCLB, and have a much more difficult time recruiting and retaining highly qualified teachers (Orfield & Lee, 2005). These schools often deal with the double- and triple-level effects according to segregation by race, class, and language, being that many of these schools have high concentrations of poverty and English Language Learners (ELLs).

This continues to be an issue of concern for urban education, because urban schools continue to be the most segregated, with African American students remaining among the most racially segregated group. Although it is not the case that White students themselves improve the learning of African American students (i.e., there is nothing "magical" about White students being in the classroom with African American students), it is often believed that positive educational benefits tend to follow these White students. Therefore, urban schools will continue to suffer the negative effects of resegregation until we decide to change their situation.

## School District/Community Issues

### *Urban Education District Leadership*

According to the Council of Great City Schools (2009), superintendents in urban school districts have one of the most challenging jobs in the United States. Urban superintendents in this era of accountability and standards are "charged with making visible and rapid improvements on the academic achievement of the nation's most vulnerable children" (p. 1). In a review of the 100 largest urban districts in the United States, researchers find that, in many instances, some of the most vulnerable children are urban African American students. Given that district leadership is of critical importance to the academic outcomes of African American students, it is imperative for us to stress that there are major leadership challenges in urban schools, particularly in terms of the tenure of its superintendents.

The Council of Great City Schools notes that the average tenure of superintendents in urban schools was 3.5 years in 2009, which is an increase from 3.1 years in 2006. A closer look at the data reveals that, as of 2009, 18% of urban superintendents had been in office for five or more years, and 33% of urban superintendents had been in office for one year or less, the same percentage as in 2006

(Council of Great City Schools, 2009). As a result of this trend, African American students in urban schools can have on the average four to five superintendents before they complete grades K–12. This type of transition in a key leadership position that is ultimately responsible for the academic achievement of students in urban schools is another great injustice that African American students have no control over but nevertheless has a great impact on their lives.

The unfortunate scenario is that, in this era of high salaries and financial incentives, little has been done to increase the tenure of these superintendents. For example, the average salary for superintendents in the nation's 100 largest urban districts was $228,000, in 2008, plus an average benefit package of $58,000. In 1998, the average superintendent's salary was $191,000, with a benefits package of $42,000 (Council of Great City Schools, 2009). However, what we learn is that the increase in urban superintendent salary has had little corresponding influence on tenure in urban school districts. This is unfortunate for African American students. Because with the instability of the superintendency in urban schools, African American students do not have stable leadership in these positions, which ultimately impacts their academic outcomes. This is another issue that the African American student has no control over but has a major impact on her future.

### *Discipline Disproportionality*

Over the past three decades, there has been a burgeoning interest in *discipline disproportionality*—the type of interest that has consequently stimulated a plethora of studies that attempt to understand why the phenomenon exists, whom it most likely impacts, and what kind of consequences it has on academic performance for students in urban settings (Butler, Joubert, & Lewis, 2010; Fenning & Rose, 2007; Ferguson, 2000; Gonzalez, & Szecsy, 2004; Monroe, 2005; Raffaele Mendez & Knoff, 2003; Skiba, Michael, Nardo, & Peterson, 2002; Skiba & Rausch, 2006). Discipline disproportionality, as it is understood in the context of classroom management, is a concept that is used to reference the overrepresentation of a group of pupils for in-school behavioral referrals. Research has often identified students of color (Bennett & Harris, 1982; Children's Defense Fund, 1975), low socioeconomic status (SES) populations (Bowditch, 1993), and the learning disabled (Balfanz, Spirikakis, Neild, & Legters, 2003; Morrison & D'Incau, 1997) as those most susceptible to disciplinary consequences. The racial disproportionality found in school discipline practices, however, has received the most extensive coverage within both the administrative (i.e., among practitioners) and academic (i.e., among scholars) sectors.

With heightened attention to the disproportional representation of students of color—namely inner-city African American males—for disciplinary action, some have argued that school-based discipline policies (e.g., zero tolerance) can be racially discriminatory (Lawson, 2003). Allegations, such as these, have led to a widespread investigation by researchers of cross-racial differences of the treatment of the male subjects that exclusionary discipline sanctions are imposed on (e.g., regarding suspensions and expulsions). In their study of out-of-school suspensions in a large, ethnically diverse school district in Florida (the 12th largest district in the nation and second largest district in Florida), Raffaele Mendez and Knoff (2003) find that African Americans accounted for 17% of the student population, yet they constituted approximately 33% of all suspensions (see also Education Trust, 1998). Gregory and Weinstein (2008) observe similar dynamics in the district they assessed; their study reveals that although African American students constituted only 30% of the total student enrollment, they made up 58% of student referrals for defiance-related infractions. In contrast, their Anglo peers made up roughly 37% of the total student enrollment, and yet they comprised just 5% of the total number of student referrals for defiance-related infractions (Gregory & Weinstein, 2008). In alignment with the previous research, Wallace, Goodkind, Wallace, and Bachman (2008) conclude in their longitudinal analysis (1991–2005) of school discipline trends among high school students in the United States that African Americans males represented a staggering 330% of the total number of suspensions and expulsions over the duration of the specified 14 years, which is roughly 3.3 times higher than the rate at which their same-gendered Anglo peers were suspended and expelled over the same span of time. As evidenced by these reports, African Americans, particularly males, undoubtedly had the highest reported suspension rates of any of their counterparts (Skiba et al., 2002).

As a result of these findings, one thing is certain: A conscious effort must be made to reduce the overall percentage of exclusionary sanctions for African American students and additionally to make discipline consequences more equitable. To do this, it is vital that the root—or rather, the source—of discipline disproportionality be uncovered. Albeit, many education theorists have speculated that the overrepresentation of African American males for disciplinary action is the product of these students' failure to behave appropriately and follow rules and instructions; others contend that such disproportionality is possibly the function of cultural and/or social misunderstandings, lack of teacher training, and classroom and/or social climate, or worse, discrimination (Raffaele Mendez & Knoff, 2003). The truth of the matter is that no one is completely sure about why discipline disproportionality exists. However, despite this uncertainty, the need to identify its source is no less important. As a result, educators, particularly those in urban settings, have the potential to not only improve classroom management but student productivity as well. As the logic concerning this improvement stands, if a student is suspended or expelled, he is not in school; hence, every day the student is not in school, he is not learning. If one can effectively reduce the percent of exclusionary sanctions imposed, it is likely that she will positively impact academic performance by simply increasing the opportunity to learn. Urban educators should not forget that these opportunities are afforded to those who have access to education; without access to an academic learning environment, the opportunity to learn is drastically minimized.

### *Disparities in Special and Gifted Education*

In considering the many influences on the school outcomes of African American students, one school-level factor that cannot be neglected is the implications of disproportionate special education and gifted education placements. African American students are vastly overrepresented in the special education spectrum of our education system and underrepresented in gifted classes (Losen & Orfield, 2002). Considering the long-term implications of such placements on the academic outcomes of African American students, these disparities must remain a part of any exploration into issues concerning urban education.

*Special education.* The obvious overrepresentation of African American students in special education and the disparities between populations have been extensively documented (see Bellanca & Swartz, 1993; Losen & Orfield, 2002; Wheelock, 1992, 1994). Indeed, students of color are overrepresented in almost every special education category in which records are kept (Losen & Orfield, 2002). However, statistics regarding special education placement are not consistent across the nation, states, or, indeed, even across school districts. They vary in interesting ways and in patterns that suggest that an unfair, biased intervention is at play. For example, African American children living in Connecticut, Mississippi, North Carolina, Nebraska, and South Carolina were found to have a four times higher chance of being labeled as mentally retarded as African American students in other states (Parrish, 2002). It is clear that students in these states are not so different from those in neighboring states as to account for such significant differences. It has been suggested that the way special education is funded in these states may incentivize them to overidentify students in need of special education services. However, although the disparities may seem quite large in some states in particular, this is a widespread and general problem, with African American children being overidentified in some special education categories in at least 45 states (Parrish, 2002). The disproportionate identification occurs specifically in high-incidence categories, such as mental retardation, emotional and behavioral disorders, and learning disabilities, which are more subjective in diagnosis. However, in low-incidence categories, such as severe or multiple disabilities, deafness, and blindness, which are more often diagnosed by medical personnel and have clearer eligibility criteria, the racial disparity all but disappears (Blanchett, 2006).

*Gifted education.* The numbers for the participation of different populations in gifted and talented (G/T) programs are not as readily available as they are for special education. This results, in large part, from the fact that schools are not required to keep track of statistics regarding the demographics of their G/T populations to the same extent that they are for special education. In accordance, educators do not have as clear a picture of the issue of underrepresentation of African American students in G/T programs. Much work in this area has focused on the lack of recruitment of students to these programs. It has also been found that there is a significant challenge in retaining these students once they are in these programs (Bonner, Lewis, Bowman-Perrott, Hill-Jackson, & James, 2009; Moore, Ford, & Milner, 2005). Other research has suggested additional variables that may impact the number of students of color in gifted education include a lack of other students of color (the problem of being the "only one"), a lack of teacher support, and a lack of culturally appropriate teaching materials and strategies, among others (Blanchett, 2006; Ford, 1996; Moore et al., 2005).

### *Social Capital*

*Social capital* is a concept that is very distinctive from all other *capital*-isms. It is not to be confused with *cultural capital* (with reference to forms of knowledge), *physical capital* (with reference to physical objects), or *human capital* (with reference to properties of individuals). Coleman (1988) suggests that social capital is defined by its function (e.g., the ability to make connections among individuals) and is best understood by how well certain outcomes can be achieved (e.g., academic achievement) that would otherwise not be possible in its absence (Dika & Singh, 2002). Social capital, here, is represented by the amount, or density, of positive interaction found between the student and her environment (i.e., family, friends, community, school, etc.; Teachman, Paasch, & Carver, 1996).

The concept of social capital, in itself, has evoked much discussion and has found a place in conversations—among urban educators—about the influence of social networks on student performance, particularly in the case of African American students (Bourdieu, 1985, Coleman, 1988; Putnam, 2000). Social scientists have long suggested that this type of connectedness—a combination of social relationships and social involvement found between the student and his environment—has the potential to translate into higher academic achievement. This maxim, although easy to argue, is rather difficult to analyze since the concept is still being developed and measured; hence, the wide speculation concerning the value of social capital.

The inability of researchers to agree upon a measurable indicator of social capital ultimately makes it that much harder to prove that the lack thereof—or the deficit of social capital—is problematic. Herein lies the real issue: As Putnam (2000) puts it, bad things—with respect to a student's opportunities and choices, behavior, and/or development—tend to happen to kids who live and learn in areas where there is a deficit of social capital. These areas are typically situated in large, diverse, impoverished communities (Orr, 1999; Monconduit, 2007).

Notwithstanding the skepticism surrounding social capital, many theorists seemingly remain optimistic about its potential benefits for African American students (Noguera, 2001; Orr, 1999; Putnam, 2000). Increasing concerns regarding the quality of education forces educators—and those alike—to look for answers to why these problematic situations occur; and it is in the evaluation of the statistical findings of the effects of social capital that many seek refuge. In essence, these proponents flesh out the positive implications of social capital from research studies in an attempt to support their claim that there is indeed value in encouraging students to build social networks.

Using the Social Capital Index (SCI), Putnam (2000) finds that social capital is the single-most important explanatory factor in students' scores on standardized tests and the rate at which they remain in school. This finding suggests that communities with increased levels of social capital, irrespective of their affluence, generally have higher SAT scores and lower dropout rates (Putnam, 2000; Orr, 1999). A similar finding, by Perna and Titus (2005), shows that social capital is positively related to higher education enrollment. This is of particular importance for students of color, who attend college at rates significantly lower than those of their Anglo peers—as evidenced by recent reports from the U.S. Department of Education (American Council on Education, 2007).

Arguments about the potential power of social capital are not just intuitive; they are empirically sound. The rationale that sociability (i.e., the involvement or participation in groups) fosters or facilitates positive outcomes for students is—as Portes (1998) suggests—"a staple notion" (p. 2). Thus, the lack thereof, or the deficit of social capital, is expected to produce less desirable effects for students (e.g., poor academic performance, an increased probability of attrition, etc.; Coleman, 1988; McGraw, 1992). With this decline in social capital permeating mainly marginalized communities located in economically depressed areas, urban schools tend to offer a critical site for building social capital (Noguera, 2001). Further investigation of the value of social capital in these institutions is warranted.

## Student-Level Issues

### *Test Score Gap*

One of the frequent "buzzwords" in the field of education, specifically in urban education, is the standardized "test score" gap between African American students and their ethnic group counterparts, in specific, White students. Although many researchers in the field of education know that a gap in test scores exists, few, if any, actually take the time to research the extent of the gap and its potential impact. Further, with so much data at the local, school, district, state, and national levels, researchers are finding many of these data sources are skewed for a variety of reasons. As a result, we examine the most reliable database—the National Assessment of Educational Progress (NAEP) from the National Center for Education Statistics at the U.S. Department of Education. The NAEP suggests that it makes "the only nationally representative and continuing assessment of what America's students know and can do in various subject areas . . . NAEP results serve as a common metric for all states and selected urban districts" (2009, p. 1). As a result, we provide a brief snapshot of the test score gap between African American students and their White counterparts—the group to which African American students are so often compared.

### *Mathematics at Grade 4 for African American Students in Urban Settings*

An examination of the documentation in Table 1 of NAEP's data from the Trial Urban District Assessment (TUDA, 2007) for mathematics illustrates that each of a sample of the largest urban school districts under examination (e.g., Atlanta, Boston, Chicago, Los Angeles, and New York City) has over 80% of their African American students that are not considered "proficient" in mathematics at grade four. New York City experienced the "best-of-the-worst" achievement rates among urban educational learners, with exactly 80% of African American fourth graders that scored below the "at proficient" category. Further, none of these urban school districts has 20% of the African American fourth-grade math students rank in the "at proficient" or the "at advanced" categories. This is particularly troubling given that the national average of urban school districts in the United States is 30% of students scoring in the "at proficient" category in grade-four math (TUDA, 2007). In comparison, the national average for White students is 40% in the "at proficient" category and 12% for African American students; this difference of 28 percentage points is so significant that the systemic causes should be considered.

### *Mathematics at Grade 8 for African American Students in Urban Settings*

Likewise, in Table 1, each of the five urban educational settings under examination has at least 49% of their African American students in the "below basic" category.

It is unfortunate that 49% to 72% of the African American students are in the "below basic" category. When examining the total percentage of African American students in the "below basic" and "at basic" categories (which is still below "at proficient"), the following results in these large urban school systems are revealed:

(a) in Atlanta, 92% are below the "at proficient" category; (b) in Boston, 88% are below the "at proficient" category; (c) in Chicago, 94% are below the "at proficient" category; (d) in Los Angeles, 93% are below the "at proficient" category; and (j) in New York City, 91% are below the "at proficient" category. For the sake of comparison, the national average of students in grade eight who reached the "at proficient" status is 23%. Also, the national mathematics average for White students who rated "at proficient" is 30%, in comparison to the dismal 8% proficiency rate for African American students at this grade level. Again, the national mathematics achievement gap for eighth graders in urban classrooms is so markedly divergent from the national average that institutional causes (i.e., racism) should be considered.

**Table 1.** *Percentage of African American Students at Each Achievement Level on NAEP Assessments in Grade 4 and Grade 8 Mathematics in Selected Urban School Districts for 2007*

| | | Grade 4 | | | | Grade 8 | | | |
|---|---|---|---|---|---|---|---|---|---|
| Urban District | Race | Below Basic | At Basic | At Proficient | At Advanced | Below Basic | At Basic | At Proficient | At Advanced |
| Atlanta | Black | 45 | 44 | 10 | — | 62 | 30 | 7 | 1 |
| | White | 1 | 18 | 59 | 22 | * | * | * | * |
| Boston | Black | 29 | 53 | 17 | 1 | 49 | 39 | 12 | 1 |
| | White | 7 | 41 | 43 | 9 | 11 | 31 | 36 | 22 |
| Chicago | Black | 52 | 40 | 8 | — | 56 | 29 | 5 | 1 |
| | White | 16 | 37 | 39 | 8 | 21 | 44 | 28 | 7 |
| Los Angeles | Black | 46 | 41 | 12 | 1 | 72 | 21 | 7 | — |
| | White | 10 | 40 | 41 | 8 | 27 | 33 | 30 | 12 |
| New York City | Black | 28 | 52 | 19 | 1 | 55 | 36 | 9 | 1 |
| | White | 9 | 38 | 45 | 8 | 23 | 37 | 27 | 13 |

*Note.* — = not enough students to equal 1 percent; * = did not meet NAEP sample requirements. Adapted from U.S. Department of Education, Institute of Education Sciences, National Center for Education Statistics, National Assessment of Educational Progress, 2007 Trial Urban District Assessment—Mathematics.

### *Reading at Grade 4 for African American Students in Urban Educational Settings*

In these same five urban educational systems (e.g., Atlanta, Boston, Chicago, Los Angeles, and New York City), the results on the reading assessment for fourth graders that documents NAEP data from TUDA (2005) reveal an equally grim record. Further, in Table 2, 58% of African American fourth graders tested at the "below basic" category in reading (an average among the five urban districts). Even more disturbing, four of the five urban school districts have numbers higher than 50% of their African American students in the "below basic." Overall, reviewing the data in Table 2, 85% to 90% of the African American fourth graders at the five urban school districts scored at the below basic or at basic levels in reading. Once again, it is interesting to note that the national average for U.S. students in the "at proficient" category in grade-four reading is 23% (TUDA, 2005). More specifically, the national reading average for White students is 30% scoring at the "at proficient" standard in this category, whereas only 11% of African American students meet the "at proficient" standard. In a dreaded but expected conclusion, urban African American fourth graders around the country contend with a disparate achievement gap in reading in comparison to their White counterparts.

**Table 2.** *Percentage of African American Students at Each Achievement Level on NAEP Assessments for Grade 4 and Grade 8 Reading in Selected Urban School Districts for 2005*

| | | Grade 4 | | | | Grade 8 | | | |
|---|---|---|---|---|---|---|---|---|---|
| Urban District | Race | Below Basic | At Basic | At Proficient | At Advanced | Below Basic | At Basic | At Proficient | At Advanced |
| Atlanta | Black | 60 | 30 | 9 | 1 | 50 | 41 | 9 | — |
| | White | 5 | 24 | 42 | 29 | * | * | * | * |
| Boston | Black | 52 | 34 | 14 | 1 | 40 | 44 | 16 | — |
| | White | 24 | 34 | 32 | 10 | 20 | 32 | 38 | 10 |
| Chicago | Black | 66 | 24 | 9 | 1 | 50 | 41 | 9 | — |
| | White | 26 | 34 | 28 | 12 | 23 | 39 | 34 | 4 |
| Los Angeles | Black | 63 | 24 | 11 | 2 | 62 | 32 | 6 | — |
| | White | 21 | 42 | 30 | 7 | 19 | 40 | 36 | 5 |
| New York City | Black | 49 | 36 | 13 | 2 | 50 | 39 | 11 | — |
| | White | 23 | 32 | 32 | 2 | 20 | 39 | 36 | 5 |

*Note.* — = not enough students to equal 1 percent; * = did not meet NAEP sample requirements. Adapted from U.S. Department of Education, Institute of Education Sciences, National Center for Education Statistics, National Assessment of Educational Progress, 2005 Trial Urban District Assessment—Reading.

### *Reading at Grade 8*

An examination of reading data at grade eight reveals similar patterns of performance among African American students in these five large urban educational settings. In Table 2, we combine the percentage of African American students in the "below basic" and "at basic" categories to yield the total percentage of grade-eight African American students testing below the "at proficient" status in reading, with the following results for each of these cities: (a) in Atlanta, 91% tested below the "at proficient" status; (b) in, Boston, 84%; (c) in Chicago, 91%; (d) in Los Angeles, 94%; and (e) in New York City, 89%. This is especially troubling given that the national average for U.S. students in the "at proficient" category in grade-eight reading was 26%. More specifically, the national average for White students was 34% in the "at proficient" category in comparison to an 11% at-proficiency rate for African American students.

The national and urban achievement NCES, NAEP, and TUDA data shared for African American fourth and eighth graders in mathematics and reading are deplorable. Only 12% of fourth graders (the national average being 30%) and 8% of eighth graders (the national average being 30%) are at the "at proficient" level in math. It is still alarming that 11% of African American fourth graders (the national average being 23%) and 11% of African American eighth graders (the national average being 26%) are "at proficient" in reading (TUDA, 2005). Given the totality of the data presented, these statistics clearly underscore the importance of this book.

## Conclusion

In this chapter, we have attempted to overview a sampling of selected issues (i.e., teacher stability, dropout rates, funding, resegregation, urban district leadership, discipline disproportionality, disparities in special and gifted education, social capital, and the standardized test score gap) that have direct and indirect impact on African American student outcomes in urban schools. We acknowledge that one chapter cannot fully explain every issue that has potential implications for African American student outcomes. However, to frame the essence of this monumental book, the field of education, particularly urban education, should be aware that student effort is not the sole criterion that has impact on African American students; there are a plethora of issues at a variety of levels that impact the achievement outcomes of African American students. As scholars and practitioners seek solutions for the education of this population, it is imperative that they understand the aforementioned complex web of issues as they seek to answer the most pressing questions for African American students in urban schools.

## References

American Council on Education. (2007). *Gaps persist in college participation rate of students of color and Whites, according to ACE's annual report on minorities in higher education*. Washington, DC: Author.

Bellanca, J., & Swartz, E. (Eds.). (1993). *The challenge of detracking: A collection*. Palatine, IL: IRI/Skylight.

Bennett, C., & Harris, J. J., III. (1982). Suspensions and expulsions of male and black students: A study of the causes of disproportionality. *Urban Education, 16*(4), 399–423.

Blanchett, W. J. (2006). Disproportionate representation of African American students in special education: Acknowledging the role of White privilege and racism. *Educational Researcher, 35*(6), 24–28.

Bonner, F. A., II, Lewis, C. W., Bowman-Perrott, L., Hill-Jackson, V., & James, M. (2009). Definition, identification, identity and culture: A unique alchemy impacting the success of gifted African American males in school. *Journal for the Education of the Gifted, 33*(2), 176–202.

Bourdieu, P. (1985). The forms of capital. In J. G. Richardson (Ed.), *Handbook of theory and research for the sociology of education* (pp. 241–258). New York, NY: Greenwood.

Bowditch, C. (1993). Getting rid of troublemakers: High school disciplinary procedures and the production of dropouts. *Social Problems, 40*(4), 493–509.

Butler, B. R., Joubert, M., & Lewis, C. W. (2010). Who's really disrupting the classroom? An examination of African American male students and their disciplinary roles. *The National Journal of Urban Education & Practice 31*(1), 1–12.

Children's Defense Fund. (1975). *School suspensions: Are they helping children?* Cambridge, MA:Washington Research Project.

Cohen, C., & Johnson, F. (2004). *Revenues and expenditures for public elementary and secondary education: School year 2001–2002* (Report No. NCES 2004-317). National Center for Education Statistics,U.S. Department of Education, Institute of Education Science. Retrieved from National Center for Education Statistics Web site: http://nces.ed.gov/pubs2004/2004341.pdf

Coleman, J. S. (1988). Social capital in the creation of human capital [Supplement]. *American Journal of Sociology, 94*, S95–S120.

Council of Great City Schools. (2009). *Urban school superintendents: Characteristics, tenure and salary sixth survey and report.* Washington, DC: Author.

Darling-Hammond, L., & Bransford, J. (2005). *Preparing teachers for a changing world: What teachers should learn and be able to do.* San Francisco, CA: Jossey-Bass.

Education Trust. (2006). *Funding gaps 2006.* Washington, DC: Author.

Fenning, P., & Rose, J. (2007). Overrepresentation of African American students in exclusionary discipline: The role of school policy. *Urban Education, 42*, 536–559.

Ferguson, A. A. (2000). *Bad boys: Public schools in the making of black masculinity.* Ann Arbor: University of Michigan Press.

Ford, D. Y. (1996). *Reversing underachievement among gifted black students: Promising practices and programs.* New York, NY: Teachers College Press.

Fossey, R. (1996). School dropout rates: Are we sure they are going down? *Phi Delta Kappan, 78*, 140–145.

Frankenburg, E. (2009). The demographic context of urban schools and districts. *Equity & Excellence in Education, 42*(3), 255–271.

Frankenberg, E., Lee, C., & Orfield, G. (2003). *A multiracial society with segregated schools: Are we losing the dream?* Retrieved from http://civilrightsproject.ucla.edu/research/k-12-education/integrationand-diversity/a-multiracial-society-with-segregated-schools-are-we-losingthe-dream

Freeman, C., Scafidi, B., & Sjoquist, D. (2005). Racial segregation in Georgia public schools, 1994–2001: Trends, causes and impact on teacher quality. In J. C. Boger & G. Orfield (Eds.), *School resegregation: Must the South turn back?* (pp. 148–163). Chapel Hill: University of North Carolina Press.

Gonzalez, J. M., & Szecsy, E. M. (2004). *The condition of minority access and participation in Arizona: 2004.* Retrieved from http://epsl.asu.edu/aepi/EPSL-0405-108-AEPI.pdf

Gregory, A., & Weinstein, R. (2008). The discipline gap and African Americans: Defiance or cooperation in the high school classroom. *Journal of School Psychology, 46*(4), 455–475.

Hanushek, E., Kain, J., & Rivkin, S. (2004). Why public schools lose teachers. *Journal of Human Resources, 39*(2), 326–354.

Kaufman, P. (2004). The national dropout data collection system: History and the search for consistency. In G. Orfield (Ed.), *Dropouts in America: Confronting the graduation crisis* (pp. 107–130). Cambridge, MA: Harvard Education Press.

Kunjufu, J. (2002). *Black students: Middle class teachers.* Chicago, IL: African American Images.

Laird, J., Cataldi, E. F., KewalRamani, A., & Chapman, C. (2008). *Dropout and completion rates in the United States: 2006* (Report No. NCES 2008-053). Washington, DC: National Center for Education Statistics. Retrieved from http://nces.ed.gov/pubs2008/2008053.pdf

Landsman, J. (2008). *Growing up White: A veteran teacher reflects on racism.* Lanham, MD: Rowman & Littlefield.

Landsman, J., & Lewis, C. (2006). *White teachers/diverse classrooms: A guide for building inclusive schools,promoting high expectations and eliminating racism.* Sterling, VA: Stylus.

Lankford, H., Loeb, S., & Wykoff, J. (2002). Teacher sorting and the plight of urban schools: A descriptive analysis. *Educational Evaluation and Policy Analysis, 24*(1), 37–62.
Lawson, E. (2003). Re-assessing safety and discipline in our schools: Opportunities for growth, opportunities for change. *Orbit, 33*(3), 23–25.
Lewis, C. W. (2009). *An educator's guide to working with African American students.* West Conshocken, PA: Infinity.
Lewis, C. W., & Moore, J. L., III. (2008a). African American students in K–12 urban educational settings. *Urban Education, 43*(2), 123–126.
Lewis, C. W., & Moore, J. L., III. (2008b). Urban public schools for African American students: Critical issues for educational stakeholders. The Journal of Educational Foundations, *22*(1–2), 3–10.
Loeb, S., & Reininger, M. (2004). *Public policy and teacher labor markets: What we know and why it matters.* East Lansing, MI: The Education Policy Center at Michigan State University.
Losen, D., & Orfield, G. (Eds.). (2002). *Racial inequity in special education.* Cambridge, MA: Harvard University Press.
McGraw, L. (1992). Social capital: A new concept for explaining failure to achieve. *Journal of Educational and Psychological Consultation, 3*(4), 367–373.
Milner, H. R., IV. (2006). But good intentions are not enough: Theoretical and philosophical relevance in teaching students of color. In J. Landsman & C. Lewis (Eds.), *White teachers/diverse classrooms: A guide for building inclusive schools, promoting high expectations and eliminating racism* (pp. 79–90). Sterling, VA: Stylus.
Monconduit, C. A. (2007). *Identifiable variables which measure the impact of social capital within schools*(Doctoral dissertation). Available from ProQuest Digital Dissertations (AAT 3293449).
Monroe, C. (2005). Why are "bad boys" always black? Causes of disproportionality in school discipline and recommendations for change. *Clearing House: A Journal of Educational Strategies, Issues and Ideas, 79*(1), 45–50.
Moore, J. L., III, Ford, D. Y., Milner, H. R. (2005). Recruitment is not enough: Retaining African American students in gifted education. *Gifted Child Quarterly, 49*(1), 51–67.
Morrison, G. M., & D'Incau, B. (1997). The web of zero-tolerance: Characteristics of students who are recommended for expulsion from school. *Education and Treatment of Children, 20,* 316–335.
National Center for Education Statistics. (2009). *School and staffing survey.* Washington, DC: Author.
Noguera, P. A. (2001). Transforming urban schools through investment in the social capital of parents. In S. Saegert, J. P. Thompson, & M. R. Warren (Eds.), *Social capital and poor communities* (pp. 189–212). New York, NY: Russell Sage.
Orfield, G. (2001). *Schools more separate: Consequences of a decade of resegregation.* Retrieved from http://civilrightsproject.ucla.edu/research/k-12-education/integration-and-diversity/schools-moreseparate-consequences-of-a-decade-ofresegregation/?searchterm=resegregation
Orfield, G., & Lee, C. (2005). *Why segregation matters: poverty and educational inequality.* Retrieved from http://www.civilrightsproject.ucla.edu/research/deseg/Why_Segreg_Matters.pdf
Orfield, G., & Lee, C. (2007). *Historic reversals, accelerating resegregation, and the need for new integration strategies.* Retrieved from http://www.civilrightsproject.ucla.edu/research/deseg/reversals_reseg_need.pdf
Orr, M. (1999). *Black social capital: The politics of school reform in Baltimore, 1986–1998.* Lawrence: University of Kansas Press.
Parrish, T. (2002). Racial disparities in the identification, funding and provision of special education. In D. Losen and G. Orfield (Eds.), *Racial inequity in special education* (pp. 15–38). Cambridge, MA: Harvard University Press.
Perna, L. W., & Titus, M. A. (2005). The relationship between parental involvement as social capital and college enrollment: An examination of racial/ethnic group differences. *The Journal of Higher Education, 76*(5), 486–518. doi: 10.1353/jhe.2005.0036

Planty, M., Hussar, W., Snyder, T., Kena, G., KewalRamani, A., Kemp, J., Bianco, K., & Dinkes, R. (2009). *The condition of education: 2009* (Report No. NCES 2009-081). Washington, DC: National Center for Education Statistics.

Portes, A. (1998). Social capital: Its origins and applications in modern sociology. *Annual Review of Sociology, 24*, 1–24.

Putnam, R. (2000). *Bowling alone: The collapse and revival of the American community*. New York, NY: Simon & Schuster.

Raffaele Mendez, L. M., & Knoff, H. M. (2003). Who gets suspended from school and why: A demographic analysis of schools and disciplinary infractions in a large school district. *Education and Treatment of Children, 26*(1), 30–51.

Rubinson, F. (2004). Urban dropouts: Why so many and what can be done. In S. R. Steinberg & J. L. Kincheloe (Ed.), *19 urban questions: Teaching in the city* (pp. 53–67). New York, NY: Peter Lang.

Skiba, R., Michael, R., Nardo, A., & Peterson, R. (2002). The color of discipline: Sources of racial and gender disproportionality in school punishment. *The Urban Review, 34*, 317–342.

Skiba, R., & Rausch, M. K. (2006). Zero tolerance, suspension, and expulsion: Questions of equity and effectiveness. In C. M. Evertson & C. S. Weinstein (Eds.), *Handbook of classroom management: Research, practice, and contemporary issues* (pp. 1063–1092). Mahwah, NJ: Lawrence Erlbaum.

Strizek, G. A., Pittsonberger, J. L., Riordan, K. E., Lyter, D. M., & Gruber, K. (2006). *Characteristics of schools, districts, teachers, principals and school libraries in the United States, 2003–04* (Report No. NCES 2006-313 Revised). Washington, DC: National Center for Education Statistics. Retrieved from http://nces.ed.gov/pubs2006/2006313.pdf

Teachman, J. D., Paasch, K., & Carver, K. (1996). Social capital and dropping out of school early. *Journal of Marriage and Family, 58*(3), 773–783.

Thompson, G. (2004). *Through ebony eyes: What teachers need to know but are afraid to ask about African American students*. San Francisco, CA: John Wiley.

Thurlow, M. L., Sinclair, M. F., & Johnson, D. R. (2002). *Students with disabilities who drop out of school: Implications for policy and practice*. Minneapolis, MN: National Center on Secondary Education and Transition.

United States Census Bureau. Population Finder. Washington, D. C.: US Census Bureau (2009). Available from: http://factfinder.census.gov/servlet/SAFFPopulation?_submenuId=population_0&_sse=on

Wallace, J., Goodkind, S., Wallace, C., & Bachman, J. (2008). Racial, ethnic, and gender differences in school discipline among U.S. high school students: 1991–2005. *Negro Educational Review, 59*(1/2), 47–62.

Wheelock, A. (1992). *Crossing the tracks: How "untracking" can save America's schools*. New York, NY: The News Press. Wheelock, A. (1994). *Alternatives to tracking and ability grouping*. Thousand Oaks, CA: American Association of School Administrators.

# PSSA for ELL

Across the page meanders a river
Of disconnected, disjointed, indecipherable
Words whose literal, figurative or metaphorical
Meanings I cannot, decipher, deduce, detect, or divine

Awash in a fathomless ocean of doubt
I diffidently dare to raise my hand
In dolorous tones the invigilator states
That she cannot explain, expound or elucidate
She is hapless, helpless, bound by the rules that so dictate
In fairness to all, she cannot deviate.

Thus, I sit staring at the endless river of words
Devastated by my diminished linguistic dexterity
I am copiously conscious of the yawning cornucopia
Of my ignorance; and am filled with the growing conviction
That while I am voluble and verbose in two languages
I am all but illiterate in the one they will use to define me.

|| SEVEN

# Through the Fire

## *How Pretext Impacts the Context of African American Educational Experiences*

Floyd D. Beachum & Carlos R. McCray

> We have a powerful potential in our youth, and we must have the courage to change old ideas and practices so that we may direct their power toward good ends. —Mary McLeod Bethune

The above quote is a challenge to all who are concerned about the plight of today's youth. The former portion of the statement affirms the ability of Black youth to take the reins of destiny and chart a course into the future. The latter part of the quote challenges us to reexamine what we have been doing and in many cases change the way we think and act for the betterment of students. Across the U.S., from politicians and public officials to students and parents, people are calling for reform, restructure, and change in schools. In response, the federal government, over the years, began to emphasize higher graduation rates, accountability, more standardized testing, more rigor in academic subjects, and educational excellence (Obiakor & Beachum, 2005). The pressure placed on schools for educational excellence can promote a paradigm or paradigms based on technical efficiency, empiricism, scientific rationalism, and modernism (Dantley, 2002; Giroux, 1997). Thus, it is assumed that the best way to improve schools is by raising test scores on standardized tests (quantitative data), the promotion of *cookie-cutter*, recipe-style, linear models, and an ideology that treats all students and communities as equals, when equity is what is needed.

To complicate matters, the 21st century has witnessed the explosion of technology, entertainment, and popular culture. Gause (2005) asked a series of relevant questions regarding popular culture and education:

> How are schools and educational leaders keeping up with this global transformation? What type of impact does this transformation of schools from sites of democracy to "bedfellows" of consumerism have upon the school and much larger global community? How are the 'souls' of schools affected? (p. 242)

These poignant questions propose significant challenges for today's educators. While trying to survive day-to-day providing students with a quality education, they must also deal with outside pressures from the national, state, and local levels. Concurrently, they must also prepare students for a future that is sure to be marked by technological advancement, the necessity of innovation, increased conceptual capacity, and the need to deal with people of different cultures, creeds, and characters (Nisbett, 2009).

Cultural collision is a clash in beliefs, cultures, or values (see Beachum & McCray, 2008a). For the purposes of our discussion, we emphasize the clash in cultures between youth (primarily youth of color in urban contexts) with the culture of educators and systems of education. A different, yet related, concept is cultural collusion, which can be described as "the negative cultural/societal implications that emerge when complex cultural cues and messages seem to influence individual and group behavior" (Beachum & McCray, 2008a, p. 104). This collusion specifically identifies "highly visible youth cultures, in this case violence, materialism, misogyny, and hip-hop culture" (Beachum & McCray, 2008a, p. 104).

In order to grasp the contemporary impact and outcomes of cultural collision and collusion, one must understand how these concepts originated and evolved. This chapter's organization is informed by the insightful work of French sociologist Loic Wacquant (2002), who proposed "not one but several 'peculiar institutions' have successively operated to define, confine, and control African-Americans in the history of the United States" (p. 42). These peculiar institutions are as follows: (1) Slavery (1619–1865); (2) Jim Crow/Segregation (1865–1965); (3) Ghetto (1915–1968); (4) Hyperghetto and Prison (1968–today). Using this framework, we will discuss historical highlights of the time period (what was happening), Blacks' attitudes toward education and shared cultural values at the time, and contradictions and complexities that caused unification or division, harmony or disagreement, and shifts in how Blacks saw themselves and the world.

## Nobody Knows the Trouble I've Seen: The Scourge of Slavery

### *Historical Context*

Slavery in the United States of America remains a painful part of the nation's history. Its psychological, economic, and educational impacts are still being felt to this day (Akbar, 1984; Kunjufu, 1995). Thompson (2007) described this institution as follows:

> Although the U.S. has been described as a melting pot of various cultures, European capitalistic values and traditions have dominated this mix since its inception, long supplanting the theocratic system imported to North America by the early settlers. The opportunity to make huge profits in the New World led colonial entrepreneurs to use any means necessary to exploit the vast untapped resources of their recently claimed land. This included using force to extract labor from unwilling participants. After a trial-and-error period with Native American and indentured European workers, the 'perfect' labor force for this harrowing task was identified on the African continent. Subsequently large numbers of Africans were brutally uprooted and shipped like cargo to strange lands hundreds of miles across the sea. (p. 50)

This quote encapsulates some of the purposes and processes regarding American slavery. Therefore, this peculiar institution promised huge profits through a massive system of forced labor. The process of obtaining this labor force meant the inhumane capture of human bodies and transporting them from one continent to another. This process would be rife with physical and psychological terror (Beachum, Dentith, & McCray, 2004; Perry, 2003). Blassingame (1979) gives yet another scathing summary:

> The chains of the American Negro's captivity were forged in Africa. Prince and peasant, merchant and agriculturalist, warrior and priest, Africans were drawn into the vortex of the Atlantic slave trade and funneled into the sugar fields, the swampy rice lands, or the cotton and tobacco plantations of the New World. The process of enslavement was almost unbelievably painful and bewildering for the Africans. Completely cut off from their native land, they were frightened by the artifacts of the white man's civilization and terrified by his cruelty until they learned that they were only expected to work for him as they had been accustomed to doing in their native land. Still, some were so remorseful they committed suicide; others refused to learn the customs of whites and held on to the memory of the African cultural determinants of their own status. (pp. 3–4)

It is quite evident and well-documented that slavery was an evolutionary industry that employed physical and psychic terror for the purposes of financial gain and the solidification of racial supremacy. It is also important to note that even in the midst of overwhelming and impossible odds, the Africans rebelled, resisted, sought ways to keep cultural traditions, and most of all reaffirmed their own humanity and forged ahead with the hope of a brighter day.

### *Educational Attitudes*

The enslaved Africans in the U.S. were certainly discouraged from learning (except for maybe the most basic information). "Law and custom made it a crime for enslaved men and women to learn or teach others to read and write" (Perry,

2003, p. 13). Once again, against these laws and customs, enslaved Africans still made attempts to become literate. The tactics used to discourage the slaves were horrific; this was countered by ingenious strategies employed by slaves in order to learn. Perry (2003) wrote:

> There are the stories of slaves who were hanged when they were discovered reading, and of patrollers who went around breaking up Sunday meetings where slaves were being taught to read, beating all of the adults who were present. Slaves cajoled white children into teaching them, trading marbles, and candy for reading lessons. They paid large sums of money to poor white people for reading lessons and were always on the lookout for time with the blue black speller (a school dictionary), or for an occasion to learn from their masters and mistresses without their knowing. (p. 13)

Here we see the desire and passion for education among slaves. At some point during slavery, slaves became aware of the importance of becoming literate (Perry, 2003). They realized the great power and potential in being educated and what it meant for changing their status. This struggle by enslaved Africans to become educated occurred against an entrenched social system that constantly reinforced the slaves' subordinate status, hopeless plight, and so-called intellectual incapability or inferiority. Interestingly, many slave owners believed that education would "spoil" a slave making them discontented instead of docile (Douglass, 1968). Thompson (2007) gives additional insight into the mentality of many Whites who supported slavery when he stated, "An educated slave was commonly viewed as dangerous and a direct contradiction to the slavery philosophy" (p. 57). Ultimately, the educational endeavor was much larger than an individualistic pursuit (even though there were obvious personal benefits); what we see is the building of a foundation to launch future freedom struggles. Education would play a critical role in not only attaining physical freedom; it also had the potential to liberate slaves from their psychological chains. In addition, education was viewed as something to be shared with the community. Again, Perry (2003) asserted:

> While learning to read was an individual achievement, it was fundamentally a communal act. For the slaves, literacy affirmed not only their individual freedom but also the freedom of their people. Becoming literate obliged one to teach others. Learning and teaching were two sides of the same coin, part of the same moment. Literacy was not something you kept for yourself; it was to be passed on to others, to the community. Literacy was something to share. (p. 14)

At the same time, we also see that education was not for education's sake; *education was synonymous with liberation* (Beachum et al., 2004). This theme would guide the slaves who would eventually be called African Americans in their long journey to freedom and beyond.

### *Complexities and Contradictions*

Indeed, the Africans faced insurmountable odds and a bleak existence in the U.S. Somehow, they maintained the high value of education, family cohesiveness, language patterns, and song. It is rather ironic that the slaves were portrayed to be intellectually inferior to Whites, but Africa was home to renowned educational institutions. "During the early 1500s, Sankore was a renowned intellectual center to which scholars from all over Africa, Asia, and Europe came to study" (Thompson, 2007, p. 57). Thus, the negative stereotyping and false imagery was clearly manufactured to support the institution of slavery (Akbar, 1984) and a dehumanization of all Africans. Africans placed a high value on family even amid the scourge of slavery. It was commonplace for slaves to be separated and sold to far off plantations by way of slave auctions (Blassingame, 1979). In many cases, fictive kinship relationships developed where another slave would become a surrogate family member. This was very important because the family proved to be an "important survival mechanism" against slavery (Blassingame, 1979, p. 191). Even though traditional African languages and dialects would slowly change to English, slaves kept their traditional cultures alive by infusing them into English. "Regardless of his previous culture, upon landing in the New World the African-born slave had to learn the language of his master. Taught by overseers or native-born slaves, the African acquired a few European words in a relatively casual and haphazard fashion" (Blassingame, 1979, p. 24) in order to perform tasks and to engage in minimal communication. The slaves retained a special reverence for spirituality, even as Christianity slowly replaced African religions. Similarly, music and dance also played a critical role not only in the lives of enslaved Africans, but also in the lives of Africans in the American diaspora.

Music is more than an avenue for entertainment only. For the slaves, it was integrated into their lives. In this particular time period, spirituals told the collective story of struggle. Stuckey (1987) wrote:

> Too often the spirituals are studied apart from their natural, ceremonial context. The tendency has been to treat them as a musical form unrelated to dance and certainly unrelated to particular configurations of dance and dance rhythm… That the spirituals were sung in the circle guaranteed the continuing focus of the ancestors and elders as the Christian faith answered to African religious imperatives. (p. 27)

Here we find that spirituals incorporated dance and collaboration (together in a circle) with multiple purposes (emphasis on Christian faith and African traditions). Blassingame (1979) summarized the focus and intent of spirituals when he stated:

> The sentiments of the slave often appear in the spirituals. Songs of sorrow and hope, of agony and joy, of resignation and rebellion, the spirituals were the unique creations of the black slaves. Since, however, the spirituals were derivations from Biblical lore and served as a means of intra-group expression in a hostile environment, they naturally contain a few explicit references to slavery… Even when slaves did model their songs on those of whites, they changed them radically. (p. 137)

From this quote we learn that spirituals were uniquely created by the slaves, and even when they adopted the songs of Whites, they changed the songs to better reflect their experiences. The really important concept to note here is that through this form of musical expression, slaves told a story, their story, and by collectively engaging in this activity it was shared with succeeding generations. Here we find that music can be more than simply an expression of art; it can be intricately intertwined with one's life. We will return to this theme later.

In sum, slavery was a dark period for Blacks in this country. Although it had an economic intent, it also reinforced notions of Black ignorance, inferiority, and incapability. Thus, the initial experiences of far too many Blacks in this nation were tainted by this peculiar institution. At the same time, the slaves still struggled to become literate, support family, maintain their culture (language, dance, and spirituals), and ultimately resign themselves to survive in the hope for a brighter tomorrow. Unfortunately, the next phase was not that bright as slavery gave way to segregation.

## I've Been in the Storm Too Long: Jim Crow/Segregation

### *Historical Context*

Eventually, slavery was totally abolished in the North while it somewhat intensified in the South. The American West would become contentious territory as the question of would slavery expand to newly admitted states arose. At the same time, the competing economic goals of the industrial North and the agricultural South slowly guided the two large factions of our country into a bloody Civil War, with the status and future of Blacks at the epicenter. The American Civil War ended with the defeat of the South and the collapse of slavery as a formal institution. A short period of relative progress called Reconstruction (1865–1877) occurred in which many former slaves attained voting rights, began to attain a formal education, and, for the first time in the U.S., saw a glimmer of hope in the darkness. This glimmer was quickly squelched as the Northern armies that provided protection and maintained order in the South pulled out. The result was a new era which could be termed Jim Crow or segregation.

Jim Crow laws were largely enforced in the South, while the North did have its forms of racism, segregation became law in Southern states. These laws were marked by the intentional separation of races (i.e., White and Black). Woodward (1974) asserted that these codes "extended to churches and schools, to housing and jobs, to eating and drinking. Whether by law or by custom, that ostracism extended to virtually all forms of public transportation, to sports and recreations, to hospitals, orphanages, prisons, and asylums, and ultimately to funeral homes, morgues, and cemeteries" (p. 7). The newly freed slaves posed a two-fold threat to the Southern social regime. First, the slaves being freed meant the immediate end to a massive free labor force and now the potential competition with Whites for jobs. Second, the new status of Blacks posed a significant threat to the system of deference, dehumanization, and racial superiority that Southern Whites had depended on for so long (Wacquant, 2001). Part of segregation's function would be to deal with both issues, "Under this regime, backed by custom and elaborate legal statutes, superexploitative sharecropping arrangements and debt peonage fixed black labor on the land, perpetuating the hegemony of the region's agrarian upper class" (Wacquant, 2001, p. 101). At the same time, "segregation laws sharply curtailed social contacts between whites and blacks by relegating the latter to separate residential districts and to the reserved 'colored' section of commercial establishments and public facilities, saloons and movie houses, parks and beaches, trolleys and buses, waiting rooms and bathrooms" (Wacquant, 2001, p. 101). These laws were supported not only by White communities, but also by local police regimes. This allowed for the growth and expansion for domestic terrorist groups like the Ku Klux Klan. What this also meant was Blacks could not rely on the police or local/state legal systems for protection, therefore they were vulnerable (West, 2004). Woodward (1974) observed, "Indeed the more defenseless, disfranchised, and intimidated the Negro became the more prone he was to the ruthless aggression of mobs" (p. 87). Although segregation was a harsh reality, Blacks created nurturing communities and endeavored to educate children and instill in them a sense of pride.

### *Educational Attitudes*

An interesting phenomenon occurred amid the ever-imposing environment of segregation. Instead of segregation totally devastating the educational aspirations of Blacks, in many cases, it actually strengthened their spirits and resolve. Segregation not only regulated the physical movement of Blacks, but it also took a psychological toll on them as well (Perry, 2003; Thompson, 2007). Schools were of course segregated, and although they were separate they were certainly not equal (even though separate but equal was the law at this time). In fact, "in many areas Negro schools were disgracefully behind schools for whites" (Woodward, 1974, p. 145). What these schools lacked in facilities and resources, they made up for in attitude and determination. While the dominant Southern social order suggested to Blacks that they were nobody (almost subhuman), schools and communities reinforced the refrain "be somebody." This meant to "be a human, to be a person, to be counted, to be the opposite of a slave, to be free" (Perry, 2003, p. 26).

Obtaining an education was the key to being somebody. Similarly, schools during this time period not only provided academic preparation to Black students, but they also prepared them for the world beyond the schoolhouse doors (including the world of segregation and Jim Crow). The academic focus was supplemented or grounded in a pedagogy that purposely cultivated student self-esteem. Another example of this would be the *110 rule*. Many educators would tell their students that 100 percent was not good enough; you had to strive for 110 percent (Kunjufu, 2002). Schools in the segregated South with effective and caring Black educators in many cases promoted academic excellence and personal mastery. In sum, Perry (2003) insightfully asserted:

> There was a systematic denial and limiting of educational opportunity for African Americans precisely because they were African Americans. The philosophy of education that developed was informed by the particular ways in which literacy and education were implicated in the oppression of African Americans. It informed the role that education and schooling would assume in resistance and the struggle for freedom from the time of slavery to the Civil Rights era. (p. 51)

The philosophy here was one that viewed education as a process and product of liberation.

### *Complexities and Contradictions*

Although it seems rather easy to totally indict the South in its determined focus on establishing and enforcing a system of segregation, it is easy to overlook the contradictory attitudes in the North. Woodward (1974) insightfully wrote, "One of the strangest things about the career of Jim Crow was that the system was born in the North and reached an advanced age before moving to the South in force" (p. 17). Although Blacks in the North did enjoy certain freedoms, such as more freedom of movement and more freedom to challenge overt forms of racism, these freedoms existed in a context of White superiority and Black inferiority. Again Woodward noted:

> For all that, the Northern Negro was made painfully and constantly aware that he lived in a society dedicated to the doctrine of white supremacy and Negro inferiority. The major political parties, whatever their devotion to slavery, vied with each other in their devotion to this doctrine, and extremely few politicians of importance dared to question them. Their constituencies firmly believed that the Negroes were incapable of being assimilated politically, socially, or physically into white society. They made sure in numerous ways that the Negro understood his 'place' and that he was severely confined to it. (p. 18)

Although this quote is primarily describing the North around the end of slavery, it is evident that such attitudes continued well past slavery's demise (Woodward, 1974). A glaring example of Northern apathy toward the newly freed Blacks is seen in the Compromise of 1877. After the American Civil War, Northern armies in the South played a key role in maintaining order while Southern resentment, outrage, and vengeance boiled beneath the surface. This compromise that on the one hand made Rutherford B. Hayes president of the U.S., on the other guaranteed the abandonment of Blacks in the South. Although some Southern politicians pledged to protect the rights of Blacks, they soon became empty rhetoric. "But as these pledges were forgotten or violated and the South veered toward proscription and extremism, Northern opinion shifted to the right, keeping pace with the South, conceding point, after point, so that at no time were the sections very far apart on race policy" (Woodward, 1974, p. 70). As White America's attitudes toward Blacks became more apathetic, Blacks found other ways to cope with the backlash. Music became one of the avenues of freedom by means of self-expression.

Music can provide unique insight into the souls of a people. Perry (2003) wrote, "To know what a people believes, one should of course pay attention to what they say, what they portray in music, poetry, and stories" (p. 27). This particular time period was marked by forms of musical expression such as gospel and blues. What we know now as gospel music grew out of the same cultural crucible as slave spirituals. In this era, Blacks now could meet in their own churches and openly worship in their own unique ways. "African American gospel represents the flip side of the blues. Spirituals are a powerful emotional testimonial to the depths of despair, atonement, and redemption, juxtaposed with an unshakeable faith that God will ultimately prevail" (White & Cones, 1999, p. 55). We discover the deep connection to spirituality here along with the belief that a brighter day was ahead. In addition, Blacks found a way to communicate and pass on a shared history and collection of experiences while acknowledging something greater than oneself. The blues, on the other hand, was a different form of musical expression.

The blues also told the story of Blacks, but in a different way than gospel. "The bluesman articulates the pain and suffering in a pattern of African-American speech and images that the listener who has lived the Black experience can understand" (White & Cones, 1999, p. 55). Here again, musical expression is not divorced from the everyday lived experiences of Blacks. It tells of struggle, strife, pity, problems, reality, and resilience. In this way, the blues was more than an impotent outlet for entertainment only; it became a way to communicate the shared cultural set of experiences complete with musical accompaniment. West (2004) wrote:

> As infectious and embracing as the blues is, we should never forget that the blues was born out of the crucible of slavery and its vicious legacy, that it expresses the determination of a people to assert their human value. The blues professes to the deep psychic and material pains inflicted on black people within the sphere of a mythological land of opportunity…The patient resilience expressed in the blues flows from the sustained resistance to ugly forms of racist domination, and from the forging of indistinguishable hope in the contexts of American social death and soul murder. The blues produced a mature spiritual and communal strength. (p. 93)

Once again, music reinforced a set of values such as spirituality, community, self-expression, self-reflection, and the undying commitment against forms of oppression in that day and time.

## What's Going On? The Urban Ghetto

### *Historical Context*

The time period from approximately 1915 to 1968 encompasses a large portion of the 20th century. This period would witness events such as two world wars, the Great Depression, and a momentous struggle to end segregation culminating in the American civil rights movement. During the first part of the century, segregation was still alive and well. Along with segregation came an era of physical and psychological terror for Blacks as evidenced by brutal lynching, beatings, harassment, and verbal abuse (Thompson, 2007; Woodward, 1974). Wacquant (2000) summarized the plight of Blacks at the time, writing:

> The sheer brutality of caste oppression in the South, the decline of cotton agriculture due to floods and the boll weevil, and the pressing shortage of labor in northern factories caused by the outbreak of the First World War created the impetus for African-Americans to emigrate en masse to the booming industrial centers of the Midwest and Northeast (over 1.5 million left in 1910–30, followed by another 3 million in 1940–60). But as migrants from Mississippi to the Carolinas flocked to the northern metropolis, what they discovered there was not the 'promised land' of equality and full citizenship but another system of racial enclosure, the ghetto, which, though it was less rigid and fearsome than the one they had fled, was no less encompassing and constricting. (pp. 4–5)

Thus, the North promised a new beginning devoid of the obvious racial barriers that were prevalent in the South. Ironically, while offering a new life, the North also offered new forms of segregation as Blacks were ushered into certain segments of Northern cities which came to be known as ghettoes.

The 20th century witnessed the migration of masses of Blacks to the industrial North from the agricultural South. According to Jackson (1996), "From 1915 to the 1930s, 1.8 million Southern Blacks migrated to industrial cities in the North and Midwest" (p. 234). Villegas and Lucas (2002) noted, "In 1940, for instance, almost 80 percent of the African American population lived in the South, and 63 percent lived in rural areas; thirty years later, only 33 percent lived in the South, and 75 percent lived in urban settings" (p. 46). It was the hope of many to find better job opportunities, to escape the segregation and violence in the South, and to possibly gain access to a small slice of the "American dream." Unfortunately, life in the North provided only minimal opportunities and a more nuanced and covert form of racism as compared to the South. Rothstein (1996) agreed, "Wherever they went, however, they found the pernicious segregation system. This affected where they went to school, where they worked, and the type of employment they were able to obtain" (p. 163). This would eventually lead to a phenomenon which would increase the "geographic isolation" of people of color from their White counterparts, called *White flight*. White flight would be the next event in a chain that would isolate urban dwellers (mainly of color) and their schools.

### *Educational Attitudes*

Whites in many urban areas began to leave as the number of Blacks (and other people of color) increased. They escaped to suburbs away from the cities, leaving a void. This process became known as "White flight." Malcolm Gladwell (2000) borrows this term in his book *The Tipping Point: How Little Things Can Make a Big Difference*; he opined:

> The expression [Tipping Point] first came into popular use in the 1970s to describe the flight to the suburbs of whites living in the older cities of the American Northeast. When the number of incoming African Americans in a particular neighborhood reached a certain point—20 percent say—sociologists observed that the community would 'tip': most of the remaining whites would leave almost immediately. (p. 12)

This quote expresses the core attitude against racial integration. The result would be exceedingly different schools: "The suburbanization of the United States has created two racially segregated and economically unequal systems of education—one urban, mostly for children who are poor and of color; the other suburban, largely White, middle-class children" (Villegas & Lucas, 2002, p. 48). This process would have detrimental effects on communities and schools of color in the inner cities. Blacks who moved to the North found a more nuanced, less overt, yet equally if not more damaging form of oppression. The experience in the industrial North gave the façade of limitless opportunities (which were actually very limited) while also making transparent a harsh reality, which included isolation, neglect, and an inferior infrastructure for schooling.

Blacks would try their best to hold on to their deep belief in education as a means of liberation. This philosophy was now challenged by the harsh reality of urban life. While isolated in segregated parts of major cities, crime rates began to increase, businesses began to leave, and the meaning of community for Blacks began to wane.

### *Complexities and Contradictions*

During this time period Blacks faced numerous challenges. In the South, segregation was still the rule of the day, undergirded by the terrorist tactics of groups like the Ku Klux Klan. By the mid-20th century, serious resistance to segregation began to mount. A watershed moment occurred with the *Brown v. Board of Education* (1954) decision.

> The landmark Supreme Court decision in the *Brown v. Board of Education* case has been hailed as the single most important court decision in American educational history. The decision in this case overturned the *Plessey v. Ferguson* separate but equal clause by establishing that segregated schools denied African American students their constitutional rights guaranteed to them in the 14th Amendment. *Brown*...would also serve as the impetus for challenging several inequities as Jim Crow laws in the South and, on a many levels, for generally protecting the civil rights of African Americans and later individuals with disabilities. (Blanchett, Mumford, & Beachum, 2005, p. 70)

While this movement impacted the physical manifestations of oppression, in conjunction, the Black Power movement started to deal with how Black people felt about themselves, by instilling self-reliance, self-sufficiency, and in some cases self-protection. Similarly, White and Cones (1999) wrote:

> At a deeper, more personal level, it was about the right of self-determination and self-definition. The Reverend Martin Luther King, Jr. used terms like "somebodyness" to define the psychological meaning of the revolution. Other terms coined to reinforce this concept were "Black pride," "Black is Beautiful," and "Black Power"...self-definition from the perspective of one's own experience is the first step in deconstructing the oppressor's negative definitions. (p. 63)

As Blacks strived to dismantle oppressive laws (i.e., Jim Crow) and deal with the psychological effects of ongoing mistreatment, music remained a means of dealing with reality as well as expressing their innermost feelings.

During this time period jazz as well as rhythm and blues (R&B) became popular. Jazz has been hailed a musical form that characterizes imagination and invention. West (2004) wrote, "These great blues and jazz musicians are eloquent connoisseurs of individuality in their improvisational arts and experimental lives" (p. 91). Dyson (1997) characterized jazz as "...its heart pumping with the blood of improvisation, its gut churning with the blues—embody the edifying quest for romantic self-expression and democratic collaboration that capture Negro music and American democracy at their best" (p. 126). With its emphasis on improvisation, individuality, and expression, jazz represented yet another form of music that transcended the boundaries of mere entertainment-laden titillation. According to West (2004), jazz was much more, "The blues and jazz made it possible to engage race in America on personal and intimate terms—with democratic results" (p. 92). West (2008) provided even more clarity when he wrote:

> What is jazz all about? It's about finding your voice. It's about that long, difficult walk to freedom. It's about mustering the courage to think critically. It's about mustering the courage to care and love, and be empathetic and compassionate… Jazz is the middle road between invisibility and anger. It is where self-confident creativity resides. (p. 118)

Thus, in the early to mid-20th century, jazz provided Blacks a unique form of musical expression in the midst of Southern segregation and Northern isolation.

The 1960s and early 1970s clearly represented a unique time period for Blacks. Dyson (2007) agrees, "In the 1960s and 1970s, black folk were struggling for the sorts of political freedoms and economic opportunities that the most fortunate members of the young black generation now take for granted" (p. 63). The movement toward Black liberation was supported by music that began to reflect the struggle. At this time you also had the Black Arts Movement (BAM). "For the members of the Black Arts Movement, there was no such thing as a serious artist who was not concerned about the struggles for self-determination and political liberty of their people, struggles which in large part inspired their art" (Dyson, 2007, p. 62). So when one hears Curtis Mayfield's "Keep on Pushin,'" James Brown's "I'm Black and I'm Proud," or Sam Cooke's, "Change Is Gonna Come," these works cannot easily be separated from the times in which these artists lived. In sum, music can be utilized strictly for entertainment value, but for Blacks, it has historically served a greater purpose. "Music has been our most powerful creative expression. Of course, the music itself is based on communal links of church, family, and social education. Our music reflects our unique sense of rhythm, harmony, and melody" (West, 2008, p. 114).

## Get Rich or Die Tryin': The Hyperghetto/Hood and 21st-Century Black America

### *Historical Context*

The last 40 years have brought even more changes to the world and to Blacks. The final institution that Wacquant proposed was the hyperghetto. Once again, his framework explains how the four institutions "operated to define, confine, and control African-Americans in the history of the United States" (Wacquant, 2000, p. 377). Our utilization of his framework in this chapter is to provide a historical model to better understand the historical, educational, and sociocultural experiences of Blacks in the U.S. The hyperghetto evolved in a post-White flight era when the residential barriers that barred Blacks from moving into White suburbs were relaxed (Wilson, 2009). Thus, White flight was followed by *Black trek* as more Blacks with greater wealth left inner-city communities leaving a dangerous void in what was the ghetto (Dyson, 2004). In addition to the spatial separation, Wacquant (2001) asserted:

> Its economic basis has shifted from the direct servicing of the black community to the state, with employment in public bureaucracies accounting for most of the growth of professional, managerial and technical positions held by African Americans over the past thirty years. The genealogical ties of the black bourgeoisie to the black poor have also grown more remote and less dense. (p. 104)

From this quote, we note the growing stratification in the Black community as the Black middle class separates themselves from the Black poor. Many scholars and authors have warned of the increasing separation, segregation, and stratification within the Black community (Dyson, 2005; Kitwana, 2002; Kunjufu, 2002; West, 2008). West (2008) elaborated, "Once we lose any sense of a black upper or black middle class or a black upper working-class connecting with the black underclass with a 'we' consciousness or sense of community, it becomes much more difficult to focus on the plight of the poor" (p. 57). The evolution of the hyperghetto has become a place of increased violence, illicit drug sale and use, economic depravity, police surveillance and brutality, and struggling schools.

It is apparent that today's Black youth (the current generation) have been impacted by certain sociopolitical forces. Kitwana (2002) identified six major phenomena that make the lives of these youth different from those of previous generations: (1) a different process of values and identity development; (2) globalization; (3) persisting segregation; (4) public policy regarding the racialization of the criminal justice system; (5) overexposure and negative exposure with regard to media representation; (6) the decline in overall quality of life for the poor and working poor. In reference to values and identity formation, there is evidence that they are influenced in different ways. In the past, church, family, and school heavily influenced Black youth identity development (Kunjufu, 1993). Regarding today's identity development, Kitwana (2002) insightfully wrote:

> Today the influence of these traditional purveyors of Black culture has largely diminished in the face of powerful and pervasive technological advances and corporate growth. Now media and entertainment such as pop music, film, and fashion are among the major forces transmitting culture to this generation of

> Black Americans…For the most part, we have turned to ourselves, our peers, global images and products, and the new realities we face for guidance. (p. 7)

In terms of globalization, today's Black youth have come of age in a time where we have witnessed the upward mobility of a select number of elites and the expansion of the middle class (including Blacks) (Dyson, 2004). At the same time, we have witnessed jobs moving away from urban areas and the increasing distancing of the haves from the have nots (Kitwana, 2002; West, 2004). Contemporary segregation is not evidenced by signs and customs as in the Jim Crow era. "We certainly live in a more inclusive society than existed in pre-civil rights America. However, continuing segregation and inequality have made it especially illusory for many young Blacks. The illusion of integration allows for some access, while countless roadblocks persist in critical areas where Blacks continue to be discriminated against in often subtle and sometimes not so subtle ways" (Kitwana, 2002, p. 13). White and Cones (1999) agree that contemporary prejudice exists mainly in the form of institutional racism. They explain:

> Institutional racism exists where whites restrict equal access to jobs and promotions, to business and housing loans, and the like. White bankers and mortgage companies can secretly collaborate to redline a neighborhood so that such loans are nearly impossible to obtain. White senior faculty members in predominately white universities (public and private) determine who gets promoted to tenured faculty positions…Good-old-boys' clubs in the corporate structure determine who will be mentored and guided through the promotional mine fields. (p. 136)

Black youth witness the continuing legacy of segregation and racism and its impact on their lives.

Related to the persistence of segregation/racism is the criminal justice system and how it is skewed against people of color (particularly Black males). This is not to say that if one commits a crime, one does not deserve punishment, but the eyes of justice should be blindfolded, making people equal before the law. For instance, young Blacks have grown up with laws that give more jail time for crimes involving crack cocaine as opposed to crimes that involve powder cocaine (largely the drug of choice for more Whites). They have been impacted by the explosive growth in prison construction, zero tolerance policies, and instances of police harassment and constant surveillance (Kitwana, 2002). Dyson (2005) asserted, "The increase in black incarceration was driven by political considerations, not a boost in, for instance, drug consumption" (p. 88).

Kitwana (2002) eloquently captured the sentiments of many Black youth when he stated, "The collapse of trust in law enforcement and the vilification of Black youth through crime legislation certainly play a role in the view Black youth share about legislation, law enforcement, and criminal justice" (p. 18).

The images of young Blacks are frequently misrepresented by the mainstream media and today's entertainment titans. Still today, young Blacks are overrepresented on the news as criminals and menaces to society (Kitwana, 2002; White & Cones, 1999). In addition, a wave of so-called reality-based television programs now depicts many young Blacks as combative, aggressive, ignorant, materialistic, and sexually obsessed (West, 2008). According to White and Cones (1999), "Not only do European Americans believe that theses caricatures represent the reality of Black male life, but Black male youths [and female youths] may aspire to live up to these images because they are popularized and romanticized" (p. 72).

Finally, today's Black youth recognize the significant issues around quality of life in America. The wealth gap between the rich and poor continues to grow (Dyson, 2005; Kitwana, 2002; West, 2008). West (2004) chides the more recent overemphasis on money-based values or obsession with wealth attainment. He asserted, "It also redefines the terms of what we should be striving for in life, glamorizing materialistic gain, narcissistic pleasure, and the pursuit of narrow individualistic preoccupations—especially for young people here and abroad" (p. 4). Kitwana (2002) discussed the impact of West's statement on the hip-hop generation when he stated, "For us, achieving wealth, by any means necessary, is more important than most anything else, hence our obsession with the materialistic and consumer trappings of financial success" (p. 6). Thus, Black youth realize the rampant wealth inequality in the U.S. and have in many cases made a conscious choice to pursue materialistic gain. West (2008) again warned, "The marketplace culture of consumption undermines community, undermines links to history and tradition, and undermines relationships" (p. 31). This quote is particularly powerful in relationship to the historical context provided here.

The phenomena presented here are provided to paint a picture of today's contemporary context, especially for Black youth. We recognize that the other time periods we examined earlier related to Blacks in general. We emphasize Black youth specifically here because of the great curiosity around their contemporary plight. Other things that inevitably impact these youth include: employment, relationships, technological growth, and political engagement (Dyson, 2004; Kitwana, 2002) to name a few. Obviously, the world around these youth would impact their outlook on education.

### *Educational Attitudes*

In the 21st century, Blacks find themselves in a place of great promise and peril. Today, there seems to be almost limitless opportunities for students who are dedicated, determined, and disciplined. We have even witnessed what some thought was virtually impossible—the election of a Black president of the United States of America. His success is powerfully symbolic for all children of color, but the structures that one must navigate remain intact. Even as we acknowledge the great progress of Black faces in high places (West, 2008) the data tell a different story. According to McKinsey & Company (2009):

- Avoidable shortfalls in academic achievement impose heavy and often tragic consequences, via lower earnings, poorer health, and higher rates of incarceration.
- For many students (but by no means all), lagging achievement evidenced as early as fourth grade appears to be a powerful predictor of rates of high school and college graduation, as well as lifetime earnings. (p. 6)

Kunjufu (2002) indicates:

- Black students comprise 17 percent of the U.S. student population. Black teachers comprise 6 percent of U.S. teachers. Black males comprise 1 percent of U.S. teachers.
- There is no staff of color in 44 percent of schools.
- Of inner-city teachers, 40 percent transfer within 5 years.
- One of every three Black males is involved with a penal institution while only one of ten male high school graduates is enrolled in college.
- Only 3 percent of Black students are placed in gifted and talented programs.
- If a Black child is placed in special education, 80 percent of the time the child will be male.
- Thirty-three percent of Black households live below the poverty line.
- In light of *Brown vs. Topeka* in 1954, schools have become more segregated since 1971. (pp. vii–viii)

These data paint a bleak picture for far too many Black youth. The obvious question for many is how can we account for the lingering challenges that continue to impede the educational progress of African Americans? The framework provided here gives some insight. Specifically, regarding educational attitudes, the emphasis on education for liberation seemed to decline with the dismantling of segregated, all-Black schools and increasing integration; the conversion of overt racist practices to covert racist practices in schools; and the change in the attitudes of students regarding the value of education. As previously noted, segregated schools provided Black children at the time with academic preparation as well as preparation for life in a world that saw them as inept, inferior, and incapable. Schools reinforced their spirits as segregated society tried its best to tear them apart. This created a kind of resiliency in these students (Perry, 2003). When segregation ended and integration came, many dedicated Black teachers and administrators lost their jobs (McCray, Wright, & Beachum, 2007). In addition, as the doors of opportunity began to open, Black students opted for other majors besides education (Kunjufu, 2002). Therefore, the educators who provided quality education were lost along with the pipeline that would replace them. In their place, White educators largely took up the task of educating Black students, with mixed results.

Today, the teaching force (along with administrators) is predominately White (McCray et al., 2007). As a matter of fact, the teaching core in the U.S. is mostly White and female (Kunjufu, 2002; Mizialko, 2005). This in itself is not inherently problematic. The key issue here is teacher expectations. "There are consequences of a primarily white, female, middle class, monolingual teaching force. The consequences are felt by multicultural, urban learners" (Mizialko, 2005, p. 177). Hancock (2006) agreed: "The reality that White women are on the front lines of urban education is clearly evident. While we continue to recruit and retain minority teachers, it is critical that we also focus our attention on helping to educate White women teachers about the realities of teaching students who may hold a different sociopolitical, sociocultural, and socioeconomic perspective" (p. 97). Additionally, Kunjufu (2002) also made the point that Black teachers could have negative attitudes and low expectations toward students of color. The great problem here is that even though we exist in a society in which the visible manifestations of segregation and alienation are absent (i.e., *Whites only* signs, *Jim Crow* laws, etc.), many students still readily get the message by other covert means that their skin color is inferior. Tatum (1997) discussed the concept of cultural racism, defined as "the cultural images and messages that affirm the assumed superiority of Whites and the assumed inferiority of people of color" (p. 6). Similarly, Delpit (1995) described specific examples where teachers would seldom interact with students of color and called this "invisible racism." It is up to all teachers to strive for equity and excellence for all students.

Black students today are strongly impacted by the world in which they live. Today's youth live in a world of high-speed information sharing, texting, and tweeting as major means of communication—life lived online on the Internet—and are used to having many options. Unfortunately, the way we still structure schools is grounded in a 20th-century philosophy. Many Black students, especially those from the inner city, seem to concentrate on immediate gratification as opposed to long-term gratification (as with a good education) (Kitwana, 2002; Kunjufu, 2002). In addition, many youth have witnessed relatives who have graduated high school or attended college and still face discrimination or unemployment (Dyson, 2005). "To be effective teaching African American students, you must convince them that there is a 'payoff' in education" (Kunjufu, 2002, p. 101). Educators must provide an accurate and convincing portrait of career choices and reinforce the importance of a good education. In addition, education must be viewed as not only a means for financial gain, but a tool for personal development and self-actualization.

### *Complexities and Contradictions*

Today, Blacks seem to be both loved and hated by mainstream society. As it stands, when a Black reaches the pinnacle of their field (sports, acting, journalism, medicine, academics, business, politics, etc.), they are hailed as examples and showered with praise. But for the vast majority of Blacks who are struggling to make a way for themselves, they are many times met with resistance, bitterness, sarcasm, and/or resentment (Bogotch et al., 2008; Dyson, 2004; Perry, 2003; Tatum, 2007; West, 2008). This dichotomized view allows the dominant culture to accept a certain select segment of the Black population while at the same time justify the unfair treatment of the great majority who have not reached such lofty heights as their privileged peers. In this manner, the illusion of true equality in American society is allowed to flourish. This is a serious and ongoing contradiction. This kind of contradiction also affects other areas such as hip-hop culture.

Hip-hop culture has emerged in recent years and clearly dominates the lives of many youth. West (2008) exclaimed, "Hip-hop music is the most important popular musical development in the last thirty years" (p. 122). White and Cones (1999) stated, "Hip-hop is a catch-all term for a contemporary, urban-centered youth lifestyle associated with popular music, break dancing, certain dress and hair styles, graffiti, and street language" (p. 96). Hip-hop culture has gone from primarily rapping, break dancing, DJ-ing, and graffiti to including dialects, attitude, expression, mannerisms, and fashion (Au, 2005; Kitwana, 2002). Regarding youth, Kunjufu (1993) asserted, "The ages between 13–17 are when they [teenagers] are particularly vulnerable to outside influence and before their values and ideas are fully developed (Kunjufu, 1993, p. 81). Furthermore, Kitwana (2002) wrote, "Today, more and more Black youth are turning to rap music, music videos, designer clothing, popular Black films, and television programs for values and identity" (p. 9). It is apparent that hip-hop culture has the ability to affect the values of youth in general and Black youth in particular.

Hip-hop (or rap) music is yet another form of musical expression that signifies, symbolizes, and structures the Black experience. The music itself, although born out of postindustrial blight and inspired by those who considered themselves outcasts, has transformed over time (Dyson, 2007; West, 2004). Some may now argue that it has become a reflection of the materialism and corporate structures it railed against during its initial phases. West (2004) elaborated:

> An unprecedented cultural breakthrough created by talented poor black youths in the hoods of the empire's chocolate cities, hip-hop has now transformed the entertainment industry and culture here and around the world. The fundamental irony of hip-hop is that it has become viewed as a nihilistic, macho, violent, and bling-bling phenomenon when in fact its originating impulse was a fierce disgust with the hypocrisies of adult culture—disgust with the selfishness, cap-

> italist callousness, and xenophobia of the culture of adults, both within the hood and in the society at large. (p. 179)

West is referring to hip-hop's more humble beginnings when the music was a form of expression, a canvas for lyrical creativity, and mechanism for sharing the trials and triumphs of urban existence.

In sum, hip-hop may very well be both overestimated and underestimated. It is overestimated by critics and detractors for blaming the music for a host of social ills that existed long before hip-hop came into being (e.g., rampant materialism, deadly violence, drug proliferation, and malicious levels of misogyny). West (2008) levied a fair critique when he wrote, "Too often, hip-hop still lacks deep vision and analysis. It's just escapism, it's thin. It's too morally underdeveloped and spiritually immature. In the end, it has to be more of a turning-to in order to constructively contribute" (p. 127). At the same time, hip-hop is underestimated because of its awesome potential to make money, motivate people, and inspire young minds. It cannot be expected to solve all of the problems in the Black community, but at the same time it does have the potential to at least "do no harm." Dyson (2007) eloquently described hip-hop as follows, "Hip hop is fundamentally an art form that traffics in hyperbole, parody, kitsch, dramatic license, double entendres, signification, and other literary and artistic conventions to get its point across" (p. xvii). If the message in hip-hop is disturbing, then its creators are trying to tell us something about the contemporary Black experience.

## Discussion

Our discussion here has covered a great majority of the Black experience. The authors acknowledge that this brief analysis cannot begin to address the comprehensive and complex nuances involved in this kind of sociohistorical critique. It is our hope to shed a modicum of light for additional insight. What follows is a summation of the information gathered from our rendering of the Wacquant (2000) framework.

### *Context Matters*

In each phase observed we acknowledged historical context. In addition, Blacks are linked to the occurrences, happenings, and experiences of the past. Moreover, this is not simply a form of misguided nostalgia when we discuss Blacks and their history. There are pitfalls to extreme forms of this. Dyson (1997) warned, "Nostalgia is colored memory. It is romantic remembering. It recreates as much as it recalls" (p. 117). Our perspective here advocates the recognition of the comprehensive historical experience, even when the memories are painful (i.e., slavery and segregation). The lesson here is to *respect* the history, and also to *protect* the history, so the next generation will not *reject* the history. The acknowledgment of our tragic past is necessary, even as Blacks begin to experience what some would consider modest success. West (2008) stated,

> It's easy to think that somehow, because there's been relative progress for a significant number of black people, that there has been some kind of fundamental transformation. Therefore, we lose sight of the degree to which the history of New World Africans, in this hemisphere for 400 years, still affects us all. (p. 50)

Ultimately, our perspectives, attitudes, and views of reality cannot be totally separated from our context.

### *Education for Liberation*

Black people have historically struggled for the right to learn, be educated, and be liberated. Education has been valued even at a time when it carried harsh penalties and was against the law (Perry, 2003). As we observe the current statistics regarding Black students in terms of dropout rates, achievement gaps, etc., we must question current practices. Earlier, we discussed several problems in the American educational system. Here are some promising ideas:

- All educators should engage in continuous self-improvement/self-development. This may include additional readings/reading groups, professional development workshops, and/or attending educational conferences. The goal is to create educational environments that value both equity and excellence (Beachum & Obiakor, 2005).
- Teachers should strive to increase the rigor of their lessons, make their lessons relevant, and continuously build relationships with their students.
- Educational leaders should provide resources to support measurable efforts to create time and space for teachers and administrators to reflect on their practice, engage in discussion/debate, and imagine as well as develop new and innovative school structures, programs, and activities.
- Parents should monitor and manage their child's educational progress. Attend parent-teacher conferences if possible; if not, schedule a specific time to talk to their child's teacher(s). Parents should provide their child with a quiet place to study as well as the proper materials (writing utensils, books, computer, globe, dictionary, calculator, etc.) (Kunjufu, 2002).
- Community members should "hold all leaders and elected officials responsible and demand that they change current policy" (Gordon, 2006, p. 34).

Improving the situation regarding Black education requires individual as well as collective action. In this chapter, we discussed what different constituencies can do individually. The collective urgency is captured in the following quote, "We must demand that local communities provide the resources to educate *all* children, that the state and federal governments provide sufficient resources. The mandate of educating all of America's children rests on all of us" (Gordon, 2006, p. 34).

### *The Continuity of Culture*

From our readings of Blacks' experiences in the U.S., we identified many complexities and contradictions. As a theme we continuously looked at the role of music in each historical epoch. The role of music is multifaceted. It was a way to communicate and share information during slavery. In segregation, it expressed the pain in the blues and the promise in spirituals. During the American civil rights/Black Power era it enhanced the struggle for freedom. Even today, the music still has the potential to do all of the things of the past or reflect the reality of today (as so much of the music seems to do). Music is indeed a form of entertainment and artistic expression. At the same time, it has meant so much more to Blacks. In all of the historical periods, the music is trying to tell us something. Encoded in the music are strife, distress, and powerful emotion. The music also can also contain joy, peace, contentment, jubilation, and hope. This is the magic of music, to be able to take listeners on a journey to places they may have never imagined, or to give the listener an in-depth look into the soul of the person or persons making the music. This is the essence of the Black experience; the highs and lows, the good and the gloom, the realization of the American dream in the midst of the American nightmare.

## Conclusion

In this chapter, we have taken a sociohistorical look at the experiences of Blacks in the United States. Wacquant (2000) provided a framework of "peculiar institutions" that informed our work: (1) Slavery (1619–1865); (2) Jim Crow/Segregation (1865–1965); (3) Ghetto (1915–1968); (4) Hyperghetto and Prison (1968–today). In each era, we delved deeper into historical context, educational attitudes, and complexities and contradictions. The core of our work may be best expressed by West (2008) when he wrote, "Black people have never had the luxury to believe in the innocence of America. Although we've experienced the worst of America, we still believe that the best of America can emerge" (p. 23).

## References

Akbar, N. (1984). *Chains and images of psychological slavery.* Jersey City, NJ: New Mind Productions.

Beachum, F. D., Dentith, A. M., & McCray, C. R. (2004). Administrators' and teachers' work in a new age of reform: Understanding the factors in African American student success. *E-Journal of Teaching and Learning in Diverse Settings, 2*(1). Available: http://www.subr.edu/coeducation/ejournal/EJTLDS.%20Volume%202%20Issue% 201.Beachum%20et%20al.pdf

Beachum F. D., & McCray, C. R. (2008). Leadership in the eye of the storm: Challenges at the intersection of urban schools and cultural collusion. *Multicultural Learning and Teaching, 3*(2), 99–120.

Blanchett, W., Mumford, V., & Beachum, F. D., (2005). Urban school failure and disproportionality in a Post-*Brown* era: Benign neglect of the Constitutional rights of students of color. *Remedial and Special Education, 26*(2), 70–81.

Blassingame, J. W. (1979). *The slave community: Plantation life in the Antebellum South.* New York: Oxford University Press.

Bogotch, I., Beachum, F. D., Blount, J., Brooks, J., & English, F. (2008). *Radicalizing educational leadership: Dimensions of social justice.* Rotterdam, Netherlands: Sense Publishing.

Dantley, M. (2002). Uprooting and replacing positivism, the melting pot, multiculturalism, and other impotent notions in educational leadership through an African American perspective. *Education and Urban Society, 34*(3), 334–352.

Dantley, M. (2005). African American spirituality and Cornel West's notions of prophetic pragmatism: Restructuring educational leadership in American urban schools. *Educational Administration Quarterly, 41*(4), 651–674.

Douglass, F. (1968). *The narrative of the life of Fredrick Douglass: An American slave.* New York: Signet.

Dyson, M. E. (1997). *Race rules: Navigating the color line.* New York: Vintage Books.

Dyson, M. E. (2004). *The Michael Eric Dyson reader.* New York: Basic Civitas Books.

Dyson, M. E. (2005). *Is Bill Cosby right? Or has the Black middle class lost its mind?* New York: Basic Civitas Books.

Dyson, M. E. (2007). *Know what I mean?: Reflections on hip hop.* New York: Basic Civitas Books.

Gause, C. P. (2005). Guest editor's introduction: Edu-tainment: Popular culture in the making of schools for the 21st century. *Journal of School Leadership, 15*(3), 240–242.

Giroux, H. (1997). *Pedagogy and the politics of hope: Theory, culture, and schooling.* Boulder, CO: Westview.

Gladwell, M. (2000). *The tipping point: How little things can make a big difference.* New York: Back Bay Books.

Gordon, E. W. (2006). Establishing a system of public education in which all children achieve at high levels and reach their full potential. In T. Smiley (Ed.), *The covenant with Black America* (pp. 23–45). Chicago: Third World Press.

Hancock, S. D. (2006). White women's work: On the front lines of urban education. In J. Landsman & C. W. Lewis (Eds.), *White teachers/diverse classrooms: A guide to building inclusive schools, promoting high expectations, and eliminating racism* (pp. 93–109). Sterling, VA: Stylus.

Jackson, K. (1996). *America is me: 170 fresh questions and answers on Black American history.* New York: Harper Perennial.

Kitwana, B. (2002). *The hip-hop generation: Young blacks and the crisis in African American culture.* New York: Basic Civitas Books.

Kunjufu, J. (1993). *Hip-hop vs. MAAT: A psycho/social analysis of values.* Chicago: African American Images.

Kunjufu, J. (1995). *Countering the conspiracy to destroy Black boys* (Vol. 4). Chicago: African American Images.

Kunjufu, J. (2002). *Black students—Middle class teachers.* Chicago: African American Images.

McCray, C. R., Wright, J. V., & Beachum, F. D. (2007). Beyond *Brown*: Examining the perplexing plight of African American principals. *Journal of Instructional Psychology, 34*(4), 247–255.

McKinsey & Company. (2009, April). *The economic impact of the achievement gap in America's schools.* New York: Author.

Mizialko, A. (2005). Reducing the power of "whiteness" in urban schools. In F. E. Obiakor & F. D. Beachum (eds.), *Urban education for the 21st century: Research, issues, and perspectives* (pp. 176–186). Springfield, IL: Charles C. Thomas.

Nisbett, R. E. (2009). Intelligence and how to get it: Why schools and cultures count. New York: W. W. Norton & Company, Inc.

Obiakor, F. E., & Beachum, F. D. (2005). Urban education: The quest for democracy, equity, and excellence. In F. E. Obiakor & F. D. Beachum (Eds.), *Urban education for the 21st century: Research, issues, and perspectives* (pp. 3–19). Springfield, IL: Charles C. Thomas.
Perry, T. (2003). Up from the parched earth: Toward a theory of African-American achievement. In T. Perry, C. Steel, & A. G. Hilliard (Eds.), *Young gifted and Black: Promoting high achieving among African-American students* (pp. 1–108). Boston: Beacon.
Rothstein, S. W. (1996). *Schools and society: New perspectives in American education*. Englewood Cliffs, NJ: Prentice Hall.
Stuckey, S. (1987). *Slave culture: Nationalist theory & the foundations of Black America*. New York: Oxford University Press.
Tatum, B. D. (1997). *Why are all the Black kids sitting together in the cafeteria?: And other conversations about race*. New York: Basic Books.
Thompson, T. L. III (2007). Historical and contemporary dilemmas facing urban Black male students today: Focusing on the past to correct present and future deficits. In M. C. Brown & R. D. Bartee (Eds.), *Still not equal: Expanding educational opportunity in society* (pp. 49–63). New York: Peter Lang.
Villegas, A. M., & Lucas, T. (2002). Educating culturally responsive teachers: A coherent approach. Albany, NY: State University of New York Press.
Wacquant, L. (2000). The new 'peculiar institution': On the prison as surrogate ghetto. *Theoretical Criminology*, 4(3), 377–389.
Wacquant, L. (2001). Deadly symbiosis: When ghetto and prison meet and mesh. *Punishment and Society, 3*(1), 95–134.
Wacquant, L. (2002). From slavery to mass incarceration: Rethinking the 'race question' in the U.S. *New Left Review*, 13, 41–60.
West, C. (2004). *Democracy matters: Winning the fight against imperialism*. New York: Penguin Press.
West, C. (2008). *Hope on a tightrope: Words and wisdom*. Carlsbad, CA: Hay House, Inc.
White, J. L. & Cones, J. H. III (1999). *Black man emerging: Facing the past and seizing a future in America*. New York: W. H. Freeman and Company.
Wilson, W. J. (2009). *More than just race: Being Black and poor in the inner city*. New York: W.W. Norton & Company.
Woodward, C. V. (1974). *The strange career of Jim Crow* (3rd ed.). New York: Oxford University Press.

# This, I believe

I believe that videogames turn our children into endorphin junkies before they learn to read
I believe that all too often we allow the people selling things on TV to raise our toddlers
And they have never had our best interests at heart
I believe that we should listen to our children's music
If we don't know what they listen to we'll never know what or how they think
I believe that abstinence, as the only form of birth control doesn't work, just ask Sarah
I believe that our children need more of our time, not more things
I believe that all parents want their children to have better lives than they did
Unfortunately, we often confuse easier with better.

I believe that education isn't, shouldn't and hasn't ever been free
The problem with free is that it has no value until it's gone
And we never know the true cost of ignorance until it's too late
I believe that who we become as a society demands that we must do more than pay lip service
To the notion that all children deserve a gifted education
I believe there is something vastly wrong with our society
When the pedophiles who abuse our children
Spend less time in jail than those who abuse animals.
I believe quality, affordable health care, like the pursuit of happiness,
Is an inalienable right.
I believe that until we place people before profits
Those we love will suffer and die needlessly on the altar of the Money God.

I believe that many on the far right of the abortion debate
Just want to control someone else's womb
I believe that pro-lifers should truly be pro-life
Why save him from destruction in the womb
So you can deny, denigrate and humiliate with a lifetime of hate
So you can kill him with a needle in his arm in that cold, dark, room
Or give him life plus 150 years
Or sell him and his soul to the merchants of death
With promises of a hero's remembrance.

I believe that hate born of ignorance and fear
Is the weapon that those who profit from prejudice amplify and use to divide and conquer
I believe that we can never truly understand those different from us
If we don't first seek to understand how they see God and their place in the universe
I believe that true understanding and acceptance (not tolerance, no-one wants to be tolerated)
Can only happen when we celebrate our similarities and our shared humanity
I believe that we have yet to learn that love truly is, color blind

I believe that our evolution is incomplete and will continue to be so
Until we free ourselves from mental slavery
Until we learn to embrace all the wonderful facets of our humanity
Until we live our lives with dignity and integrity
Until we see the many faces of God in all the children we meet
I believe that until we love our neighbors as we love ourselves
Our extinction as a species, will always be heartbeats away

This, I believe.
**©H$^2$12**

|| EIGHT

# Dealing with Cultural Collision

## *What Pre-Service Educators Should Know*

Floyd D. Beachum & Carlos R. McCray

I think your ears have lied to you
And your eyes have implied to you
That Urban means undeserving and absent of purpose
So give me back!!
Give me back my identity!!
Give me the opportunity
To break free of influential essentials that my community seeks
And have been led to believe
Either from Hip Hop vultures disguised as moguls
Or mass media outlets that televise and overemphasize
What is deemed a destructive culture
Broadcast and typecast misguided black youth
That lives below the reality of broken homes, economic oppression, and a multitude of Half-truths
And finding no salvation in my inner city school
Because educators aren't there to educate
But instead baby-sit and dictate
Further reinforcing and filtrating the messages that distort who I am
And who I could grow to be
So I ask why haven't you extended your hand
To enhance my ability, expand my ideals and possibilities Versus leaving me to discover my identity through manipulated mediums And an environment that welcomes my bemused condition I mean more to this society My articles of clothing, vernacular, or demographic Do not define me. Contrary to popular belief I am also aspiring, inspiring, and operating as a prodigy born out of art So it is evident that I have the ability to play more than just this part But I am also a product of my surrounding…and my underdeveloped mind often

has no protection . . . Then difficult to discover my identity and direction This
is a burden that I cannot overcome alone Give me something additional to relate to before I become prone To embracing what is put into the universe to be
adopted as my own Way of thinking, living, feeling…I am a king on my way to
being dethroned Understand me rather than abandon me and pierce me with
labels This is when you find distrust, despair, and anger I need positive influence
to rival the issuance of negative imagery so common in my
world I am young, black, impressionable, but imperiled Look at me!!

–"Look at Me," a poem by Krystal Roberts (of Atlanta, GA)

This poem gives an acute voice to the legions of voiceless young people who are trapped in neglected neighborhoods, segregated schools, and cultures of chaos. Addressing this reality, Smith and Sapp (2005) stated,

> The goal of educational psychology is to effectively solve problems. In many urban schools, many educational problems remain unsolved. As it stands, we can clearly identify the epidemic of failures for ethnic minorities.…Urban practitioners must become problem-solvers and functional decision-makers. As problem-solvers, they must value ethnic, linguistic, and racial differences to effectively teach in urban schools. (p. 109)

The dispositions and beliefs of pre-service educational professionals are of extreme importance. The fate of urban school children largely rests in the hands of educators who may not share the same cultural backgrounds as their students or clients (Kunjufu, 2002; Landsman & Lewis, 2006). Therefore, it is critically important for these individuals to understand social context, appreciate differences, and champion change for a more multicultural organization (Cox, 1994; Cox, 2001; Irvine, 2003). Sometimes the problem is cultural, where the culture of educators clashes with that of their students, thereby creating a phenomenon called cultural collision (Beachum & McCray, 2004). By critically examining and understanding youth culture, teachers can gain educational insight (i.e., how to tailor teaching strategies and arrange classroom management policies) and make significant connections with their students, which could help reduce many of the problems Black youth face in schools.

African American youth identity is unique and multi-faceted. Like all youths, it can be affected by a multitude of factors including parents, peers, music, school, television, religious influences, and life experiences (Harro, 2000). But for inner-city youth in particular, self-identity is a combination of unique complexities. These youth may face several critical issues such as socioeconomic despair, pressure from gangs, a lack of faith in institutions, and society's concentration on materialism and individualism (Berman & Berreth, 1997). Of the numerous influences and factors that shape youth identity, two sometimes conflicting factors,

Black youth popular culture (hip-hop culture and television) and school culture are of particular importance.

In this chapter, we will concentrate on the development of secondary school-aged urban youth (i.e., those in grades 7–12). The popular culture of urban Black youth will be examined by means of hip-hop culture and the media. Both of these variables have the awesome potential to shape youth identity. The American phenomenon known as hip-hop can affect youth in both positive and negative ways (Kunjufu, 1993). In a like manner, television too can exert a powerful influence over youth. The media has the power to alter the habits, feelings, and minds of young people, especially Black youth (Kunjufu, 1990), as will be discussed. This chapter was written to assist in the understanding of psychological and cultural/social forces on urban youth, with special emphasis on Black youth culture. This information is critically important for emerging teachers who will work with these impressionable young people.

## Notions of Contemporary America and Schools

If you work hard, can you really be "successful" in America? How much of your success is due to individual merit (your own efforts)? To what extent do structural barriers inhibit the life chances of certain groups in America? Are schools agents of change or do they perpetuate the inequalities found in American society? Though they may not seem so at first, these are complex questions, and of vital importance for educators and professionals who deal with diverse populations.

Why can't we readily identify oppression, inequity, and injustices? The answer might very well be that we are socialized into believing and acting out various roles as related to race, class, gender, ability, status, age, and social class (Harro, 2000). Tatum (1997) stated that this socialization process is similar to smog in the air; we all breathe it and are inevitably impacted. This "smog" is found in notions of meritocracy, individualism, and old-fashioned hard work. The cultural ethos of the United States is full of idealistic concepts such as the Protestant work ethic and the Horatio Alger myth (belief in the idea of going from rags to riches, as applied to everyone equally). Such ideas are ingrained into the psyches of nearly all Americans. Writing about pre-service educators, Villegas and Lucas (2002) asserted:

> They are insensitive to the fact that power is differentially distributed in society, with those who are affluent, white, and male having an advantage over those who are poor, of racial/ethnic minority groups, and female. They lack an understanding of institutional discrimination, including how routine practices in schools benefit young people from dominant groups while disadvantaging those from oppressed groups; and they have an unshakable faith that American society operates according to meritocratic principles and that existing inequalities in social outcomes are thereby justified. (p. 32)

Thus, pre-service educators must be willing to question deeply held beliefs and to challenge foundational assumptions. Of course, one might think, "I made it, why can't anyone else?" Villegas and Lucas responded, "Because the educational system has worked for them [pre-service teachers], they are not apt to question school practices, nor are they likely to doubt the criteria of merit applied in schools" (p. 31). The next factor in understanding how cultural collision operates is to realize how people are affected by the geographic isolation of many urban areas.

## The Urban Context and Popular Culture

For the purpose of this discussion, it is important to understand the significance of the urban context. Many urban areas across the nation are plagued with all types of social and community problems, and schools in these areas face challenges such as inadequate funding and teacher apathy. Neglect from external powers fuels the fire for the marginalizing and criticism of these schools (Ayers, 1994). The urban context clearly creates an environment that affects urban schools and the youth within them. "The situation in far too many schools is one of despair, poverty, isolation, and distress" (Obiakor & Beachum, 2005, p. 13). Noguera (2004) wrote, "In poor communities, the old, persistent problems of overcrowded classrooms, deteriorating facilities, and an insufficient supply of qualified teachers and administrators remain largely unaddressed" (p. 176). These are but some of the serious problems urban schools, and sometimes districts, encounter. Inevitably, the attitudes and behaviors of urban youth of color begin to reflect the structural inequities that have created their environments. Kozol (2006) traced the segregation, poverty, and inequity found in such schools in his book, *Shame of the Nation*. At the same time, these problems have resulted in the increasing pseudo-police state found in many urban areas and schools (Wacquant, 2001), as well as feelings of alienation (Rothstein, 1996; Yeo & Kanpol, 1999).

Black popular culture tends to originate from this urban context. According to Damen (1987), "Culture is learned and shared human patterns or models for living; day-to-day living patterns; those models and patterns pervade all aspects of human social interaction; and culture is mankind's primary adaptive mechanism" (p. 367). Black popular culture was born amidst "social, cultural, political, and economic segregation—initially as a vibrant expression of black political and cultural strivings" (Guy, 2004, p. 48).

Gause (2005) stated that "popular culture is the background noise of our very existence" (p. 336). When we consider the origin, expansion, and influence of "Urban America," we realize that its inhabitants are molded and shaped by history, experience, and social context. The global phenomenon known as hip-hop culture can be viewed as an expression of Black popular culture with its roots found in the plight and promise of the urban context.

### *Hip-Hop Culture*

Hip-hop culture has a great influence on American youth. Hip-hop culture is a broad term that encompasses rapping, dj-ing, danicng, langauge patterns, slang, fashion, graffiti and artistic expression, and attitude (Dyson 2001; Kitwana, 2002; White & Cones, 1999). In reference to its wider appeal, Kitwana (2002) asserted that, "Rappers access to global media and their use of popular culture to articulate many aspects of this national identity renders rap music central to any discussion of the new Black youth culture" (p. 11). This emphasis on media opens up rap artists to audio and visual media. McCall (1997) wrote:

> Dr. William Byrd, a black clinical psychologist, pointed out that for young, impressionable people the mere fact that explicit gangsta lyrics are aired on the radio lends credence to their messages as truth. 'When you bombard someone with those messages, it causes conflict, even with those young people who may have been taught other values. With these rap messages, not only are they being bombarded with radio, they also get video.' So it's what you hear and what you see. It confirms that these are acceptable values in a subculture. (p. 60)

Therefore, this "message bombardment" can be influential to impressionable youth. Kitwana (2002) agreed, "Today, more and more Black youth are turning to rap music, music videos, designer clothing, popular Black films, and television programs for values and identity" (p. 9).

Hip-hop culture has become an integral part of the lives of many urban youth. Through its influence, they develop various ideas about sex, relationships, success, and life (Kunjufu, 1993). These influences can have positive or negative effects on youth identity. Hip-hop culture is expressed through songs on the radio, glamorized by video, and reinforced by peers. The result is a particularly powerful form of infiltration and indoctrination. Again, this influence can be good or bad. Most of the controversy surrounding hip-hop culture has to do with its emphasis on male chauvinism, open gunplay, and illegal drug usage.

Much of the criticism revolves around a certain mode of hip-hop expression called gangsta rap. Gangsta rap usually refers to a style of rap that emphasizes drug selling, hyper-macho posturing, disrespect for authority, the use of violence to settle disputes and gain respect, and negative attitudes towards women (Guy, 2004; Kunjufu, 1993; White & Cones, 1999). In reference to this form of rap, Dyson (1997) wrote:

> The gangsta rap genre of hip-hop emerged in the late '80s on the West Coast as crack and gangs ruled the urban centers of Los Angeles, Long Beach, Compton, and Oakland. Since hip-hop has long turned to the black ghetto and the Latino barrio for lyrical inspiration, it was inevitable that a form of music that mimicked the violence on the streets would rise. (p. 113)

In recent years, the label gangsta rap has seemed to apply less to the contemporary forms of hip-hop displayed in popular culture. Today, much of the music incorporates strands of hip-hop along with other themes, making it into an eclectic combination of macho-posturing, misogyny, violence, and materialism. Thus, gangsta rap is less identified as a societal pariah of previous years, but is now a common part of "normalized" hip-hop culture. Hip-hop culture affects the values of Black youth through various media, television being the most significant.

## Television Media

The American media are a source of news, entertainment, and information that include radio, newspapers, the Internet, and television, to name a few. For our purposes, the authors will concentrate on the media as represented by television. The media have the ability to spread truthful and positive knowledge or to misrepresent people, events, and data. Unfortunately, the latter is often the case. Moreover, television is responsible for imagery that negatively influences youth and can affect youth identity (Bush, 1999).

Television is an important part of life to many Americans. Black youth, in particular, watch seven to eight hours of television a day, as compared to four and a half hours for white youth (Browder, 1989). Bush (1999) noted that "negative images presented in all of the media conspire with many hours of television viewing to produce a negative effect on Black children's self-image" (p. 36). In reference to Black youth and television, Browder (1989) observed the following:

- Black children tend to use TV as a source of role models. They imitate other people's behavior, dress, appearance, and speech.
- TV provides examples of relationships with members of the opposite sex.
- TV is used as a primary source of learning and perfecting aggressive behavior.
- Black children closely identify with television characters—particularly the Black characters. (p. 47)

Given the amount of television watched by Black youth and its influence on their development, the images portrayed by the television media become extremely important.

Television many times promotes gender stereotypes and negative images of Blacks. A study conducted by Patricia D. Mamay and Richard L. Simpson (as cited in Bush, 1999) concluded that "women in commercials were typecast according to three stereotypical roles: mother, housekeeper, and sexual objects" (pp. 35–36). This research indicates that television has the ability to affect the way people view gender roles.

In addition to its role in shaping gender stereotypes, the television media also influence many youth towards violence. For instance, a 14-year-old Black male was sentenced to life in prison for the murder of a 6-year-old girl; he had been imitating pro wrestling moves he watched on television (Ripley, 2001). Today's Black youth are many times criticized and labeled as violent or rebellious (Dyson, 1997; Kitwana, 2002). Though violent acts are sometimes perpetrated, Wilson (1990) asserted, "Deeds of violence in our society are performed largely by those trying to establish their self-esteem, to defend their self-image, or to demonstrate that they too are significant" (p. 54). This is not to excuse individuals for violent behavior, but it does provide helpful insight into fundamental (or other) influences that impact behavior. Moreover, the television media promote a value system based on materialism and immediate gratification (Kunjufu, 1990). Enticed by these values, too many youths resort to violence. Thus, television exposure to negative imagery could possibly encourage an inner-adversarial conflict of self-identity.

## Identity Theory and Black Youth

Black youth who are matriculating through middle and high school deal with a considerable amount of transition. The transitions are related to grade levels, geographic location of schools, maturation, and identity development (to name a few). Considering the latter, young adults share a certain amount of curiosity, exploration, and discovery with regard to the development of identity (Tatum, 1997). However, Black youth in particular begin to examine their own ethnic/racial identities even more than their White counterparts (Negy et al., 2003). Tatum (1997) posited that "Given the impact of dominant and subordinate status, it is not surprising that researchers have found that adolescents of color are more likely to be actively engaged in an exploration of their racial or ethnic identity than are White adolescents" (p. 53). It is in this state of heightened identity awareness that salient and unconscious messages and imagery can influence ideas and values. Black youth are also more sensitized to society's view of them with regard to race. "Our self-perceptions are shaped by the messages that we receive from those around us, and when young Black men and women enter adolescence, the racial content of those messages intensifies" (Tatum, 1997, p. 54). Hence, identity development for Black youth is complicated by notions of race/ethnicity more than for their White peers, making adolescence a time of complexity and vulnerability. This situation creates the need for direction and guidance from influential individuals and institutions, one of which is the school.

## School Culture

The school itself can have a major impact on the development of students. During school, students are afforded opportunities for academic, emotional, and social growth. Students interact with teachers and administrators within the educational environment that is founded upon certain values. Academics, opportunities for growth, different types of interaction, and value systems all play a role in a school's culture; school culture also shapes student identity.

A school is commonly defined as a place of teaching and learning. The culture of an organization is the set of values and beliefs of the organization, and these values and beliefs are normally shared with the majority of people in the organization (Cunningham & Cordeiro, 2006; Fullan, 2004; Karpicke & Murphy, 1996). Thus, school culture is the shared value system of a given school. Specifically, school culture involves certain components. According to Pawlas (1997), "The key components of a strong effective school culture include shared values, humor, storytelling, empowerment, a communication system for spreading information, rituals and ceremonies, and collegiality" (p. 119). School culture is important to all who are involved with the school.

The school culture can affect student identity. Banks (2001) noted that

> the school culture communicates to students the school's attitudes toward a range of issues and problems, including how the school views them as human beings and its attitudes toward males, females, exceptional students, and students from various religious, cultural, racial, and ethnic groups. (p. 24)

When the school's culture is characterized by value disagreement, lack of communication, and little collegiality among teachers and students, many students see themselves as incapable, incompetent, and worthless. However, when an environment promotes a school-wide value system, good communication, collegiality, and the utilization of ceremonies, students' attitudes are much more positive. Karpicke and Murphy (1996) agreed that a healthy school culture has a great impact on the success of students.

Taking all of this into account, we find that those teachers who are interested in changing a culture must first try to understand the existing culture. To do this, teachers would have to begin by understanding the various cultures that come to the schoolhouse on a daily basis, before attempting to impose another culture.

## Intersection of School Culture and Black Popular Culture

Certain negative values as dictated by hip-hop culture and media influence many times conflict with the values of the school. Kunjufu (1990) noted that gangs and negative media promote immediate gratification and materialism, while many parents and teachers promote long-term gratification and qualities such as moral integrity and honesty. Kunjufu (1993) also stated that there is a concern about some hip-hop artists' misogynistic and violent messages. In effect, students obtain certain values from this segment of hip-hop culture and television media and then bring those values to the school. As a result, there is a conflict of value systems, which sometimes results in discipline problems and a lack of communication between students and educators. In addition, peers can have a great influence on each other, even more so than the influence of adults (Kunjufu, 1990). Thus, negative or unhealthy values can become pervasive because of the influence of peer communication and pressure. Furthermore, Black youth spend much more time with peers listening to music and watching television than they do having meaningful conversations with teachers and parents (Bush, 1999; Kitwana, 2002; Kunjufu, 1994). The task for educators, therefore, is to familiarize themselves with youth culture/value systems and realize the subsequent effect on youth identity.

Hip-hop culture has undergone tremendous growth as an artistic form of expression and fashion, as well as a money-making venture. Many have advocated censorship in order to curtail the negative influence of rap music. However, censorship may not be an appropriate or realistic response; for it sends the message that artistic expression can be stifled by those who simply disagree. But what are we to make of the violent themes readily found in hip-hop culture? In response to the overemphasis on violence in hip-hop, Dyson (2005) explained,

> Hip-hop has been nailed for casting glamour on thuggish behavior and for heartlessly painting violent portraits of urban life. It's all true, but still, the whole truth of hip-hop as art form and, because of generational lag, as agitator of adults, must not be overlooked.…At its best, hip-hop summons the richest response in the younger generation to questions of identity and suffering. (p. 115)

Dyson (1996) wrote, "While these young black males become whipping boys for sexism and misogyny, the places in our culture where these ancient traditions are nurtured and rationalized—including religious and educational institutions and the nuclear family—remain immune to forceful and just criticism" (p. 186). Therefore, a certain amount of responsibility must be placed on parents, guardians, and school officials. In effect, parents and educators should take a greater role in involving themselves in the lives of these youth. One must remember that hip-hop culture has a business aspect and the supply will meet the demand. What would happen if the consumers demanded more positive images?

The media also have to be held accountable for their negative imagery. If not, then youth identity remains imperiled. Chideya (1995) wrote, "In the final analysis, it's up to the reader and viewers to keep the media honest…pointing out times that the media has [sic] misrepresented the African-American community can only make the community better. The media belongs [sic] to all of us. If we want it to work, we have to work" (p. 11).

### *Implications for Educators*

In summary, there are many factors that influence the identities of urban Black youth. Hip-hop culture, television media, and school culture do have a serious impact on this particular group. At the heart of this analysis is the creation of a healthy and positive value system. Consequently, those students who develop a strong value system have less chance of being affected by negative aspects of hip-hop culture and misrepresentation in television media, and more of a chance to be influenced by the "positivity" exemplified in a healthy school culture.

Educators have a critical role to play in students' academic and social development. First, they must recognize the inherent inequities within our society and how they impact people, especially those in urban areas. Second, it is important they realize how cultural collision plays out in our schools. By acknowledging the background experiences of urban students, which includes their cultural expressions, educators can gain insight into addressing student behavior, communication, and values. Lastly, Milner (2006) proposed some questions for educators to consider as they begin to self-examine, referring to such self-examination as *relational reflection*. The questions are as follows: "(1) Why do I believe what I believe? (2) How do my thoughts and beliefs influence my curriculum and teaching [managing and disciplining] of students of color? and (3) What do I need to change in order to better meet the needs of all my students?" (p. 84). Serious attention to these issues and questions can cultivate greater understanding, thereby helping educators to be more effective.

Educators engage students in a mutual process of liberation for completeness: "Completeness for the oppressed begins with liberation. Until liberation is achieved, individuals are fragmented in search of clarity, understanding, and emancipation. This liberation is not outside of us or created or accomplished through some external force. Rather, it begins with a change in thinking" (p. 85). The essence of this "education for liberation" is a change in thinking for educators, causing them to realize their own power with students and their potential in society.

Due to the increasing amount of cultural and social diversity in our schools, educators must embrace some degree of cultural pluralism as they find the right balance that promotes a healthy school climate (Villegas & Lucas, 2002). There should be a willingness and effort among educators to structure the school culture to ensure that individuals of diverse backgrounds are well-positioned to achieve, regardless of their predispositions in life. A school culture structured in a pluralistic manner can foster self-efficacy and self-determination in students who, as a result, may bring conflicting values from their environment (Banks, 1995). Thus, Banks (2001) insisted that"The culture and organization of the school must be examined by all members of the school staff…in order to create a school culture that empowers students from diverse racial and ethnic groups" (p. 22). This is extremely important because it helps to ensure that students are not being labeled incorrectly and are not subjugated because of inadequate cultural capital. Therefore, it is important for educators to help such students develop the kinds of value systems that encourage positive self-identities, and to give them the legitimate opportunity to become successful in school, as well as in life.

## Note

This chapter is a reprint from:
Beachum, F. D., & McCray, C. R. (2008). Dealing with cultural collision: What pre-service educators should know. In G. Goodman (Ed.), *Educational psychology: An application of critical constructivism* (pp. 53–70). New York: Peter Lang Publishing.

## References


Ayers, W. (1994). Can city schools be saved? *Educational Leadership, 51*(8), 60–63.

Banks, J. A. (1995). Multicultural education: Development, dimensions, and challenges. In J. Joll (Ed.), *Taking sides: Clashing views on controversial education issues* (pp. 84–93). New York: The Dushkin Publishing Group, Inc.

Banks, J. A. (2001). Multicultural education: Characteristics and goals. In J. A. Banks & C. A. McGee Banks (Eds.), *Multicultural education: Issues and perspectives* (4th ed.) (pp. 3–30). New York: John Wiley & Sons, Inc.

Beachum, F. D., & McCray, C. R. (2004). Cultural collision in urban schools. *Current Issues in Education, 7*(5). Available: http://cie.asu.edu/volume7/number5/

Berman, S., & Berreth, D. (1997). The moral dimensions of schools. *Educational Leadership, 54*(8), 24–27.

Browder, A. (1989). *From the Browder file: 22 essays of the African American experience*. Washington, DC: The Institute of Karmic Guidance.

Bush, L. (1999). *Can Black mothers raise our sons?* Chicago: African American Images.

Chideya, F. (1995). *Don't believe the hype: Fighting cultural misinformation about African-Americans.* New York: Penguin Books.

Cosby, B., & Poussaint, A. F. (2007). *Come on people: On the path from victims to victors.* Nashville: Thomas Nelson.

Cox, T. H. (1994). *Cultural diversity in organizations: Theory research and practice.* San Francisco: Berrett-Koehler Publishers.

Cox, T., Jr. (2001). *Creating the multicultural organization: A strategy for capturing the power of diversity.* San Francisco: Jossey-Bass.

Cunningham, W. G., & Cordeiro, P. A. (2006). *Educational leadership: A problem-based approach* (3rd ed.). Boston: Allyn and Bacon.

Damen, L. (1987). *Culture learning: The fifth dimension on the language classroom.* Reading, MA: Addison-Wesley.

Dantley, M. (2002). Uprooting and replacing positivism, the melting pot, multiculturalism, and Dyson, M. E. (1996). *Between God and gangsta rap: Bearing witness to black culture.* New York: Oxford University Press.

Dyson, M. E. (1997). *Race rules: Navigating the color line.* New York: Vintage Books.

Dyson, M. E. (2001). *Holler if you hear me: Searching for Tupac Shakur.* New York: Basic Books.

Dyson, M. E. (2005). *Is Bill Cosby right? Or has the Black middle class lost its mind?* New York: Basic Civitas Books.

Fullan, M. (2004). *Leading in a culture of change: Personal action guide and workbook.* San Francisco: Jossey-Bass.

Gause, C. P. (2005). Navigating the stormy seas: Critical perspectives on the intersection of popular culture and educational leader-"ship." *Journal of School Leadership, 15*(3), 333–345.

Guy, T. C. (2004). Gangsta rap and adult education. *New Directions for Adult and Continuing Education, 101*, 43–57.

Haberman, M. (2005). Personnel preparation and urban schools. In F. E. Obiakor & F. D. Beachum (Eds.). *Urban education for the 21st century: Research issues and perspectives.* Springfield, Ill: Charles C. Thomas Publishers, LTD.
Harro, B. (2000). The cycle of socialization. In M. Adams, W. J. Blumenfield, R. Castaneda, H. W. Hackman, M. L. Peters, & X. Zuniga (Eds.), *Reading for diversity and social justice: An anthology on racism, anti-Semitism, sexism, heterosexism, ableism, classism* (pp. 79–82). New York: Routledge.
Irvine, J. J. (2003). *Educating teachers for diversity: Seeing with a cultural eye.* New York: Teachers College Press.
Karpicke, H. & Murphy, M. E. (1996). Productive school culture: Principals working from the inside. *National Association of Secondary School Principals, 80,* 26–32.
Kitwana, B. (2002). *The hip-hop generation: Young blacks and the crisis in African American culture.* New York: Basic Civitas Books.
Kozol, J. (2006). *The shame of the nation: The restoration of apartheid schooling in America.* New York: Crown Publishers.
Kunjufu, J. (1990). *Countering the conspiracy to destroy black boys* (vol. III). Chicago: African American Images.
Kunjufu, J. (1993). *Hip-hop vs. MAAT: A psycho/social analysis of values.* Chicago: African American Images.
Kunjufu, J. (1994). *Countering the conspiracy to destroy black boys* (vol. IV). Chicago: African American Images.
Kunjufu, J. (2002). *Black students—Middle class teachers.* Chicago: African American Images.
Landsman, J., & Lewis, C. W. (Eds.). (2006). *White teachers/diverse classrooms: A guide to building inclusive schools, promoting high expectations, and eliminating racism.* Sterling, VA: Stylus.
McCall, N. (1997). *What's going on.* New York: Random House.
Milner, H. R. (2006). But good intentions are not enough: Theoretical and philosophical relevance in teaching students of color. In J. Landsman & C. W. Lewis (Eds.), *White teachers/diverse classrooms: A guide to building inclusive schools, promoting high expectations, and eliminating racism* (pp. 79–90). Sterling, VA: Stylus.
Negy, C., Shreve, T. L. Jensen, B. J., & Uddin, N. (2003). Ethnic identity, self-esteem, and ethnocentrism: A study of social identity versus multicultural theory of development. *Cultural Diversity and Mental Health, 9*(4), 333–334.
Obiakor, F. E., & Beachum, F. D. (2005). Urban education: The quest for democracy, equity, and excellence. In F. E. Obiakor & F. D. Beachum (Eds.), *Urban education for the 21st century: Research, issues, and perspectives* (pp. 3–19). Springfield, IL: Charles C. Thomas.
Pawlas, G. E. (1997). Vision and school culture. *National Association of Secondary School Principals, 81*(587), 118–120.
Ripley, A. (2001). Throwing the book at kids. *Time, 157* (11), 34.
Rothstein, S. W. (1996). *Schools and society: New perspectives in American education.* Englewood Cliffs, NJ: Prentice Hall.
Smith, R., & Sapp, M. (2005). Insights into educational psychology: What urban school practitioners must know. In F. E. Obiakor & F. D. Beachum (Eds.), *Urban education for the 21st century: Research, issues, and perspectives* (pp. 100–113). Springfield, IL: Charles C. Thomas.
Tatum, B. D. (1997). Why are all the Black kids sitting together in the cafeteria?: And other conversations about race. New York: Basic Books.
Villegas, A. M., & Lucas, T. (2002). Educating culturally responsive teachers: A coherent approach. Albany, NY: State University of New York Press.
Wacquant, L. (2001). Deadly symbiosis: When ghetto and prison meet and mesh. *Punishment and Society, 3*(1), 95–134.
White, J. L. & Cones, J. H., III (1999). *Black man emerging: Facing the past and seizing a future in America.* New York: W. H. Freeman and Company.
Wilson, A. (1990). *Black on black violence.* New York: African World Info Systems.

Yeo, F., & Kanpol, B. (1999). Introduction: Our own "Peculiar Institution": Urban education in 20th-century America. In F. Yeo & B. Kanpol (Eds.), *From nihilism to possibility: Democratic transformations for the inner city* (pp. 1–14). Cresskill, NJ: Hampton Press, Inc.

# How Do You, How Do I

How do you
Just say no
When your daddy's holding down a corner
And your brother's blunted eating down the kitchen

How do you
Share family stories in school
When daddy's doing hard time
And momma's a junkie

How do you
Practice abstinence
When your uncle visits every night
Talkin' 'bout he likes his girls tight

How do you
Do as they ask
And turn the other cheek
When you know that on your street
There's no place for the meek

How do you
Abandon the ghetto
When you fear it's all
You'll ever know
How do you
Focus on trigonometry
When you worry that the idiot down the street
Is just trigger happy

How do you **not**
Take your fears
And frustrations out on your teachers
When they are the only ones who can't
**Make you**
Sit down,
Shut up
And pay attention
How do I
Reach you
Teach you
Help you keep hope alive…

|| NINE

# How Do We Locate Resistance In Urban Schools?

Luis F. Mirón

Like most institutions funded with taxpayer monies, public schools must honor the laws of the country. Beginning with passage of the Civil Rights Act of 1964, discrimination because of race, ethnicity, gender, sexuality, or religion has become forbidden. For example, it is against the law for any public school or university to deny admission to immigrants (legal or illegal) because of their noncitizen status. However, many building administrators and classroom teachers believe that if they follow the guidelines of federal laws, their schools will be protected from discrimination, racism, and prejudice. Educators assume that by following the letter of the law, the spirit of the law will be honored and respected. Research and knowledge of professional practice tell us differently. More precisely dejure desegregation is equated with educational equality.

Desegregation of Little Rock, Arkansas, public schools after the passage of the historic *Brown v. Board of Education* decision unleashed nearly a half century of externally generated reforms of urban public schools. Today public schools are situated differently as the global political economy, and the worldwide concentration of capital in particular, has caused a host of demographic and other pressures on urban schools (see Lipman, 2002). Urban schools are now resegregated, and notoriously underfunded in comparison with their more affluent suburban counterparts. Furthermore, they are perhaps somewhat academically weakened owing in part to the influx of immigrant populations who arrive at school with limited English, low family incomes, and a lack of cultural support for learning. This context is similar to the historical circumstances of inner-city schools serving poor students of color; however, I want to argue that the pressures are exacerbated with waves of immigration from Mexico and Latin America as well as the heavy-handed role of the state in exacting academic standards.

Between 1993 and 1998, I conducted a qualitative study of four public inner-city high schools enrolling large percentages of students from ethnic and language minority groups in New Orleans. The study consisted of approximately 50 interviews with students lasting between 30 and 90 minutes (Mirón, 1996; Lauria & Mirón, 2003). In these interviews I sought to ascertain the extent to which students from similar socioeconomic backgrounds and varying school cultures (magnet vs. neighborhood) and with different levels of academic success (A's and B's vs. C's and D's) expressed widespread "resistance" to both the formal and the hidden curriculum and to pedagogical practices.

Drawing upon this research, I will attempt to answer the question, How do students resist in urban schools? In addition I summarize important demographic data on educational inequality in Chicago to provide a comparative glimpse of substantial contextual issues found in the majority of urban schools and districts nationwide. I begin by addressing the uniqueness of the urban school "problem."

## Are Urban Schools Different?

Inner-city schools are different. Lipman (2002, pp. 385-389) paints a rich picture of public education in Chicago, the "dual city." As Chicago strives to become a "global city" like Los Angeles and New York, academic and social inequalities have deepened. Lipman cites the often noted economic shift in the United States from a manufacturing to a service and knowledge base. As a result, the country has experienced a "highly segmented and increasingly polarized labor force." Lipman states that service jobs, for instance, are highly segmented by wage/salary levels, education, and benefits. Growth in highly skilled technical, professional, and managerial jobs at the high end are dominated by white males, while an abundance of low-end, low-skilled jobs are held mostly by women and people of color.

In addition, Lipman notes the widespread expansion of contingent, provisional labor: multitask, part-time, and temporary work performed mainly by women, workers of color, and immigrants who often hold down two, three, and even four jobs to make ends meet. A quickly growing informal economy employs primarily immigrant and women workers who provide specialized consumer goods and services for the well-to-do (designer clothing and live-in child care) and cheap goods and services for poor or lower-income households (e.g., unlicensed day care). He claims that there is little opportunity for gainful employment in the formal economy for large sectors of the population, specifically African American and Latino youth.

Paradoxically, as the global economy grows and capitalism intensifies, economic and social inequalities widen. For instance, the overwhelming majority of new jobs pay lower wages and offer less protection (heath insurance, pensions). Between 1973 and 1995 real average weekly wages for production and nonsupervisory workers decreased from approximately $480 to $395. More dramatically, the wealthiest 1 percent of households increased their wealth by 28 percent from 1983 to 1992, while the bottom 40 percent saw their income decrease by nearly 50 percent.

Like most "global cities," Chicago has experienced widening inequalities that are mirrored in geography. These social and economic inequalities, moreover, are vividly illustrated in the move to gentrify old neighborhoods with expensive upscale housing and restaurants, high-tech employment, and (central to our goals here) academically achieving public schools. (Although the site of my research [see Lauria & Mirón, 2003] is not a "global city," it too is not immune to the processes and effects of globalization.) These escalating inequalities linked to the worldwide consolidation of capital have been well documented. I argue that it is the intensification of educational inequality, on a meta level, that inner-city high school students most resist and resent. The processes of globalization deny them access to a quality education and thus the possibility of social mobility.

### *How does the global economy produce educational inequality?*

Using secondary sources, Lipman (2002) documents the economic shift in Chicago from manufacturing to service/information employment. From 1967 to 1990, the number of jobs in manufacturing fell an astounding 41 percent, from a total of 546,500 to 216,190. In comparison, nonmanufacturing jobs rose by an equally impressive 59 percent, from 797,867 to 983,580. Most significantly, as the *Chicago Tribune* reported in 1999, the trend saw manufacturing employment with average salaries of $37,000 being replaced by service jobs whose wages paid only $26,000. Since 23 percent of workers in the city belong to a union, the impact on the working class has been even more severe, often resulting in the loss of health insurance and retirement benefits. This economic transformation led to what Lipman refers to as the "production of educational inequality."

In brief, the efforts of two generations of rule by the Daleys (Richard Daley Jr. was recently reelected to a third term) have resulted in the marketing of Chicago as a "world class" city that attracts businesses in the new knowledge economy. In order to "sell" the city to affluent and well-educated professionals who will staff the kinds of firms the city covets, Chicago has embarked on the most ambitious urban school reform agenda in the nation. This reform agenda, moreover, has created a system of high-stakes testing and accountability, college preparatory "magnet schools" as well as remedial high schools, and a pedagogical culture that rewards achievement on standardized tests. For example, in some of the schools in Lipman's study, nearly two months of the academic year were spent in preparation for tests, complete with cheerleading and pep (or prep?) rallies. These everyday practices are being reproduced in urban school districts besieged by underachievement all over the country.

## The New Orleans Experience: From Political Resistance to Political Agency

Unlike previous scholarly notions of resistance, the concept demonstrated in my work extends beyond mere moments in time or simple expressions of acting out. Resistance involves a discourse practice that is an expression of human agency. This expression may take the form of political agency. The question that ensues is, How can human agency become transformed into political agency? In this section I would like to outline a new conception of how a return to the political may develop. But first I need to sketch in broad strokes the conceptual (sociological) underpinnings of this move.

### *Social Structures*

Sociologists have long indicated that social structures serve a dual function. At their heart is an understanding that they exist interactively with human agents. Social structures both (1) constrain the actions that agents can perform and (2) provide the space to act. This includes political (collective) actions. For example, social structures are neither organic, self-regulating systems nor freewheeling spaces where agents can roam without rules. The point is that structures are products of history—people acting in behalf of their beliefs—and, once constructed, tend to re-create themselves time and time again. So: where do resistance and political agency come into play within this conception?

More likely to employ passive resistance, inner-city students in particular seem to lack the capacity to exercise political agency. Subjected in many instances to a prescripted curriculum and pedagogy, they lack cultural and historical knowledge of their social situation, their "situatedness." For example, many students I interviewed in the neighborhood high schools in New Orleans were unaware of how construction of interstate highways through the city in the 1950s devastated local communities and residential neighborhoods. People and families were displaced. On the other hand, inner-city students from approximately the same socioeconomic backgrounds enrolled in magnet schools were treated to a rich curriculum emphasizing cultural diversity, oral history, and writing programs that placed students at the center of pedagogy. Therefore, given a curriculum and instructional practices that ignore students' lived cultural experiences and history, political agency is almost nil. Social reproduction happens. Students do, however, resist these structures. I argue that this form of resistance largely results in high school students disengaging from school, often dropping out or, as the data indicate below, accommodating to teachers' busywork. Though these forms of resistance may seem similar on the surface, we should bear in mind that a strategy of accommodation leading to leaving school versus remaining in school—and choosing to graduate—obviously has different outcomes and should be kept analytically separate.

Inner-city students armed with culturally relevant knowledge and coming out of a school culture that places a premium on racial/ethnic pride are more free to act. They possess the capacity to exercise political agency, which means that in cities like Chicago and New Orleans, they can petition local school boards to establish schools such as Roberto Clemente High School, serving Puerto Rican students in Chicago, and programs like "Students at the Center" at McDonough #35 magnet high school in New Orleans, a writing program built on oral history and creative arts. Such students learn to view inner-city high schools as vehicles for local community development and lobby the school board to enact these curricular models in other high schools as antidotes to dropping out of school or, worse, incarceration.

It was not unreasonable to predict such intense student resistance, because the setting of our study—an urban center beset by economic restructuring and a sagging tourist economy—left high school graduates few prospects for employment besides working in fast-food restaurants or busing tables in one of the area's numerous upscale eateries. In short, high school students had few viable career options and thus little incentive to do well in school. Surprisingly, what my colleagues and I found was that all the students we interviewed were highly motivated to graduate from high school—many of them aspired to attend college. There was, indeed, student resistance; however, the forms of student resistance varied to a certain degree by the form of school organization and culture. At times, forms of resistance converged. In general, student resistance in this urban center characterized at the time by widespread poverty, illiteracy, and violent crime was directly tied to students' perceptions of their teachers' academic expectations and everyday practices of racial stereotyping.

For instance, African American high school students in particular often complained that teachers believed that all Asian American students (e.g., upper-class Vietnamese) were intelligent and highly motivated and enjoyed strong family support for learning. By contrast, African Americans (especially males) were seen as mostly hoodlums and disinterested in learning. Moreover, some of these students complained that the principals shut down student assemblies and cultural activities. In hopes of curbing actual and perceived student violence, school administrators disbanded clubs and organizations. On the other hand, students enrolled in college preparatory magnet schools (see Lauria & Mirón, 2003; Mirón, 1996) took pride in the caring school atmosphere, the challenging curriculum, and rich extracurricular opportunities. I call this pedagogical phenomenon *academic discrimination.* Furthermore, the kinds of student resistance I will disclose below are based on high school students' relationship to this form of discrimination and institutional racism, especially their perceived capacity for human agency, expressions of student voice, and their own representations of racial/ethnic identities.

### *Prototypes of Student Resistance*

Based on the student interview data, students manifested two broad strategies of resistance: accommodation and mobilization. These strategies of resistance, moreover, were direct responses to students' relationship to the formal and hidden curricula. As we gleaned from the ethnographic interviews, their overall goal in both of these kinds of strategies of resistance was to secure their right to a quality education (Mirón & Lauria, 1998, p. 191).

What is most striking is that, like the Chicago school reform summarized above, school cultures matter. In magnet schools in New Orleans, generally characterized by an emphasis on "diversity," the curriculum differed sharply from that of the neighborhood public schools. In the magnet schools, we found a culturally relevant curriculum and a sense of racial/ethnic pride. On the other hand, students in neighborhood schools were seemingly denied a quality education owing primarily to a curriculum that emphasized busywork and a lack of student voice. The intensity of student resistance, moreover, as will be disclosed below, largely depended on the type of school organization and corresponding everyday lived culture. Urban students' capacity for agency—the ability to act on perceived alternatives—closely paralled the form of resistance.

### *Accommodation*

For students at the magnet schools, accommodation meant being fully engaged in the rich formal curriculum, a sense of racial/ethnic pride, and a broad array of student activities. These students perceived the school-based activities as connecting them to the wider society by providing them with practical social skills as well as instruction in global affairs. In other words, their teachers made explicit connections between local context and the processes of globalization. Furthermore, teachers, administrators, and counselors fostered student voice, in the process "authorizing" students to have a role in curriculum policy and engaging them in the mission and cultural traditions of magnet schools. Students perceived that these connections protected them from the callousness of the outside world, a societal attitude that reduced African American males in particular to a nameless statistic.

By contrast, the widespread curtailment of student assemblies, organizations, and clubs obviously hindered student voice at the neighborhood secondary schools. There, a school climate existed that systematically disengaged students from the curriculum and from the broader school culture more generally. Some of these students enrolled in neighborhood schools employed a form of passive resistance, telling the interviewers that they "did what they had to do to get by." These students were not "silenced" and they were obviously not pushed out of school, as they maintained passing averages by the end of the year. Following Anthony Giddens' theory of structuration, I want to argue that these students were not merely passive victims. Just the reverse was true: They made the decision to remain in school and graduate, thus at least securing the possibility, however limited, that they could improve their life chances.

### *Mobilization*

All of the students we interviewed made an important strategic decision: to remain in high school. I say that this was a *decision* because, at least in the neighborhood schools, there were keen pressures to disengage stemming from the low expectations of teachers, peers, and administrators. As I stated earlier, as researchers we tacitly bought into lowered expectations when we believed students would show evidence of giving up on school for economic reasons. Just the reverse turned out to be true. I argue that this decision represents a kind of human agency. At times this converts into political agency.

Deciding to remain in inner-city public high schools, despite a weak economy, constitutes a discourse practice. Most of the neighborhood students would voice this discourse as an "antagonism" expressed to the researchers. There was little opportunity to organize collectively, as leadership practices astutely separated students from one another, in effect enacting an extreme psychological paradigm of learning. Other students, however, mobilized in behalf of their civil rights, which they perceived entitled them to access to a quality education. In other words, they formed strategic alliances with parents, school board members, and community leaders to make their demands heard on behalf of educational justice. Many of these students told us again and again: "The teacher can't take away my grades. If she does, I will tell my mama. And if my mama can't change my teacher's mind, she will take it all the way to the school board if she has to." This mobilization was grounded in a collective ideology among African Americans in New Orleans in particular that their parents and community struggles for civil and human rights during the civil rights movement of the 1950s and 60s left them with a near moral obligation to succeed academically and give something back to their local communities. At one of the magnet schools, students frequently told us, "You must remember where you came from," and, "Our teachers remind us to stand on the shoulders of those who came before us." Resistance here was clearly tied to a sense of racial/ethnic pride, respect for elders, and a collective recognition that white society was a common "enemy."

The following narratives of student resistance illustrate the prototypical forms of resistance, which at once support the capacity for political agency and vividly demonstrate how the structures of inner-city schools constrain agency. The narratives are organized by actual interview questions posed to high school students in New Orleans.

### *1. What is everyday life like as a student in your school?*

The first question in the interview protocol of this five-year ethnographic case study asked inner-city secondary students to describe what it was like to be a student in their school. Stark differences existed between the organizational cultures of magnet vs. neighborhood high schools. Yet these differences blurred a bit as we documented how students resisted. At the neighborhood public schools, students often complained of boredom with class activities. Furthermore, the administrative practice of curtailing student assemblies ("shutdown") exacerbated boredom and isolation.

The research uncovered an unexpected finding. When we coded the interview transcripts of nearly 1000 pages, these emotions, coupled with an apparent distrust of students by their teachers in regard to completion of homework assignments, related to the conditions of violent crime, both at school and in the local community. This is ironic given the strong regulation of student behavior. Naturally students resisted these practices and social conditions, yet the form of this resistance was voiced in accommodationist terms. As the administration in the neighborhood schools moved to shut down student assemblies, and therefore preempted student voice, the students seemed to get angrier. This may have exacerbated the conditions for violent crime, an ironic unintended consequence.

> The curriculum and everything else here is way below. I used to have a 3.9 average and [at my old school] they used to motivate us better than back here. Like the teachers here really don't teach. If you get it, you get it. If you don't, you don't. Well you didn't bring up anything about violence. One week we had four fights in one day.
>
> I think the African American students are treated fairly by the administration. I mean that if they do something wrong, then they will just have to suffer the consequences. African American students treat Asian American students very differently. I mean they would make fun of them because of the language that they use. I say there is no need to do that because if you came from another country and you couldn't speak fluent English either, you wouldn't want anybody doing that to you.

There were stark contrasts at the magnet high schools. The interviewers recorded few negative comments about what it was like to be a student in this kind of urban high school. More typical was this statement:

> It's fun, exciting. You get involved with a lot of community activities. . . . Especially being a black male like myself, you get a lot of prestige and a lot of pushing from your teachers and the principal. And I really enjoy that, especially from the principal. It's just a sort of love here—and it really helps a lot of children.

### 2. *What is schoolwork like?*

Since we found the curriculum to be much richer at the magnet schools, and the pedagogy more tuned in to community concerns as well as global affairs, I will underscore this type of school:

> To be a student here, it's a lot of hard work, but after you get the hang of it, you know it's fairly easy if you do all of your work. You have to study, and once you study and catch up and you know the work, then you can go ahead of the rest of the students. Then it would be easier for you. The teacher explains it, and then you already know it.
>
> I try very hard because at my school there are a lot of people who make very good grades—and you want to be just like those people. I find myself up some nights until 3 or 4 in the morning just studying, you know, working the material in my head.

At the magnet schools, academic work implied an application of the competitive work ethic to students' studies in order to become successful. Students appeared to learn collaboratively from and to model themselves after other students (some of whom attended the same school), and to compete with students in their ethnic group for top honors.

By contrast, students at the neighborhood high schools tended not to push themselves as much. They often told us that they "did what they had to do to get by" and to graduate. Apparently they strategically chose not to do more. Some of the students actually blamed the teachers for holding low expectations, which did not require them to work harder or learn anything of substance. They frequently complained of busywork. We gleaned from these admonishments that students at these schools do in fact desire to compete academically.

On the one hand, students at the neighborhood high schools resisted: In our interviews with them, they expressed antagonisms because they perceived that they were unjustly denied a quality education. But their resistance took the form of an accommodation to the wishes of their classroom teachers, who appeared to engage in an implicit (hidden) social contract of controlling students by holding out the carrot of a passing grade, and eventually a high school diploma. More precisely, this form of student resistance was tied to students' notion of agency by accepting the quid pro quo of paying attention, completing seat assignments, and especially not challenging the teacher's authority, in order to just get out of there. This strategy guaranteed them, in their minds, the prerequisite of completing high school, as the first step in the long pursuit of a middle-class life.

### 3. *With whom do you identify?*

In trying to understand students' behaviors and relationships at school, at home, and in their neighborhoods, we asked them if they changed behavior in each of these social environments. We wanted to know whether they were able to move comfortably among "multiple identities" that were located in different discourses, for example, between studiousness and being focused in school and clowning around and hanging out at home and in the neighborhood. Could students from the magnet schools, for instance, keep discursively separate who they were at school from the peer pressures of the street? The most interesting finding was that 38 percent of all students—from both types of school—felt alienated from their neighborhood (had no friends, were fearful), whereas another 38 percent felt comfortable.

These results varied inversely between the two types of school organization. Among students at the magnet schools, 58 percent felt alienated in their neighborhoods and 25 percent felt comfortable. At the neighborhood schools, 16 percent felt alienated, while 58 percent felt comfortable. Furthermore we generally expected that the dynamics of students' identity politics would play out among their friends in the neighborhood. Therefore, students of varying academic performance (A's/B's vs. C's/D's) or similar social class background would express similar degrees of affiliation and identification with the home vis-à-vis the high school. This turned out to be false. The only students we found at the neighborhood schools who felt alienated from their neighborhoods were females. Inversely the only students from the magnet schools who felt comfortable in their neighborhoods were males. Secondly, when these students enrolled in the magnet schools, they had the feeling of escaping to a safer, less chaotic social environment. This was coupled with the prevailing ideology of the magnet school, i.e., that it provides a ticket to college admission. Paradoxically the magnet schools reproduced this dominant ideology, and there too the students willingly accommodated with apparent ease.

Students in the magnet schools seemed to experience greater difficulties separating their academic identities from their personal identities. Their peers who did not attend magnet schools, which offered academically rich and culturally relevant curricula, apparently could not understand why their friends changed. This caused conflicts. On the other hand, students in neighborhood schools felt less conflicted, as their friends generally attended less challenging schools as well. Of course, these are generalizations, as there is not space in this chapter to closely examine the nuances.

The interviews disclosed that at the magnet schools, students generally felt that teachers were there to help them academically, socially, and emotionally. Teachers cared. In sharp contrast, students in the neighborhood high schools generally perceived that their teachers treated segments of the student population differently. For example, Black males widely perceived that their (mostly white) teachers discriminated against them by holding lower expectations for them and stereotyping most of them as hoodlums:

> Some teachers have their favorite student, but it isn't [necessarily] racism. My teacher thinks that I'm a hoodlum or a gang member. A lot of other teachers say that, though. I hear the other teachers say that.
>
> The teachers expect more from the Vietnamese students, that they are always smarter and stuff. It's like the Vietnamese student is always smarter, and my teachers never expect a black [male] student to be smarter than a Vietnamese student, you know. They always automatically think that we're dumb.
>
> From what I know, some teachers may think that, well, if a person is white, well, they are better than the rest, you know. If another [black] student makes a higher grade, then the teacher will say, well, the white student must have had a bad day. The teachers won't put them down or announce their grade in class, or anything like that. They will just keep it to themselves and come talk with the student privately.

These interview narratives disclose the perceptions among the students in the neighborhood high schools of the authoritarian school climate. Democratic practices, to say nothing of deep racial/ethnic democracy, are apparently void. Students felt stuck "back here" in their neighborhood schools, seemingly isolated from the wider society and even from each other. "Shutdown" was the norm. However, by accommodating, going along with, their teachers, students resisted. They specifically exercised their "situated" agency and made the one strategic choice available. They chose to pass their grade level and go on to graduate. This kind of student resistance obviously differs from that characterized by Robert Everhart (1983) and others as an escape from anxieties. I argue that this form of student resistance is inherently political and, perhaps more evocatively, "collective." It begins the pedagogical move from human to more political agency.

## Toward a New Urban Pedagogy

Classroom teachers in inner-city public schools, whether they are white or teachers of color, find themselves in an unenviable position. They are daily besieged by the demands of the state to lift student achievement and struggle with the social realities of widespread inequality. Despite this contradictory location, teachers must strive to become transformative intellectuals.

Their first pedagogical imperative is to foster their students' racial/ethnic identity and pride. So as not to become mired in factionalism, however, classroom teachers must demand greater awareness of the identity of "the other." During these uncertain times, knowledge of the plight of Muslims, Middle Eastern women, and oppressed populations around the world is indispensable. Why is this important?

On ethical grounds alone, classroom teachers in urban centers must find the means to resist the increasing surveillance of schooling, and perhaps more perniciously the trend toward standardization of teaching and learning. These trends are clearly linked to processes of globalization and in particular the overwhelming propensity of the nation-state to converge upon neoliberal market ideologies. On pragmatic grounds, however, teachers coalescing around broader concerns, and linking these issues to global processes and events, make their political positioning stronger. They are less vulnerable. Students and teachers are thus partners in the struggle for democracy in urban schools—sites where the appeal of the "global city," like Chicago or Los Angeles, makes imperative the regulation of student bodies and teacher pedagogy through high-stakes testing and accountability.

In this regard Henry Giroux (1983) has argued that curricula that lay bare the colonizing legacies of western Europe enable classroom teachers to transform their roles. They become cultural workers who, together with their students, "take seriously the identities of subordinate cultures" (p. 154). Public schooling for racial/ethnic minorities in inner cities, therefore, can potentially assume a counterhegemonic purpose by becoming a site for cultural politics. Though institutionally rare, there are countless examples of these transformations, such as the Roberto Clemente School and other schools serving Puerto Rican students in Chicago. These schools have implemented a critical pedagogy based on the principles of Paulo Freire. Here I want to extend Giroux's argument and assert that procedurally, only by understanding how students construct their racial/ethnic identity—and finding pedagogical space to accomplish this task—is the transformation of teachers from bankers of knowledge to cultural workers institutionally possible. Schools are sites of both meaning and morality.

### *A Vision of Urban Student Resistance*

The resources that urban students possess, as shown in our study, are uniquely situated sociocultural perspectives from their shared experiences relating to violence and the material hardships of poverty. Whether they are conscious of this or not, they share collective struggles for quality public schooling.

Educators should form coalitions with students to design interventions, forged at the national, state, or local levels, that confront (and hopefully interrupt) the perceived moral transgressions articulated in the student narratives. Specifically principals and classroom teachers must deliberately foster a school climate or school/community partnerships, whereby students may occupy safe pedagogical spaces and places to construct the production of meaning and morality.

This issue of creating safe spaces for student dialogues and collaborative learning environments may be more complicated than first imagined. Our data show that even when presented transactional opportunities for information sharing with teachers, the students in our study remained skeptical. Students' collective attitude, especially in the neighborhood schools, was, What's in it for the teacher? Building trust takes time, but it is our contention that teachers need to constantly remind themselves that sensitive issues such as teenage pregnancy, home difficulties, and ordinary adolescent angst are everyday concerns for students. Secondly, students should lead discussions of private issues and their relationships to the formal and informal curriculum. This will help prevent the perception that teachers gossip about personal concerns. Students would feel psychologically more comfortable. Classroom practices that facilitate the articulation of student voice, for example, those at Roberto Clemente High School, should be replicated.

In general, what the student interviews revealed as necessary, but perhaps insufficient, was a school climate that increased self-discipline and provided caring in a nonpaternalistic manner, along with a more culturally relevant curriculum. Pedagogically what seemed to distinguish the magnet schools most centrally was their relevant and engaging curriculum. Students at these two public schools above all were connected to the world. A common complaint voiced by students at the neighborhood schools was: "[The adults there] are ignorant on the subject, so therefore how can you teach somebody something you don't know?" Globalization was a process that meant something in the everyday world of student learning. Urban school curriculum architects need to keep foremost in mind the processes of globalization and issues that can potentially unite high school students with their teachers, for example, against global economic oppression.

Public schools are not institutional isomorphs. Classroom leaders and administrators understandably often function as if schools had no connections to the broader community and political economy. They do. Moreover, many of the high school students we interviewed voiced a desire to make these relational interconnections explicit in the curriculum. They wanted help in overcoming their social class backgrounds and cultural biases. One student from a neighborhood school told us, "I don't live in the best neighborhood. I don't think society really cares about me."

What is crucial, I believe, from a pedagogical perspective is to authorize student voices as "learning subjects." Despite denied access to quality public schooling and high-paying jobs owing to the disappearance of work in the inner city, demonstrated income inequality, and persistent low wages for many racial minority groups, inner-city students nonetheless choose to remain in school. Nationwide approximately 50 percent of students in urban centers do so. High school students in our study perceive that they have few material options other than to stay in school and graduate. Moreover, those students who do graduate and eventually enroll in college often must learn to navigate separate personal and cultural identities and set spatial distances from their everyday life in their residential neighborhoods. High school students in urban centers, especially those enrolled in neighborhood schools, often have to develop new academic self-images to succeed and gain admission to college. Potentially, these students could experience an inexorable estrangement from their nonacademically oriented peers, who may get pushed out of school as a result of policy structures and school practices. They must negotiate between, on the one hand, new identities located in academic discourses and spaces embedded in their "moral strategy" to obtain quality public schooling, and, on the other, broader social and economic connections to the world.

## References


Everhart, Robert (1983). *Reading, writing, and resistance: Adolescence and labor in a junior high school.* Boston: Routledge and Kegan Paul

Giroux, H. (1983). *Theory and resistance in education: A pedagogy for the opposition.* South Hadley, MA: Bergin and Garvey.

Lauria, Mickey, & Mirón, Luis F. (2003). *The new social spaces of resistance.* New York: Peter Lang.

Lipman, Pauline (2002). Making the global city, making inequality: The political economy and cultural politics of Chicago school policy. *American Educational Research Journal*, 39, 379–423.

Mirón, Luis F. (1996). *The social construction of urban schooling: Situating the crisis.* Cresskill, NJ: Hampton Press.

Mirón, Luis F., & Lauria, Mickey (1998). Student voice as agency: Resistance and accommodation in inner city schools. *Anthroplogy and Education Quarterly, 29,* 189-213.

# Fathers and Sons

The son of my son
Smiled as I held him today
Perhaps it was simply because I held his bottle
Perhaps he recognizes me as someone benign
Another helpless adult he has caused to lose his mind
Spewing silly nonsense words and regressing beyond reason
Perhaps he smiled because he already knows that this world is his to hold.

The son that is my son
Smiled as he held his son today
I read pride and love in that smile
Perhaps he was merely dreaming of the many things
They will do as father and son
Perhaps he was happy to be father and somehow no longer simply son
Perhaps it was because the world had finally given him something to hold.

The son that is me
Smiled as I held my son today
I held him close and told him I love him
Perhaps I smiled because I know his son will change him
Perhaps I smiled at the prospect of watching them both grow
Perhaps it was knowing that we three will have memories to hold.

The son that is my father
Smiled as I told him the news
Perhaps it was because great-grand sounds just as grand
As all the other titles he now holds
Perhaps it was just amazement that the bridge
That links fathers and sons is one span longer today
Perhaps it was simply the notion of having another little one to hold.

This is for my son for choosing to be present
This is for my father for having been present
This is for my grandson in whose life I intend to be present
This is for all fathers who choose to be present
This is for those who work to make the future brighter than the present
This is for the intergenerational bridge builders.

# TEN

# Urban Dropouts

## *Why Persist?*

Greg S. Goodman & Adriel A. Hilton

As we are keenly aware, the national educational statistics tell a very troubling and foreboding story about life for students within America's urban classrooms (Banks & Banks, 1989; National Center for Education Statistics, 2006). African American students embody 17 percent of the total US student population, but African American teachers represent only 6 percent of all teachers in the US ("*Leaving Schools,*" 2004). For Hmong and other minority groups, the gap can be even more acute African American male teachers constitute just 1 percent of America's total teaching force. Underscoring those dismal numbers is the fact that there are no staff of color in 44 percent of the nation's schools (National Center for Education Statistics, 2006). Based upon these demographics and the cultural mismatch they portray, is it any wonder that inner city schools are failing their students and continuing to fall further behind (Beachum & McCray, 2008)? This is failure by design (Duncan-Andrade & Morrell, 2008) Why persist? Indeed.

The Children's Defense Fund reports the alarming fact that one American high school student drops out every nine seconds ("*Leaving Schools,*" 2004). In 2007, that statistic equated to 6.2 million students in the United States between the ages of 16 and 24 dropping out of high school. These data are further substantiated by the Center for Labor Market Studies at Northeastern University and the Alternative Schools Network ("High School," 2009): the demographics represent roughly 16 percent, or one student in eight, of all of the students in the United States who were in that age group. As these data consistently show, most of the students who are dropping out of school are minority youth, specifically African American and Hispanic (National Center for Education Statistics, 2006), and they are living in our nation's largest urban areas. Seventy-one percent of students nationwide graduate from high school, but less than half of the students of color graduate (Greene & Forster, 2003). These data spotlight the fact that our young African American and Hispanic men are the most prone to drop out of high school. For most urban youth, the question "why persist?" is a metaphor of their dilemma in the struggle for survival.

## Why Do Urban Students Fail to Persist in School?

Angela Pascopella (2003) pulls no punches when she states that the schools themselves are to blame for most students dropping out of high school. Why persist when the school is large and alienating, students are confronted with less experienced teachers in their classrooms, schools are given fewer resources and support, and it is clear that the majority White policy-making community is complicit in undermining the education of its urban youth (Duncan-Andrade & Morrell, 2008)? According to Pascopella (2003), even the teachers unions work to support a corrupt system of ineptitude. Teacher contracts can result in the more knowledgeable and skilled teachers being rewarded for their performance by moving from low-performing schools to escape the ghetto. These systems support a vicious cycle of cultural reproduction. Students who lack qualified teachers and pupil personnel services in their schools fall further behind (Bourdieu, 1993; White & Cones, 1999). Why persist when the scene is set for failure? Research also demonstrates that a significant number of students drop out of urban high schools because their schools are not offering real life opportunities for learning (Duncan-Andrade, 2008). The curriculum is not relevant, and student lives and the experience within the classroom are grossly disconnected. Teachers are presenting materials that are prescribed by central office administrators in a misguided attempt to increase standardized test scores (Goodman & Carey, 2004). When students are exposed to the mandated curriculum within their classrooms, the subject content often has no relevance to the real problems they confront on a daily basis. Schools must be held accountable for what they are teaching and how it translates to the real world of their community, not to the dictates of the Educational Testing Service (ETS) or a central office oligarchy fearful of losing cushy, politically parceled jobs (Carnevale & Desrochers, 2003).

Researchers tie at least part of the problems facing urban schools to their makeup. Although these schools are populated mainly by students of color, educators within these settings are mostly White and female (National Center for Education Statistics, 2006). Hancock (2006) notes,

> The reality that White women are on the front lines of urban education is clear. While we continue to recruit and retain minority teachers, it is critical that we also focus our attention on helping to educate White women teachers about the

> realities of teaching students who may hold a different sociopolitical, sociocultural, and socioeconomic perspective. (p. 97)

The effect of the cultural mismatch is supported by the work of Malloy and Malloy (1998). These researchers have discovered that many urban teachers consider the culture of the student and the culture of the classroom to be very different. A solid example of this mismatch is found in the debate concerning the use of Ebonics in schools. To teachers supporting White curriculum, the wealth of opportunity that a mix of experiences brings to the classroom is threatening, unappreciated, and devalued (Goldenberg et al., 2003). In urban school districts, as many as 95 percent of the students are minority. Large urban states such as New York report 86 percent of the teachers are White (National Center for Education Statistics, 2006). In rural states such as New Hampshire and Maine, the population of White teachers climbs to 98 and 99 percent, respectively! According to Cross (2003), concerns related to race and culture are of tremendous significance in today's educational environment. Issues of an irrelevant curriculum and the attitudes, color, and disposition of the educators charged with teaching our youth bring additional evidence to support our fundamental question: Why persist? Why persist when you cannot see yourself represented in any of the identifications of your school?

An urban school is so designated, generally, because of its location, rate of poverty, percentage of students of color, and proportion of students who are limited in English proficiency (i.e., Hispanic and other English Language Learner [ELL] students). Most teachers going into urban schools for the first time face unexpected challenges as they confront the everyday problems of inner city classrooms (McKinsey & Company, 2009). For inexperienced and untrained White teachers, the adjustment is even more profound. Season four of the critically acclaimed, award-winning HBO series *The Wire* focuses on the stories and the lived experiences of several young boys in Baltimore City Public School System. The youth featured in this dramatic television series continuously grapple with authentic problems within their homes and the Baltimore ghetto/community. In this fourth season, the writer/producer David Simon focused on an urban middle school in West Baltimore that faced a critical shortage of teachers, especially in the important areas of science and math. *The Wire* provides viewers with a drama accurately representing most urban school districts. The drama exposes the policy of urban school systems that elect to employ teachers who are not certified but are offered alternative methods for certification such as teaching residency programs. The training represented in *The Wire* is positively ludicrous. Teachers are instructed to chant "I am lovable and capable" with their charges. This 1960s pablum nourished hippies, but in this episode of *The Wire* it effectively demonstrates how out of touch trainers and administrators are with the urban classroom of the twenty-first century.

David Simon is acutely aware of both the research and the lived experience of the people existing within the inner city of Baltimore. *The Wire* is set in an urban district that is one of the largest in the nation. Baltimore includes a very highly educated and affluent community, yet it also is home to a significantly large number of undereducated and poor. In 2006, 33 percent of the population aged 25 and older had a college degree, yet conversely, Baltimore had one of the highest rates of people over the age of 25 without a high school diploma (*Greater Baltimore State of the Region Report,* 2007).

Season four of *The Wire* features a suspended police detective who seeks a career change with the goal of impacting the lives of youth. Naively, our protagonist decides to teach math in an urban school district. Driving the drama, this White male with little experience in urban schools has no idea what challenges are ahead. As he begins to struggle with gaining command and order within the classroom, the students are more engaged in creating a brutal and hectic culture reflective of their lives on the street. As one could expect, our protagonist was surprised to learn just how little help was available to teachers or students. The program depicts a system characterized by a lack of intervention and support mechanisms, a system designed to perpetuate failure. Why persist as either teacher or student within this mismatch?

*The Wire* reveals many of the reasons why urban students drop out of high school. A recurring theme in the show identifies the role of the gangstas and their grip on the young and vulnerable wannabes. To fulfill the need for quick, if not always easy, money to take care of themselves and their loved ones, the gangstas enlist the children of their block to distribute drugs (mules) to drive-through customers. As the show deftly demonstrates, the lure of quick money in real time makes education for a future and distant reward appear meaningless and disconnected Within a culture of violence, the lure of gangs is clear. Joining can help young people feel and be more protected within the violent inner city neighborhoods where they live. Gangs are a support network that fills the void manifested by society's abandonment of the ghetto's inhabitants. The gang is the family, the court, the administration, and the authority.

Urban school districts, such as Baltimore, are facing major problems, made worse by a very nomadic student and teacher population. Of inner city teachers, 40 percent will transfer within five years of placement. Sara Neufeld (2006), a reporter with the *Baltimore Sun,* stated that only 38.5 percent of Baltimore's high school students graduate four years after entering. Too much of the city's workforce is undereducated and poorly prepared for the economy of today, much less the future. The ripple effect on quality of life issues throughout our nation is apparent—it leads to more crime and a less healthy, less wealthy population. Employment opportunities are few because businesses will not locate in areas where schools are subpar. Further driving the economic and social downturn, businesses choose to relocate away from communities with such issues, meaning fewer jobs, a declining population and, of course, higher taxes for those who stay.

When segregation ended to make way for integration, many dedicated African American teachers and administrators lost their jobs. Black schools were closed and their students were bused to White schools (McCray et al., 2007). Also exacerbating the lack of Black educators for our urban students, young African American college students opted to major in fields of study other than education (Kunjufu, 2002). These shifts left a void of teachers who had traditionally provided quality education to America's Black students. In their place, White educators largely took on the job of educating African American and other urban students. Despite multiple efforts to recruit minority candidates within urban school districts, the teaching force (along with administrators) continues to be predominately White (McCray et al., 2007).

While we live in a more inclusive society than that which existed in pre-civil rights America, continuing segregation and inequality have made the hope of living "The American Dream" illusory and an irony for many young Blacks. "The illusion of integration allows for some access, while countless roadblocks persist in critical areas where blacks continue to be discriminated against in often subtle and sometimes not so subtle ways" (Kitwana, 2002, p. 13). White and Cones (1999) agree that contemporary prejudice exists mainly in the form of institutional racism:

> Institutional racism exists where whites restrict equal access to jobs and promotions, to business and housing loans, and the like. White bankers and mortgage companies can secretly collaborate to redline a neighborhood so that such loans are nearly impossible to obtain. White senior faculty members in predominately white universities (public and private) determine who gets promoted to tenured faculty positions. Good-old-boys' clubs in the corporate structure determine who will be mentored and guided through the promotional mine fields. (p. 136)

African American youth witness the continuing legacy of segregation and racism and its impact on their lives. They see their schools continuously underfunded, lacking in modern facilities, supplied with inadequate and inappropriate textbooks, and staffed with teachers who are poorly trained and who have low expectations of youth. Why persist when those who need to support you are so conspicuously absent?

Wacquant (2000), a noted sociologist, takes the racism theory several steps further, proposing the notion of hyperghetto to describe African Americans who were steered to certain areas of northern cities, areas that came to be known as ghettoes. Wacquant created the neologism hyperghetto to identify the environment of urban African Americans from 1968 to the present day. He points out the relationship between hyperghetto and prison in the way African Americans are forced to live. According to Wilson (2009), hyperghettos are characterized by increased crime, illegal drug activity including addiction, economic depravity, police surveillance and brutality, and struggling schools, all of which force businesses to relocate to the suburbs.

The hyperghetto evolved in a post-White flight era when the residential barriers that barred African Americans from moving into White suburbs were relaxed (Wilson, 2009). When Blacks move up and make it to middle or upper class status, they often move out of inner cities and develop amnesia concerning where they come from, neglecting to reach back and uplift their former community. The lack of involvement in their old community, including the schools, can only be described as abandonment. This alienation between middle and upper class Blacks and the hyperghetto exacerbates the recurring problems of inadequate urban school funding, parental detachment from the schools, and the continuing cycle of conditions detrimental to student success. Many scholars and authors have warned of the increasing separation, segregation, and stratification within the African American community (Dyson, 2005; Kitwana, 2002; Kunjufu, 2002; West, 2008). West (2008) elaborates, "Once we lose any sense of a black upper or black middle class or a black upper working-class connecting with the black underclass with a 'we' consciousness or sense of community, it becomes much more difficult to focus on the plight of the poor" (p. 57).

> Urban school districts have their share of problems that are not often experienced by suburban schools. Dropout rates of 70 percent or higher are common in many inner city schools (Alexander et al., 1997). The impact of these students' decision to drop out can be felt throughout their communities and into society as a whole. Communities already plagued by high rates of crime and physical and mental challenges often find those problems are exacerbated by high numbers of citizens experiencing disenfranchisement. Dropouts, for example, have been shown to account for half of the nation's prison population (Coley, 1995; Goodman, 2007). One of every three African American males spends time in a penal institution, but only one of ten male high school graduates is enrolled in college. (Coley, 1995)

## Urban Dropouts: People Make the Difference

The recurring question, why persist? gets a resounding round of reinforcement: it's cool, schools sucks, my teachers hate me, I don't fit, America ain't right, everybody else does. It is the truth that arguments for dropping out too often outweigh the cries for persistence. "The situation in far too many schools is one of despair, poverty, isolation, and distress" (Beachum & Obiakor, 2005, p. 13). As we stated in the first half of this chapter, the student dropout problem is reinforced with obsolete and counterproductive pedagogical practices that extend beyond the individual classrooms into the halls, cafeteria, bathrooms, and the entirety of the culture known as school. Often the result of this complex ecology is a "cultural collision" in which "the culture of educators clashes with that of their students" (Beachum & McCray, 2008, p. 55), and the mismatch is devastating. Jeff Duncan-Andrade and Ernest Morrell (2008) take this argument one step further and make the claim that urban schools are performing exactly as they were designed to function. "If urban schools have been decried for decades as 'factories for failure' (Rist, 1973), then their production of failures means they are in fact successful at producing the results they are designed to produce. To the degree that we continue to misname this problem by calling schools designed to fail 'failing schools' we will continue to chase our tails" (p. 5).

Consequently, for students facing the paradox of successful "factories for failure" (Rist, 1973), what could be the counternarrative to the urban question: why persist? What factors contribute to students' resiliency and school persistence? In this second half of our investigations into the questions of urban middle and high school dropouts, we will explore some of the successful initiatives that have been utilized in building healthy learning communities. The complex ecologies of these learning communities will be explored and deconstructed to reveal the ways in which they work to keep students connected and on track toward graduation. These are not presented as simple panaceas to the huge problem of dropouts. All of these initiatives require hard work, courage, tenacity, intelligence, emotional toughness, and, as Barack Obama observed, audacious hope.

James Comer (1980) has been one of the undisputed leaders in the development of successful learning communities for the past 30 years. Comer was one of the first urban educators to identify the holistic nature and the complex ecology of the learning community. "When satisfactory home and school conditions exist the caretaker and the school staff constitute an alliance and are both able to interact with a child in a series of social and teaching experiences in which the child can gain personal control, motivation for learning, a balance between individuality and cooperation, interpersonal and social skills, and a sense of responsibility for his or her own behavior" (Comer, 1980, p. 33–34). Although Comer's work centered on preschool and elementary school children in New Haven, which is not New York or Los Angeles, his model School Development Program (SDP) was innovative for its attention to all of the ecological factors contributing to student success: the school, the home, and the community. This early work applied social and behavioral science to the operation of the whole school and community environment.

Comer's SDP also has spurred the growth of interest in addressing the myriad elements of each of these complex ecologies. "Our work over the years shows that curriculum and instruction are at the heart of the education enterprise, but that relationships must be such that young people can imitate, identify with, and internalize the attitudes, values, and ways of the meaningful adults around them in order to be motivated to learn academic material and, eventually, to become self-motivated, disciplined, self-directed learners capable of taking advantage of the resources of our society" (Comer, 1980, p. 295). Comer redefined and revitalized the role of psychology and social science within the school.

Unfortunately, attempts to widely reproduce Comer's SDP have proved limited in their possibilities for replication. The reality is that people, not programs, are the change. Within the culture of each school and the community they represent, there are key individuals who are responsible for the myriad factors that contribute to the success or failure of the school organization's complex ecology Dropouts are the result of the failure to successfully resolve the issues of "cultural collision" (Beachum & McCray, 2008), and each community needs a leader who can interpret both the existing research on urban school reform and translate this into a workable program for their unique community.

California's Clovis East High School is an example of an urban high school that has developed a culture effective in reducing school dropouts and in creating strong and personally meaningful bonds within its community's shareholders. Clovis East High School's 3,000 students, drawn from a mix of diverse socioeconomic and cultural subcommunities located in California's Central Valley, are typically Californian, as exemplified by being mainly minority in racial identification. In addition to the racial diversity of the student body, the academic abilities of the students are wide-ranging. Most students are well below grade level in both reading and math scores.

When the school opened in the fall of 1999, there was a new principal, Jeff Eben, greeting the students as they walked onto the campus. Jeff Eben is a quadriplegic, yet his stature in his Quickie wheelchair resembles that of a professional basketball center. His presence on campus is ubiquitous, and his sensitivity to issues of culture is unparalleled. "On the day we opened, our students brought with them varied experiences in school. When we looked at the test results on the academic records of our first group of students, almost 70 percent couldn't read at grade level. Many of them had never been on teams or part of performing groups. School had not been a friendly place for a large portion of our clientele and our community didn't come in with a great deal of trust in education. We had no credibility, and it felt like we were actually starting at whatever comes before square one" (Eben, 2006, p. 193). The tasks were daunting, but the persistence of this principal and many of the staff caused the culture to form and take hold.

In his autobiography, *How Many Wins Have YOU Had Today?,* Eben (2006) recounts his experiences from the early days of Clovis East High School:

> If we were going to have any academic success, we had to be able to teach our kids how to read, a tough task with teenagers. A struggling reader will have trouble in every discipline, so we had to find instructional practices that were innovative and effective, and we aren't necessarily trained at the secondary level for that type of instruction. Motivation was critical, and I thought our students would try harder if they participated in activities outside of class. We wanted to create opportunities for our young people to participate in sports, the arts, agriculture, and any other programs that would make their school experience more fun. Many of our students had not been part of high profile groups, but they would be here. We even adopted a schedule with eight class periods as opposed to the typical six to force students to take elective classes. Finally, I wanted students to feel safe and was concerned about how well our different cultures would interact with each other. It seemed natural to use our diversity as an on-going tool to teach inclusion, social tolerance and justice, and caring. So we took our Feel the Love motto and defined it with three words: "Competence, Connectedness, and Compassion." These words combined our goals of helping students achieve academically, provide them with a sense of belonging, and create an environment where we care about each other. We put these words on a poster and hung them in every room and office in the school. It became who we were and caught on quickly. Two of my colleagues even gave us the name of "The Love Shack" and our marching band still plays the song as a way of celebrating our identity. (p. 194)

Eben's work at Clovis East follows a line of thought well accepted and articulated within current critical constructivist pedagogical perspectives. Constructivists subscribe to the belief that the individual must invest of themselves in order to acquire knowledge. Using a combination of external and internal motivations, the individual learner is engaged in learning and meaning-making. Critical constructivists further the championing of an individual's self-efficacy as a learner with an application of social justice education. Social justice education is focused upon the liberation of all individuals from the destructive forces of racism, sexism, poverty, and the oppression of ignorance and hate. Dropping out of school reflects the victory of these destructive forces by being self-perpetuating and contributing to the cultural reproduction of failure (Bourdieu, 1993). More than any other factors, critical constructivist pedagogy can provide a positive intervention for ecological and educational success. "Understanding the problem of high school dropouts requires looking beyond the limited scope of individual student characteristics to include school (read: ecological) factors in student decisions to stay in or leave school" (Knesting, 2008, p. 3).

Eben's culture of caring has replicability. In her research on dropout prevention in high school students, Knesting (2008) lists a caring culture and three other factors as key to promoting student school persistence and dropout resistance. "Four factors emerged as critical for supporting student persistence: (*a*) listening to students, (*b*) communicating caring, (*c*) the school's role in dropout prevention, and (*d*) the students' role in dropout prevention" (p. 3). The generalizability of caring and compassionate teachers is clear. What is not so obvious is the tremendous effort and persistence that is required of staff. Knesting concludes: "Developing caring, supportive, and mutually respectful relationships with students in a large, comprehensive high school is not an easy task" (p. 9). This is why people, not programs, are the key to success in creating 'wins' with our students.

Another important and successful school reform for improving students' school persistence is found through the creation of charter schools, school within a school, and other alternative ecologies for learning, for example, smaller learning communities (SLC). Transitions from grade to grade and school to school are disrupting and threatening to adolescents. When these transitions from school to school are not supported with the creation of solid bonds to either the new school's culture, individuals such as teachers or counselors, or another emotional and/or social anchor for the student, the risks of dropout loom large. Conversely, the literature is replete with examples of reclaiming youth through the development of alternative educational programming featuring adventure activities, relevant curriculum, and the development of close bonds between students and staff (Goodman, 2007; Brendtro et al., 2002). SLCs have been proven to significantly contribute to student school persistence (Darling-Hammond, 2002).

Very often the failure of students to bond with the new school and its culture results in social frustrations and academic failure (Diller, 1999). Across the nation, the dropout rate for freshmen in urban settings hovers around 40 percent (EPE, 2006). In many schools, students get stuck in ninth grade, and their experience is one of a continuing cycle of repeating because of a failure to win the credit-banking game of high school (Freire, 1970). Patterson et al. (2007) explain:

> For many urban school districts, the response to the dehumanizing condition of the large urban high school has been the creation of smaller learning communities (SLC). The impressive benefits of SLCs have been well-established in the literature, with increasing examples of success across the country (Cotton, 2001; Darling-Hammond, 2002). Hundreds of SLCs have been created in urban areas, including Chicago, Denver, Los Angeles, New York, Philadelphia, Seattle, and Ohio. Small school researchers are careful to assert, however, that shrinking the size of schools is not a panacea; rather, smaller environments make it easier to give kids the things they really need to succeed: collegiality among teachers, personalized teacher-student relationships, and less differentiation of instruction by ability (Cotton, 2001; Gladden, 1998; Raywid, 1999). (p. 128)

Although this process of creating dropout preventions can sound simple as described in these pages, what is not easy is finding instructional and support staff with the strength, courage, conviction, and love of humanity to pull this off. Jeff Duncan-Andrade is a professor who walks the talk. A member of the faculty at San Francisco State University, Jeff was also the teacher of a twelfth-grade English literature class at the Oasis Community High School (now closed), in Oakland, California. Jeff understands and communicates caring as a primary value, but he demonstrates his love (Freire, 1970) for his students by providing them with a rich, culturally relevant curriculum. This curriculum places students' cultural identification and icons at the center of their educational experience. Duncan-Andrade (2008) says,

> A curriculum that draws from youth culture would embrace expanding definitions of literacy by viewing students as producers of and participants in various cultural literacies, such as: image, style, and discursive practices. This more inclusive approach to literacy instruction recognizes students as cultural producers with their own spheres of emerging literacy participation. This pedagogy of articulation and risk (Grossberg, 1994) values and learns from the cultural literacies students bring to the classroom and assists them as they expand those literacies and develop new ones. Teachers should aim to develop young people's critical literacy, but they should also recognize students as producers of literacy and support that production. (p. 140)

Duncan-Andrade also trusts his students. He believes in their ability to know the truth and their skills in detecting elements of the popular and school's culture that enhance and scaffold their success. This is the ultimate show of respect and caring. Students don't drop out of Duncan-Andrade's class: they are practically breaking down the doors to get in. Within his classroom, students have the opportunity to learn how to create an activist agency to transform themselves and their community's ecology by applying an authentic social justice and critical pedagogy. Duncan-Andrade has dubbed this process "Doc ur block":

> The Doc Ur Block project was a commitment to those principles of humanization by providing young people an education that prepares them to analyze their world critically. It put tools of critical thinking, research, and intellectual production in the hands of young people so that they could counter-narrate pathological stories of their families and communities. Along the way, many students discovered that they too had come to believe the dominant discourse about their community and had lost sight of the countless indicators of hope and strength that are present on their blocks every day. (Duncan-Andrade & Morrell, 2008, p. 147)

## Conclusions

The examples we have provided are evidence of some of the successes that can be achieved in countering successful factories of failure, of promoting school persistence, and reversing the tsunami of student dropouts. All of these examples are the products of individuals' efforts—the real results of work by teachers and staff who are leading a revolution in education (Ladson-Billings, 1994). These individuals are bucking social and political forces that act to perpetuate the dropouts; and their work is nothing shy of courageous. As we witnessed in *The Wire,* standing in front of a class of urban youth and chanting "I am lovable and capable" is an exercise in pretending to make the changes that real love can bring (Freire, 1970). Perpetuating absurd, trite, trivial, and outdated practices maintains the hegemony of the dominant culture upon a failed community and its main socializing institution: the school.

Resisting hegemony, schools can produce a counternarrative to the forces trying to perpetuate student failure (as success). Although the story was typically Hollywood, the portrayal of Erin Gruwell's struggle to transform her students through her own metamorphosis is absolutely on point (Gruwell, 2006). Many urban sites are centered in 'the war,' and winning these battles begins with the courage to transform one's self into a warrior's character much like heroine Erin Gruwell: to fail and to come back, to risk defeat and to refuse to accept losing, to persist and not to yield! This is the circle of courage required to answer the question: Urban dropouts: Why persist? This is what the pedagogy of love means.

## References

Beachum, F. D., & McCray, C. (2008). Dealing with cultural collision in urban schools: What preservice educators should know. In G. Goodman (Ed.), *Educational psychology: An application of critical constructivism.* New York: Peter Lang

Beachum, F. D., & Obiakor, F. E. (2005). Educational leadership in urban schools. In F. E. Obiakor & F. D. Beachum (Eds.), *Urban education for the 21st century: Research, issues, and perspectives* (pp. 83–99). Springfield, IL: Charles C Thomas.

Bourdieu, P. (1993). *The field of cultural production: Essays on art and literature.* New York: Columbia University Press.

Brendtro, L., Brokenleg, M., & Van Bockern, S. (2002). *Reclaiming youth at risk: Our hope for the future.* Bloomington, IN: National Educational Service.

Carnevale, A. P., & Desrochers, D. M. (2003). *Standards for what? The economic roots of K-16 reform.* Princeton, NJ: Educational Testing Service.

Coley, R. (1995). *Dreams deferred: High school dropouts in the United States.* Princeton, NJ: Educational Testing Services.

Comer, J. P. (1980). *School Power: Implications of an intervention project.* New York: The Free Press.

Cotton, K. (2001). *New small learning communities: Findings from recent literature.* Portland, OR: Northwest Regional Educational Laboratory.

Cross, B. E. (2003). Learning or unlearning racism: How urban teachers transfer teacher education curriculum to classroom practices. *Theory into Practice, 42*(3), 203–209.

Darling-Hammond, L. (2002). Redesigning schools: What matters and what works. Stanford, CA: School Redesign Network. Retrieved October 20, 2009 from http://www.schoolredesign.net

Diller, D. (1999). Opening the dialogue: Using culture as a tool in teaching young African American children. *Reading Teacher, 52,* 820–827.

Duncan-Andrade, J. (2008). Your best friend or worst enemy: Youth popular culture, pedagogy, and curriculum in urban classrooms. In G. Goodman (Ed.), *Educational psychology: An application of critical constructivism* (pp. 113–143). New York: Peter Lang.

Duncan-Andrade, J. & Morrell, E. (2008). *The art of critical pedagogy: Possibilities for moving from theory to practice in urban schools.* New York: Peter Lang.

Dyson, M. E. (2005). *Is Bill Cosby right? Or has the Black middle class lost its mind?* New York: Basic Civitas Books.

Eben, J. (2006). *How many wins have you had today?* Clovis, CA: Garden of Eben Press.
Educational Projects in Education (EPE). (2006). Ohio graduation report. *Education Week.* Retrieved October 20, 2009 from http://www.edweek.org/ew/toc/2006/06/22/index.html
Freire, P. (1970). *Pedagogy of the oppressed.* New York: Continuum.
Gladden, R. (1998). The small school movement: A review of the literature. In M. Fine & J. Sommerville (Eds.), *Small schools, big imaginations: A creative look at public schools* (pp. 113–133). Chicago: Cross City Campaign for Urban School Reform.
Goldenberg, I. I., Kunz, D., Hamburger, M., & Stevenson, J. M. (2003). Urban education: Connections between research, propaganda & prevailing views of education. *Education, 123*(3), 628–634.
Goodman, G. S. (2007). *Reducing hate crimes and violence among American youth: Creating transformational agency through critical praxis.* New York: Peter Lang.
Goodman, G. S., & Carey, K. T. (2004). *Ubiquitous assessment: Evaluation techniques for the new millennium.* New York: Peter Lang.
*Greater Baltimore state of the region report.* (2007). Greater Baltimore Committee: Retrieved June 15, 2009 from http://www.gbc.org/reports/GBCSOR2007.pdf
Greene, J., & Forster, G. (2003). *Public high school graduation and college readiness rates in the United States.* New York: Manhattan Institute for Policy Research.
Gruwell, E. (2006). *Freedom writers. How a teacher and 150 teens used writing to change themselves and the world around them.* New York: Broadway Books.
Hancock, S. D. (2006). White women's work: On the front lines of urban education. In J. Landsman & C. W. Lewis (Eds.), *White teachers/diverse classrooms: A guide to building inclusive schools, promoting high expectations, and eliminating racism* (pp. 93–109). Sterling, VA: Stylus.
"High school dropout crisis" continues in U.S., study says. (2009). CNN: Retrieved June 18, 2009 from http://www.cnn.com/2009/US/05/05/dropout.rate.study/index.html
Kitwana, B. (2002). *The hip-hop generation: Young blacks and the crisis in African American culture.* New York: Basic Civitas Books.
Knesting, K. (2008). Students at risk for school dropout: Supporting their persistence. *Preventing School Failure, 52* (4). Retrieved June 3, 2009 from ERIC EBSCO.
Kunjufu, J. (2002). *Black students—Middle class teachers.* Chicago: African American Images.
Ladson-Billings, G. (1994). *The dreamkeepers: Successful teachers of African American children.* San Francisco: Jossey-Bass.
*Leaving schools behind: When students drop out.* (2004). University of Minnesota: Retrieved June 16, 2009 from http://education.umn.edu/research/ResearchWorks/checkconnect.html
Malloy, C. E., & Malloy, W. M. (1998). Issues of culture in mathematics teaching and learning. *The Urban Review, 30,* 245–57.
McCray, C. R., Wright, J. V., & Beachum, F. D. (2007). Social justice in educational leadership: Using Critical Race Theory to unmask African American principal placement. *Journal of Instructional Psychology, 34*(4), 247–255.
McKinsey & Company (2009). *The economic impact of the achievement gap in America's schools.* New York: McKinsey & Company.
National Center for Education Statistics. (2006). *Status and trends in the education of racial and ethnic minorities.* Retrieved July 10, 2009 from http://nces.ed.gov/pubs2007/minoritytrends/
Neufeld, S. (2006). Schools challenge report: Journal says city graduates 38.5 percent of students; Only Detroit fared poorer. *The Baltimore Sun.* June 26, 2006. Retrieved June 12, 2009, from http://www.redorbit.com/news/education/551340/schools_challenge_report_journal_says_city_graduates_385_percent_of/index.html
Pascopella, A. (2003). Drop out. *District Administration, 38*(11), 32–36.
Patterson, N. C., Beltyukova, S. A., Berman, K., & Francis, A. (2007). The making of sophomores: Student, parent, and teacher reactions in the context of systematic urban high school reform. *Urban Education, 42*(2). Retrieved May 24, 2009 from http://uex.sagepub.com
Raywid, M. (1999). *Current literature on small schools.* Retrieved September 20, 2009 from http://www.ael.org/eric/digests/edorc988.htm

Rist, R. (1973). *The urban school: A factory for failure.* Cambridge, MA: MIT Press.
Wacquant, L. (2000). The new "peculiar institution": On the prison as surrogate ghetto. *Theoretical Criminology, 4*(3), 377–389.
West, C. (2008). *Hope on a tightrope: Words and wisdom.* Carlsbad, CA: Hay House, Inc.
White, J. L., & Cones, J. H. III (1999). *Black man emerging: Facing the past and seizing a future in America.* New York: W. H. Freeman & Company.
Wilson, W. J. (2009). *More than just race: Being Black and poor in the inner city.* New York: W. W. Norton & Company.

# Catharsis

I write to drown the screams of quiet insanity
I write for the little black boys chasing 21st century bling-dreams
Ensnared by meaningless pursuits that guarantee futures
As cannon fodder for an army of one

I write to still my creeping impotence
As we kill each other for the same baubles and trinkets
That triggered the Black Holocaust

I write because 500 years later
Mother Africa still grieves from her greatest loss
Still staggers from wounds that never heal.

I write for the little girls who've lost their
Laughter and their innocence
To predators with the conscience of zombies
Ghouls and demons masquerading as men

I write to find my voice
I write to lose my voice
To the endless struggle to become more human

I write to save my sanity
I write to give voice to the madness that consumes me

I write to lend my voice
To the destruction of a millenniums old status quo
That relegates me and mine to second class citizenship
And meaningless scraps from the table of plenty

I write to find my spiritual purpose
I write to touch the god within
I write to ease the pain
I write to find peace
I write in search of love

I write with the hope
That the revolution is more than a forgotten, abandoned dream
I write because I still believe that the pen is my mightiest sword
I write so that you may know the WORD
And perhaps join the fight to save the world.

## ELEVEN

# Urban Education Challenges

## *Is Reform the Answer?*

Susan Fuhrman

My topic for this address is Urban Education Reform. Clearly, there are challenges in urban schools, but what's important, and what I want to focus on, is that there is no shortage of reforms intended to address them. The question I want to address is: Why is reform so prevalent and so disappointing?

I think that there are three sets of reasons, some having to do with political factors, some having to do with an overemphasis on structural solutions, and some having to do with the research base that is supposed to guide us as we choose from the different ones. So, if "reform" is not the right metaphor for addressing urban challenges, as I believe it is not, what is? And, what should we do? I will try to address these questions here, and I'll refer to some things we're doing right, and maybe not so right, here at Penn's Graduate School of Education. I would like you all to help us improve as a graduate school of education that cares deeply about urban problems.

### Urban Educational Challenges

To start with the background, you all know how concentrated students are in urban settings. Over 31% of all students attend school in 226 large school districts among the 15,000 or 16,000 school districts in America. That translates into 31% of all students in just 1.5% of school districts (Ladd & Hansen, 1999). So, urban education is where the challenge is, and for my money, if you are not focusing on urban education, especially for a school of education located in Philadelphia, you are not focusing on the important issues of our time.

I don't need to dwell on the litany of challenges that accompanies the concentration of students in large districts. You know that there are higher-than-average proportions of students in poverty, of students with poorly educated parents, of immigrants and other students with limited English skills, and of students from unstable family settings, and you also know that there are greater rates of student mobility. There are greater shortages of teachers, and more teachers with emergency credentials; there are also poor facilities, and low achievement—generally, significantly lower achievement than in suburban districts.

And, there are, of course, fiscal challenges. Great disparities related to wealth still exist. Districts with 25% or more of their school-age children in poverty have an average total per-pupil revenue that is only 89% of the average total per-pupil revenue elsewhere. So, poor districts spend less. And that's *total* revenue. If you adjust for the needs and the costs of educating children in urban areas with all the challenges I just outlined, and for the higher costs in urban areas where there are higher prices to be paid for labor and virtually everything else, then you will find the really significant disparities.

Just to take some figures that emerged from Standard and Poor's School Evaluation Service's recent release of Pennsylvania school district data: when you adjust for costs and needs, Philadelphia spends as much as 23% below the state average expenditure per pupil. Now this is not to say that all of Philadelphia's problems, such as extraordinarily low achievement, are related to money, but it is certainly to make a point about the disparities between the richer and poorer areas in this country. On top of that, we know that Philadelphia citizens and other urban citizens are paying high taxes for every service that they must provide, not just schooling, and are overburdened with all of these taxes.

## Urban Reform

Given these challenges, it is no surprise that most urban districts are extensively engaged in reform. The following section from a book called *Building Civic Capacity* by Stone, Henig, Jones, and Pierannunzi (2001) is a description of the recent reform efforts in the District of Columbia.

> As part of the decentralization effort, every school had been required to establish a local school restructuring team. And over forty "enterprise" and "renaissance" schools had been given special discretion to shape their own policies at the school level. Many schools offer specialized programs that had developed loyal constituencies. These included an elementary school with dual language (English and Spanish) immersion, another elementary school with an Afrocentric curriculum, and special "academies" designed to provide high school students with career-relevant education (including a Health and Human Services Academy, a Public Service Academy and a Trans-Tech Academy). Public/

> private partnerships were in place in dozens of schools; many of these provided enriched career-related training, including separate programs for Culinary Arts, Interior Design, and Landscape Architecture, International Studies, Pre-Engineering, Business and Finance, and Travel and Tourism, and COMSTAT's computer and science partnership with Jefferson Junior High. In addition, during the early 1990s, an aggressive deputy superintendent spearheaded the expansion of the District's Early Learning Years program, which involves more child-friendly curriculum, and a heavy emphasis on making certain that teachers and principals receive the training and support they need to put the curriculum into place. The district is perhaps the only large urban school district to offer a full-day early childhood education program in every elementary school. And the program has been expanding to incorporate many three-year-olds. In 1995 Congress passed legislation initiating a major charter school program in D.C., but even before Congress acted, the public system had experimented with "School-within-School Charters," including a Montessori school, a Non-graded School, and a Media-Technology Social Research School. (p. 148)

That description could take place in any city in America except for the fact that Congress mandated part of it, because in the case of the District of Columbia, Congress is the big school board. So, this amount of reform is quite common. Frederick Hess (1999), the author of *Spinning Wheels: The Politics of Urban School Reform*, studied 57 large school districts and reported that the mean district proposed 11.4 reforms over a 3-year period in the 1990s (Hess, 1999). The problem is not the absence of reform. In fact, what we see is a picture of too much reform. Too many reforms, few of which are effective; too many reforms that are undertaken, and too few that are implemented. Further, the reforms are hardly coordinated; they seem to lurch in all different directions, reflecting opportunism more than any coherent improvement strategy.

Why this "policy churn," to use Hess's (1999) term? As I said before, I think that there are three sets of factors. Let me start with the political factors, and draw heavily from Hess (1999), who writes about how institutional incentives encourage a focus on proposing symbolic change, not on improving schools; on inputs, not outputs.

### *Political Factors*

It is obvious that it is much easier to propose a reform than it is to implement it. That explains part of the "policy churn." But there are a number of other factors that are particularly characteristic of urban schools that lead to this emphasis on symbolic reform, or this posturing around change. For one thing, it is hard to hold urban schools accountable for performance, even in the current climate of accountability.

There are so many complicating factors in urban schools—high mobility, teacher turnover—that it is really hard to determine the value added by schools. Leaders can escape accountability for performance, so it does not matter much if the reform actually works because if it does not work, there are many reasons we can give for why it did not work, such as, "Well, the kids weren't here two thirds of the year when we tried to implement this new curriculum." And it is true, not a made up excuse; it is absolutely true.

Another factor is executive turnover. Urban superintendents hold office for about 3 years, which is much too short a time for reforms to really take effect. They are not around long enough to be accountable for results, so they tend to be held accountable for what they propose. And, in fact, superintendents' careers are built on advancing from district to district, to larger and larger districts with more and more prestige. Superintendents have to be active to build a reputation, and since they have a short term, they have to be active in that short term. And that means proposing and starting reforms, and calling attention to oneself for doing that, or in Hess' (1999) terms "overindulging in innovation."

This posture is reinforced by the foundation, corporate, government, and, yes, academic communities surrounding education. We get benefits when they adopt our ideas so we push our ideas on them, and these are always "new" ideas because we are not about to push somebody else's ideas on them. No one gets paid for working on old ideas, so we contribute to the problem.

The high visibility of education, particularly in urban areas, also contributes. There is much at stake. You cannot work quietly. The public thinks you're doing nothing if you're not attracting attention. You have to convince the community that you're acting, if you're an urban school leader, and proposing reforms is a way of rallying community support and resources. Also, reforms bring notoriety and prestige to a community. Unlike the quiet, much less glamorous work of improvement, school boards support reforming superintendents because it enables them to claim credit too. They can say, "We were the school board that initiated X, Y, and Z reforms."

Clarence Stone et al. (2001) saw additional reasons for urban school reform challenges such as the absence of civic capacity. Civic capacity is the ability of a community to collectively problem-solve with a supportive array of relationships across elected and district leaders. Without it, long-term support for reform is missing. Elected leaders have even more incentives than superintendents and boards to engage in eye-catching reforms; their electoral cycle drives them to short-term, catchy initiatives. Getting their cooperation for hard, long-term work requires an investment in education that has to be deeply felt and that is not present in many communities.

One of Stone's coauthors, Jeffrey Henig, and his colleagues Hula, Orr, and Pedescleaux (1999) noted in the *Color of School Reform* that in the four cities they studied—Atlanta, Baltimore, Detroit, and Washington, DC—racial factors made long-term civic collaboration on education that much more difficult (Henig et al., 1999). There was distrust and much history that was never overcome.

## Structuralism

A second characteristic of urban reform that impedes its effectiveness is the emphasis on structural reforms: on centralization or decentralization, on school-based management, on charters and choice, and on altering patterns of authority within the district. The resort to structure characterizes American education reform efforts historically. We've played around with how to organize schools around grade levels with graded vs. ungraded classrooms, with large vs. small schools, and with creating large, centralized bureaucracies—in Tyack's words, the "one best system"—and then breaking them up.

Why the preoccupation with structures? Because structures are visible, manipulable, and easy, relative to the hard work of really improving teaching and learning. Structural reforms are tangible, you can see them; if you have a 3-year time frame, structural change may be something that you can do. You can see why, given the political incentives just discussed, people would gravitate to big, structural reforms.

But these reforms don't necessarily lead to meaningful improvement in teaching or learning. They focus on changing the incentives around which people work, "empowering" them, or monitoring them more closely, theoretically affecting people's will to work harder.

But sometimes, that theory of action is just wrong. For example, people don't necessarily work harder on instruction when they are "empowered" through school-based management. They may be tied up in meetings on keeping hallways clean, or determining how council representatives are elected. Even if they do work harder, motivation is just a part of effectiveness. These structural reforms don't necessarily affect the other aspects that make educators effective, i.e., their knowledge, skills, and beliefs about whether children can learn. This is the "myth of omnipotent structure," to borrow a title from public administration literature (Anne Marie Houck Walsh as cited in course material, 1973). Policy wonks and educators alike seize on structural solutions without fully elaborating the connections between the structural change and the desired results. School-based management may give teachers more authority, but what conditions would be necessary for them to use that authority to realize improvement?

Structure can, of course, be enabling, but it should not be seen as the entire solution.I find the emphasis on structuralism particularly troubling in the case of charters and choice. They are clearly today's "silver bullets," the panaceas that are going to change everything. "Break it up," one hears often with respect to large urban districts; but the next question, "and then what?" rarely gets asked.

## The Research Base

This leads us naturally into the third area I will discuss: the research base underlying the reforms that cities are so busy adopting. Choice and charters are a good example of the kind of guidance, or lack thereof, that the research base gives us. With respect to those reforms, the evidence about their effects is increasingly clear: it is inclusive. There is no clear evidence of achievement gains; for example, there are gains in certain grades, certain subjects, and certain populations, and not in others.

Why don't we have better research to guide us about reform, and if we did, would it matter? Would urban educators use research to choose reforms, instead of selecting the more visible, structural reforms we just discussed?

Let me address the more sensitive topic first, which is the quality of the research. The research base is much weaker than it could be. There are many important questions about which we could use more guidance. I think education research needs to be improved in several ways. In 2000, I gave a speech at AERA about three studies that had gained a lot of policymaker attention (Fuhrman, 2000). Deborah Nelson, who worked with me on this, and I, chose three studies that policymakers were interested in and referred to in a way that they don't often do with other research. The three studies are the Perry Preschool study of early childhood education (Schweinhart et al., 1993[1]), the Tennessee STAR experiment on class size (Nye, Hedges & Konstantopoulos 2000), and the NICHD (National Institute for Child Health and Human Development) studies of reading (2000). I cited four qualities of these studies that enhanced their credibility, along with a host of contextual factors, such as the presence of research brokers to help popularize their results.

First, the studies did not try to answer a question with an inappropriate design. To state that positively, the studies tried to address a question with an appropriate design. Much education research tries to get at the "what works" question, with studies that might show relationships between treatments and achievement, but cannot answer the causal question as definitively as possible. Research rigor has everything to do with matching the design to the question, something, by the way, that I don't think we as a field think enough about or pay significant attention to in the training of new researchers. I know that we at Penn GSE have excellent methods courses—both quantitative and qualitative—but I often wonder how well we prepare students with the prerequisites they need to really benefit from the methods courses. How well do we prepare them with the ability to frame a good research question and to match it with a good design that employs one or more of these methods?

I certainly don't mean to imply, by focusing on those three big studies or by the causal question, that all research should be experimental or quasi-experimental. I don't mean that at all. The "what works?" question is not the only question to be asked about reform options. We also want to know the manner in which policies exert an influence, not just whether they exert influence. We want to know how various design options play out in practice. We want to know more about the dimensions of problems, such as whether different population groups or types of schools experience issues differently. In other words, there are many things we want to know that don't require an experimental design. The important point is that research suited to the question is more likely to be considered rigorous by policymakers and by us than is research that is stretched to answer questions that it cannot.

A second point about these studies is that they were longitudinal. Either the original study, or the follow-up studies, looked at effects over a period of time, giving the results staying power and helping to sell them to policymakers. It is much easier to justify a program expense when the results of the program last, and there's no way to know that, unless some longitudinal research is conducted.

Third, these studies were replicated by other studies, confirming their findings and lending them much greater power. Replication is a way to test findings; it is through repeated studies that we learn whether original findings can be confirmed, whether they hold up. If repeated studies get different results, there's good reason to question the original findings. Lack of replicability is what did that in cold fusion, as I'm sure you all remember. But replication serves other purposes as well, purposes especially important to education reform. Repeat studies can confirm findings in different contexts, proving to policymakers that results are not just situational but have broader applicability. In other words, policymakers want to know that "this will work in my city." It is easier to make that case with studies done in a variety of settings than with evidence from just one.

And, replication creates a body of research that multiplies the importance of any one study, telling policymakers that a variety of researchers, perhaps even of different perspectives, agrees on a conclusion. This last point is very important to policymakers. Few things irk them more about research than the fact that researchers often disagree with one another and cannot provide clear guidance. It leads them to discredit and underfund research altogether.

Finally, these studies were incorporated into syntheses that helped make sense of the findings. This is what we need to do in order to create and understand the weight of the evidence. Policymakers want to know how the latest study affects what was known before, how new work fits into the total body of work, and how the research aggregates to form a conclusion.

We can do more to assure the credibility of research. We can assure that designs are suited to questions, that more studies are longitudinal, that replication takes place, and that work is synthesized to provide cumulative answers. It is true that much of this cannot be done without additional funding, and lack of adequate support for education research creates a real challenge. Elaborate designs, longitudinal studies, and replication are very expensive. And funders tend to put a premium on new work, just like reformers do, rather than on repeating existing work or doing follow-up studies. Each funder wants to claim its own unique contribution, so it is hard to get both public and private funders to support confirmatory work that's not likely to be as splashy as the original. In the case of dissertations, we can also accept some blame. We push the new and the unique no matter how narrow and arcane it can make the topic. And we rarely think about the importance of replication and confirmatory studies when encouraging students to undertake research projects.

The fact that too few large-scale, longitudinal, and replication studies are done is not all our fault, but we cannot escape the blame. We value newness over replication ourselves—in our training of future researchers and our guidance about dissertations. We argue among ourselves over paradigm rather than spending the time necessary to see how the evidence accumulates across qualitative and quantitative work and across different research approaches. We are too rarely concerned that students become adept in combining methods. Certainly, we must convince funders that we need more money to do the kind of work that they value, the kind of work that has meaning for policy and practice. But we also need to prove that we are interested in doing the sort of work that can justify a much larger investment.

There are some encouraging signs. One example that I am very proud of is the Campbell Collaboration, which is taking shape under the leadership of Bob Boruch. This collaboration, a new multi-national effort, will prepare, maintain, and promote access to systematic reviews of studies on the effects of social and educational policies and practices. The organization will provide regularly updated syntheses intended to help policymakers and other users by presenting the weight of the evidence. And it's no coincidence that by deciding what research to include in syntheses, the Collaboration can have a great deal of influence over research standards.

However, it would be naïve of us to assume that better research would automatically have stronger sway in the marketplace of ideas that surrounds urban school reform. In fact, we have reason to worry about the climate for research and the value placed on evidence by practitioners. Tom Corcoran, Cathy Belcher, and I studied the adoption and support for comprehensive school reforms in two large districts. We called them River City and Metropolis. We found that while district personnel wanted to use evidence about student learning in choosing reforms, and talked about "best practice" in a way that implied research-based decisions, they often made choices based on ideology rather than results. At the school level, there was even less pretense about the importance of research.

Our major finding was that school personnel value the opinions of other educators much more than published research. The teachers we surveyed placed strong value on the endorsements of other teachers, with between 80% and 90% agreeing that these were the "best" source of evidence on quality. On the other hand, only around 60% gave such support to published research on evidence of effects. In fact, 35% of the teachers we surveyed in these 2 cities think that the findings published by education researchers should not be trusted. Almost the same proportion is likely to distrust anything but their own eyes and own measures as evidence of effectiveness in education.

Surely there is reason to distrust educational research, as I have just discussed, but we have not built a culture of attending to evidence in education either. Of course, the relationship between a research culture that produces good evidence and a culture of use of evidence is circular. We need to work on both sides if we want to improve evidence-based decision making. It is important that we worry about the quality of the research we produce, but it is also important that we focus the education of practitioners on evaluating, and benefiting from, evidence. I know that the new mid-career leadership program we are designing at GSE takes evidence-based practice as one of its starting points. I'm encouraged by that development.

## Improvement Not Reform

If "reform" is not the answer for urban schools because they already do too much of it, because they tend to rely on structural reforms, and because picking reforms that "work" is difficult to do based on existing evidence, and educators might disregard the evidence anyway—what *is* the answer?

I would like to shift the metaphor around urban school progress from "reform," to "improvement." This is not a new concept. Fifteen years ago, Richard Elmore and Milbrey McLaughlin (1988) wrote a very influential little book called *Steady Work*. Improving teaching and learning, the heart of schooling, is slow, unending, not particularly glamorous, and hard work. It is not a matter of policies coming in from the outside, swooping down. It is a matter of continued attention to the basics and to what matters in teaching and learning. It involves deep investment in teacher quality and knowledge, through recruiting, compensating, and developing teachers. It involves thoughtful, well-funded professional development. Professional development must be intensive, extensive (over a period of time), focused on the curriculum the teachers are teaching, and followed up by coaching and other on site support.

At the Consortium for Policy Research in Education, we surveyed elementary school mathematics teachers in California who had taken a variety of kinds of professional development in mathematics. Some of them took content-focused units based on the curriculum that the students were learning on fractions. Some of them took equally worthy courses that were disconnected from the curriculum: collaborative learning, diversity training, things that we think of as important but that weren't directly connected to the 4th grade mathematics curriculum. What we found was that the teachers who took the curriculum-related professional development, provided that it was intense enough and had enough follow up and support, changed their practice in ways that were envisioned by the reforms, and also had gains in student achievement that the other teachers who were engaged in other kinds of professional development did not have (Cohen & Hill, 2001). When I tell this story to a lay audience, the story that professional development focused on curriculum that students are learning has a bigger effect than professional development that is disconnected from what the students are learning, they look at me strangely, thinking, "you were paid to have that study done?" The answer is so commonsensical. In fact, that kind of intensive curriculum-related professional development is not what we do in education. We know that we do scatter-shot workshops. We teach about Lyme disease and Right-to-Know with chemicals and all things that are important for the safety of our kids, but don't influence student learning. If we want to influence student learning, if we want to improve students' knowledge of subjects and skills, then we have to think seriously about the professional development in which we engage. At Penn GSE, in programs such as the Penn Literacy Network, the Philadelphia Writing Project, and the Penn-Merck Collaborative for the Enhancement of Science in Education, we have content-focused professional development, and we need to promote that force.

Improvement over the long run and steady work involves good curriculum design. We don't make enough time for teachers to collectively develop curriculum. We also don't provide adequate choices through the web or other means if they don't want to make their own curriculum. We have this enormously romantic notion that teachers want to teach all day and come home and write curriculum all night. The teachers that we studied in our research that are implementing the various reforms that we are studying do not want to do that. They'd like to have good curricula available to them so that they can make wise choices about what to use. Improvement involves developing leaders—administrators and teachers—who know good instruction and can evaluate and support it. It means developing a collective vision for, and responsibility for, good instruction, and overcoming the norms of isolation and building communities in which teachers are accountable to one another for good instruction. This is much like what we're starting at the new Penn Assisted School, where teachers are in each other's classrooms all the time and where they talk about their practice regularly. Granted, the school has only been open for two months, but so far, it is a model; we hope that this kind of teamwork continues.

Steady improvement involves changing the culture of low expectations surrounding urban schooling. As we at CPRE have examined instruction in many settings across the nation, we see countless examples of teachers "protecting" their students by not presenting material that is more challenging. Believing that the students they teach from "disadvantaged" backgrounds need discipline, order, and basic skills, even teachers who try to teach more complex material, even those who may be better prepared than others in terms of their own knowledge and skills, even those with supportive principals and other factors in their favor, doubt that poor and under-prepared students can reach challenging and complex understandings. Encouragingly, experience—through professional development, observing experts teach their classes, seeing their own children engage in problem solving and more complex activities—can change these beliefs. In Kentucky, in 1994, only 35% of teachers agreed with the Kentucky reform principle that all children can learn, and most at high levels. By 1999, 68% agreed. How did this change occur? In the context of a stable reform environment, which Kentucky had over all these years, teachers made incremental changes in their practice, and student performance, even in the most disadvantaged settings, improved. Teachers could see that as they changed their practice, the students were learning.

Some of the efforts that I have described can be achieved by reallocating resources. Some will require new money, and while certain structural reforms might make them easier, they don't necessarily require structural change. We can see some schools and classrooms undertaking such efforts with more central direction, such as District #2 in New York City, or San Diego, or with less central direction and more flexibility from district operating procedurism, such as we see in our own Penn Assisted School.

The tough work of improvement must be separated from the glamour of reform. It requires steady work. It requires realism rather than romanticism. It requires the efforts of all of us.

## Notes

1. The most recent report of this important longitudinal study was published after this lecture in 2005 by Schweinhart and colleagues. This citation is also included in the references.

## References

Cohen, D., & Hill, H. (2001). *Learning policy: When state education reform works.* New Haven, CT: Yale University Press.

Elmore, R., & McLaughlin, M. (1988). *Steady work: Policy, practice, and the reform of American education*. Washington, DC: Rand Corporation.

Fuhrman, S. (2000). *Education policy: What role for research?* Division L Vice Presidential address at the annual meeting of the American Educational Research Association, New Orleans, LA.

Henig, J., Hula, R., Orr, M., & Pedescleaux, D. (1999). *The color of school reform: Race, politics, and the challenge of urban education*. Princeton, NJ: Princeton University Press.

Hess, F. (1999). *Spinning wheels: The politics of urban school reform*. Washington, DC: Brookings Institution Press.

Ladd, H. F., & Hansen, J. S. (1999). *Making money matter: Financing America's schools. Committee on education finance. Commission on Behavioral and Social Sciences and Education*. Washington, DC: National Research Council, National Academies Press.

Nye, B., Hedges, L.V., & Konstantopoulos, S. (2000). The effects of small classes on academic achievement: The results of the Tennessee Class Size Experiment. *American Educational Research Journal, 37* (1), 123–151.

Stone, C., Henig, J., Jones, B., & Pierannunzi, C. (2001). *Building civic capacity: The politics of reforming urban schools*. Lawrence, KS: University of Kansas Press.

PART THREE

# The Praxis of Urban Education: What Do I Do Now?

# Behind the Smile

The brilliant smile
She so carefully applies each morning
Is as ancient as the smiles that hid
The agony, anguish and bitter hate
Of the generations who bent their heads
To hide the hate in their eyes as they broke their backs in servitude

Her beguiling smile
Hides the painful knowledge that
She cannot, must not, will not, speak to her birth mother
Whenever and wherever she should, by chance, encounter her.
A mother from whom she sought only love
And from whom she learned that there is no love or peace
To be found at the end of a crack pipe.

The radiant smile
With which she blesses me each morning
Conceals the tears glistening behind her eyes
For siblings lost to the system,
Brothers and sisters whom she may never see again
A dysfunctional family
Devoured and decimated by a dysfunctional system
Created by a society that values possessions over people

The impish, bewitching smile
Is an elaborate mask for wounds that may never heal
She hasn't seen or heard from her father for
More than nine of her fourteen years
The woman she now calls mom
She's known for less than a year
The promise of a place to call home
And a family not quite her own
Are almost enough to quell her fears

And so, she smiles
Unaware of the miles of sorrow and pain
Etched between the curves of that smile
I smile and softly whisper—I believe in you!
Armor pierced, her façade crumbles and in a quiet voice
She hesitantly shares her sorrowful story……
With tears glistening in my eyes I whisper
I still believe in you.

TWELVE

# What Does "Good" Urban Teaching Look Like?

Rochelle Brock

What is my philosophy of good urban education? How does it reflect my pedagogical style? How do I understand myself as an urban teacher? The answers to these questions are constantly changing and growing, because the more I learn about myself, the more I learn about my purpose as an urban educator. I am able to ask my students the right questions when I can ask myself the right questions. Although there are always common themes running throughout my philosophy of urban education, it is constantly in flux. The more I learn and experience life, the better able I am to teach my students.

I hold certain beliefs based on my life assumptions. I accept that there are certain facts and truths based on my life experiences. The combination of my beliefs and truths becomes my philosophy and pedagogy A truth: minority and poor people are always fighting to get through the back doors of educational systems. A truth: in a colonial system, the colonizer has a dual purpose in educating the colonized. The first is socialization into accepting the value system, history, and culture of the dominant society. The second is education for economic productivity. A truth: the oppressed are treated like commodities imbued with skills that are bought and sold on the labor market for the profit of capitalists. These are my truths as an African American woman and an urban educator.

We live in a society that places people based on their race, class, and gender. I believe that students who are poor and/or minority exist under a system that accepts and promotes their failure. I know that in most schools, World History equals Western History; children celebrate Thanksgiving by dressing as Indians with art class feather headbands and are told that Columbus discovered America.

I know that students of color are hungry for knowledge about their culture, not tolerance. I know that Black and Brown children are tracked into special classes where they typically remain for the entirety of their school career. I know that the ideology under which America exists constructs these children as nothing and ensures through that construction that these children believe they are nothing. All of these things I know, and I cannot accept—not when I feel the failure of a large segment of the population. My knowledge and observations contextualize my beliefs.

As an urban teacher, I must teach all of my students, especially my minority and disenfranchised students, to think critically and to deconstruct the world. I must provide them with the tools to analyze their everyday life through the lenses of race, class, and gender oppression. They must think politically and see the connections between what they see on a comedy sitcom, to what they read or don't read in the newspaper. My pedagogy is educating my students for struggle, survival, and the realization of their humanity. I believe I must teach to demystify the injustices of the world by becoming a radical teacher, facilitating students in the understanding of their self-identity and outside constructed identity, the structures working against them, what they must fight, and the form the fight will take—education of self and activism for the community.

How do I go about enacting my truths and my beliefs as they change and I change, although my truths and beliefs manifest themselves differently depending on the needs and identities of my students? What stays constant, and what all my students recognize about me is that they will leave my class more aware than when they entered.

The following is a fictional constructed conversation with my African goddess Oshun. Using a Black feminist theoretical framework, the reader becomes privy to our conversation on urban education and teaching Black feminist thought is a useful tool in framing this chapter because, as Patricia Hill Collins (1991) asserts, it furnishes a space for voice by challenging prevailing approaches to studying oppressed groups. These approaches support the notion that the oppressed identify with the powerful and are seen as less human, and therefore less capable of interpreting their own oppression. A feminist perspective allows a language of critique to be developed that questions this assumption. This language of critique is developed through an epistemological framework, which is useful in understanding urban teaching. Collins (1991) delineated a Black feminist epistemology which has the following four characteristics: (1) "concrete experience as a criterion of meaning," (2) "the use of dialogue in assessing knowledge claims," (3) "the ethic of caring," and (4) "the ethic of personal accountability."

Epistemology, the study of how knowledge is constructed, lets us construct the questions to delve more deeply into the realities of the urban family. Moreover, we are better able to understand the answers we receive from those questions. For the purpose of this chapter the first two characteristics will be used to frame how we look at urban teaching and to help us understand what we ultimately see.

The conversation is based on the group conversation method, which is a culturally relevant qualitative ethnographic strategy. Taking the group conversation method one step further, the constructed conversation is based on the tenets of Black feminist thought and allows a fictional dialogue to personalize the subject by creating a connectedness between the words. A constructed conversation asks us to momentarily suspend reality. The essence of the constructed conversation is the "use of dialogue in assessing knowledge claims," the second characteristic of a Black feminist epistemology (Brock, 2005).

Dialogue implies talk between two subjects, not the speech of subject and object. According to Collins (1991), "a primary epistemological assumption underlying the use of dialogue in assessing knowledge claims is that connectedness rather than separation is an essential component of the knowledge validation process." Collins further states that people become human and empowered only in the context of a community, and only when they "become seekers of the type of connections, interactions, and meetings that lead to harmony." Dialogue allows this to happen.

Dialogue presupposes that we talk with each other not at each other. In addition, dialogue is an important aspect of both African American language and Latino(a) language. It assumes an understanding that language is more than words and cannot be a singular event as in one-sided talk. A feminist epistemology demands discourse. In order for ideas to be tested and validated, everyone in the group must participate. As in the first characteristic, which speaks of the importance of community, as well as knowledge and wisdom, dialogue occurs within a community of individuals.

The use of dialogue in assessing knowledge claims supports the methodology of constructed conversation. The method of constructed conversation is "in tune with" the African American and Latino(a) tradition of dialogue within a community setting. In addition, the constructed conversation methodology allows research to be presented in a more realistic format.

In this context, I address the nuances involved in teaching urban kids of color, specifically Black and Brown students.

**OSHUN:** Rochelle, tell me about your classroom. How do you enact your philosophy of urban education?

**ROCHELLE:** I teach through a pedagogy of wholeness which allows me to work with all parts of the student (Brock, 2005). I see and talk to so many students who are struggling to believe in themselves and end up doubting their existence, their right to be. The most important issue to me as a teacher and as a political activist working toward social justice and equity for all students is to bridge that disconnect. I want a conversation about the curriculum or pedagogy needed for urban and minority students. What type of education is needed? What type of education will be empowering? How do I as an instructor foster in my students a commitment toward radical agency?

These are questions I have asked myself and am still struggling to answer. I realize that there are inequalities, poor schools, racist teachers, bad curricula, and children coming into the class ill-prepared to learn There are countless reform movements aimed at making urban schools better Some movements blame the teachers; others blame the students, and others are convinced that urban schools are destined to fail. The movements are not successful. Despite the failures in urban school reform and teaching reform movements, we can't give up. Effective teachers of urban students understand the symbiotic relationship between their teaching philosophy and their pedagogy and how both have been influenced by their culture (Bartolome, 2008; Dimitriadis, 2008; Joyce, 2008; Foster, 1994). How can I take my intellectual knowledge and make it work in urban settings? How can I dance with theory in a rhythm which is indigenous to my culture?

**OSHUN:** Gestalt—understand all the parts of your whole. As a minority in a society that devalues us at every turn, survival is often the main goal. From negative depictions on television to negative depictions in the ideology of America, we are under a constant siege, battling for survival. How do you enact this pedagogy of wholeness in your classroom?

**ROCHELLE:** Let me use as an example of my pedagogy a class I teach called *The African American Woman.* As a critical teacher, I try to facilitate my students to understand the anger and the pride I feel in my Black identity. I attempt to lead them to an understanding of the *culture of survival* that Black people have historically possessed. In my class, my students and I discuss the insidious ways Black women are constructed in society. We discuss the social, historical, political, and economic realities of an urban environment. I begin the class with a word list scribbled on one half of the bulletin board: "ideology, epistemology, deconstruction, hegemony, devaluation, Other, dichotomy, binary opposition, stereotypes." I then ask the students for adjectives they think of when describing Black women. Of course they begin with politically correct, positive words—strong, beautiful, mother—until I tell them to be honest and tell me the words that most of society uses to describe Black women. At that point a fervor is created, as students hurl words at me faster than I can write them down—slut, ho, matriarch, ugly, sexual, aggressive, demanding, fat, unattractive, teen mothers. Once the board is filled I just let them look at the words, allow them to seep into their consciousness. (We also do this exercise discussing Latina women; many of the descriptors are the same.)

**OSHUN:** Aren't the words already part of their consciousness?

**ROCHELLE:** Singularly, maybe, but not together. There is an impact on students when the students see the board dripping with the venomous lexicon.

**OSHUN:** Kind of a drama queen, aren't you?

**ROCHELLE:** Whatever it takes. It's important that the students realize from the start that this is not a history class and we are not going to go through a long litany of historical facts on Black women. We analyze the construction of Black womanhood and the etymology of these words through the lenses of ideology, epistemology, the Other, deconstruction, hegemony, devaluation, dichotomy, binary opposition, stereotypes. They learn these concepts, pay close attention to them in their readings; it is through an understanding of these concepts that they will begin to partially open the door in their realization of Black women. Whatever time remains in the class on that first day is spent talking about the meaning of Black feminist thought—its purposes, goal, and benefit to our understanding of Black and Brown women. It is also important to understand that many, many Brown women are included in the categories, situations, and assumptions that are placed on Black women. Given the conditions of slavery and indenture in the Caribbean, South and Central America, and the diaspora which blended Black and Brown together, we are looking at complex racialized groups. For the purpose of this conversation, I relate to Black and Brown women through Black feminist thought.

Borrowing from Patricia Collins (1991), I divided the discussion of African American women, and to a large part, Latina women, into five themes:

- Black Feminist Thought
- Legacy of Struggle
- Representation and Controlling Images
- Search for Voice
- Empowerment in Everyday Life

Through readings, documentaries, films, and class discussions, the class dissects the life of African American women. This dissection allows the students (Black, Brown, and White—male and female) to understand the various ways ideology has attempted to control and dominate Latina and African American women. In addition, an understanding of Black feminist thought allows the students to see the ways Black and Brown women are not only deconstructing the race, gender, and class oppression of women but also Black and Brown female activism and empowerment.

I am aware of the need to assess the abstract through concrete experience. Although I use *Black feminist thought* to teach students the theory that underlies Black women's lives, I also weave in *We Are Your Sisters: Black Women in the Nineteenth Century,* an anthology of Black women's writings edited by Dorothy Sterling (1984). In this excellent volume, students read firsthand accounts of Black women under enslavement, freedom, the Civil War, and post-World War I through letters, diaries, interviews, and Freedmen's Bureau records. In this way two purposes are served: the first is the women become subjects in their own history and are no longer objectified by present-day scholars Students are allowed to hear their voices, concerns, and intelligence, and then relate that voice to the tenets of Black feminism. For example, they receive a glimpse of the bewilderment and confusion the concept of freedom caused some enslaved people. Take, for example, the following passage from Sterling's *We Are Your Sisters* (1984):

> Member de fust Sunday of freedom. We was all sittin' roun' restin' an' tryin' to think what freedom meant an' ev'ybody was quiet an' peaceful. All at once ole Sister Carrie who was near 'out a hundred started in to talkin':
>
> Tain't no mo' sellin today,
> Tain't no mo' hirin' today,
> Tain't no pullin off shirts today,
> Its stomp down freedom today
> Stomp it down!
> An' when she says Stomp it down, all de slaves commence to shoutin' wid her:
> Stomp down freedom today—Stomp it down! Stomp down Freedom today.

**OSHUN:** You trouble and layer the realities of knowledge or in some cases what we think we know. Speaking of knowledge I remember once how you used the book to lay a guilt trip on your students.

**ROCHELLE:** As soon as I realize my class is not doing the assigned reading, I recite a passage from *We Are Your Sisters* where various women discussed their struggle to learn to read during enslavement, despite fear of death if discovered. I have to bring it home to the students. Personal accountability (Collins, 1991; Villaverde, 2008) is not just a notion. In my class, students are accountable for their actions and when they aren't I let them know Tapping into my Black matriarchal self—we have had that guilt trip laid on us since we were babies. I like to think of it as more of a reality check.

**OSHUN:** It's the juxtaposition of accountability within the ethic of caring; both are qualities of effective and affective teaching.

**ROCHELLE**: In addition, students begin to appreciate that African American women who were enslaved understood their objectification and oppression at the hands of a cruel system and found ways to survive. Either due to a lack of education or miseducation, many students believe that other than Sojourner Truth and Harriet Tubman, slave women were just singing in the fields and accepting their conditions. Black women have always participated in the legacy of resistance and struggle from the social, historical, and political conditions of society. For example, Lewis Hayden, a leader of Boston's Black community in the 1900s, tells of how his mother kept her children from being sold:

> My mother often hid us all in the woods, to prevent master selling us. When we wanted water, she sought for it in any hole or puddle formed by falling trees or otherwise. It was often full of tadpoles and insects. She strained it, and gave it round to each of us in the hollow of her hand. For food, she gathered berries in the woods, got potatoes, raw corn & c. After a time, the master would send word to her to come in, promising he would not sell us. (Hayden, in Sterling, 1984, p. 58)

It is important for my students to understand the strength that these women possessed despite the hell they were living in. I often remind them of the words and images we wrote on the board the first day of class so that they can see the dichotomy between the reality of Black women and the perception of Black women.

Although I occasionally use the didactic method when there was particular information the students needed, my pedagogy is built around the second characteristic of an African American epistemology, the use of dialogue in assessing knowledge claims. In the African American community, words carry power. An African American epistemology demands discourse and pursues the connectedness of dialogue (Collins, 1991). Connectedness, an important part of African American roots, asserts that the importance of community outweighs the need of the individual in African American thought, which is related to a sense of being human (Asante, 1991; Collins, 1991; Hurtado, 1996; Jocson, 2008). Asante (1991) believes that becoming human or realizing the promise of becoming human is the only task of the person. Likewise, Collins asserts that people become human and empowered only in the context of a community and only when they "become seekers of the type of connections, interactions, and meetings that lead to harmony" (p. 185).

In my class I strive to create a community of learners through dialogue where the talk is simultaneously distinct and collective. I create a safe space where the freedom exists to explain self and others. When a teacher engages a class in personal introspection, they must be prepared to hear the painful questioning of students. In one log entry a Black female student cried, "Me questioning me am I the source of the friction never forgetting or forgiving?" (log entry, July 10, 1997). She went on to say:

> I started to question the fact if there was racism, because the people in that circle would never express or better yet have or entertain an ill thought against a black person. BULLSHIT! I know that when I have people look at us strange.

> I know that when I am with a white guy people stare. I know that my colored skin matters. I know when people see me some tell me I'm pretty *for a Black girl.* I know when I talk to people about State they assume I'm here on scholarship or because of affirmative action. I know that people give me grief because I am an African American. I know that I was scared for my boyfriend every time he

drove home. *I know that I know.* Being in that class made me wonder. Made me wonder about reasoning and logic. (log entry, July 10, 1997)

**OSHUN:** Do you think you make learning meaningful for your students?

**ROCHELLE:** I believe that to make learning a meaningful experience students must become active in the attainment of knowledge. In order for this to happen, it is critical to create a space within the class in which student–teacher and student–student discourse can occur. For this reason, at least 70 percent of class time is spent in discussion, where we critically analyze the class readings in a sociohistorical context. We need to know how we got here, why we got here, and how power worked in creating the current context in urban schools, with Black and Brown students. Each semester, many students enter the class afraid to speak, fearful that their knowledge will not be valued or they will have nothing important to add to the discussion. Students of all colors and classes, though to different degrees, have been silenced through years of schooling in a system that operates on the belief that non-credentialed knowledge is unimportant. Although at first apprehensive to speak, eventually most students begin to use their voice and engage in dialogue where they are using their specialized knowledge to theorize about the taken-for-granted or personal feelings and experiences they hold.

If I become too theoretical, I can lose sight of the subjugated knowledge, which has helped Black people survive in this country since the 1600, as well as Brown people who have entered the US to seek a better life. Finding a method to combine my empirical and experiential way of knowing is paramount to my survival both as a teacher and a Black woman. More importantly, it is paramount that I use my personal dilemma to appreciate the realities of students and better equip my pedagogical philosophy to foster a mental–spiritual decolonization of the mind and spirit.

**OSHUN:** Simmons (1962) states, "Trying to write beyond the assignment of language to a medium of personal expression I have been cognizant that writing does not translate a reality outside itself but, more precisely, allows the emergence of a new reality." I think of Moraga and Anzaldúa's questions, "How do we organize ourselves to survive this war? To keep our families, our bodies, our spirits intact?" (Moraga & Anzaldúa, 1981).

In response to both Simmons and Moraga and Anzaldúa, I say we develop a language of critique, but one in our own voice, filled with anger, emotion, and caring.

**ROCHELLE:** Often in heated class discussions, White students feel under attack because of the emotional mode of expression that some Black and Brown students engage in. Often it is the first time White students have been physically and socially close (as in proximity) to Brown and Black students. As the teacher and facilitator, I am left with either the choice of silencing students of color, encouraging them speak in a dry, detached style, or utilizing the teachable moment and opening a discussion on different styles of communication. Of course the discussion is more than a simple talk on different communication styles; instead, it is a view into the historical and social effects on the construction of culture. Safety for all students to tell their truth takes time and patience.

An ethic of caring is developing the capacity for empathy. We share with others when we empathize with them and they with us. For example, an interesting conversation took place among several students when I asked them to discuss the class so that I could use their words for a paper I was writing at the time. The discussion eventually turned to the topic of hate and the question of whether we as a society ever get beyond it. Lisa, an extremely emotional and caring person, sincerely attempts to deal with her Whiteness and understand Black culture.

> **Lisa:** (White female) I want to touch it [the pain of Black people] and make it better. I have to watch it and can't do anything about it. My White friends don't understand when I talk about the importance of this class and the fact that I have learned so much.
>
> **Tina:** (North Indian female) I understand your pain and I feel bad for it but Black people have to go through the pain every day of being the Other and as much as I feel for what you are experiencing you will never understand the daily pain that Black people experience.

Tina empathized with Lisa's frustration but also was not going to allow Lisa to become wonderful *in-your-face-with-the-truth* white savior community. The respect and understanding they had for each other were evident when they joked with Lisa about her constant crying and said they were going to make her a stronger person by the end of the semester. In my classroom I attempt to invoke an ethic of caring in my teaching as well as the ways students interact with each other.

The last theme of the class, Empowerment in Everyday Life, attempts to show students how Black and Brown women are redefining and empowering themselves and their community and also how each student has the responsibility to take the learning beyond the class into everyday life. Tell me, Oshun, have you ever given birth?

**OSHUN:** From my womb I have given birth to a civilization.

**ROCHELLE:** Yeah, well, I can't lay claim to a civilization, but one night for three hours I felt like I gave birth to the consciousness of 40 students.

**OSHUN:** Sounds painful.

**ROCHELLE:** It was. My labor pain lasted four months. But seriously, the birth was actually the fruition of a teaching dream. See, every time I develop a new syllabus for *The African American Woman,* I have the final assessment a major class project—a collective project. A cultural production, with song, dance, and drama. It's very hard to pull it all together. I am usually little scared of tying a large portion of the students' grades into one assignment. It came about as I neared my last semester teaching at State, and I knew I most likely would never get the chance to teach this particular class again.

**OSHUN:** There are times when life forces us to take action.

**ROCHELLE:** My pending graduation gave me the freedom to pull together everything I hoped I had taught my students. The development of a pedagogy of wholeness that had consumed me for two years, more or less, coalesced in the final class project. Understand, I didn't want my students to leave with disconnected bits of information. The class, or my pedagogy, wasn't meant to present factoids of information but rather to paint a realistic picture of the African American woman, specifically, and women of color, in general. Earlier I talked about the connection between thought and action being a central part of Black feminist thought. Well, my challenge was how that connection could manifest itself in a semester-length class.

**OSHUN:** Why a class project?

**ROCHELLE:** I wanted to see the students bring together and make whole all of the knowledge from the entire semester. I attempted to utilize an alternative mode of assessment to really force the students into new ways of thinking. The celebration as I pictured it would allow students to not only express their individual talents but also concentrate on the specific aspect of the class that had been of greatest significance to their growth. I guess there were two central reasons why I decided on the class project. First, I believe in the importance of public pedagogy—taking what we had learned into the public sphere, beyond the confines of our classroom. I tried to instill in my students the commitment to teach what they had learned throughout the semester. Second, a social justice component had to be part of the project in order for it to be real. Again, it's not just about regurgitating the info back to me but making a difference.

With the project as 40 percent of their grade, I asked the students to design a program celebrating Black women. The only parameters were that it would be held on the last evening of the semester and that it would be open to the campus community. Many times throughout the semester I regretted my decision. Despite my best efforts and pedagogical strategies most students refused to take the project as seriously as I had hoped they would. Their initial lack of commitment left me with two choices—give failing grades or have a serious, open discussion with the class. I love to expose myself in class.

**OSHUN:** Isn't that against the law?

**ROCHELLE:** A goddess with a wicked sense of humor—I love it. Maybe the law of a traditional removed pedagogy, but I prefer to create an open, safe environment in my class where we share our feelings, so I had no choice but to choose the latter and spend an entire class period expressing my disappointment. I wanted the students to know that although I cared about their learning, I was not going to accept their lack of respect for me as an African American woman. I told them I felt as though they were treating me with less respect, based purely on my race and gender, thereby proving to me that they were not learning anything. I also gave them the alternative assignment in a very long research paper.

**OSHUN:** Don't try to make light of what happened. I know you were upset with the class and with yourself for not giving them what they needed.

**ROCHELLE:** You're right, I was upset and I blamed myself for the disaster that the class project had turned into, more than I blamed the students. But I did not hide my hurt and disappointment from the class. Instead I gave the students an honest expression of my feelings and the power to either disappoint the class mandate and me, or make rise to the occasion, do what they were capable of doing and create in me, a happy Black woman.

They did the latter. They pulled it together and held a program for the community celebrating Black women. Not only did they have poetry, African and modern dance, skits, and monologues, but they also raised $200 for the local women's shelter.

Learning is, and should be, messy, confusing, and painful. Although at times I doubted the effectiveness of my pedagogy, in the final analysis it worked. The students ultimately developed a sense of social commitment: they cared about the subject, they took responsibility for their failures, and made the needed changes. They acted as a community. Importantly, they began to understand the connectedness of social forces on the perceptions of Black women because they could see their actions as a manifestation of those forces. Ultimately, the students had empowered themselves and in turn empowered me as a teacher. They joined the pedagogical community.

**OSHUN:** A synergistic relationship exists between what you as a teacher and they as students receive from each other. As long as both you and the students through your interaction provided the force to keep the synergy alive, growth occurs If either retreated from the interaction, the synergistic relationship would cease to exist.

**ROCHELLE:** I infuse Black feminist thought and critical pedagogy to gain a better understanding of myself, my students, and the ways in which I design my teaching strategies. I use the tenets of Black feminist thought, critical pedagogy, and critical multiculturalism as I try to foster in my students not only a love of knowledge but also a commitment to political activism and dedication to social change in the urban environment. I think I am a good teacher, but often in the midst of my inner turmoil I ask myself whether I am leading them far enough. Am I really giving my students what they need or just disconnected bits of knowledge that will not provide the necessary inner strength? Have I taken my students far enough, to the level of healing necessary to go beyond the Other? This was perhaps the most important question, and I needed to find the answer.

Education should provide students "care for their being," with a pedagogy that teaches love of self and others, inner strength, humanity and humanness, survival and struggle, and hope and knowledge. King (1994) declares that "the potential to exist fully in alignment with one's human spirit is already present in each of us" (p. 270) and a task of education "is to help us learn hopeful principles of human existence" (p. 273). According to King, Afrohumanity is a soul-freeing liberatory education that nourishes well-being in the individual and helps a person reconnect with their humanity. When education does not provide a person with the right tools to tap into their humanity, it is impossible for hope to survive (Bartolome, 2008; Brock, 2005; Hollins, 2008). A freeing legacy in a curriculum of hope and Afrohumanity affords the acceptance of the humanity of everyone without being entangled in the web of proving legitimacy of any individual or group. In contrast to the effects of justifying self, Afrohumanity allows students to see the benefits of engaging with others on an equal basis. As long as North American cities—urban environments—are racially encoded with Black and Brown, I believe Black feminist thought and critical liberatory pedagogy are what we need to infuse in the education of new urban teachers.

We see our brothers and sisters as human and we understand the urgency in our "getting it together." Finally, we realize and act on the socioemotional intimacy of sharing in truth seeking and truth speaking amid gender equitableness. One of my students in the class *The African American Woman* gave me the answer when she said:

> I've been given to deal with myself. I now know I have a foundation from which to start to build my own Black consciousness, my own female consciousness and bring them together to where they impact me so that I can then turn around and impact people. The most important thing I got out of this class was that it's so important for me to go back and get them little Black girls. It's so important because a lot of us didn't have that and a lot of the Black girls right now don't have it. It's important for me to get them, you know, while they're young as opposed to older, so they don't go through this. They'll have some more different issues, but at least those will have some balance for them instead of just finding out now. So that's it.

## References

Asante, M. K. (1991). The Afrocentric idea in education. *The Journal of Negro Education,* 60, 170–179.

Bartolome, L. I. (2008). *Ideologies in education: Unmasking the trap of teacher neutrality.* New York: Peter Lang.

Brock, R. (2005). *Sista Talk: The personal and the pedagogical.* New York: Peter Lang.

Collins, P. H. (1991). *Black feminist thought: Knowledge, consciousness and the politics of empowerment.* New York: Routledge.

Dimitriadis, G. (2008). *Studying urban youth culture primer.* New York: Peter Lang.

Foster, M. (1994). The power to know one thing is never the power to know all things: Methodological notes on two studies of Black American teachers. In A. Gitlin (Ed.), *Power and method: Political activism and education research.* (pp. 129–146) New York: Routledge.

Hurtado, A. (1996). *The color of privilege: Three blasphemies on race and feminism.* Ann Arbor, MI: The University of Michigan Press.

Jocson, K. M. (2008). *Youth poets: Empowering literacies in and out of schools.* New York: Peter Lang.

Joyce, P. A. (2008). *School hazard zone: Beyond the silence/finding a voice.* New York: Peter Lang.

King, J. E. (1994). Being the soul-freeing substance: A legacy of hope and humanity. In M J Shujaa (Ed.), *Too much schooling too little education: A paradox of Black life in White societies* (pp. 269–294) Trenton, NJ: Africa World Press.

Moraga, C. & Anzalduá, G. (Eds.) (1981). *This bridge called my back: Writings by radical women of color.* New York: Kitchen Table Women of Color Press.

Simmons, D. (1962). Possible West African sources for the American Negro dozens. *Journal of American Folklore 75,* 339–340.

Sterling, D. (Ed.) (1984). *We are your sisters: Black women in the nineteenth century.* New York: W. W. Norton.

Villaverde, L. E. (2008). *Feminist theories and education primer.* New York: Peter Lang.

# Messiah to the $N^{th}$ Power

I have come in many guises before
And I'll assume many more
Until you all know the score
There's only one family of man
Only one, no more

I came as Marcus
Asked you to hold your head up
And revel in the beauty of your blackness
Taught you that darkest Africa
Was once a land of kings, queens, nations,
Empires and ancient civilizations
You told me to take my black ass back
So I gave you the Black Star Liner
Some of you made it to Liberia and Sierra Leone
I died jailed, cold, broke and alone.

I came to you as Martin the Dreamer
Asked you once again to lift up the family of man
Taught you that truth and justice
Will not be denied by lynchings, jails, hoses, hoods
Dogs, bullets or bombs
We built a coalition of colors fighting peacefully
For justice and equality
The world added Doctor to my names
And gave me a bullet for my pains

I have come in a hundred guises before
And I'll assume even more
Until you all know the score...
There's only one family of man
Only one, no more

I came as Malcolm
A little red man among black men
Jails and bars couldn't hold me 'cause
Allah's wisdom was there to mold me
Muhammad's nation gave me propers
When misguided and bitter
I taught hate in the name of Allah
A trip to Mecca
Opened my eyes

And I returned with true knowledge
As my prize
Love, not hate, is truly the answer

An assassin's bullet snuffed me out
Like radiation does a growing cancer

I came as Marley
Marcus's Rastafarian messenger
I asked you simply to:
"Get up and stand up for your right"
You heard the rhythms
Your heart still pounds to the beat
But I want your mind to resound
With the magic of the lyrics
So, don't tap your feet
Don't jump to the beat
Listen with your head and heart
To the Natural Mystic of
Our Redemption Song

In the jungles of Southern Africa
Many heard our song
Among them Nkomo and Neto
And so, I came once again
As Nyerere called Mwalimu
Knowledge in my right hand
Lightning and thunder in my left
Taught you that niggers and kaffirs
Will not be denied
By any system of Apartheid
I am not the Dalai Lama
Before we can talk ujamaa
We must stand as equals
Through the language of Uhuru

Yes, I have come in many guises before
And, I'll assume a thousand more
Until you all know the score
There's only one family of man
Only one, no more

I came as Mandela
Showed you that twenty seven years in isolation

Would only lead to the strengthening of my nation
With dignity and integrity
Carried forward the legacy
Of King Shaka Zulu
I am Abel, your brother and your nemesis
You can never slay the source of your genesis
Each time, like the Phoenix, I shall rise
To lead you ever close to the prize.

I have come in many guises before
There is only one family of man
Only one, no more
Some day you'll learn the score

|| THIRTEEN

# The Quest for Social Justice in the Education of Minoritized Students

Christine Sleeter

A pressing problem facing nations around the world today is the persistence of educational disparities that adversely affect minoritized students, and by extension, the nation as a whole. As Shields, Bishop and Mazawi (2005) explain, the term "minoritized" refers to those who, while not necessarily in the numerical minority, have been ascribed characteristics of a minority and are treated as if their position and perspective is of less worth. Exactly who are the minoritized students varies somewhat from country to country, but they generally include Indigenous students, students of color, students whose families live in poverty, and new immigrants whose parents have relatively low levels of schooling. As populations of minoritized students expand, the urgency of addressing disparities increases.

For example, in the United States, one can see the future population mix in the current school-age population, which is more racially, ethnically, and linguistically diverse than ever due to higher birth rates among communities of color, who tend to be younger than the White population, and net immigration of minoritized peoples. In 2008, students were 58% White, 22% Hispanic, 16% Black, 4% Asian and Pacific Islander, and 1% Native American (U.S. Department of Education, 2010). Yet, this growing proportion of students continues to experience disparities in school achievement from early childhood through university level. Villegas and Lucas (2002) noted that "[h]istorically, members of economically poor and minority groups have not succeeded in schools at rates comparable to those of their white, middle-class, standard English-speaking peers" (p. xi). As one snapshot indicator, according to Aud, Fox, and KewalRamani (2010), White, African American, and Asian 4-year-olds demonstrated higher rates of proficiency in letter recognition than Latino and American Indian 4-year-olds in a 2005 comparison. In reading, on the 2007 National Assessment of Educational Progress assessment, higher percentages of Asian/Pacific Islander and White 4th and 8th graders scored at or above Proficient than did African American, Latino, or American Indian students at the same grade levels, as did a higher percentage of White than non-White 12th graders. In mathematics, on the 2005 and 2009 National Assessment of Educational Progress assessment, higher percentages of Asian/Pacific Islander students in 4th, 8th, and 12th grades scored at or above Proficient than did White, Black, Latino, and American Indian students at the same grade levels. On the Scholastic Aptitude Test for entry into university, White students had the highest average critical reading score in 2008 and Asian students had the highest average mathematics score.

Similar disparities are evident in New Zealand schools. In 2010, students were 55% New Zealand European, 22% Indigenous Māori, 10% Pacific Nations, and 10% Asian immigrant and other (Ministry of Education, 2010). In mainstream schools Māori students are overrepresented in special education programs, leave school early with fewer qualifications, and are overrepresented in school expulsion and suspension figures compared with the dominant New Zealand European students (Ministry of Education, 2006). One finds the same picture with respect to Aboriginal students in Canada (Cherubini, Hodson, Manley-Casimir & Muir, 2010; Kanu, 2007), and in Australia, where in 2002 the 38% retention rate for Indigenous students contrasted sharply with a 76% retention rate for non-Indigenous students (Moyle, 2005). In India, rapidly expanded access to schooling has resulted in schools having much more diverse populations in terms of language, caste, gender, family income, and religion. At the same time, disparities in educational attainment are sharp (Kumar, 2010).

In Europe, particularly "old Member states" of the European Union, migrations of people from previous colonies and other sending countries, with their different age structures and birth rates, have expanded the diversity of its school-age population. Now sizable groups of ethnic and religious minorities are evident in most towns and cities (Luciak, 2006). As Liégeois (2007) put it, "The convergence of these two phenomena, migration and the emergence of minorities, has reconfigured the demographic, social, cultural, and European political landscape, a landscape now marked by pluriculturalism or multiculturalism" (p. 12). This pattern of increasing diversity is coupled with persistent and increasing educational disparities, primarily between those from dominant cultural groups as well as relatively well-educated immigrants (Holdaway, Crul & Roberts, 2009), and those of minoritized children, which include African Caribbeans, Roma, Travellers in Ireland, and Muslims in Greece (Luciak, 2006). For example, in Britain, despite fluctuations in the magnitude of the gap in various indicators of school achievement between White and African Caribbean Black students, the gap itself remains constant (Gillborn, 2008).

The situation of increasingly diverse student populations being taught by persistently non-diverse teaching forces exacerbates the problem of disparities in achievement. For example, in the U.S. in 2008, while about 58% of the students were White, about 82% of public school teachers were White, proportions that had not changed markedly over the years (U.S. Department of Education, 2010). In New Zealand, while 55% of the students identify as New Zealand European, 74% of teachers do so while only 9% of teachers identify as Māori, 3% as Pasifika, and 14% as other (Ministry of Education, 2010). In Canada, the growing numbers of Aboriginal children in classrooms are being taught largely by non-Aboriginal teachers who generally lack the background and training to teach them well (Cherubini, Hodson, Manley-Casimir & Muir, 2010). Teachers with a limited range of cross-cultural experiences and understandings are often unaware of the "funds of knowledge" that children of different backgrounds can call upon in classrooms, and may not understand the cultural cues that people use to indicate their willingness to enter into dialogue fundamental to learning (Gay, 2010; Gonzalez, Moll & Amanti, 2005). As a result, one commonly finds teachers using pedagogical practices and models of education more appropriate to the dominant populations than to the diverse populations in their classrooms, drawing on deficit discourses when these do not work (Bishop, 2005).

## Common Approaches to Understanding and Addressing Disparities

Because of the urgent need to address educational disparities, countries, states, provinces, and cities commonly have plans in place, at least at the level of policy documents. For example, the legislation known as No Child Left Behind in the U.S. announces this goal prominently. In the United Kingdom, speaking to the DfE Single Equality Scheme, Secretary of State for Education Michael Gove proclaimed that "Raising standards and narrowing gaps are the central goals of the government's education policy" (Department for Education, 2010). The Hon. Julia Gillard MP, formerly Minister for Education, Minister for Employment and Workplace Relations, and Minister for Social Inclusion, now Prime Minister of Australia, announced policy commitment to "Closing the gap between Indigenous and non-Indigenous Australians" (Gillard, 2008). Indian Prime Minister Manmohan Singh stated in 2009 that "The role of education is to uphold equity and tolerance . . . these are all-important in a country like ours which has diversities, to emerge as a strong nation" (Kumar, 2010, p. 41).

Yet, the successes of such plans are generally underwhelming. In the U.S., for example, although newspaper announcements often tout achievement gaps that are being closed as a result of No Child Left Behind, careful perusal of student achievement data does not warrant enthusiasm (Ravitch, 2010). Below, three approaches to understanding and addressing disparities are reviewed. I will argue that deficit-oriented approaches, while the most common, are least helpful, while emancipatory approaches that include culturally responsive pedagogy, while least common, have the most power to bring about lasting change.

## Deficit-Oriented Approaches

Deficit-oriented approaches to understanding and addressing disparities, though inherently problematic, continue to be very common. For example, in a discussion of the persistent racial disparities in U.S. education, Noguera (2002) noted that the most commonly held explanations evaluate presumed cultural characteristics of racial and ethnic groups: "it is widely believed that Asian-American students do well academically because they come from a culture that emphasizes the importance of hard work and the pursuit of academic excellence. . . . In contrast, African-American and Latino students are perceived as being held back by attitudes of opposition and a culture of poverty" (p. 6). Similarly, writing about Indian teachers' beliefs, Kumar (2010) pointed out that teachers commonly connect children's ascribed identities with assumptions about their educability that teachers regard as rooted in the parents' level of schooling.

Deficit-oriented perspectives find data-based support in surveys that correlate student achievement with student background factors without examining school processes. For example, in a large-scale survey of factors that correlate with reading achievement in 30 countries, Marks, Cresswell and Ainley (2006) found that cultural resources operationalized as books in the home and possession of classic literature and art explained more of the variance in student reading achievement than did family economic resources or several school factors. However, missing from the study was information about classroom pedagogy, teacher expectations, and the extent to which schools capitalize on non-mainstream cultural resources students do have.

The 'solution' from a deficit perspective, is to 'free' students from 'pathological' cultures of their homes by helping them to acquire more of the dominant culture. Writing about Māori education in New Zealand, Penetito (2010) remarked that

> The mainstream system has always accepted Māori students, but it has consistently treated them paternalistically. . . . For Māori, the message has always been: to achieve comparability in any aspect of the education system, you are to set aside your Māoritanga (qualities that distinguish you as a Māori) in favor of acquiring P¯aket¯atanga (qualities that demonstrate your socialization into P¯akeh¯a).[1] (p. 15)

Compensatory education has been the main deficit-oriented solution to disparities. It has taken a variety of forms, ranging from remedial basic skills education (Woolfolk, 2001), to transition bilingual programs that aim to move students into the dominant language as quickly as possible (Billings, Martin-Beltran & Hernandez, 2010), to offering minoritized students supplementary schooling so they can catch up. In a critique of deficit-oriented approaches to working with immigrant students in Spain, Rodríguez Izquierdo (2009) noted that such is manifest in:

> la concepción de la educación compensatoria como dispositivo para adecuar a los niños al ritmo de la clase, en la utilización de métodos de tratamiento de los trastornos del lenguaje para la enseñanza del castellano como segunda lengua, en la reducción de la diversidad a problema lingüístico.
>
> [the concept of compensatory education as a device to bring children into the rhythm of the classroom, the use of methods of treating disorders of language for teaching Castilian as a second language to reduce the diversity of the language problems.]

While compensatory education rests on problematic assumptions about minoritized communities that ignore systemic racism, and many such programs do not in fact improve students' learning (e.g., Rodríguez Izquierdo, 2009), some do produce small achievement gains. For example, in the U.S., Head Start provides a range of services to preschool children and their parents that more affluent families already have access to. Although evaluation studies of the impact of Head Start have been mixed, partly because of the varied quality of programs, they tend to find modest positive gains for children who have participated in Head Start in comparison to those who have not (Jung & Stone, 2008; Nathan, 2007). As another example, Title I authorizes funds to states and local educational agencies that have high concentrations of children in poverty to provide supplemental remedial education services. The initial intent was to enable schools to close the achievement gap between children in poverty and children from more affluent communities. Early evaluations found most Title I interventions to be largely ineffective. However, due to revisions in the nature of programs that qualify, they have become somewhat more effective in boosting the achievement of children in poverty (Borman, 2005).

Although minoritized communities critique and often reject deficit-oriented approaches because of their inherent devaluing of family and community cultures (e.g., Penetito, 2010; Yosso, 2005), such approaches refuse to go away. This is so probably because of the small successes of some compensatory programs, but even more because such approaches suggest that dominant communities have no culpability for the existence of disparities. In fact, educators from dominant groups often deny the deficit orientation within their own deficit explanations for disparities. The current popularity of Ruby Payne in U.S. schools is an example. Payne is an entrepreneur who consults with schools about how to teach children in poverty. Her message is largely one of offering strategies teachers can use to help children in poverty acquire aspects of middle class culture. Payne (2009) argues that her approach is not deficit-oriented because it focuses on how to help children escape the culture of poverty.

In a critique of Payne's message to educators, however, Bomer, Dworin, May and Semingson (2009) pinpoint several central problems with deficit-oriented approaches that arise from a failure to acknowledge the cultural resources children and their families have, and the way discrimination becomes institutionalized when programs and practices are built around that failure:

> Deficit perspectives, when educators hold them, have been shown in much research to lower the quality of education for children from low-income households (see e.g., Ansalone, 2003; Anyon, 1980; Connor & Boskin, 2001; Dudley-Marling, 2007; Gamoran & Berends, 1987; Moll, 1988; Moll & Ruiz, 2002; Oakes, 1985; Rist, 1970; Valenzuela, 1999). The kinds of conversations available to them are diminished, the scope of the curriculum contracts, the modalities in which they are asked to represent their learning are constricted.

And yet, deficit orientations persist as dominant groups attempt to maintain control over the education system into which minoritized students might assimilate. As Penetito (2010) argued with reference to Māori education in New Zealand, the mainstream system has always selected and filtered which aspects of Māori culture are admissible into the schooling system. Deficit thinking, then, normalized in the minds of many educators and in the routinized ways schooling is done, is bound up with the politics of who gets to exercise control.

## Structural Approaches

Structural approaches to understanding and addressing disparities focus on equalizing student access to inequitably distributed resources, such as high quality programs or teachers (e.g., Haycock & Hanushek, 2010). Rather than viewing the home and community culture of students as the main source of disparities, structural approaches look to systems in which students are educated.

For example, in a comprehensive study of the underachievement of English language learners in California (the great majority of whom speak Spanish as their first language), Gándara, Rumberger, Maxwell-Jolly and Callahan (2003) identified the following specific inequitable structures that place English learners at a disadvantage: access to qualified teachers and to teachers who are trained to teach English learners, access to good instructional materials and schooling conditions, meaningful assessment that identifies what students actually know rather than what they can communicate in English, access to rigorous coursework and to school counselors, time in classrooms that is used specifically for instruction, and segregation of English learners. They argued that all of these forms of inequitable resource distribution can be addressed, and that doing so would meaningfully address disparities in student learning. Similarly, in a "parsing" of the achievement gap in the U.S., Barton and Coley (2009) examined 16 inequitable conditions for learning for students of color and for students from low-income families. School conditions included access to the following: an academically rigorous curriculum, qualified and experienced teachers, lower class sizes, instructional technology, and a safe learning environment. The study also examined home and community factors such as exposure to environmental toxins and time spent viewing television. The authors argued that achieving equitable conditions of learning would substantially narrow achievement gaps; they also noted that inequitable conditions have deep roots that require a broad and comprehensive set of policies to address.

Similar kinds of structural barriers in schools have been identified in countries around the world. For example, Luciak (2006) describes segregation of minoritized students in many European countries, where they tend to be placed in "schools that are less academically challenging and of shorter duration," and in which students are "overrepresented in special education" (p. 76). In England, school processes of "selection and separation" support racism, particularly "setting" pupils into hierarchical "ability" groups, creating pathways for "gifted and talented" students, and creating specialist schools. In this system, which purports to be colorblind, Black Caribbean students end up with disproportionately less access to academically advanced curricula and teaching than White students and Indian immigrants (Gillborn, 2007).

Unlike a deficit orientation to understanding the underachievement of minoritized students, a structural analysis points toward systemic changes that could be made, such as reducing or eliminating tracking/streaming, ensuring that students who need excellent teachers the most get them, ensuring that all students have access to an academically challenging curriculum, reducing or eliminating segregation, ensuring that assessment systems are culturally fair, and so forth. Many current school reforms do, in fact, explicitly focus on some of these structural inequities, particularly access to a challenging academic curriculum.

For example, a prominent model in the U.S. is a system of charter schools known as the Knowledge Is Power Program (KIPP). KIPP's mission is to prepare minoritized students for university, and its schools are experiencing high rates of success in closing achievement gaps. Based on a study of three KIPP schools, Macey, Decker and Eckes (2009) synthesized the connected strategies that appear to contribute to KIPP schools' success. Strategies that address structural issues include ensuring students access to a rigorous college preparatory curriculum that is taught by teachers who are hired for their dedication, many of whom graduated from prestigious institutions; increased instructional time (a longer school day, school every other Saturday, and summer school); and consistency of expectations, rewards and sanctions across classrooms. Other factors include hiring relatively young, enthusiastic teachers and principals who are dedicated to the mission of KIPP and willing to do whatever is needed to close the achievement gap (significantly, almost half of the teachers were of color), and hiring instructional coaches who observe teachers and offer them feedback and help regularly. These important additional factors suggest limitations of a structural analysis alone, as they indicate the importance of culture as well as of how teachers position themselves toward their students and students' families.

No Child Left Behind addresses disparities by focusing on a selection of structural factors, particularly access to a rigorous curriculum, then legislating that schools must bring all students up to the same achievement standards. But it ignores other significant structural factors such the institutionalization of poverty (Anyon, 2005; Berliner, 2006). And, while ostensibly rejecting a cultural deficiency approach, spotlighting achievement disparities without offering a very deep analysis of why they exist, coupled with implying that treating the growing diversity of students as if they were identical will reduce disparities, fails to counter deficit thinking when disparities remain.

## Emancipatory Approaches

Emancipatory approaches to understanding and addressing disparities locate both how the problem is defined and why it continues to exist in unequal power relationships in schools as well as the broader society. From an emancipatory perspective, disparities exist because schools are institutionalized to produce them, through practices such as assigning students to schools based on race and class segregated residential patterns, staffing schools mainly with members of the dominant society, structuring curriculum and assessment around the knowledge and worldview of the dominant group, and classifying and streaming students based on their mastery of this curriculum. While confronting structural disparities, emancipatory approaches begin with the premise that those who experience disparities know best what the problems are, thus shifting who defines the problems and their solutions from members of the dominant society to marginalized communities, as part of a broader effort to claim, share, and use power for the community's benefit.

Within contexts that the dominant society controls, even when that control seems benevolent, children and youth from minoritized communities internalize deficit perspectives about themselves and their communities, which impacts negatively not only on their school achievement but also on their mental health. Research studies investigating students of color in different regions of the U.S., for example, have consistently found a relationship between academic achievement, level of awareness of race and racism, and identification with students' own racial group. Students who have a strong ethnic identity and are aware of barriers of discrimination are likely to see education as a tool of liberation, thereby taking it seriously (Altschul, Oyserman & Bybee, 2006; Chavous et al., 2003; Miller & MacIntosh, 1999; Sanders, 1997). For example, Altschul, Oyserman and Bybee (2008) surveyed 185 Latino/a 8th graders in 3 low-income middle schools where students ranged from being recent immigrants to second- and third-generation; most were of Mexican descent. Students with higher grades tended to have bicultural identities, identifying with their ethnic origin as well as focusing on overcoming obstacles within mainstream society. Students who identified little with their ethnic origin tended to achieve poorly, as did the relatively fewer students who identified exclusively with their culture of origin and not at all with the mainstream society. Based on in-depth interviews with high-achieving African American adolescents, Carter (2008) and O'Connor (1997) found that having a critical consciousness of race and racism and a strong Black identity helped the students develop an achievement ideology and a sense of agency.

Emancipatory knowledge counters perspectives generated by dominant social groups. For example, in addition to common use of cultural deficiency explanations, mainstream explanations of the underachievement of minoritized students are often couched in terms of psychological factors such as motivation or self-perception of competence (e.g., Pershey, 2010). While such analyses may suggest school interventions, they still tend to locate the problem within the student. Conversely, work such as Ladson-Billings's (1995) study of successful teachers of African American children, which was generated within the African American community, interpreted through African American professional thought, and explicitly designed to improve teaching of African American children, focused on classroom pedagogy that made a difference. In generating a vision of culturally relevant pedagogy, Ladson-Billings and the teachers placed culture and analysis of political oppression at the fore, constructing teaching as a tool of intellectual liberation, a vision that has long been common among African American educators (e.g., Woodson, 1933). Significantly, culturally relevant pedagogy describes what teachers do with minoritized students that both produces academic success as well as validating who they are. Similarly, writing with regard to the limits of conventional approaches to addressing the academic underachievement of Māori students, Penetito (2010) argued that Māori do have "remedies for this problem," but that "the system has continually set out to address the problem of disparity between Māori and non-Māori academic performance rather than explain the marginalization of Māori knowledge, history, and custom within the system" (p. 58). In other words, the dominant society tries to maintain control by addressing minoritized students' underachievement itself, rather than turning to and learning directly from minoritized communities.

Several somewhat different but related theoretical strands and practices can be considered emancipatory approaches. Critical race theory, for example, which emerged in the U.S. during the early 1980s as scholars of color in legal studies began to examine the intransigence of racism following the civil rights movement and the role of the law in maintaining unequal race relations, serves as a counter to analyses of diversity and disparity that do not specifically examine race and power (Dixson & Rousseau, 2006; Ladson-Billings & Tate, 1995; Solórzano & Delgado Bernal, 2001). Its main goal is to expose hidden systemic and customary ways in which racism works, drawing from a wide variety of sources ranging from statistics to social science research to personal experience. While much initial work in critical race theory was articulated largely within a Black/White binary, scholars of color have found the focus on racism immensely helpful, and many have adapted it to the histories, experiences, and concerns of specific communities of color. For example, developing TribalCrit theory with respect to American Indian tribes, Brayboy (2005) points out that for Indigenous peoples, colonialism is more fundamental than race. He argues that TribalCrit scholars "must expose structural inequalities and assimilatory processes and work toward debunking and deconstructing them" as well as working "to create structures that will address the real, immediate and future needs of tribal peoples and communities" (p. 440). He emphasizes that the entire process of both exposing the roots of disparities as well as addressing them must be conducted "with Indigenous Peoples" rather than "for" them (p. 440).

In New Zealand, Kaupapa Māori theory, research, and approaches to schooling emerged during the 1980s as a process through which Māori name the world, its problems, and their solutions (Bishop, 2003; Fitzsimons & Smith, 2000). According to Penetito (2010), "the kaupapa Māori agenda is about both the reproduction of Māori culture through schooling and the transformation of dominant structures within the broader context of education" (p. 225). Schools (kura) based on a Kaupapa Māori orientation have greatly expanded over the past 20 years, having a transformative impact on thousands of Māori students. As Penetito explains, reproduction of Māori culture does not mean returning to the culture of a century ago, but rather the power of Māori today to define their own goals and processes for achieving those goals.

While emancipatory approaches to addressing disparities focus on a wide range of power relations, there is a clear emphasis on classroom pedagogy that values students' cultural communities and that directly addresses the conditions of oppression their communities face. Critical pedagogy and culturally responsive pedagogy are forms of emancipatory pedagogy that relate to this book.

## Critical and Culturally Responsive Pedagogy

Freire (1972, 1973, 1976) argued throughout his life that oppressed people must develop a critical consciousness that will enable denouncing dehumanizing social structures, and announcing social transformation. In the process of teaching literacy to adults, he created a process of culture circles in which students took up topics of concern to them, discussed and debated them in order to clarify and develop their thinking, and developed strategies for acting on their concerns. A fundamental task in culture circles was to distinguish between what humans have created and what nature created, in order to identify what role humans can play in bringing about social change. Freire's connection between critical education and political work for liberation became an important basis for critical pedagogy.

Critical pedagogy engages students to analyze inequities in their own lives and advocate for justice. Duncan-Andrade and Morrell (2008), for example, explain that in their own secondary school teaching, while critical pedagogy did not preclude them from using traditional canonical texts, and it definitely involved teaching to very high academic expectations, critical pedagogy also meant using practices that were "explicitly aware of issues of power, oppression, and transformation, that honored the non-school cultural practices of the students, and that included the students in authentic dialogue about inequity and advocacy for justice" (p. 51). Their teaching tapped into students' everyday life experiences and deep familiarity with popular culture "to scaffold academic literacies" (p. 54), while simultaneously helping students learn to read and act on the world politically.

Similarly, culturally responsive pedagogy situates teaching and learning within an analysis of oppression. Gay (2010) defines culturally responsive pedagogy as teaching "to and through [students'] personal and cultural strengths, their intellectual capabilities, and their prior accomplishments" (p. 26); culturally responsive pedagogy is premised on "close interactions among ethnic identity, cultural background, and student achievement" (p. 27). Ladson-Billings (1995) proposed three dimensions of culturally relevant pedagogy: holding high academic expectations and offering appropriate support such as scaffolding; acting on cultural competence by reshaping curriculum, building on students' funds of knowledge, and establishing relationships with students and their homes; and cultivating students' critical consciousness regarding power relations. While these definitions overlap, they are not identical: Ladson-Billings's conception includes critical pedagogy in its emphasis on developing students' critical consciousness, while Gay's conception focuses more strongly on culture. In an attempt to operationalize culturally relevant pedagogy as reflected in 45 classroom-based studies of teacher practice, Morrison, Robbins and Rose (2008) found 12 kinds of actions that they classified into three broad categories, following Ladson-Billings's (1995) theoretical framework. Significantly, none of the 45 studies depicted all 12 key actions, although each study depicted several of them. Nonetheless, there was agreement that culturally responsive pedagogy, however it is specifically defined, is a significant emancipatory approach to addressing disparities.

Research on the impact of culturally responsive pedagogy on student outcomes, however, is rather thin, consisting mainly of case studies, program descriptions, and anecdotes (Brayboy & Castango, 2009; Gay, 2010). Many studies illustrate what it looks like in practice, although most of these do not report student outcome data (e.g., Cazden, 1989; Duncan-Andrade, 2007; Ladson-Billings, 1994; Lee, 2001; Matthews, 2003; Sleeter & Stillman, 2007). There are case studies that connect culturally responsive pedagogy with student engagement, suggesting that academic learning follows from engagement (e.g., Hill, 2009; Howard, 2001; Nykiel-Herbert, 2010). Several promising projects demonstrate positive impact on students, including the Algebra Project and the Kamehameha Early Elementary Project for Native Hawaiians (see Gay, 2010 for a detailed review).

Only a few projects that currently exist embody a robust conceptualization of culturally responsive pedagogy, and have produced published data demonstrating their impact on student outcomes, including achievement. Math in a Cultural Context (MCC) connects Yup'ik Alaska Native culture and knowledge with mathematics as outlined in the National Council of Teachers of Mathematics standards. The project was developed through collaboration between math educators, Yup'ik teachers, and Yup'ik elders. A few small-scale experimental studies report that students in classrooms using MCC make more progress toward the state mathematics standards than students in classrooms not using it (Lipka & Adams, 2004; Lipka et al., 2005).

Lee's (2006) Cultural Modeling project "is a framework for the design of curriculum and learning environments that links everyday knowledge with learning academic subject matter, with a particular focus on racial/ethnic minority groups, especially youth of African descent" (p. 308). Lee posits that African American life affords young people a wealth of cultural scripts and contexts that can be used in the classroom to develop literary analysis strategies students can then apply to unfamiliar texts, and that pedagogy that enables students to use their cultural frames of reference immediately engages them in much higher levels of cognition than is usually the case with a traditional curriculum. Lee's small-scale studies find that African American students learn literary analysis better through this culturally responsive pedagogical strategy than through traditional teaching (Lee, 1995, 2001, 2006).

Cammarota and Romero (2009) report data on the impact of the Social Justice Education Project on secondary Chicano students in high poverty schools in Tucson, Arizona. Their model of "critically conscious intellectualism" has three components: (1) curriculum that is culturally and historically relevant to the Chicano students, focuses on social justice issues, and is academically rigorous; (2) critical pedagogy in which students develop critical consciousness by gathering data on a problem involving racism in their own community and analyzing the problem using social science theoretical frameworks; and (3) authentic caring in which teachers demonstrate deep respect for students as intellectual and full human beings. The authors have documented a direct connection between student participation in the program and subsequent academic achievement on the state basic skills test, as well as high school graduation and subsequent university entrance.

As these examples show, culturally responsive pedagogy is promising. Based on their review projects such as these, Brayboy and Castagno (2009) note that

> There are a number of examples in the literature of programs that have successfully developed and implemented CRS [culturally responsive schooling] for Indigenous youth. What many of these case studies have in common is a 'grass roots' approach in which local communities play a key role in developing and sustaining the program, sustained financial support, and careful record-keeping of both achievements and setbacks. (p. 45)

The project that is the subject of this book—Te Kotahitanga—focuses on helping teachers shift the nature of pedagogy in their classrooms in a way that enables minoritized students to participate and learn. In subsequent chapters, we not only show what the implementation of culturally responsive pedagogy looks like in classrooms, but also link its use with student outcome data. We fully recognize that this focus on classroom pedagogy addresses one significant layer of a much larger system of institutionalized disparities and control. However, for students, what happens in the classroom is central.

## Teacher Professional Development

This book takes up the question of how teachers can be supported in learning to work with culturally responsive pedagogy, given the cultural, experiential, and social gaps between the majority of teachers and minoritized students. Ideally an emancipatory approach would staff schools with teachers who bring a critical consciousness and a keen understanding of students' lives and cultural backgrounds. However, if schools on a widespread scale are to address disparities in student outcomes, it is necessary to work with the teachers who are already there. The importance of doing so is supported by Hattie's (2009) comprehensive meta-analysis that highlights that the predominant influence on student achievement is the teacher.

The literature suggests that professional development that is most likely to have an impact on teaching is sustained over time, focuses on specific instructional strategies or content areas, involves teachers collectively rather than individually, is coherent, and uses active learning (Garet et al., 2001; Snow-Runner & Lauer, 2005). Peer coaching in the classroom is emerging as an important facet of teacher professional development that is linked with improved student learning (Joyce & Showers, 2002; Neufield & Roper, 2003). Yet, as is highlighted in Chapter 4, surprisingly little research directly links professional development with student learning. Yoon et al. (2007) reviewed more than 1,300 studies that purport to address the impact of teacher professional development on student learning, finding only 9 of the studies to meet rigorous criteria of evidence. The 9 studies found that student achievement increased by an average effect size of 0.54, or put another way, an improvement index of 21 percentile points, as a result of teachers' professional development, which Yoon and colleagues described as a "moderate effect" (p. 2). Clearly, there is a compelling need for well-designed, larger scale research on the impact of teacher professional development on student achievement.

Overall, research on teacher professional development for culturally responsive pedagogy is thin, examining impact on teachers, but not on students. None of the studies Yoon et al. (2007) reviewed focused on culturally responsive pedagogy. Most case studies that have been done explore the impact of specific kinds of professional development programs, such as a series of workshops (DeJaeghere & Zhang, 2008), inquiry-based graduate courses (Jennings & Smith, 2002; Sleeter, 2009), teacher networks (El-Haj, 2003), teacher collaborative inquiry groups (Hynds, 2007), community-based learning (Fickel, 2005; Moll & González, 1994), and sustained workshops combined with classroom-based coaching (Zozakiewicz & Rodriguez, 2007). But there has been no systematic research program into how teacher professional development on culturally responsive pedagogy changes teacher practice, let alone impacts on students.

I will suggest how one conceptualizes the nature and basis of disparities is important in the design of professional development for culturally relevant pedagogy. One can distinguish between two quite different designs: technical-rational designs in which experts teach pedagogical practices to teachers, and designs that attempt to reposition teachers as learners in relationship to their students and students' communities.

## Technical-Rational Models of Professional Development

Technical-rational models have long dominated education (Mehan, Hubbard, & Datnow, 2010). Sleeter and Montecinos (1999) explain that under a technical-rational model, "teaching entails a series of technical decisions made by experts who have a claim to authority. This claim rests on two premises: ownership of a domain of a morally neutral set of facts and the belief that those facts represent law-like generalizations that can be applied to particular cases" (p. 116). It follows then that professional development based on a technical-rational approach assumes that underachievement of minoritized students can be addressed by experts teaching teachers specific skills and understandings to use in the classroom. Two examples illustrate, both of which were structured in accordance with research on effective professional development.

Haviland and Rodriguez-Kiino (2008) reported the results of a program designed to shift White professors' deficit thinking about Latino students in a small college in the western part of the U.S. They explain that the course was based on the assumption that professors would shift their practices if they were more aware of the problem and knew more about culturally responsive pedagogy. The program entailed a 6-week online course teaching about Latino culture and culturally responsive teaching, and a 3-day summer institute where professors could share ideas and work together. Pre- and post-interviews, structured classroom observations, and student surveys revealed mixed results across the faculty. While some professors reported large gains in awareness, others found the program irrelevant to their practice.

Zozakiewicz and Rodriguez (2007) studied the impact of professional development for elementary and middle school teachers in California, towards making science gender-inclusive, inquiry-based, and multicultural. This program included a summer institute, classroom visits, a workshop focused on teacher-identified needs, and meetings to discuss progress. The summer institute taught theoretical underpinnings for sociocultural transformative teaching, and classroom practices that connect science with learning. Interview, focus group, and survey data revealed high satisfaction with the program and self-reported improvements in teaching for most teachers. However, Zozakiewicz and Rodriguez found that some of the teachers focused more on science aspects of the professional development rather than issues of culture and equity.

In both of these cases, while there was some self-reported shift in understandings and practices, there was also a significant amount of resistance that took the form of teachers viewing culture as irrelevant. While improving teaching of minoritized students may well require teachers to learn new knowledge and skills, unlearning deficit theorizing also requires that teachers reframe their construction of students. Timperley et al. (2007) reviewed 8 empirical studies of professional development programs designed to reframe teachers' constructions of students. The focus of the various programs differed, ranging from gender positioning, to disability positioning, to expectations for achievement of low-income students. The authors identified characteristics common to the programs, such as infrastructural supports, teacher engagement in the learning process, and use of external expertise. What strikes me, however, is that most of the programs used a technical-rational approach to teacher learning in the sense that "experts" taught knowledge and skills to teachers that teachers could then use with minoritized students. Implicitly, the programs replicated power imbalances in the wider society in which minoritized students themselves have little or no voice. Teachers occupy the position of "expert" in relationship to the students, just as professional developers occupy the position of "expert" in relationship to the teachers.

## Professional Development that Repositions Teacher Student Relationships

A co-construction model of teacher professional development that repositions teachers as learners, and minoritized students as teachers, would seek to reconstruct this power imbalance, placing students as the 'experts' who know best what works for them. In that way, this model fits with emancipatory approaches to addressing disparities. But, as Cook-Sather (2006) argues, repositioning students as active agents in the reform of schooling is both profoundly democratic and profoundly difficult, "Because schools are set up on premises of prediction, control, and management, anything that challenges those premises is hard to accomplish within formal educational contexts" (p. 381). She argues that convincing educators not only to listen to students, but to develop an ongoing process of engaging with what students say, even when what they say destabilizes core assumptions teachers hold, contradicts deeply held norms about teaching. Yet, one might truly regard students as the "experts" about teaching and learning since they are the beneficiaries of what happens in school every day.

Several published studies have examined what students have to say about school, with the intention that student voice should inform school reform and teacher learning. In the U.S., these include Poplin and Weere's (1992) study in Southern California, Wilson and Corbett's (2001) extensive body of interviews with students in Philadelphia, and Storz's (2008) study of more than 200 students in four Midwestern urban schools. There has been a small amount of research on teachers' learning through listening to their students. Martin and Hand (2009) report a case study of a science teacher in the U.S. learning to shift from teacher-centered to student-centered teaching; as student voice increased in the teacher's classroom, the researchers found that students' ownership over their learning and the quality of students' argumentation also increased. In New Zealand, Baskerville (2011) reported a process of using storytelling in the classroom to activate student voice and build cross-cultural understandings and relationships; as the two teachers took part in the storytelling alongside the students, everyone in the classroom was positioned as both teacher and learner.

There has been some investigation into engaging preservice teachers with student voice as a way of prompting them to rethink their assumptions about students. Cook-Sather (2010) in the U.S. has developed a well-conceptualized process in which high school students act as consultants to preservice teachers about teaching and learning. Her process intentionally disrupts the traditional positioning of the teacher as the source of knowledge and students as passive receivers of knowledge, and works to build a reciprocal relationship in which teachers and students can talk with each other about classroom teaching and learning.

But missing is research that links teacher professional development in culturally responsive pedagogy with an impact on not just the teacher, but also the teacher's students. Documenting that link, especially through a program designed around repositioning, is the focus of this book.

## References

Altschul, I., Oyserman, D., & Bybee, D. (2006). Racial-ethnic identity in mid-adolescence: Content and change as predictors of academic achievement. *Child Development, 77*(5), 1155–1169.

Altschul, I., Oyserman, D., & Bybee, D. (2008). Racial-ethnic self-schemas and segmented assimilation: Identity and the academic achievement of Hispanic youth. *Social Psychology Quarterly, 71*(3), 302–320.

Ansalone, G. (2003). Poverty, tracking, and the social construction of failure: International perspectives on tracking. *Journal of Children and Poverty, 9*, 3–20.

Anyon, J. (1980). Social class and the hidden curriculum. *Journal of Education, 162*, 67–92.

Anyon, J. (2005). Radical possibilities. New York: Routledge.

Applebee, A. (1996). Curriculum, as conversation. Chicago: University of Chicago Press.

Aud, S., Fox, M. A., & KewalRamani, A. (2010). Status and trends in the education of racial and ethnic minorities. National Center for Education Statistics. Retrieved February 14, 2011, from http://nces.ed.gov/pubs2010/2010015/index.asp

Barton, P. E., & Coley, R. J. (2009). Parsing the achievement gap. Princeton, NJ: Educational Testing Service.

Baskerville, D. (2011). Developing cohesion and building positive relationships through storytelling in a culturally diverse New Zealand classroom. *Teaching and Teacher Education, 27*, 107–115.

Berliner, D. (2006). Our impoverished view of educational reform. *Teachers College Record, 108*(6), 949–995.

Billings, E. S., Martin-Beltran, M., & Hernandez, A. (2010). Beyond English development: Bilingual approaches to teaching immigrant students and English language learners. *Yearbook of the National Society for the Study of Education, 109*(2), 384–413.

Bishop, R. (2003). Changing power relations in education: Kaupapa Maori messages for 'mainstream' education in Aotearoa/New Zealand. *Comparative Education, 39*(2), 221–238.

Bishop, R. (2005). Freeing ourselves from neocolonial domination in research: A Kaupapa Maori approach to creating knowledge. In N. Denzin & Y. Lincoln (Eds.), *The Sage Handbook of Qualitative Research* (3d ed.) (pp. 109–138). Thousand Oaks, CA: Sage.

Bomer, R., Dworin, J. E., May, L., & Semingson, P. (2009). What's wrong with a deficit perspective? *Teachers College Record,* Date Published: June 03, 2009. Retrieved February 14, 2011, from http://www.tcrecord.org ID Number: 15648.

Borman, G. D. (2005). National efforts to bring reform to scale in high-poverty schools: Outcomes and implications. *Review of Research in Education, 29*, 1–28.

Brayboy, B. M. J. (2005). Toward a tribal critical race theory in education. *The Urban Review, 37*(5), 425–446.

Brayboy, B. M. J., & Castagno, A. E. (2009). Self-determination through self-education: Culturally responsive schooling for Indigenous students in the U.S.A. *Teaching Education, 20*(1), 31–53.

Cammarota, J., & Romero, A. (2009). The Social Justice Education Project: A critically compassionate intellectualism for Chicana/o students. In W. Ayers, T. Quinn, & D. Stovall (Eds.), *Handbook for Social Justice Education* (pp. 465–476). New York: Routledge.

Campbell, D. & Stanley, J. (1963). Experimental and quasi-experimental designs for research. Chicago: Rand-McNally.

Carter, D. (2008). Achievement as resistance: Development of a critical race achievement ideology among Black achievers. *Harvard Educational Review, 78*(3), 466–497.

Cazden, C. B. (1989). Richmond Road: A multilingual/multicultural primary school in Auckland, New Zealand. *Language and Education, 3*, 143–166.

Chavous, T., Hilkene, D., Schmeelk-Cone, K., Caldwell, C. H., Kohn-Wood, L., & Zimmerman, M. A. (2003). Racial identity and academic attainment among African American adolescents. *Child Development, 74*(4), 1076–1090.

Cherubini, L., Hodson, J., Manley-Casimir, M., & Muir, C. (2010). "Closing the gap" at the peril of widening the void: Implications of the Ontario Ministry of Education policy for Aboriginal education. *Canadian Journal of Education, 33*(2), 329–355.

Connor, M. H., & Boskin, J. (2001). Overrepresentation of bilingual and poor children in special education classes. *Journal of Children and Poverty, 7*, 23–32.

Cook-Sather, A. (2006). Sound, presence, and power: "Student voice" in educational research and reform. *Curriculum Inquiry, 36*(4), 359–380.

Cook-Sather, A. (2010). Students as learners and teachers: Taking responsibility, transforming education, and redefining accountability. *Curriculum Inquiry, 40*(4), 555–575. Covey, D. (2004). Becoming a literacy leader. Leadership, 33(4), 34–35.

DeJaeghere, J.G., & Zhang, Y. (2008). Development of intercultural competence among U.S. American teachers: Professional development factors that enhance competence. *Intercultural Education*, 19(3), 255–268.

Department for Education. (2010). DfE Single Equality Scheme 2010. Retrieved March 4, 2011, from http://www.education.gov.uk/schools/pupilsupport/inclusionandlearnersupport/ inclusion/equalityanddiversity/a0069463/ses-2010

Dixson, A.D., & Rousseau, C.K. (Eds.). (2006). Critical race theory in education. New York: Routledge.

Dudley-Marling, C. (2007). Return of the deficit. *Journal of Educational Controversy, 2*. Retrieved May 22, 2009, from http://www.wce.wwu.edu/Resources/CEP/eJournal/v002n001/a004.shtml

Duncan-Andrade, J. (2007). Gangstas, wankstas, and ridas: Defining, developing, and supporting effective teachers in urban schools. *International Journal of Qualitative Studies in Education, 20*(6), 617–638.

Duncan-Andrade, J.M.R., & Morrell, E. (2008). The art of critical pedagogy. New York: Peter Lang.

El-Haj, T.R. (2003). Practicing for equity from the standpoint of the particular: Exploring the work of one urban teacher network. *Teachers College Record, 105*, 817–845.

Fickel, E. H. (2005). Teachers, tundra, and talking circles: Learning history and culture in an Alaskan native village. *Theory and Research in Social Education, 33*(4), 476–507.

Fitzsimons, P., & Smith, G. (2000). Philosophy and indigenous cultural transformation. *Educational Philosophy and Theory, 32*(1), 25–41.

Freire, P. (1972). Pedagogy of the oppressed. New York: Continuum.

Freire, P. (1973). Education for critical consciousness. New York: Seabury Press.

Freire, P. (1976). Education and the practice of freedom. London: Writers and Readers Publishing Cooperative.

Gamoran, A., & Berends, M. (1987). The effects of stratification in secondary schools: Synthesis of survey and ethnographic research. *Review of Educational Research, 57*, 415–435.

Gándara, P., Rumberger, R., Maxwell-Jolly, J., & Callahan, R., (2003). English learners in California schools: Unequal resources, unequal outcomes. Education Policy Analysis Archives, 11(36). Retrieved October 28, 2005, from http://epaa.asu.edu/epaa/v11n36/

Garet, M.S., Porter, A.C., Desimone, L.M., Birmann, B.F., & Yoon, K.S. (2001). What makes professional development effective? Results from a national sample of teachers. *American Educational Research Journal, 38*(4), 915–945.

Gay, G. (2010). Culturally responsive teaching. Theory, research and practice (2nd ed.). New York: Teachers College Press.

Gillard, J. The Hon. (2008, May 13). Joint media release: Closing the gap between Indigenous and non-Indigenous Australians. Ministers' Media Centre. Retrieved March 4, 2011, from www.deewr.gov.au/ministers/gillard/media/releases/pages/article_081030_143929.aspx

Gillborn, D. (2007). Accountability, standards, and race inequity in the United Kingdom: Small steps on the road of progress, or defense of White supremacy? In C. E. Sleeter (Ed.), *Facing accountability in education: Democracy & equity at risk* (pp. 145–158). New York: Teachers College Press.

Gillborn, D. (2008). Coincidence or conspiracy? Whiteness, policy and the persistence of the Black/White achievement gap. *Educational Review, 60*(3), 229–248.

Gonzalez, N., Moll, L.C., & Amanti, C. (2005). Funds of knowledge: Theorizing practices in households, communities, and classrooms. Mahwah, NJ: Lawrence Erlbaum Associates.

Hattie, J.A.C. (2009). Visible learning: A synthesis of 800+ meta-analyses on achievement. Oxford: Routledge.

Haviland, D., & Rodriguez-Kiino, D. (2008). Closing the gap: The impact of professional development on faculty attitudes toward culturally responsive pedagogy. *Journal of Hispanic Higher Education, 8*, 197–212.

Haycock, K., & Hanushek, E. A. (2010). An effective teacher in every classroom. Education Next, 10(3), 46–52.

Hill, M. L. (2009). Wounded healing: Forming a storytelling community in hip-hop lit. *Teachers College Record, 111*(1), 248–293.

Holdaway, J., Crul, M., & Roberts, C. (2009). Cross-national comparison of provision and outcomes for the education of the second generation. *Teachers College Record, 111*(6), 1381–1403.

Howard, T. C. (2001). Telling their side of the story: African American students' perceptions of culturally relevant teaching. *The Urban Review, 33*(2), 131–149.

Hynds, A.S. (2007). Navigating the collaborative dynamic: 'Teachers' collaborating across difference. Unpublished PhD thesis, Victoria University of Wellington. Wellington, New Zealand.

Jennings, L. B., & Smith, C. P. (2002). Examining the role of critical inquiry for transformative practices. *Teachers College Record, 104*(3), 456–81.

Joyce, B., & Showers, B. (2002). Student achievement through staff development (3rd ed.). Alexandria, VA: Association for Supervision and Curriculum Development.

Jung, S., & Stone, S. (2008). Sociodemographic and programmatic moderators of early Head Start: Evidence from the National Head Start Research and Evaluation Project. *Children and Schools, 30*(3), 149–157.

Kanu, Y. (2007). Increasing school success among Aboriginal students: Culturally responsive curriculum or macrostructural variables affecting schooling? *Diaspora, Indigenous, and Minority Education, 1*(1), 21–41.

Kumar, S. (2010). Inclusive classroom, social inclusion/exclusion, and diversity: Perspectives, policies and practices. Delhi, India: Deshkal Publication.

Ladson-Billings, G. (1994). The dreamkeepers. San Francisco: Jossey-Bass.

Ladson-Billings, G. (1995). Toward a theory of culturally relevant pedagogy. *American Educational Research Journal, 47*(3), 465–491.

Ladson-Billings, G., & Tate, W.F. (1995). Toward a critical race theory of education. *Teachers College Record, 97*(1), 47–68.

Lee, C.D. (1995). A culturally based cognitive apprenticeship: Teaching African American high school students' skills in literary interpretation. *Reading Research Quarterly, 30*(4), 608–630.

Lee, C.D. (2001). Is October Brown Chinese: A cultural modeling activity system for underachieving students. *American Educational Research Journal, 38*(1), 97–142.

Lee, C.D. (2006). "Every good-bye ain't gone": Analyzing the cultural underpinnings of classroom talk. *International Journal of Qualitative Studies in Education, 19*(3), 305–327.

Liégeois, J.P. (2007). Roma education and public policy. *European Education, 39*(1), 11–31.

Lipka, J., & Adams, B. (2004). Culturally based mathematics education as a way to improve Alaska Native students' math performance. Appalachian Collaborative Center for Learning, Assessment, and Instruction in Mathematics. Retrieved December 27, 2010, from http:// www.uaf.edu/mcc/award-recognition-and-oth/

Lipka, J., Hogan, M.P., Webster, J.P., Yanez, E., Adams, B., Clark, S., & Lacy, D. (2005). Math in a cultural context: Two case studies of a successful culturally-based math project. *Anthropology & Education Quarterly, 36*(4), 367–385.

Luciak, M. (2006). Minority schooling and intercultural education: A comparison of recent developments in the old and new EU member states. *Intercultural Education, 17*(1), 73–80.

Macey, E., Decker, J., & Eckes, S. (2009). The Knowledge Is Power Program (KIPP): An analysis of one model's efforts to promote achievement in underserved communities. *Journal of School Choice*, 3, 212–241.

Marks, G.N., Cresswell, J., & Ainley, J. (2006). Explaining socioeconomic inequalities in student achievement: The role of home and school factors. *Educational Research and Evaluation, 12*(2), 105–128.

Matthews, L.E. (2003). Babies overboard! The complexities of incorporating culturally relevant teaching into mathematics instruction. *Educational Studies in Mathematics*, 53, 61–82.

Mehan, H., Hubbard, L., & Datnow, A. (2010). A co-construction perspective on organizational change and educational reform. *Yearbook of the National Society for the Study of Education, 109*(1), 98–112.

Miller, D., & Macintosh, R. (1999). Promoting resilience in urban African American adolescents: Racial socialization and identity as protective factors. *Social Work Research, 3*, 159–169.

Ministry of Education. (2006). Ngahaeatamatauranga: Annual report on Māori education. Wellington, New Zealand: Ministry of Education.

Ministry of Education. (2010). Education counts: Teaching staff. Retrieved February 15, 2011, from http://www.educationcounts.govt.nz/statistics/schooling/ts/teaching_staff

Moll, L. (1988). Some key issues in teaching Latino students. *Language Arts, 65*(5), 465–472.

Moll, L.C., & González, N. (1994). Lessons from research with language-minority children. *Journal of Reading Behavior, 26*(4), 439–456.

Moll, L., & Ruiz, R. (2002). The schooling of Latino students. In M. Suarez-Orozco & M. Paez (Eds.), *Contexts for learning: Sociocultural dynamics in children's development* (pp. 19–42). New York: Oxford University Press.

Morrison, K.A., Robbins, H.H., & Rose, D.G. (2008). Operationalizing culturally relevant pedagogy: A synthesis of classroom-based research. *Equity & Excellence in Education, 41*(4), 433–435.

Moyle, D. (2005). Quality educators produce quality outcomes: Some thoughts on what this means in the context of teaching Aboriginal and Torres Strait Islander students in Australia's public education system. *Primary & Middle Years Educator, 3*(2), 11–14.

Nathan, R.P. (2007). How should we read the evidence about Head Start? Three views. *Journal of Policy Analysis and Management, 26*, 673–689.

Neufield, B., & Roper, D. (2003). Coaching: A strategy for developing instructional capacity. Washington, DC: The Aspen Institute Program on Education and the Annenberg Institute for School Reform.

Noguera, P. (2002). Understanding the link between race and academic achievement and creating schools where that link can be broken. *Sage Race Relations Abstracts, 27*(3), 5–15.

Nykiel-Herbert, B. (2010). Iraqi refugee students: From a collection of aliens to a community of learners. *Multicultural Education, 17*(30), 2–14.

Oakes, J. (1985). Keeping track: How schools structure inequality. New Haven, CT: Yale University Press.

O'Connor, C. (1997). Dispositions toward (collective) struggle and educational resilience in the inner city: A case analysis of six African-American high school students. *American Educational Research Journal, 34*(4), 593–629.
Payne, R.K. (2009). Using the lens of economic class to help teachers understand and teach students from poverty: A response. *Teachers College Record*, Date Published: May 17, 2009. Retrieved February 14, 2011, from http://www.tcrecord.org ID Number: 15629.
Penetito, W. (2010). What's Māori about Māori education? Wellington, New Zealand: Victoria University Press.
Ravitch, D. (2010). The death and life of the great American school system: How testing and choice are undermining education. New York: Basic Books.
Rist, R. (1970). Student social class and teacher expectations: The self-fulfilling prophecy in ghetto education. *Harvard Educational Review, 70*, 257–301.
Rodríguez Izquierdo, R.M. (2009). La investigación sobre la educación intercultural en España, Archivos Analíticos de Políticas Educativas, 17(4). Retrieved February 16, 2011, from http://epaa.asu.edu/epaa/
Sanders, M. G. (1997). Overcoming obstacles: Academic achievement as a response to racism and discrimination. *Journal of Negro Education, 66*(1), 83–93.
Shields, C., Bishop, R., & Mazawi, A.E. (2005). Pathologizing practices: The impact of deficit thinking on education. New York: Peter Lang.
Sleeter, C.E. (2009). Developing teacher epistemological sophistication about multicultural curriculum: A case study. *Action in Teacher Education, 31*(1), 3–13.
Sleeter, C.E., & Montecinos, C. (1999). Forging partnerships for multicultural education. In S. May (Ed.), *Critical multiculturalism: Rethinking multicultural and anti-racist education* (pp. 113–137). London: Falmer Press.
Sleeter, C.E., & Stillman, J. (2007). Navigating accountability pressures. In C.E. Sleeter (Ed.), *Facing accountability in education: Democracy & equity at risk* (pp. 13–29). New York: Teachers College Press.
Snow-Runner, R., & Lauer, P.A. (2005). Professional development analysis. Denver, CO: Mid-continent Research for Education and Learning.
Solórzano, D.G., & Delgado Bernal, D. (2001). Examining transformational resistance through a critical race and LatCrit theory framework: Chicana and Chicano students in an urban context. *Urban Education, 36*(3), 308–342.
Storz, M.G. (2008). Educational inequity from the perspectives of those who live it: Urban middle school students' perspectives on the quality of their education. *Urban Review, 40*, 247–267.
Timperley, H., Wilson, A., Barrar, H., & Fung, J. (2007). Teacher professional learning and development: Best Evidence Synthesis (BES). Wellington: New Zealand Ministry of Education. Retrieved February 12, 2011, from http://www.educationcounts.govt.nz/publications/series/2515/15341
U.S. Department of Education, National Center for Education Statistics. (2010). The condition of education, Chapter 3. Retrieved February 14, 2011, from http://nces.ed.gov/programs/coe/2010/section4/indicator27.asp
Valenzuela, A. (1999). Subtractive schooling: U.S.-Mexican youth and the politics of caring. Albany: State University of New York Press.
Villegas, A.M., & Lucas, T. (2002). Educating culturally responsive teachers: A coherent approach. Albany: State University of New York Press.
Wilson, B.L., & Corbett, H.D. (2001). Listening to urban kids: School reform and the teachers they want. Albany: State University of New York Press.
Woodson, C.G. (1933). The mis-education of the Negro. Trenton, NJ: First Africa World Press.
Woolfolk, A. (2001). Educational psychology (8th ed.). Needham Heights, MA: Allyn & Bacon.
Yoon, K.S., Duncan, T., Lee, S.W.Y., Scarloss, B., & Shapley, K. (2007). Reviewing the evidence on how teacher professional development affects student achievement (Issues & Answers Report, REL 2007–No. 033). Washington, DC: U.S. Department of Education, Institute of Education Sciences, National Center for Education Evaluation and Regional Assistance, Regional

Educational Laboratory Southwest. Retrieved February 1, 2011, from http://ies. ed.gov/ncee/edlabs

Yosso, T. (2005). Whose culture has capital? A critical race theory discussion of community cultural wealth. *Race Ethnicity and Education, 8*(1), 69–81.

Zozakiewicz, C., & Rodriguez, A. J. (2007). Using sociotransformative constructivism to create multicultural and gender-inclusive classrooms: An intervention project for teacher professional development. *Educational Policy, 21*(2), 397–425.

# Glow

I glow with the light
Of a million coalesced stars
I am the whale song filling the ocean deep
I am the void of the beginningless beginning
I am the world made whole
I am the buffalo on the plain
I am the thunder and the rain
I am unspeakable joy and unutterable pain
In this now, that is future passed
I am the cry of the first child
The sigh of the last
I am the breath and song
Of every living being
I am death the beginning
I am love without limit
I am divine
I am everything
I am nothing
I simply
Am

|| FOURTEEN

# The Next Chapter of Our Story

## *Rethinking African American Metanarratives in Schooling and Society*

Ebony Elizabeth Thomas

*We are one people! We are one nation! And together, we will begin the next chapter in the American story...* —President Barack Obama, New Hampshire Primary Concession Speech, January 8, 2008

*We have come over a way that with tears has been watered,*
*We have come, treading our path through the blood*
*of the slaughtered,*
*Out from the gloomy past,*
*'Til now we stand at last Where the white gleam of our bright star is cast.*
—James Weldon Johnson, "Lift Ev'ry Voice and Sing"
(Negro National Anthem), February 12, 1900

On the eve of President Barack Obama's 2008 Democratic presidential nomination, African American author and literary critic Charles Johnson asked in the *American Scholar* if "the old Black American narrative has outlived its usefulness as a tool of interpretation" in the early twenty-first century (Johnson, 2008, p. 42). The unprecedented rise of the junior United States senator from Illinois to the highest office in the land has inspired popular and scholarly debates about the possibility of moving beyond race as a definitive factor of our national consciousness. Anticipating Obama's success in the November election, Johnson was among the first to call for reinterpretation of what he viewed as an inaccurate singularity—an African American metanarrative or "master story" centered around victimization. In place of the familiar civil rights era tale of an oppressed people struggling against injustice and providing a prophetic cipher for the ideology of the American experiment, Johnson proposed "new and better stories, new concepts, and new vocabularies and grammar based on not the past but on the dangerous, exciting, and unexplored present" (Johnson, 2008, p. 42). What these stories might be or become was not specified. Nonetheless, Johnson's proposition that the ways that we have been preconditioned to think about the Black presence in the United States might be obscuring lived realities and experiences is provocative and deserves serious consideration.

The story of the Black presence in the United States of America is deeply rooted in the very founding of the nation. It is (or should be) impossible to study literature, history, or culture in our nation's schools without taking Black America into account. Yet I posit that this story is not a singular and uncontested narrative, and never was. It consists of multiple, contested accounts of what happened in the past and what continues to happen to Black people in America. Indeed, there have always been competing master stories—metanarratives—that purported to explain the phenomenon of the Black presence in the United States. The anti-slavery rallying cry "Am I not a man and a brother?" was the rhetorical question that early metanarratives about the Black presence in America sought to answer (Carpenter, 1903, p. 167). Writing from a Black abolitionist perspective, David Walker, in his 1829 *Appeal to the Coloured Citizens of the World*, asserted that "America is more our country, than it is the whites—we have enriched it with our *blood and tears*" (Walker, 1995[1829], p. 76, emphasis in original), explicitly referring to the primacy of unpaid Black American labor in the founding and expansion of the United States. U.S. Supreme Court Chief Justice Roger B. Taney stated in his proslavery opinion in *Dred Scott v. Sandford*, 60 U.S. 393 (1857) that all persons born in the United States of African descent were "regarded as beings of an inferior order and altogether unfit to associate with the White race, either in social or political relations; and so far inferior that they had no rights which the White man was bound to respect; and that the Negro might justly and lawfully be reduced to slavery for his benefit" (Taney, 2009, p. 22). Both Walker and Taney wrestled with questions about of African American citizenship and human rights, and reached different rationales rooted in competing metanarratives that would ultimately lead to the Civil War.

In contemporary times, post–civil rights era narratives about race still consider these questions. Former Secretary of State Condoleezza Rice characterized the presence of slavery in the early United States as the nation's "birth defect" (Kralev, 2008), drawing ire from fellow members of the Republican Party. During his famous speech on race in Philadelphia as he ran for the Democratic presidential nomination, President Obama stated that the Declaration of Independence was incomplete at the time of its writing, stained by the original sin of slavery (Obama, 2008). These statements are all derived from various stories in the popular and political consciousness about who African Americans are, their positioning within the context of the American story, and what American citizens believe it means for a nation founded on the principles of liberty and equality to have held millions of human beings in bondage for generations. Although they are positioned on opposite sides of the contemporary political spectrum, both Secretary Rice and President Obama evoked similar critiques of the nation's founding and early history. Their critiques, much like those from previous eras, are rooted deeply in American metanarratives about who we are as a nation and whether we have truly lived up to the ideals of our founding. These stories about Black America raise questions that many believe remain unanswered today.

In this chapter, I briefly describe four metanarratives about the African American presence in the United States—secular triumph, spiritual pilgrimage, sociological reaction, and cultural or biological deficit. Each of these master stories is delineated in its own section. In doing so, I wish to stress that these four metanarratives are merely an exemplar of all the ways that the Black American presence is and has been narrated in our culture and society. For instance, as Johnson's essay focuses primarily on the persistence of a metanarrative of perpetual African American *victimization*, I do not treat it here. Another metanarrative that I will not treat due to time and space constraints is that of African Americans being always *already foreign or non-American.* Black Americans descended from enslaved persons in the antebellum South quite obviously have native-born ancestry that predates that of many, if not most, other citizens of the contemporary United States, yet their loyalty, citizenship, and "American-ness" are often questioned. I have chosen the four metanarratives of this chapter not exclusively because they are more salient in the current moment than others, but also as exemplars to demonstrate how the ways that we talk about, think about, and represent race and ethnicity in the present are deeply rooted in our collective past, have continuing import for the future, and are implicated in our teaching of African American literatures, cultures, and experiences.

Given Johnson's call, my definition of metanarrative has been influenced by French philosopher and literary theorist Jean-Francois Lyotard's *The Postmodern Condition: A Report on Knowledge* (1984). According to Lyotard, one of the defining features of postmodernism is incredulity toward the master stories that purport to explain human history. Before modernity, these metanarratives were used to legitimate knowledge. However, the ascent of science and technology over metaphysics and the humanities, along with the new ability to widely broadcast the atrocities of the mid-twentieth century, did much to undermine the dominance of many of these master stories, from the biblical creation narrative to Manifest Destiny. Thus, since "the status of knowledge is altered as societies enter what is known as the postindustrial age and cultures enter what is known as the postmodern age" (Lyotard, 1984, p. 3), then the ways that knowledge about societies and cultures are transmitted must also be altered. Given the social changes in the United States over the past 50 years that have resulted in the descendants of slaves going from *de jure* segregation in the South to one of their number becoming the First Lady of the United States, this changing and altering of knowledge received from earlier generations and eras applies to African American metanarratives as well.

One of the disciplines that is the most responsible for teaching African American metanarratives to each new generation of young students in the United States is my own field of English language arts education. Literacy researcher Allan Luke has suggested that we characterize the purpose of English education as "political interventions, struggles over the formation of ideologies and beliefs, identities and capital" (Luke, 2004, p. 86). These interventions and struggles happen in elementary language arts and secondary English classrooms all over the nation through instruction in language, literature, and history. Sociologist Basil Bernstein (1996) characterizes this process as developing horizontal solidarity through the transmission of mythological discourses. Mythological discourses, analogous to metanarratives, serve two functions: (1) to celebrate and produce a united, integrated, apparently common national consciousness; and (2) to obscure or render less visible the relationships between social hierarchies within and outside of schools. The transmission and internalization of these mythic metanarratives about the American nation's origin, achievements, and destiny are critical to societal and cultural reproduction (Bourdieu & Passeron, 1990, pp. 11, 47). Furthermore, we know that in classrooms "narratives... express views about what should count as knowledge and as displays of knowledge and of achievement" (Rex, Murnen, Hobbs, & McEachen, 2002, p. 789). The process of guiding students as they connect seemingly disparate stories about similar groups into a coherent (or messy) politically and socially acceptable whole is a critical yet invisible function of English language arts pedagogy.

If one of the ways that we engage in political interventions and ideological struggles is by transmitting shared metanarratives through curriculum and pedagogy, the discipline of secondary English language arts, along with history, carries much of the burden of being the site within schooling that transmits the social and cultural norms of society. However, unlike history, this function of secondary English teaching is implicit instead of explicitly stated, transmitted through instructional content and in the ways that teachers and students talk together about historical and contemporary fictional and biographical texts (Sassi & Thomas, 2008, pp. 25–26). Within this specific context, if our master stories about African American literature, culture, and history are not informed by contemporary literary theory, politics, and cultural criticism, as well as the lived experiences of African Americans across a variety of spectra, we run the risk of perpetuating myths that have little basis in fact or, perhaps worse, that present only a portion of the entire story.

My intent is not to provide an exhaustive account of the ways that the presence, experiences, or legacy of persons of African descent has been read or talked about in the past. It would be impossible to do so, as metanarratives about Black America circulate broadly in the culture among Blacks, Whites, and other American ethnic groups and range across various age, gender, religious, orientation, and socioeconomics distinctions. These master stories about Black lives and experiences are incredibly resilient, yet evolve with each new cultural event of import. Instead, my aim is to position these metanarratives within the unique social and political cultures of the Obama presidency and to analyze the ways that each of these master stories influence our readings of the African American experience. From this, I will propose new directions towards a theoretical framework for the teaching of African American literature in contemporary English education that will contextualize Black experiences for young readers from all backgrounds during the Obama era and beyond.

## Ways of Reading African American Experiences: Four Metanarratives

### *Stories of Triumph*

> *African Americans were brought to this country under extreme duress in conditions that from modern and postmodern perspectives would be considered genocidal. Despite slavery, Jim Crow, and historic and continuing racism, African Americans have thrived in the United States. Exceptions to this rule are individual or socioeconomic and are not indicative of a deficit inherent in African American culture.*

Earlier, I quoted David Walker's assertion that African Americans belonged more distinctly and rightfully to the United States than many other ethnic groups because of their forced labor under inhumane conditions during slavery. His statement, "we have enriched it with our blood and tears," is an early representation of the triumph metanarrative. The metanarrative of African Americans as suffering servants whose righteous travails would bear future fruit is a master story told throughout the Black literary canon, in the Black church, and in Black musical and comedic traditions. The imminent secular triumph of Black America is alluded to in Charles Johnson's essay, as well as in the recent work of other renowned scholars (see, for example, Ifill, 2009). Yet stories about the trials and victories of "many thousands gone" have deep roots. Antecedents of today's triumphalist metanarratives include the Afrocentricity of the Black arts movement of the 1960s and 1970s[1] as well as the earlier Harlem Renaissance's "New Negro Movement," which ultimately were both influenced by another metanarrative, that of Marxism.[2] Maulana Karenga, the founder of the holiday Kwanzaa, used Marxist lexis when defining the seventh day, Imani: "to believe with all our heart. . . in our people and the righteousness and victory of our struggle" (Karenga, 2008, para.

7). It is also notable that the genesis of the Harlem Renaissance is contemporaneous with the Russian Revolution and Leninism—although the Renaissance was most concerned with folk culture, the class struggle mirrored the struggle for racial equality. As Claude McKay wrote in "If We Must Die" after the Red Summer of 1919:[3]

> O kinsmen we must meet the common foe!
> Though far outnumbered let us show us brave,
> And for their thousand blows deal one deathblow!
> What though, before us lies the open grave?
> Like men we'll face the murderous, cowardly pack,
> Pressed to the wall, dying, but fighting back! (1997[1919], p. 104)

In McKay's poem, as in other African American literature that tells stories of secular struggle and eventual triumph, Black people are not passive reactors to racism and dehumanization. They are active agents fighting for their own physical, social, and economic liberation from stifling oppression. Thus, the triumph metanarrative is reparative, telling celebratory tales about the victories and the achievements of African Americans in spite of collective trauma and monumental odds. Positioning the African American master story as a triumph makes it an integral part of the American story-myth—tragedy to triumph, rags to riches, unimpeded progress for those whose lives embody the Puritan work ethic and other spiritual virtues that have entered the American secular consciousness.

The ultimate symbol of the triumph metanarrative is President Barack Obama. Initially, there was a great deal of anticipation about the potential social impact of the 2008 election of Barack Obama as the 44th president of the United States. Specific attention was paid to the election's impact on the African American community, for whom the first decade of the twenty-first century had been both the best and the worst of times. The Black middle and upper-middle classes had expanded considerably in the two generations since the civil rights movements of the middle twentieth century. The number of African Americans with postsecondary education had skyrocketed, with increasing Black representation across many professions. At the time of Obama's election, many of the most visible Americans hailed from African descent, from comedian Chris Rock to media mogul Oprah Winfrey. Two African Americans held the position of secretary of state during the 2000s, Colin Powell and Condoleezza Rice, and the attorney general of the United States at the time of this writing is Eric Holder, an American of African-Caribbean descent. Immigrants from the African diaspora were among the most successful new entrepreneurs in the United States, and represented a majority of students of African descent at the nation's most selective colleges (Bennett & Lutz, 2009). Many successful African Americans are descended from these immigrants, including Powell and Holder.

The election of Barack Obama was at first considered the pinnacle of Black America's secular triumph. However, the expanding gap between a triumphant Black professional class and a growing Black underclass cannot be ignored. For those African Americans who live in impoverished urban and rural communities, life has become quite desperate indeed. The corporate takeover of agricultural production in the South and the deindustrialization of America's urban centers have devastated historic Black communities (Hoppe & Bluestone, 1987; Sugrue, 1996). Where schools, churches, and community centers once thrived, urban blight, failing school systems, and a palpable sense of despair have led to a sharp increase in families in distress, unsafe neighborhoods, and poor mental and physical health. At the same time, conservative rhetoric has made social programs that were taken for granted in the mid-twentieth century unpopular with a plurality of Americans. One danger of the triumph metanarrative is the perpetuation of the meritocractic myth (for example, "President Obama/ Condi Rice/Oprah Winfrey became successful through hard work and sacrifice—what's *your* excuse?"). The sentiment that the election of the first president of African descent should have ameliorated all uncomfortable aspects of American history and transported us into a postracial era is pervasive. Thus, the challenge created by the triumph metanarrative is that it encourages indifference towards the continued suffering in Black communities on many levels, ignoring structural realities that cannot merely be explained away by social and economic class.

The implications for the ways that we teach African American literature, history, and culture in our middle and high schools are manifold. Of course, the triumph metanarrative—African Americans achieving despite all odds—can and has provided students with models of success. The impetus behind African-centered curriculum and pedagogy is rooted in this perspective, and research clearly shows that it is important for children and youth to have positive images of their culture and heritage in order to be successful in schooling (Murrell, 2002; Hilliard, 1995). However, the triumph metanarrative does *not* provide students with satisfactory explanations for why many African Americans have not thrived in post–civil rights era America. When educators focus primarily on individual and collective victories of certain African Americans without providing sufficient and credible evidence for why some individuals and groups succeeded in the United States at particular times, and why others did not, students are robbed of a critical interpretative lens to deconstruct and understand the totality of African American lives, both today and in the past.

## Stories of Pilgrimage

*The African American story has many parallels to religious traditions and stories (for example, the Bible, the Koran, the Torah). African Americans' individual and col-*

*lective spiritual traditions have successfully countered the challenges of slavery, Jim Crow, and historic and continuing racism, and will continue to help African Americans overcome. Continuing problems and pathologies in the African American community are due to a "turning away" from spirituality and community.*

Author and cultural critic James Baldwin observed that "the hymns, the texts, and the most favored legends" of African Americans come from the Old Testament of the Bible: "the flight from Egypt, the Hebrew children in the fiery furnace, the terrible jubilee songs of deliverance . . . the covenant God made in the beginning with Abraham . . . is a covenant made with these [Black American] latter-day exiles also: as Israel was chosen, so are they" (Baldwin, 1985, pp. 7–8). The African American story has been narrated as a story of pilgrimage since colonial times. The earliest slave narratives were part and parcel of an abolitionist tradition that appropriated the predominant value system of the time, Christianity, to warrant moral arguments against the bondage of fellow human beings. In his introduction to the *Classic Slave Narratives,* Henry Louis Gates noted that

> the Black slave narrators sought to indict both those who enslaved them and the metaphysical system drawn upon to justify their enslavement. . . . Each slave author, in writing about his or personal life experiences, simultaneously wrote on behalf of the millions of silent slaves still held captive throughout the South. Each author, then, knew that *all* Black slaves would be judged—on their character, integrity, intelligence, manners and morals, and their claims to warrant emancipation—on this published evidence provided by one of their number. The slave authors therefore had to satisfy the dual expectations of shaping the random events of their lives into a meaningful and compelling pattern, while also making the narrative of their odyssey from slavery to freedom an emblem of every Black person's potential for higher education and the desire to be free. (Gates, 2002, p. 2)

The metaphysical system to which Gates refers is the Christian religion.[4] The collective narrative that enslaved writers and composers as disparate as Olaudah Equiano, Harriet Jacobs, Frederick Douglass, Jupiter Hammon, Phillis Wheatley, and the anonymous writers of the spirituals turned to was found in the Scriptures. There, the writers found both their oppressors' justification for their bondage (the stories of Cain[5] and Ham[6]) as well as accounts of deliverance from bondage and freedom (the stories of Moses and the Israelites in the Promised Land[7]). The writers used these tales of wandering and pilgrimage to refute slaveholders' arguments in favor of White supremacy, as well as construct their own arguments for liberty and personhood. Phillis Wheatley's admonition to "Remember, Christians, Negroes, Black as Cain / May be refined, and join the angelic train" (Wheatley, 2006[1773], p. 13) was a radical statement during an era when there were still debates about whether or not peoples of African descent had souls. Several decades later, Frederick Douglass drew upon another biblical story to question the celebration of the Declaration of Independence: "It was fashionable, hundreds of years ago, for the children of Jacob to boast, we have 'Abraham as our father,' when they had long lost Abraham's faith and spirit. That people contented themselves under the shadow of Abraham's great name, while they repudiated the deeds which made his name great. Need I remind you that a similar thing is being done all over this country to-day?" (Douglass, 2001[1852], p. 105). In addition to the written tradition of pilgrimage, the Black spirituals were used as oral metanarratives pointing toward liberty through song, inspiring thousands to undertake the perilous journey from slavery to freedom: "Deep river, my home is over Jordan"; "Swing low, sweet chariot / Coming forth to carry me home"; "Go down, Moses, way down to Egypt-land / Tell old Pharaoh / Let my people go!"

A century later, metanarratives of pilgrimage were echoed once again in the religious rhetoric of the civil rights movement. Dr. Martin Luther King, Jr., viewed himself as an itinerant messenger of nonviolence, heir to the same jeremiadic tradition as Walker and Douglass (Jordan, this volume), and compared himself to another evangelist at the very beginning of his famous letter from a Birmingham jail.

> I am in Birmingham because injustice is here. Just as the prophets of the eighth century B.C. left their villages and carried their "thus saith the Lord" far beyond the boundaries of their home towns, and just as the Apostle Paul left his village of Tarsus and carried the gospel of Jesus Christ to the far corners of the Greco Roman world, so am I compelled to carry the gospel of freedom beyond my own home town. Like Paul, I must constantly respond to the Macedonian call for aid. (King, 2003, p. 177)

For the centuries of the African American story prior to the civil rights movement, the metanarrative of spiritual pilgrimage was one of the most treasured within the culture. Many religious African Americans from a number of faith traditions besides Christianity view the "stranger in a strange land" metaphor as useful for understanding the Black presence in America, even viewing the experience of slavery and freedom as prophetic (for example, the Nation of Islam). One finds much rhetoric in Black communities today about current maladies being caused by a rejection of the traditions of a spiritual people whose spirituality liberated them and their forebears, and whose spirituality has the potential to liberate their children. However, statistics show changes in religious practices among African Americans. According to the Pew Forum on Religion and Public Life (2009), while 87% of African Americans reported a religious affiliation, and even those without affiliation reported belief in God and prayer more often than the nonreligious of other ethnic groups, only 53% of African Americans reported attending services on a weekly basis. Although one cannot draw definitive conclusions about faith and belief from participation in religious activities alone, these figures show that what has been previously assumed about the centrality of religion in the lives of African Americans may be shifting.

In our secondary classrooms, the metanarrative of pilgrimage is useful for those charged with teaching the African American story and is generally positive for students. This "master story" connects the African American struggle for freedom and equality under the law with the struggles of other oppressed peoples from historical accounts and religious literature. Many who have transmitted this metanarrative refer to the fellowship, purification, and virtue found in suffering, as well as the moral righteousness of those who suffer. Dr. King was famously inspired by Reinhold Niebuhr, an American forerunner of liberation theology, and by Mahatma Gandhi, whose wisdom and faith through adversity was shaped by Hinduism. Narratives of pilgrimage provide students with a moral or ethical framework for understanding the story of Black America and its place within the American story. Much like the metanarratives of secular triumph, the spiritual pilgrimage is also reparative, giving purpose to persecution and meaning to collectively traumatic historical memories.

As a rule, thinking of Black experiences as having metaphysical significance is comforting. The pilgrimage metanarrative has inspired artists and abolitionists alike. Its major characters and themes are heard in the call and response during sermons in the Black church, as well as in secular and spiritual discourses of the civil rights movement. However, returning to Lyotard, this present era challenges the very notion of pilgrimage as explanatory. Spiritual comfort is intangible. Spiritual experiences cannot be commodified or coded for a postmodern, information-driven age. The pilgrimage metanarrative does not provide a satisfactory explanation for those who are secular. Neither does it necessarily attend to the social justice elements of Black American literature and history. Cynics might assert that if it was truly God's divine will that people of African descent should suffer untold misery for nearly half a millennium—if righteousness is truly only earned in the crucible of suffering—then one might dangerously argue that slavery and segregation were not atrocities or crimes against humanity, but somehow beneficial in the end for Black Americans (a view that has been expressed by some conservative commentators across ethnic groups). For a growing number of people, the pilgrimage metanarrative simply does not do enough to address issues of social justice and human rights here on Earth.

## *Stories of Reaction and Assimilation*

> *African Americans, as an involuntary minority group, have created a reactive culture in response to slavery, Jim Crow, and racism. Since most or all elements of this culture are in response to historic and continuing racism, once racism has been eradicated,*

*African Americans will be able to fully assimilate into mainstream–White American society.*

The work of educational anthropologist John Ogbu provided another way of thinking about the storied place of African Americans within the fabric of the United States. Ogbu famously used ethnic group histories and self-perceptions to separate them into two categories: voluntary minorities who traveled to the United States in search of religious freedom and economic opportunity, and involuntary minorities who became part of the United States due to conquest, land seizure, or slavery (1987). In his seminal article, "Variability in Minority School Performance: A Problem in Search of an Explanation," Ogbu posited that cultural inversion is a form of resistance to the dominance of the majority (Foley, 2004, p. 387). It "usually results in the *coexistence of two opposing cultural frames of reference* or ideal ways orienting behavior, one considered by the minorities as appropriate for themselves and the other as appropriate for White Americans" (Ogbu, 1987, p. 323, emphasis in original).

Since oppressive majorities often ascribe to involuntary minorities negative stereotypes and derogatory images, cultural inversion is one way that oppressed groups repudiate imposed identities. Ogbu theorized that academic and societal achievement is perceived by many involuntary minorities as "acting White." Thus, high-achieving individuals from involuntary minority groups risk losing group membership through perceived association with the oppressive majority. Over the two decades since his theory first appeared, Ogbu's thesis has been challenged by numerous critics (for one exhaustive treatment, please refer to Foley, 2004). However, there are those who believe that African American culture arose as a distinct entity during slavery and segregation, when access to the mainstream was unavailable and Black Americans were viewed as second-class citizens. Adherents to "melting pot" theories of American immigration and proponents of assimilation believe that many of these distinct elements of Black American culture—historically Black colleges and universities, Black Greek-lettered organizations and Masonic lodges, Black churches with their unique worship styles, and even soul food cuisine and Black American English—have served their historical purpose. Many of those who adhere to or espouse this particular metadiscourse may not have a full understanding of the origins or the purposes of these cultural phenomena, but they nonetheless believe that African Americans who choose to engage in these practices are segregating themselves from a supposed undifferentiated American mainstream.

Education scholars and practitioners have examined the psychosocial dimensions of Black academic underachievement for the past 40 years. Many have critiqued aspects of the reaction metanarrative, such as the "sour grapes" phenomenon that Black high achievers are perceived to be "acting White." For the sake of our youth and young adults, perhaps examining the origin and purpose of some cultural practices may lead to deeper analysis about the evolution and persistence of creative elements of Black American culture (for example, soul food, African American English, and so on). The reparative aspect of the reaction metanarrative is that it tells the story of a people who have been adaptive, creative, and resilient, thriving for many generations in the face of oppression and discrimination. Nonetheless, the danger of this "master story" is that some proponents advocate subsuming the unique features and practices of African American culture into a supposedly undifferentiated American mainstream. This metanarrative may be particularly difficult for teachers to address within the classroom context, especially if students conclude as a result that "Black kids just don't try hard enough," or that they ought to subsume their cultural and ethnic identities in order to be successful in schooling and society. This is neither desirable nor possible.

### Stories of Deficit

> *Due to slavery, Jim Crow, and historic and continuing racism, African American achievement and resilience is the exception, not the rule. African Americans remain on or near the bottom of many quality-of-life demographic indicators, and matters are only getting worse. There are no coherent or productive solutions for these challenges and problems. The individual achievements of African American athletes, entertainers, and professionals are not enough to counter the crisis in the African American community as a whole.*

The final metanarrative and metadiscursive tradition that I will examine is perhaps the one that has had the most negative and painful effects on the lives of Americans of African descent. Returning once again to the introduction, recall that I quoted Justice Roger B. Taney's opinion about the inherent inferiority of Black people in order to establish some of the ways that these master stories were essential to the founding of the nation, and continue to shape what it means to be American today. The deficit narrative is one of the most pernicious answers to the question that Taney set forth in the Dred Scott decision.

> Can a negro, whose ancestors were imported into this country, and sold as slaves, become a member of the political community formed and brought into existence by the Constitution of the United States, and as such become entitled to all the rights, and privileges, and immunities, guaranteed by that instrument to the citizen? (Taney, 2009, p. 21)

As the quote from the introduction illustrates, Taney responded to this question by denying the fundamental human rights of Black Americans. He went on to describe persons of African descent as "ordinary articles of merchandise and traffic" (p. 21). By denigrating the status of Black people, he was thus able to deny

Dred Scott's legal rights to due process as an American citizen. This argument had its genesis not in the founding of the nation, as Taney erroneously asserted in his opinion, but in the scientific racism that arose in response to global abolitionist movements of the late eighteenth and nineteenth centuries. As anthropologist Lee D. Baker observed,

> On the heels of Nott and Gliddon's first edition (of *Types of Mankind*), and in the middle of the escalating tensions between the North and the South, the U.S. Supreme Court decided *Dred Scott v. Sanford* (1857). Chief Justice Roger B. Taney authored the majority opinion, which was supposed to be only about the right of a manumitted slave to sue across state lines in federal court. By broadening the scope of the case, Taney decreed that all African American (enslaved or free) had no rights as citizens under the U.S. Constitution. Taney framed his argument by detailing how "far below" Negroes were from Whites "in the scale of created beings," in effect constitutionalizing the racial ideology articulated by the scientific discourse and the opinion of proslavery interests. (Baker, 1998–1999, p. 90)

Metanarratives about the supposed biological, intellectual, and cultural deficiencies of African Americans were engrained in not only academic discourse, but also in policy and in legislation throughout the nineteenth and early twentieth centuries (Baker, 1998–1999, p. 93). Ethnology and scientific racism were the dominant perspectives until the pioneering work of Franz Boas in the midst of the nadir period of race relations. Postwar revelations of the horrors of Nazism, followed by anticolonial, anti-apartheid, and civil rights movements during the second half of the twentieth century, further discredited deficit narratives about racial and religious minorities. However, although technological advances antiquated racism justified by scientific or cultural studies, adherents to deficit theories remained. Under such cloaked terms as "race realism" and "human biodiversity," a minority of scientists, cultural critics, and social commentators are starting to articulate opinions about the inherent deficiencies and limitations of Black people in the public sphere, reinvigorated by genetic studies (Carter, 2007, p. 547). Public figures have recently made questionable comments about the abilities of people of African descent, from DNA pioneer and Nobel laureate James Watson's comments that "all our social policies are based on the fact that their intelligence is the same as ours—whereas all the testing says not really" (Nugent, 2007) to Democrat Harry Reid's observations of President Obama as a "light-skinned" African American "with no Negro dialect, unless he wanted to have one" (Heilemann & Halperin, 2010, p. 34). These and other incidents, while electrifying the public, show that views from previous eras have not entirely disappeared from the national consciousness.

This metanarrative is particularly dangerous for schooling. Proponents (whom I am making a conscious, political choice *not* to cite here) use discredited pseudoscience from the age of scientific racism in order to claim that people of African American descent are genetically less intelligent than others. Cultural deficit metanarratives are derived from many of the same racist roots, sown during a time when Black people were caricaturized by a society that regarded their speech as broken English, their food as unpalatable, their music and dance as vulgar, and their religious worship as primitive (Riggs, 1987). Even today, public intellectuals like Michael Eric Dyson, Cornel West, and Tim Wise are still engaged in educating the public en masse about the brilliance and inherent worth of Black folkways while highlighting the persistence of structural racism that impedes the progress of many in the underclass.

Should the deficit metanarrative be considered when teaching African American literature, history, and culture in schools? All Americans should be aware that deficit views of African Americans still influence social policy and political discourse, as well as daily interactions between individuals and groups. Even during an era where there is an African American president, racism still has implications for the real conditions of Black people from all walks of life. Teachers and other stakeholders engaged in the telling of African American stories through their work are ethically obligated to challenge stories of deficit as outdated, discredited nonsense. Presenting the work of Franz Boas and other pioneering social scientists in historical context alongside W. E. B. Du Bois' *The Souls of Black Folk* (1998 [1904]) should be essential reading in high school English classes, where we sometimes jump from teaching the slave narratives to King's "I Have a Dream" speech in our American literature anthologies without providing sufficient explanations for how race relations changed over time. For it is only when the metanarrative of deficit is exposed that it can be challenged.

## Conclusion: The Black American Story as Twenty–First Century Classroom Cipher

Stories about race in society have implications for schooling, especially secondary English education, where students are usually first introduced to the American literary canon. When and *if* the story of Black America is taught in our literature classes, it is often introduced as a singular, uncontested metanarrative, privileging only certain stories as appropriate ways of talking about the African American experience. However, as the earlier sections have illustrated, there have always been multiple ways of reading, talking about, and teaching what it means to be Black in America. Whether Black histories, lives, and letters are taught as stories of triumph, pilgrimage, reaction, or deficit, or in other ways, each of our readings of the phenomenon of American Blackness is rooted in specific philosophies and ideologies that are directly correlated to the identities, social subjectivities, and sociopolitical concerns of the individuals and groups who espouse them, both today and in the past. At the time that I write these words (mid-2010), metanarratives about race are pervasive in contemporary media and culture. With a plethora of information available to the public and competing frames for analyzing this often hyper-racialized information, it has become difficult for many adults today to process current events, statistics, and data about race and distill fact from fiction, let alone for teachers of adolescents and young adults.

Given these stakes, we would do well to examine how the Black American story has been taught historically during similarly fraught time periods. Learning more about the histories of successful African American literary pedagogies is imperative for the success of not only Black students, but also for millennial and post-millennial generations that will spend their entire adult lives in a complex, diverse, multiethnic, multilingual, and multimodal world. While we do not have access to video recordings of their lesson plans, some of the teachers of the freedmen, their children, and their children's children certainly pulled back the curtain of the American literary canon and held it up to scrutiny. Otherwise, the evolution of the African American protest tradition in literature would not have been possible. The conditions of these schools, largely segregated, were deplorable, but the metanarratives taught in some of these classrooms may have been something other than the regulatory discourse of the textbook and official curriculum. African American scholar bell hooks attests to the potential for structurally transformative agency within the segregated classroom: "To be changed by ideas was pure pleasure. But to learn ideas that ran counter to values and beliefs learned at home was to place oneself at risk, to enter the danger zone. . . . School was the place where I could forget that self and, through ideas, reinvent myself" (hooks, 1994, p. 3). She describes her teachers as linguistically and culturally similar "women on a mission." Providing students with frames to analyze the ways in which texts are raced in explicit and implicit ways can help further their appreciation for African American and American stories, both old and new.

Although my aim is certainly and emphatically not to advocate for the resegregation of American schools, it may be worth asking how American education in general and English education in particular can benefit from the transformative metanarratives obviously employed by hooks's teachers. In an excellent recent account of the history of Black education, *A Class of Their Own: Black Teachers in the Segregated South*, Adam Fairclough (2006) carefully delineates the sociopolitical position of African American teachers towards the end of the Jim Crow era and the beginning of the civil rights movement: "Black teachers felt a duty to protect their students. They wanted Black youth to be dissatisfied with discrimination, but they did not wish to use them, or see them used by others, as cannon fodder . . . teachers had to walk a fine line between encouraging righteous indignation over an unjust system and enabling their students to cope with that system. Teachers in the public schools . . . trained their children's eyes on the past and the future, not just the present" (Fairclough, 2006, p. 337). Instead of dismissing the poorly funded schools of the segregated South as uniformly deficient, Fairclough illustrates how Black education evolved from northern missionaries and former slaves teaching an entire race how to read and write into the training ground for one of the most profound social movements of the twentieth century. "Black teachers had also encouraged a more general sense of racial pride that played a more important role—so pervasive that it was taken for granted—in motivating the civil rights movement" (p. 389). For nearly one hundred years between the Emancipation Proclamation of 1863 and the Civil Rights Act of 1964, these test cases of systematically revealing the next chapter of our story to the linguistically and culturally marginalized in segregated schools like the ones attended by bell hooks certainly produced social and cultural movements that shook the globe.

Charles Johnson's call for new and better stories, new concepts, and new vocabularies and grammar is timely and has import not only for English language arts educators, but also for our early twenty-first century society. Our youth and young adults really are "reading and writing differently," to quote the title of a recent *Council Chronicle* brief (Gere, et al. 2008, p. 15). They are digital natives who harness the Internet's social resources in order to propel their preferred presidential candidate to the White House. They are the most racially and ethnically diverse generation in American history. While this chapter does not take the position that we are "postrace," I contend that educators have now arrived at a moment where the role of race in our literacy teaching must be repositioned for a new century. The rethinking of the African American metanarrative is central to the essential work of encouraging students to move from passive consumption to thoughtful analysis of *all* of the diverse narratives in our society. Providing students with frames to analyze the ways in which texts are raced in explicit and implicit ways can help further their appreciation for American stories both old and new.

## Notes

1. Although beyond the national scope of this chapter, the Black arts movement was also influenced and cross-pollinated by postcolonial movements in post–World War II Africa, Latin America, and Asia.
2. The Marxist metanarrative purports to explain human history as consisting of stories of perpetual struggles between social classes, and privileging the interests and the struggles of the proletariat (see, for example, Marx, 1998; Althusser, 1998). As an oppressed group, many African Americans, including Richard Wright and James Baldwin, during the nadir (lowest point), Great Depression, and post–World War II periods found in Marxist theory a useful interpretative lens to define their own struggles.
3. The Red Summer of 1919 was the apex of the nadir of race relations in the United States. Fueled by the end of World War I and fears generated by the Russian Revolution, bloody race riots occurred in over two dozen cities.
4. Many slaves practiced syncretized Christianity—a mixture of European Christian and African spiritual traditions.

5. According to the book of Genesis in the Bible, Cain was the eldest son of Adam and Eve, the first human couple ever to be created, expelled from the sinless and deathless Garden of Eden for partaking of divinely forbidden fruit. Their curse fell upon Cain, who in a fit of jealousy killed his younger brother, Abel, for offering a sacrifice that was acceptable to God (Cain's was rejected). In punishment, Cain was cursed and condemned to wander, but to protect him from those who might kill him in revenge, God marked him and his descendants. The biblical account does not specify what this mark was, but in the eighteenth century, some assumed that it was dark skin.
6. Genesis also gives an account of a great flood, which only one man, Noah, along with his wife, sons Shem, Ham, and Japheth, and their wives survived. After the floodwaters receded, Noah planted a vine, made wine, became drunk, and fell asleep naked. Noah's son Ham "saw his father's nakedness" (what this refers to has been disputed), and mocked him to his brothers. When Noah awoke and sobered up, he knew what Ham had done, and cursed Ham's son Canaan, declaring him to be "a servant unto his brothers." During the slave trade, Ham and Canaan's curse was popularly assumed to have fallen upon peoples of African descent.
7. In the biblical book of Exodus, the children of Israel were enslaved in ancient Egypt after losing favor once their revered ancestor Joseph was long dead and forgotten. Through a series of events, one of the Israelites, Moses, was reared in the house of the Pharaoh (Egyptian god-king) and was then expelled after killing an Egyptian in defense of an Israelite slave. After spending 40 years in the wilderness, God speaks to Moses from a burning bush, choosing him to be the deliverer of Israel. When Pharaoh refuses to let Moses' people go, Moses and his brother Aaron unleash 12 plagues on their Egyptian oppressors. Pharaoh agrees to free the slaves, then has a change of heart and pursues them to the edge of the Red Sea. Through divine power, Moses splits the sea, allowing the Israelites to cross on dry land and drowning the pursuing Egyptian army. The rest of Exodus and the Old Testament is about the Israelites' perilous journey to, in, and in exile from their Promised Land.

## References

Althusser, Louis. (1998). Ideology and ideological state apparatuses: Notes toward an investigation. In Julie Rivkin & Michael Ryan (Eds.), *Literary theory: An anthology* (pp. 693-702). London: Blackwell.

Baker, Lee D. (1998–1999). Columbia University's Franz Boas: He led the undoing of scientific racism. *The Journal of Blacks in Higher Education*, 22 (Winter), 89–96.

Baldwin, James. (1985). The Harlem ghetto. In *The price of the ticket: Collected nonfiction*, 1948–1985. New York: Macmillan.

Bennett, Pamela R., & Lutz, Amy. (2009). How African American is the net black advantage? Differences in college attendance among immigrant blacks, native blacks, and whites. *Sociology of Education*, 82(1), 70–99.

Bourdieu, Pierre, & Passeron, Jean-Claude. (1990). *Reproduction in education, society, and culture*. London and Thousand Oaks, CA: Sage.

Carpenter, George Rice. (1903). *John Greenleaf Whittier*. New York: Houghton Mifflin and Company.

Carter, Robert. (2007). Genes, genomes, and genealogies: The return of scientific racism? *Ethnic and Racial Studies*, 30(4), 546–56.

Douglass, Frederick. (2001[1852]). What to the slave is the Fourth of July? In Richard P. Horwitz (Ed.), *The American studies anthology* (pp. 105–123). Lanham, MD: Rowman & Littlefield.

DuBois, W. E. B. (1998 [1904]). *The souls of Black folk*. Rockville, MD: ARC Manor.

Fairclough, Adam. (2006). *A class of their own: Black teachers in the segregated South*. Cambridge, MA, and London: Harvard University Press.

Foley, Douglas. (2004). Ogbu's theory of academic disengagement: Its evolution and its critics. *Intercultural Education*, 15(4), 385–97.

Gates, Henry Louis. (2002). Introduction. In Henry Louis Gates (Ed.), *The classic slave narratives* (pp. 1–14). New York: Penguin.

Gere, Anne Ruggles, Laura Aull, Hannah Dickinson, Tim Green, Stephanie Moody, Melinda McBee-Orzulak, Ebony Elizabeth Thomas, & Evelyn Moody. (2008). Reading and writing differently: A policy brief produced by the National Council of Teachers of English. *Council Chronicle*, 18(2), 15–21.

Heilemann, John, & Halperin, Mark. (2010). *Game change: Obama and the Clintons, McCain and Palin, and the race of a lifetime*. New York: HarperCollins.

hooks, bell. (1994). *Teaching to transgress*. New York: Routledge.

Hoppe, Robert A., & Bluestone, Herman. (1987). *Black farmers and the economic and social conditions where they live: Some policy implications*. A study prepared by the Economic Research Service, United States Department of Agriculture. Retrieved September 24, 2010 from http://www.ag.auburn.edu/auxiliary/srsa/pages/Articles/SRS%201987%205%2041-58.pdf

Ifill, Gwen. (2009). *The breakthrough: Politics and race in the age of Obama*. New York: Doubleday.

Johnson, Charles. (2008) The end of the Black American narrative. *American Scholar*, 77(3), 32–42.

Karenga, Maulana. (2008). Nguzo Saba (Seven Principles). In *Kwanzaa: A celebration of family, community, and culture*. Los Angeles, CA: University of Sankore Press. Retrieved September 24, 2010 from http://www.officialkwanzaawebsite.org/NguzoSaba.shtml.

King, Martin Luther, Jr. (2003). Letter from a Birmingham jail. In Roger Gottlieb (Ed.), *Liberating faith: Religious voices for justice, peace, and ecological wisdom* (pp. 177–187). Lanham, MD: Rowman & Littlefield.

Kralev, Nicholas. (2008, March 28). Race hits U.S. birth defect: Secretary sees legacy of race in effect today. *Washington Times*, p. A01.

Luke, Allan. (2004). The trouble with English. *Research in the Teaching of English*, 39(1), 85–95.

Lyotard, Jean-Francois. (1984). *The postmodern condition: A report on knowledge*. Minneapolis: University of Minnesota Press.

Marx, Karl. Capital. In Julie Rivkin & Michael Ryan (Eds.), *Literary theory: An anthology* (pp. 665–72). London: Blackwell.

McKay, Claude. (1997[1919]). If we must die. In Arnold Adoff & Benny Andrews (Eds.), *I am the darker brother: An anthology of modern poems by African Americans* (p. 104). New York: Simon & Schuster.

Nugent, Helen. (2007, October 17). Black people less intelligent, scientist claims. *London Times*, Retrieved July 5, 2011 from http://www.timesonline.co.uk/ tol/news/uk/article2677098.ece

Obama, Barack. (add New Hampshire primary concession speech citation)

———. (2008, March 18). A more perfect union. As transcribed byNational Public Radio, *Transcript: Barack Obama's speech on race*. Retrieved September 24, 2010 from http://www.npr.org/templates/story/story.php?storyId=88478467

Ogbu, John. (1987). Variability in minority school performance: A problem in search of an explanation. *Anthropology and Education Quarterly*, 18(4), 55–88.

Pew Forum on Religion and Public Life. (2009). *A religious portrait of African Americans*. Washington, DC: Pew Research Center. Retrieved from http://pewforum. org/docs/? DocID=389

Rex, Lesley A., Timothy J. Murnen, Jack Hobbs, & David McEachen. (2002). Teachers' pedagogical stories and the shaping of classroom participation: "The dancer" and "Graveyard shift at the 7-11." *American Educational Research Journal*, 39(3), 765–96.

Riggs, Marlon, Dir. (1987). *Ethnic notions*. [documentary]. California Newsreel.

Sassi, Kelly & Ebony Elizabeth Thomas (2008). "Walking the talk: Examining privilege and race in a ninth-grade classroom." *English Journal*, 97(6), 25–31.

Sugrue, Thomas J. (1996). *The origins of the urban crisis: Race and inequality in postwar Detroit*. Princeton, NJ: Princeton University Press.

Taney, Roger B. (2004). *The Supreme Court and American democracy: Case studies on judicial review and public policy*, Earl E. Pollock (Ed.). Westport, CT: Greenwood.

Tate, N.W. & Hamilton, J.P. (2012). Taking the pulse of our communities the state of Black public health in the Obama era. In Ebony Elizabeth Thomas & Shanesa R.F. Brooks-Tatum. *Reading*

*African American experiences in the Obama era: Theory, advocacy, activism.* (pp. 227-240). New York: Peter Lang.

Walker, David. (1995 [1829]). *Appeal in four articles; together with a preamble, to the coloured citizens of the world, but in particular, and very expressly, to those of the United States of America.* New York: Macmillan.

Wheatley, Phillis. (2006[1773]). On being brought from Africa to America. In David Lehman (Ed.), *The Oxford Book of American Poetry* (p. 13). New York: Oxford University Press.

# Blue

I been blue so long
I'm indigo blue
Blue like an Ethiopian Jew
Blue like those fleeing the Hutu
Blue, like lost Timbuktu
Been blue so long
So blue I can hardly be seen by you
Moving from blue to invisible
The invisible hue
Of a Ugandan AIDS orphan
Blue of a hanged man
I am cyanide suicide blue
I am raging inside blue
Poisoned sushi blue
See beyond my otherness blue
Brother to the brotherless blue
Child of the motherless blue
Lost voice in the wilderness blue

I am the ocean two miles wide blue
I am the ocean two miles deep blue
Octopus ink blue
Oh yeah.... that's black
Been blue so long
Trying to get from black
To simply human—blue

|| FIFTEEN

# Encouraging the Discouraged

## *Students' Views for Elementary Classrooms*

Julia Ellis, Susan Fitzsimmons & Jan Small-McGinley

Every teacher is faced with students whose troubled behavior challenges the teacher's sense of pedagogical responsibility. But what would the nature of that pedagogical responsibility be under such conditions, and how could one research this question in a way that retained the living voice of the child? This chapter reports on a project that attempts to address those questions. In the context of a video production project we sought to engage students with a history of behavioral difficulties in sharing their views about how elementary school teachers can transform modes of discouragement into modes of encouragement.

The students discussed many aspects of helpful teacher practices. In this paper we provide a brief overview of the ideas they related and then focus on their specific suggestions and experiences related to encouragement. In examining the encouragement or discouragement stories they shared, we saw that encouragement became linked with experiencing teachers as caring and discouragement became linked with experiencing teachers as punishing. Because punishment interfered with both a student's ability to concentrate on schoolwork and the student's relationship with the teacher, frustration, punishment, alienation and discouragement easily became a self-perpetuating cycle of despair. Students wanted teachers to recognize their limits and provide appropriate help or at least calming, encouraging words. The students prized personal recognition for accomplishment or improvement and treasured any concrete mementos of those instances of recognition. The students listened closely for genuine praise when constructive criticism was given. They needed their teachers to communicate hopefulness for them and trust in their abilities and intentions. Without knowing students well, it can be difficult for teachers to recognize students' limits or correctly discern their intentions or preoccupations. Taken together, the students' stories suggest the value of erring on the side of preserving relationships with students in the same ways one might with any other person. If relationships aren't positive, it is unlikely that they can become genuinely pedagogical.

## Background

Our work began with a concern for students whose troubled behavior can render them unwelcome in regular classrooms by the time they complete elementary school. These are students who, because of behavioral difficulties in the classroom or school, are often required to attend alternative programs at the junior high level. We wondered how such students experience the classroom in their elementary school years and what we could learn from them about circumstances in classrooms that could have a positive impact on their experiences.

Given the complexity and breadth of social and biological issues that can contribute to students' troubled behavior, teachers and school administrators may sometimes feel at a loss as to what to do or where to begin in order to make any real difference. Further, because school programs are not the apparent "cause" of troubled behavior, it may not seem that changes in school practices are likely to provide any substantial solution. Nevertheless, in this study we endeavoured to learn students' views about how classroom practices could better support students who tend to develop a history of behavioral difficulties in school. We are concerned that educators' awareness of challenging social and cultural conditions can detract attention from what schools can be doing to support students.

We met with the students in a junior high alternative program in a small urban school district and asked for volunteers to work with us to make a video program that would present their views about how elementary school teachers can be helpful to students. Each of the 10 participating students was interviewed 2, 3 or 4 times. The students also expressed their ideas in writing after the second to last interview. All of the last interviews were videotaped, 8 of the first interviews were videotaped, and all interviews were audiotaped.

All of the videotapes, transcripts, and students' writing were coded to identify topics, subtopics and recurring ideas. The professionally produced video program, *Listen Up!: Kids Talk About Good Teaching* (1997), was composed with a view to providing a representative cross-section of all of the students' ideas. Table 1 provides a categorized listing of the students' ideas. The 23-minute video is used in a number of teacher education programs to stimulate discussion about ways that teachers can be proactive regarding classroom management concerns. It is available for purchase very inexpensively. Some teachers show it on the first day of school to stimulate class discussion about how students want their classroom to work. It has been publicly broadcast several times a year on ACCESS Television in Alberta.

When the video was completed, our colleagues expressed surprise that what the students said they wanted wasn't radical at all—what they were asking for was basic. After seeing the video, parents with teenage children typically asked their sons and daughters what they wanted from teachers and were surprised to hear the same ideas our 10 alternative program students had expressed.

The students' ideas about good teaching are not novel. Other researchers (e.g., Loman, 1996; Phelan, Locke Davidson & Cao, 1992) have also found that students want teachers to be friendly, respect them, relate to them as people, be

*Table 1: Students' Views on Helpful Teaching Practices*

Practices that are not helpful for misbehavior:

- blaming the wrong student
- believing a student's "enemies"
- blaming the "victim"
- yelling
- using time-out for a young child who already feels isolated and abandoned
- requiring a student to miss recess or physical education
- overusing the principal's office
- becoming angry with the whole class because of one student's behavior
- using time-out for a student who is "goofing off" (as opposed to a student who is angry and needs to calm down)
- failing to respond to misbehavior and then "blowing up" when it persists
- dwelling on or reminding students of past infractions and punishments

Practices that are helpful for misbehavior:

- "coming back after" in order to ask students why they're misbehaving and whether anything is upsetting them
- if a student has "an accident," providing comfort and assistance rather than increasing distress by blaming or accusing about behavior that may have led to the accident
- if a student has done something wrong, explaining it rather than assuming that the student knows what was wrong with the action that is being reprimanded
- if a student persists in talking, calmly asking the student to move to another seat
- helping students learn how to get their anger out and giving them opportunities to do so

- being a "friendly father figure" who "shows the way" rather than a stern lecturer
- helping the "class clown" learn when it is or is not appropriate to "entertain" the class (and finding ways to give him/her some attention)
- letting kids know that by succumbing to peer pressure they'll be the only ones getting into trouble and will in fact lose popularity because other kids will then not be allowed to keep company with them
- diffusing tension in the classroom (or the teacher's own negative mood) by interjecting an activity that is fun or relaxing for everybody
- using whole-class incentives such as a movie on Friday afternoon to work towards

"Winning over" is the best way to prevent misbehavior. Winning over entails:

(a) Respecting students
(b) Providing encouragement
(c) Caring
(d) Making learning enjoyable
(e) Discerning and supporting students' learning needs
(f) Being a nice person

(a) Respecting students

- If students feel respected they don't want to be "bad" and risk losing that respect.
- If students feel respected by the teacher, then they respect the teacher in return.
- If students don't respect the teacher, then they don't want to do anything "for" the teacher.
- Students respect a teacher who is "friendly," i.e., asks how they are, participates in games/sports with them in the gym, talks to them at recess or lunch, greets them if they see them at the mall or elsewhere.
- Students respect a teacher who trusts them and is willing to reason and compromise with them.

(b) Providing encouragement

- Give recognition for an individual's improvement.
- Respond positively to inept work; e.g., "Close, but good try."
- Say, "You can do it! Leave the hard question, go on and do the others, and then come back to it."
- Make a fuss over creative work; e.g., put story in newspaper, take photograph of artwork or construction.

- Be careful with "constructive criticism"; i.e., make it clear that the work is already good and that if the student wants to add things, then provide some ideas.
- Help a child achieve success on a unit or upcoming test by identifying the component pieces of learning and acknowledging success in each part along the way.
- Give compliments, compliments, and more compliments.

(c) Caring

- means "being there for" a student.
- means noticing if a student needs help in some way and making sure he/she gets it.
- means making sure that students have a feeling of belongingness and safety in the classroom.
- means letting a student tell you his/her troubles and letting him/her know that you care and that you understand how he/she feels.

(d) Making learning enjoyable

- Use humor.
- Use the school grounds for math activities.
- Use games.
- Use group work.
- Focus attention with a riddle before starting class.
- Use decorative or thematic drawings or symbols on the board.
- Give choices.
- Use variety.

(e) Discerning and supporting students' learning needs

- Use a different way to explain something if a student hasn't understood the initial presentation or instruction.
- Notice a student who is struggling and provide an alternative task or set of materials.
- Support the learning needs of students whose strengths are in different modalities; e.g., visual, kinesthetic.
- Provide or obtain extra help for students who have difficulties.
- Allow time for slower students to complete a test rather than collecting it whenever most students seem to be finished.

(f) Being a nice person

- "A good teacher is a nice person,...easy to get along with, fun to be around."

caring, make them feel safe and accepted, encourage them, motivate them, make learning active and enjoyable, use variety, use group work, and have a good instructional repertoire. In undertaking this research, however, we did not expect that students would suggest practices that were previously unheard of. Instead we hoped that students' stories and voices would return the dramatic tension and significance to many good ideas that have become dry, abstract prescriptions. As Crites (1971) has argued, without the human story, abstractions can become hostile to life itself. We also hoped to gain insight into the dynamics of classroom experience from the perspectives of students with histories of behavioral difficulties in that context; that is, to learn how, in their experience, everything was connected to everything else, or how one thing led to another.

We have had some success with both expectations or research purposes. Many teachers who have viewed the video and completed evaluation forms have indicated that the video caused them to reflect and deepened their commitments to supportive practices for students. In terms of the classroom dynamics for students with troubled behavior, we have discerned how easy it can be for students who are most in need of belonging or of encouragement to get even less than their more advantaged classmates. It is obviously easier to offer approval, affirmation, and encouragement to students whose academic work is strong. It can require more care and imagination to formulate encouraging comments for students who are less adept with assigned tasks. Thus students who come to school with fewer academic skills can become increasingly discouraged where schoolwork is concerned. Similarly, if students do not experience a secure sense of belonging and affiliation in their life outside of the school, they can have particularly high needs for connection, inclusion, and belonging in the classroom itself. Sadly, their lack of emotional nurturance outside of school can lead to troubled behavior in the classroom that may in fact diminish their opportunities for experiencing inclusion there. We realize that teachers can experience disruptive students as taking up more than their fair share of the teacher's time and attention. The nature of the attention they receive, however, is often not experienced as affirming or as enhancing their feeling of belonging in the classroom.

We have revisited the students' stories of events related to belonging or encouragement to attend to the dynamics and meanings of these events for the students. Our work with the theme of belonging has been presented elsewhere (Ellis, Hart, & Small-McGinley, 1998b). A brief overview of key ideas related to belonging and encouragement has also been reported (Ellis, Hart, & Small-McGinley, 1998a). In this paper we wish to offer a more in-depth examination of students' stories of how they experienced encouragement, or in some cases, discouragement, during their elementary school years. The students' perspective can be a rich source for informing reflection on one's own teaching.

## Methodology

### *Researching Students' Perspectives*

While recognized as an expensive and labor intensive undertaking, researching students' perspectives interpretively or ethnographically is understood to be a necessary means for understanding students' behavior. It is the students' own interpretations of classroom dynamics that guide their thoughts and actions in those contexts. Because the child's viewpoint can be distinctively different from the adult's viewpoint, misreadings or misunderstandings of students and their perceptions can impede teachers' best intentions. As Sanders (1996) and others (e.g., Christensen & James, 2000; Graue & Walsh, 1998; Greig & Taylor, 1999; Mergandollar & Packer, 1985; Peevers & Secord, 1973; Shedlin, 1986; Weinstein, 1983; Whitfield, 1976) have contended, children can reliably describe events and experiences in the school setting. In sharing their perceptions, they also reveal their understandings of the events that give structure to their lives. Without access to the meanings of events for students, teachers' best efforts can be hampered by their own broad assumptions about students' perceptions.

### *The Pilot Study*

As a field test for the methodology, an interview was conducted with a grade 7 student who was enrolled in an alternate program because of behavioral difficulties in the classroom and school. As the opening question for the interview, the student was asked what advice he would offer to teachers about how to make the classroom a supportive place. The student talked for 40 minutes with no further prompting. Then he was asked to put his ideas in writing. He was offered an honorarium if he could use his computer word processing equipment to produce 20 double-spaced pages of text on the topics he had discussed. He produced 4 double-spaced pages showing 12 paragraphs on separate coherent topics and then said he couldn't think of anything else. He was paid the whole honorarium. The analysis of the pilot study has been presented elsewhere (Ellis, 1997).

### *Site and Participants*

A small urban school district in Alberta agreed to support our research and made it possible for us to meet with 29 students (24 boys and 5 girls) to extend our invitation for participation. All of the students were in the same junior high alternate program. Of these 29 students, 23 were interested, and 10 finally submitted all required signed consent forms. Of the 10 students, 7 were boys and 3 were girls. In age, 1 student was 13, 7 were 14, and 2 were 15.

### *Data Collection*

Each of the participating students was interviewed 2, 3, or 4 times and completed a piece of writing to express his/her ideas. The four students who were slower to submit signed consent forms had a smaller number of interviews. Students were paid an honorarium for their writing work. All interviews were audiotaped and transcribed. One or two of each student's interviews were also videotaped. Excerpts from videotaped interviews were used in a video program entitled *Listen Up! Kids Talk About Good Teaching* (1997). All interviews and writing took place in October and November 1996.

### *Interviews*

The interviews with students were unstructured and open-ended. At the beginning of the first interviews students were asked to reflect back on elementary school experiences and to formulate advice they would offer to student teachers or beginning teachers about how to make the classroom a more supportive place for all students. When students ran out of ideas to bring forward, they were prompted to think about memories from specific grade levels or teachers they had particularly admired or appreciated. In follow-up interviews, students were asked to clarify or expand points they made in previous interviews and to offer any further ideas that they could think of. Through this open-ended approach and through following the students' lead in terms of topics, we hoped to avoid introducing language or terminology and ideas that did not come from the students' own perspectives.

Students were asked to write about a number of their ideas after their second to last interview. All students completed four double-spaced typed pages of writing focusing on five or more of the topics that had been of high interest to them in their interviews.

### *Data Analysis*

Through our analysis of the students' interview transcripts and writing, we sought to understand the significance of various teaching practices to these students. There were a number of teaching practices or teacher characteristics that were commonly mentioned by the large majority of the students interviewed. Examples of these were making learning fun, providing choice, providing help, using humor, using group work, respecting students, encouraging students, caring, talking to students, using incentives and consequences, and using helpful ways to respond to misbehavior. Each of the students also brought forward a unique topic that was particular to his/her own experience. Examples of these topics were: protecting a child who is being bullied or picked on; how to respond helpfully to a class clown; the importance of talking to students about peer pressure; responding to the troubled behavior of a child who is already feeling isolated and alienated; helping a student un-learn the rhythm of frustration and despair with schoolwork; diffusing rather than exacerbating tension or anger in the class; and refraining from asking prying, sensitive questions unless the parents are there.

Although the students' ideas were not necessarily novel, their modes of expressing these ideas often served to remind us of the deep reciprocity in relations between teachers and students. For example, one student talked about the relationship between caring and respect in the following way:

> Like, if a kid thinks a teacher cares about him, it's kind of like how you treat your mother. Some of the ways you treat your mother might start rubbing off on your teacher. Without even thinking, you'd start treating the teacher with more respect. Just because the teacher was nice to you that one time would make the kid feel like there is someone who does care out there and someone who does care where you're going in life.

The majority of the ideas listed in Table 1 have been presented in the students' own voices with their own stories in the video program *Listen Up!* (1997).

For this paper, we have studied all of the students' stories that pertain to encouragement and endeavour to highlight key ideas about how these students have experienced and understood this dimension of elementary school.

### *Encouragement*

Encouragement was a recurring theme in the general advice that students said they would offer to teachers. The following excerpts are from interviews with five of the students.

> "Give compliments, compliments, and more compliments!!"

> "It [encouragement] makes you want to do more work!"

> "Say: 'You can do it! Just try your hardest. And if you can't get that one, go on and do the other ones and then come back and try it again.'"

> "And if I didn't get it, she would say 'Close, but good try' and that made me feel like she appreciated my effort."

> "Your self-esteem is like a balloon. If someone says to a kid, 'Oh, you're so stupid,' that's just like letting air out of the balloon."

During the interviews, students were asked to share any striking memories they had from earlier grades. They were also asked to recall teachers they had appreciated and any special things these people had done. Students most frequently answered these questions by either describing a "winning over activity" a teacher had used (e.g., letting each child have a turn at being "principal" of the classroom for a day; giving a picnic at the teacher's home), or by relating an event they experienced as extremely encouraging or discouraging.

### *The Salience of Encouragement Experiences*

When students shared memories of events from elementary school years, they became particularly animated when telling stories about encouragement. If the stories were positive ones, their eyes sparkled and their faces lit up as they appeared to re-experience the uplifting quality of the remembered moment. If the stories were negative ones, the heaviness and disappointment of those experiences were palpable in the retelling.

In the following interview excerpt, a student shares a memory of discouragement from the first day of school in grade 1. Notice how at the end of the story he reminds the interviewer of another happier story about a caring teacher who remembered and recognized his August birthday on the last day of school in June. Experiencing encouragement and caring may be closely intertwined for some of these students.

> I had a Grade 1 teacher, and on the first day of Grade 1 she said to everyone, "Write a word on a piece of paper." I didn't really understand the question, so I just started picking letters off the wall and writing this big, long line. She went around to everyone else, saying, "That's really good. Look at this! Look at that!" and I think I was the only one that didn't write a word or something that made sense. I said, "Look how long my word is," and she said, "That isn't a word." It made me feel like I was stupid because I didn't know how to do any of that. That gave me a bad impression for when I got in Grade 2. When I did get that teacher that did give me a pencil and a cupcake because my birthday was in August, that was a good experience, and it prepared me for Grade 3, 4, and so on.

In the following excerpts from interviews with two students, the students share positive memories of experiencing encouragement. Interestingly, both students explicitly connect the encouraging event to feeling cared for.

> STUDENT: I wrote a 19- or 20-page story. I was only in Grade 1. It was a Halloween story, and she liked it so much and I liked it so much that she decided to publish it in the newspaper.
>
> INTERVIEWER: How did that make you feel?
>
> STUDENT: It made me feel that people actually cared and made me feel really proud of myself.
>
> INTERVIEWER: Tell me about your Grade 6 teacher.
>
> STUDENT: She acted like she cared about what you did regardless of the importance of it. This one time I wasn't doing very good in school and I got a 75 on a test, and she said, "That's really good." She let me take a pencil out of this pencil jar, and I thought it was really great. It made me try harder. It picked up my marks too because I thought it was just the best.

Another student told a story about how his teacher took a photograph of a structure he had built out of blocks. Thereafter, he said, he always went to get her whenever he made something out of blocks again, just to see if she'd take another photograph. As we re-visit these encouragement stories, we feel that we see glimpses of the magic of teachers who know how to let students know that they care by seizing any available opportunities to affirm and celebrate students' accomplishments. We hope that these stories will help teachers remember what they always already knew and reassure them of the value of these kinds of encouragement efforts.

### *Prize as Artifact*

The students' stories about recognition that was accompanied by a concrete prize helped us to appreciate the significance of their concrete materiality. Individual recognition for accomplishment or improvement was prized by these students. The concrete materiality of the pencil or the newspaper publication of the Halloween story forever froze these moments of recognition into their memories and into their stories about their own capabilities. The possession of a concrete prize also gave them the opportunity to extend the moment of recognition. One boy spoke insistently and at length about how he preferred it if a teacher wrote a note to his parents about his improved math work during the week rather than simply telling them by telephone. He appreciated being able to present the note to the parent of his choice at the time of his choice. The note was his prize. In concretely presenting it himself, he could count on extending his moment of recognition. Another student treasured a certificate he had received for making the largest improvement in a particular subject area. The certificate remained on the refrigerator at home for three years. We wonder what can explain the potency of these "trophies." Have they been so hard to come by? Have they served as lifelines in a sea of self-doubt? Whatever their meaning, teachers can know that these forms of thoughtfulness on their part are not wasted.

## Constructive Criticism That Encourages

The students seemed to be incredibly sensitive detectors of either encouragement or discouragement. They were very ready and able to "teach" us how to "do" encouragement.

One of the students in our study spoke at length about how he experienced constructive criticism as detrimental rather than helpful. He said that if a teacher used constructive criticism all the time, a student would feel that there was always one more thing to improve on, that his/her work would never be good enough. He gave the following example in one of his interviews:

STUDENT: A student gets 75% on a language arts assignment, and the teacher comes along and says, "You know, this is not a bad mark, but if you just sound out your words a bit better, you could get 80s on it. You just have to try harder." I took that as a put-down. She thinks I could do better; she's not happy with what I did.

INTERVIEWER: What would you suggest instead?

STUDENT: She could have said, "This 75% is really good!" She may not have thought it was really good, but she could have said that just to keep on good terms with me. She could have said, "Do you want me to give you a secret on how you can do better on tests?" And I'd say, "Yeah," and she'd say, "You know those long words. Sound them out; it might help you a lot. That 75% was really good." Another student explained the art of constructive criticism metaphorically. It's like when someone builds a sand castle. Another person might come along and say "You could put a door there." Your response might be "Well, yeah" or you might just knock the whole thing down and say "Build it yourself." Instead the person could say "That's a really great sand castle. Do you want to add something to it?"

The first student above used the phrase "to keep on good terms with me." Perhaps the students are reminding us of the importance of preserving relationships. In our relationships with loved ones, do we not endeavour to exercise tact or discretion when we consider offering constructive criticism? At the very least, the students remind us of the difficult work of teachers who must help students progress while also supporting their sense of accomplishment and capability.

### *Establishing the Cycle of Discouragement*

Students' difficulties with schoolwork, coupled with their behavioral difficulties, sometimes meant that punishment became implicated in discouraging experiences and failed relationships with teachers. Everything became connected to everything else, eventually creating a "knee-jerk" response of high frustration whenever new, difficult tasks were presented.

In the following interview excerpt, a student asks that teachers recognize a child's limits, provide help that may be needed, and if that's not feasible, leave the child with the encouraging words, "That's better. Try a bit more."

STUDENT: I'm a really messy writer because I'm dyslexic, and my handwriting is really messy. My l's didn't look good enough, and she would just go, "Do them right!" and I couldn't do them right. And then she would go, "Go! Go sit down and do it again!"

INTERVIEWER: So that's some advice you'd give student teachers—to encourage students?

STUDENT: Yeah, not hassle the students; encourage them so they will feel better about what they are doing.

INTERVIEWER: Okay, what do you mean by hassle?

STUDENT: So instead of "Do this! Make those letters!" I think, Why should I try? That's a hassle right there. That's just like pushing the student too hard to do something that they might take a bit longer to learn how. Instead of that I would try to make the student feel better about what they are doing. You know, say, "That's better. Try a bit more." Encourage them so they feel better about what they are doing, so they will get it done right. Instead of keeping them in for recess or lunch hour because they didn't get it right, sit down with them some other time and let them work, and help them get it right.

Some of the students in this study come to school already upset by their social or biological conditions. They can be easily agitated by negative experiences. As much as other students, and perhaps more than most students, they welcome a calm, patient, encouraging manner. The difficulties they may exhibit with schoolwork or behavior can very likely make teachers feel frustrated and impatient. The students remind us to consider whether our words and our tone can be experienced as encouraging.

The following is a brief excerpt from the above student's lengthy discussion about how he began to experience pressure and frustration in early elementary grades:

INTERVIEWER: Can you give me an example of a teacher hassling a student?

STUDENT: Well, like, the student is sitting in class and does his work, talks to someone, with the teacher being the authority figure, that would be like, "You get down and you do your work, and after, for talking, you can do this and this and this!" Then the student goes back to their work and looks at the question 6 times 7, and instead of getting, like, 42, right off the bat they will be, "Uh, ah, what about the work I have to do after school? What about this? Oh, no! Oh, no!"

The student's discussion of this example and related experiences extended over several pages of transcripts. He talked to the interviewer about how even simple "consequences" for small infractions like talking can be emotionally upsetting and preoccupying for a young child who may already have "problems from home" on his mind. So, for example, if he were told of a pending consequence such as staying in after school and missing play with friends, he would become preoccupied with that and then, in his words, "freeze up" and not be able to figure out his schoolwork. This would be followed by the teacher asking him why he was unable to do his work. This created more frustration because he knew it would be confrontational to tell the teacher the real reason.

Some punishments were also experienced as humiliating and created a feeling of rage. For example, for throwing things into the wastepaper basket from a distance, he was made to not only stay in at recess but also to vacuum the entire classroom floor while the teacher and custodian watched. His stories gave meaning to a simple statement by another one of the students who said that punishment wasn't a good idea and that, yes, "We can learn from it, but it doesn't help us out much." It seems that for students who are already upset about one thing or another, punishment gives them even more to be upset about, distracts them from schoolwork, and distances them from the teacher who is the only present adult who might have been "helpful" in some way. Even the punishment of being yelled at by the teacher in front of the class was a strong one. When asked how that feels, one student replied that "it makes you feel like everyone else in the class is better than you." Just as encouragement was associated with caring on the part of the teacher, discouragement seemed to be connected to a punishing attitude on the part of the teacher.

### *Hope and Re-establishing Encouragement*

The Latin root word for courage is *cor,* meaning heart. If one considers the word *encourage,* what would it mean to *en-hearten* a student? Would it mean to give love? Would it mean to give life force? Would it mean to give hope? In the following interview excerpt, a student offers contrasting stories of ways that teachers can dis-hearten or en-hearten students:

> STUDENT: Well, like at some schools it is harder to be there with teachers that pressure you. Like this one teacher, when you were having problems with your work he'd say, "If you don't get this right you ain't going to pass."
>
> INTERVIEWER: How did that make you feel?
>
> STUDENT: Well, that made me feel that I wasn't going to pass no matter what I did. It made me feel that I wasn't going anywhere. And other teachers encourage students, and they make you feel that you have a really, really good chance to pass, which makes the students feel better. Teachers should have a happy attitude.

Can teachers, being fearful about their students' likelihood of success, communicate that fear, discouragement, or despair to the students? This story suggests that in order to be hopeful themselves, students draw strength, inspiration, courage, and serenity from the teacher's "happy attitude." A teacher who is en-heartening or encouraging is one who communicates hopefulness and a sense of possibility in their interactions with students. If students are to have courage and confidence, they have to see that teachers are at least trying to have confidence in them. As one of our students said, "Encouragement is like a railroad track. It keeps you going."

The student discussed in the section above, "Establishing the Cycle of Discouragement," explained how some teachers were able to support him in breaking out of that cycle.

> STUDENT: Teachers like Mr. ________ made me feel like I had the choice to do my work. Like, if I didn't want to do it, I was allowed to take a little time out and go to a little table alone to re-gather my thoughts until I was ready to do it.
>
> INTERVIEWER: So you mean he gave you a break to go re-gather your thoughts. What do you mean?
>
> STUDENT: Like, if I wasn't getting something right and I was getting frustrated about it, he let me go sit in a corner and read a book, put down the book, and then think about what I was just doing, to figure it out when I was not under pressure. When I have all that done I come back to the class. That made it a lot easier because I wouldn't want to sit there for the whole class, getting frustrated. So he gave me five minutes to go figure it out. He didn't pressure me. That makes people feel more mature and more secure about themselves. And they actually feel that they can do it if they set their mind to it. Some students like to do it that way because they know they can get it done. Like, me, I like taking my time and think things out. With the right teachers and the right principals, I can do that.

One of our students said, "You have to trust students; and even if you don't, you have to try." In this story of the student being allowed or invited to take a break to "re-gather his thoughts," we see an example of how teachers can demonstrate trust and communicate confidence in students' abilities.

## Closing Reflections

As we searched for a theoretical framework that could most adequately account for or hold together the ideas students had expressed, we found Eric Fromm's (1956) model of positive relationships to be most satisfying and parsimonious. In this model, Fromm identifies *caring, responsibility, respect,* and *knowledge* as four elements that are common to positive relationships. *Caring* entails concern for the life and growth of the person in the relationship. *Responsibility* means being ready to act to meet the needs, expressed or unexpressed, of another human being. *Respect* entails having the ability to see an individual as s/he is and allowing that person to develop without exploitation. *Knowledge* includes not a superficial awareness but genuine understanding of the other's feelings, even if they are not readily apparent.

We expect that elementary school teachers choose their profession because of their *caring,* that is, their willingness to be concerned for the life and growth of students in their classrooms. However, their ability to exercise *respect* and *responsibility,* that is, to recognize a child's limits and to take appropriate action to meet a child's needs, depends on their *knowledge* of the child. *Knowledge,* in Fromm's sense, means being able to read a child's feelings, intentions, and responses. If a child is misread, actions which may be intended as helpful can work at cross-purposes.

Getting to know a student can sometimes require more than listening to the stories a student comes forward to share. A number of student teachers and teachers have used a particular interview schedule to invite students to discuss a variety of topics that are most salient for them. This interview schedule and procedures for its use have been reported in previous articles and a book chapter (Ellis, 1992; Ellis, 1994; Ellis, 1998). Many student teachers using this interview activity often found that simply conducting the interview was enough to transform a previously "difficult" student into a cooperative one. The following is an excerpt from a student teacher's written reflection on the interview experience.

> Finally, the interview served to encourage me to think that I am able to develop the same close, warm rapport with Junior [grades 4, 5, and 6] boys as with girls—and indeed of the value of the interview as a tool for building trust and friendship. Ryan was tremendously supportive following the interview, and volunteered continually for demonstrations, solo musical performances, and generally anything in which I sought input or assistance from the class. He also raised his hand to answer any question I ever posed—all of which reinforced the notion that elementary-aged children typically enjoy only with very few adults a relationship that allows them to talk openly and share concerns.

Although a primary benefit of the interview activity is the relationship it cultivates, the topics the students discuss also alert teachers to their preoccupations, motivations, fears, hopes, and loves. Increased awareness of the student's perspective enables the teacher to support connections between the student's story and the classroom story.

We are also aware that the pressures many teachers may experience to have their "performance" and "achievement" as teachers meet certain standards can discourage them from providing the kinds of support some of their students may need. A number of the students in our study said that they often needed time to calm down or time to just talk to other students, and that a class in which everyone had to be "on-task" at all times was not a good one for them. One of the boys talked about the value of group work as providing a space for "talking about feelings," which he said isn't feasible during the physical activity of recess. Teachers need more space, not less, to accommodate the growth needs of all students in their classrooms.

Teachers in our graduate courses have also reported that the percentage of high needs students in their classes has increased dramatically during the last 10 years. Recognizing that teachers cannot individually provide all the support that so many students need, we turned our research efforts in the direction of school-based mentorship programs, peer support and student leadership programs. These are programs that provide students with opportunities for attachments with adult mentors, contribute to a climate of caring, or empower students to care. In our research with such programs we have endeavored to

- work with schools to collaboratively develop and research mentorship programs for students in the early school years.
- locate and study other existing mentorship programs spanning the years of K-12.
- locate and study peer support programs spanning the years of K-12.
- locate and study student leadership program.

Our intent was not to develop a comprehensive list of existing programs in any specific geographical area, but rather to conduct case studies of a wide range of programs with a view to learning how they work and what their benefits are. We collected data on each of the programs through whatever means were feasible including: audiotaped and videotaped interviews with program coordinators, students, mentors, parents; students' written narrative reports; and program documents. Because most of the programs we found and studied had been in operation for five to seven years, the program coordinators were well informed about program benefits and the practicalities of operating such programs successfully.

In the mentorship programs that we helped to develop, we conducted three intensive studies on the following questions:

- In a short-term mentorship program (8–10 weeks) with minimal training and structure for mentors, do the mentors and children achieve mutually satisfying relationships and are the mentors effective in providing academic support to the children?
- How does the mentor's pedagogy work? What informs or guides the mentor's instructional planning and decision-making? To what extent is the mentor's pedagogy shaped by the child or the child's responses?
- How do the mentors and children develop their relationships? What are the dynamics or key components of non-related adults cultivating relationships with young children in one-hour per week mentorship sessions over an 8- to 10-week period?

These research questions were considered important given that the schedules of schools and available mentors make short-term programs most feasible. Further, there is little research available on mentorship programs for young children and little in-depth qualitative research on mentorship programs for older students. The findings from these three studies were expected to clarify the potential value of such programs and the processes for their successful implementation. An understanding of the dynamics of mentoring young children would be useful to program developers who must make many decisions about the structure, resources, and support for such programs. The results of the completed research have been made available through several publications (Alberta Teachers' Association, 1999; Ellis & Small-McGinley, 1998a; Ellis & Small-McGinley, 1998b; Ellis & Small-McGinley, 1999a; Ellis & Small-McGinley, 1999b; Ellis, Small-McGinley & Hart, 1998; Ellis, Small-McGinley, & De Fabrizio 1999; Ellis, Small-McGinley, & De Fabrizio, in press).

This paper has focused on students' views about how elementary school teachers encourage achievement. Their stories revealed how difficult it was for them to separate discussions about encouragement from discussions about the nature of their relationships with teachers. To support their growth, to give them strength and courage, students need affirmation and encouragement from adults who are oriented to them in a positive way. The students have given many examples of how teachers accomplish this. With so many students needing school to be their primary site for experiencing belonging and encouragement, it makes sense for teachers to be encouraged to give emphasis to their relationships with students. It also makes sense for schools to coordinate programs such as mentorship, peer support, and student leadership to provide further support for the growth of all students in the school.

In closing we wish to express our own tribute to the many teachers who have taken time to listen to the stories of individual students and who have used their art, heart, and imagination to help students find supportive places in their classrooms. We also thank the students who participated in this research for their trust and their efforts to help us understand their experience.

## References

Alberta Teachers' Association, Edmonton. (1999). *Volunteer Mentorship Programs.* Videotape. Website for ATA's Safe and Caring Schools Project: http://www.teachers.ab.ca/projects/safe.html

Christensen, P. & James, A. (Eds.) (2000). *Research with children: Perspectives and practices.* New York: Falmer Press.

Crites, S. (1971). The narrative quality of experience. *Journal of the American Academy of Religion, 39*(3), 291–311.

Ellis, J. L. (1992). Teachers undertaking narrative inquiry with children. *Analytic Teaching, 12*(2), 9–18.

Ellis, J. L. (1994). Narrative inquiry with children: A generative form of preservice teacher research. *International Journal for Qualitative Studies in Education, 7* (4), 367–380.

Ellis, J. (1997). What a seriously at-risk 12-year-old would really like to say to teachers about classroom management. *Education Canada, 37*(2), 17–21.

Ellis, J. (1998). Narrative Inquiries with Children and Youth. In J. Ellis (ed.) *Teaching from Understanding: Teacher as Interpretive Inquirer* (pp. 33–56). New York: Garland.

Ellis, J., Hart, S., & Small-McGinley, J. (1998a). Classroom management: The views of "difficult" students. *The Canadian Association of Principals' Journal, 8*(1), 39–41.

Ellis, J., Hart, S., & Small-McGinley, J. (1998b). "Difficult" students' perspectives on belonging and inclusion in the classroom. *Reclaiming Children and Youth: Journal of Emotional and Behavioral Problems, 7*(3), 142–146.

Ellis, J. & Small-McGinley, J. (1998a). *Peer Support and Student Leadership Programs.* Edmonton: Alberta Teachers' Association.

Ellis, J., & Small-McGinley, J. (1998b). *Volunteer Mentorship programs K-12.* Edmonton, AB: Alberta Teachers' Association.

Ellis, J., & Small-McGinley, J. (1999a). Students' perspectives on student leadership programs. *Canadian Association of Principals' Journal, 8*(2), 35–37.

Ellis, J. & Small-McGinley, J. (1999b). *Volunteer Mentorship Programs: A Practical Handbook.* Edmonton: Alberta Teachers' Association.

Ellis, J., Small-McGinley, J., & Hart, S. (1998). Mentor-supported Literacy Programs in Elementary Schools. *Alberta Journal of Educational Research, 44*(2), 149–162.

Ellis, J., Small-McGinley, J. & De Fabrizio, L. (1999). "It's So Great to Have an Adult Friend…": A Mentorship Program for At-Risk Youth. *Reaching Today's Youth: The Community Circle of Caring Journal,* August, 46–50.

Ellis, J., Small-McGinley, J. & De Fabrizio, L. (in press). *Caring for Kids in Communities: Using Mentorship, Peer Support, and Student Leadership Programs in Schools.* New York: Peter Lang Publishing.

Fromm, E. (1956). *The art of loving.* Toronto: Bantam Books.

Graue, M.E. & Walsh, D.J. (1998). *Studying children in context: Theories, methods and ethics.* Thousand Oaks, CA: Sage Publications.

Greig, A. & Taylor, J. (1999). *Doing research with children.* Thousand Oaks, CA: Sage Publications.

*Listen up! Kids talk about good teaching.* (1997). Videotape. Calgary, AB: Mighty Motion Pictures. Telephone: 800–471–5628. Fax: 403–439–4051

Loman, J. (1996). Characteristics of exemplary teachers. *New Directions for Teaching and Learning. No. 65,* Spring, 33–40.

Mergendollar, J.R. & Packer, M.J. (1985). Seventh graders' conceptions of teachers: An interpretive analysis. *The Elementary School Journal, 85,* 581–600.

Peevers, B.H. & Secord, P.F. (1973). Developmental changes in attribution of descriptive concepts to persons. *Journal of Personality and Social Psychology, 27,* 120–128.

Phelan, P., Locke Davidson, A. & Cao, H.T. (1992). Speaking up: Students' perspectives on school. *Phi Delta Kappan, 73*(9), May, 695–704.

Sanders, S. W. (1996). Children's physical education experiences: Their interpretations can help teachers. *JOPERD, 67*(3), 51-56.

Shedlin, A. (1986). 487 sixth graders can't be wrong. *Principal, 6,* 53.

Weinstein, R.S. (1983). Student perceptions of schooling. *The Elementary School Journal, 28,* 286–312.

Whitfield, T. (1976). How students perceive teachers. *Theory into Practice, 15,* 347–351.

# Ode to My Old Man

At five foot three
You were a titan among mere men
Possessed of an intellect unsurpassed
I loved you more than I feared your wrath
Now as I tend your wizened frame
I wonder if memory is nothing more
Than a child's game.

This intimate touch comforts me
Perhaps more than it eases your pain
For as much as I have loved you
I have never held you close or
Called you by your given name

I learned life lessons at your knee
What it means for a black man to be truly free
To see my blackness as a gift
Not a curse
To hold my head up and tell the world
To do it's worst 'cause life on this plane is but a verse
In the spiritual journey back to the everlasting source.

My fingers knead the ropy muscles
Beneath your silken skin
That age and time have rendered paper thin
I wish that I could eat your pain
And find a way to make you whole again

You taught me to be present and accounted for
In the lives and laughter of those who bear my name
And when things go wrong not to seek others to bear the blame
Taught me that without dignity and integrity
You have no true claim to fame

For more than a decade
You've held the monster at bay
And like the song, you did it your way
You kept the twins, avoided the needle and the knife
With wit and wisdom you've continued to live your life

I touch you and memories of you touch me
I now know that as long as me and mine
Breathe in sunshine you'll never live in shadow
And your legacy will never die.

## SIXTEEN

# Schools of Hope

## *Teaching Literacy in the Obama Era*

Jane Bean-Folkes

> "We know that the success of every American will be tied more closely than ever before to the level of education that they achieve. . . . The jobs will go to the people with the knowledge and skills to do them. It's that simple." —President Barack Obama, U.S. Chamber of Commerce, 2010[1]

The statement President Obama made to the U.S. Chamber of Commerce in March of 2010 can be seen as a call to further the goal of increasing accountability for student performance. Until early in 2009, the focus of the Department of Education, through the No Child Left Behind Act (NCLB), was on school performance rather than student performance. Under this act, the standard of performance varied from state to state, and although America's schools were challenged to educate all students so they would be ready to meet the demands of the workforce, student achievement continued to vary widely across the country and across sectors of society. According to recent U.S. Department of Education data, only 60% of those African Americans who entered as freshmen graduate from high school nationwide (U.S. Department of Education, National Center for Education Statistics [NCES], Common Core of Data [CCD], 2010).[2] The Obama administration's blueprint for revising the Elementary and Secondary Education Act, released in March of 2010, aims to address this disparity. Ultimately, the Obama reform effort seeks to ensure that students leave school with skills that allow them to compete in the global workforce, and attempts to achieve this goal primarily by linking teacher compensation to student performance. This chapter sheds light on important challenges faced by teachers and by students of color as they strive to achieve the high level of literacy needed to compete in today's global workforce. This chapter also addresses and offers recommendations for support that school, parents, and communities can provide in order to assist in these efforts.

The National Governors Association (NGA) Center for Best Practices and the Council of Chief State School Offices (CCSSO) recently took up the challenge of increasing high school graduation rates. Their research and collaboration led to the creation of the Common Core State Standards, which were released in August 2010.[3] The mission of the Common Core State Standards is to provide a clear, consistent understanding of what students are expected to learn in order to help teachers and parents be aware of what they need to do to help our young people. The standards provide a detailed outline for literacy across grades K–12, with strong emphasis on reading, writing, listening and speaking, as well as on language in the social and natural sciences. The focus is on ensuring that all of America's students leave school with the ability to read, write, and think effectively and critically so that they are ready to compete in the global economy. The standards are designed to be robust and relevant to the real world, reflecting the knowledge and skills that our young people need in order to succeed in college and in their future careers.

The Obama administration and the nation's governors have emphasized that the current initiatives to increase student performance are not a top-down mandate for curricular content or materials in the manner of the scripted programs that were favored under NCLB[4] Rather, states are encouraged to improve schools from the bottom up, with the goal of enhancing outcomes for all children—Black, White, Asian, Native American, Latino, and multiracial children alike. In response, many states have taken steps to recruit and train quality teachers so that every child in America receives a good education and has a fair chance of success. In this regard, an emphasis on literacy is crucial. Literacy plays a major role in education because without the ability to read critically and with comprehension, it is difficult to learn subjects such as science and math (Allington, 2001). The changes in the literacy standards are robust, in that they require students to read and to think using higher levels of analysis and critique.

What does it mean to read and to think critically? Peter Freebody and Allan Luke (1990) describe proficient and critical reading as a social practice that consists of four key elements: coding competence (learning your role as a code breaker: How do I decode this?), semantic competence (learning your role as text participant: What does this mean?), pragmatic competence (learning your role as text user: What do I do with this, here and now?), and critical competence (learning your role as a text analyst: What is this text trying to do to me? In whose interests?).[5] Literacy instruction in school too often addresses the first two elements and perhaps the third, but leaves out critical competence. Freebody and Luke assert that developing this critical awareness of the implications of texts needs to be an integral part of any reading program. These authors suggest that teachers should strive to make such awareness part of their teaching and to guide their students in learning to perceive the implications of the texts that they read.[6]

Literacy for advanced students involves reading at the critical level of awareness, whereas others learn at best only to break the code of a text. This is, at the very least, problematic. Too often, it is students in high-need schools in urban settings who learn only to decode. The failure to achieve consistent standards more than half a century after the historic Supreme Court *Brown v. Board of Education of Topeka* ruling rejecting "separate but equal" education both runs contrary to the spirit of post–civil rights movement notions of equality and has negative implications for the U.S. economy. America needs to graduate students at higher literacy rates so that they can be viable candidates for success in the U.S. and global workforces (Orfield, Losen, Wald & Swanson, 2004). This is especially imperative for students of color, who too often still need to outperform others in order to gain a foothold in the workplace, and who seldom are provided with good opportunities to attain the skills to do so. The power of literacy—the ability to read, write, think, listen, and speak clearly and critically—is absolutely necessary for Americans of all backgrounds if we are to forge links between literacy, power, and humanity in a nation where all things are supposedly possible for all people. The current measures that emphasize both teacher performance and student learning, together with the leadership and example of such articulate, educated Americans of color as Barack and Michelle Obama, provide the potential for a major uplift in literacy rates and standards for all Americans. Nonetheless, historical obstacles affecting African Americans and others continue to stand in the way of achieving our educational, social, and economic goals (Baugh, 2000; Greene & Abt-Perkins, 2003; Fisher, 2009). Continued, well-informed vigilance is needed in order to transform good intentions and good policies into success.

## Teacher Quality, Teacher Training, and the Challenge of Literacy Instruction for All

As a staff developer within a university-school partnership, I often encounter teachers who struggle with whether to focus on sustaining basic reading skills (decoding and fluency) or on reading for deeper meaning (synthesis, analysis, and critique). Teachers realize the importance of learning how to decode a text, and much instructional time is devoted to this aspect of reading. However, many are unsettled by the fact that they seldom have enough time to teach students how to analyze the text and to think critically about what they have read. In an effort to create uniformity across districts, teachers are often given strict timelines to complete unit materials in order to meet scheduled benchmark assessments. Many are also given scripted programs to follow that incorporate phonemic awareness, phonics, fluency, spelling, and comprehension. Moreover, even when time and assessment demands permit, many teachers feel uncertain about how to teach students higher-level critical reading and thinking skills, especially in schools where many of the children come from backgrounds that involve limited literacy at home or considerable difference between home and school languages—even, in many cases, where both of those languages are forms of English. Teachers worry that the prescribed reading program may leave some students, particularly African American students, behind. Nonetheless, in my work in schools I have observed many seasoned literacy teachers achieving good results in teaching complex analysis. These teachers are able to do so because their knowledge allows them to utilize the unit materials in ways that meet student needs, rather than merely fulfilling the letter of curricular demands. In fact, Richard Allington (2002) argues that "teachers, and teacher expertise, matter much more than which reading series a school district might choose" (p. 6). Therefore, it is imperative to ensure that all literacy teachers are provided with the training and support to make the kind of difference in student outcomes that we know they are capable of making.

In fact, education researchers recognize teacher quality as a key element in student performance (Cooper, 2003; Gere & Berebitsky, 2009; Sirota & Bailey, 2009). At the same time, literacy instruction is too complex to be entrusted to the sort of "factory education" model (Newkirk, 2009) prescribed by recent federal and state-level mandates. It requires teachers to be knowledgeable educators who are capable of assessment, evaluation, and intervention in order to meet student learning needs. This is particularly crucial for teachers who work in high-poverty schools, in which students often represent a wide range of learning abilities with a wide range of challenges. However, acquiring quality teachers who are effective in teaching diverse populations and high-needs students is a perennial challenge (Cooper, 2003; Duncan-Andrade, 2007; Gere & Berebitsky, 2009; Sirota & Bailey, 2009). The majority of high-quality teachers typically choose to teach in more affluent districts, where they face fewer challenges. Those who wind up—and especially those who remain—in so-called difficult schools are often the most well-meaning of educators and may well be skilled and knowledgeable as well; nonetheless, their training and resources—and therefore they themselves—often fall short of meeting their students' needs. Jeffrey Duncan-Andrade (2009) writes that at the end of the day, effective teaching depends most heavily on one thing: deep and caring relationships (p. 191). One such teacher is Ms. McMillan.

Ms. McMillan,[7] a veteran fourth-grade teacher in an urban public school, was faced with a dilemma. Although she had been provided with a program to address the literacy needs of her students, she realized that her students were experiencing difficulties and that the reading assessment tools were not sufficient to inform her about their literacy needs. Nonetheless, she struggled with how to go beyond what the program provided. Moreover, even if she had felt confident about what changes or additions to make, Ms. McMillan told me that she was not allowed to make any changes to the curricular plan, which dictated what pages she was to teach each day. Thus, even though Ms. McMillan was a knowledgeable teacher, she expressed that she felt ineffective, both because she had to follow the scripted lessons and because her training and classroom resources did not enable her to fill the gaps in this program or to fulfill the various needs of the diverse students in her class.

To be highly effective, Ms. McMillan not only needed to be committed and caring. She also needed knowledge and to be empowered as well. Schools of education can support teacher knowledge by providing more courses on literacy instruction and on the teaching of reading in both pre-service and in-service programs. Through such instruction and support, teachers like Ms. McMillan can and should be made to feel comfortable with assessment tools and to have confidence in their knowledge of how and when to intervene with instruction in order to promote the success of all students. In addition, teachers themselves must be consistently willing to take on the challenges of literacy instruction by meeting each student at his or her own present level of development, rather than pitching all instruction to the level at which the group is expected to be. Unfortunately, NCLB had the broad effect of stripping many teachers of their knowledge confidence by demanding the use of scripted programs (Morgan, 2008). Clearly, a change was called for, and the federal education funds allotted by the current administration are more appropriately targeted at supporting teacher quality, which is now understood as being closely tied to student learning rather than to test scores alone. Moreover, the intention is that the funds received by states will help to provide teachers with an equivalent level of preparation, curricular materials, and professional development across school districts. In the following section, we will see some of the reasons why this equal distribution is so crucial.

## Literacy Stories of Three African American Learners

To exemplify the challenges in high-needs school districts in a more personal and hands-on manner, I relate in this section an account of some of my own experiences as an African American literacy learner, as well as some of the experiences of students with whom I have worked. My own experiences took place as a young African American woman growing up on Long Island, New York, in the late 1970s. The other students profiled here were ones that I encountered recently during my research in an elementary school in the Mott Haven section of the Bronx. In what follows, I will share the stories of two students who, like me, struggled with literacy learning. I share these stories to illustrate the importance of authentic materials, teacher preparation, and quality, targeted instruction in the lives of literacy learners.

**Jane:** As an African American literacy learner, I had to navigate my way through a number of special challenges on the path to becoming proficient, even though my parents were neither poor nor uneducated. Early in my academic career, I was often the only person of color in my classes, and teachers, without malicious intent, would ask me to speak about the African American perspective on current issues. They assumed that my membership in the African American ethnic group enabled me to understand that group as a whole and to inform others about it. Later, I had professors who assumed that, because of my skin color, I was from a working-class or poor home, and I was even advised not to enter certain programs because it was assumed that I could not compete academically. Nonetheless, I learned to be persistent at finding answers to my questions, which often required that I shift from my home language to using academic English.[8]

If my professors had focused on communicating with me by inquiring about my goals and ambitions, they might have had the chance to learn more about me and my needs. Instead, they focused on the "incorrect" English usage in my oral dialect. In effect, they followed the same pattern encountered in John Baugh's (2003) study on linguistic profiling. Baugh called prospective realtors requesting an apartment, alternating between using African American Vernacular English (AAVE) and a mainstream middle-class speech pattern. Whenever he used AAVE, he was told no apartments were available. However, when he called the same realtor using the mainstream dialect, he was often told to come right over to look at the apartment. Similarly, my professors heard the "errors" in my oral dialect and made erroneous assumptions about my capacity to learn. Over time, I developed radar for when my speech might be problematic for my audience. I also learned more about oral and written English grammar, as well as about reading texts critically and analytically. These skills are, as noted at the beginning of this chapter, crucial for success in college and in many careers.

**Tyree:** As a fifth grader in an urban elementary school, Tyree—one of the many students whose literacy struggles I have observed—was always reading. In fact, Tyree was a prolific reader who was able to decode the words in a text and could read aloud fluently. He was just entering the O-P level, which was the standard for his grade level in reading, according to the Fountas and Pinnell (2002) leveling system used by many schools. However, whenever Tyree was asked about what he had read, he would draw a blank. When tested, he did not quite meet the comprehension standard for his grade level.

In working with Tyree, I found that he read words smoothly and was able to decode a text with few miscues or errors, which meant that he could read with 95% to 100% accuracy. However, when I reviewed the responses that Tyree gave to comprehension prompts, I noticed that they were literal and lacked the inferential work of a more sophisticated reader. He was able to retell what he had read in the text, but he lacked the comprehension of the deeper meaning needed to speak about the character's feelings or about the significance of the plot in the context of the story. Why was Tyree able to read well, but not at the same level as his White counterparts, in terms of comprehension, analysis, and critique? His teacher was happy that, at least, Tyree was close—as measured by benchmark assessments—to meeting the reading standards established by the school district. It may be that she set her expectations too low for Tyree on account of his ethnicity. In any case, I noticed that she herself was still learning about higher-level comprehension and in some ways lacked the instructional methods that could have supported Tyree's growth.

**Deshawna:** At age nine, Deshawna believed that school was important and that it was the place to learn better English. Deshawna had learned from her mother and from other adults that it was important to learn "good" speech and to be proficient in writing. I learned from Deshawna's comments—such as, "peoples going to think I live on the streets"—that she recognized that "poor" speech and writing skills are associated with lower-class status. What Deshawna had not learned was how to acquire the higher standard of English that she sought. For Deshawna, the belief in meritocracy was all it took to succeed.

Sitting side-by-side on the steps outside the gym one day, I told Deshawna that I wanted to talk with her about her literacy learning. I had been observing her in class and noted that she was tenacious in asking questions of her teacher. In our short conversation, she shared that her mother—who had taught Deshawna that going to school and learning should be her major focus—considered asking questions until you get an answer to be an important skill for learning. However, the reality was that, despite all of Deshawna's hard work, she fell short of consistent use of Standard American English (SAE). Deshawna tried her best to acquire SAE by diligently working on her language exercises, asking questions, and producing writing from the units of study, yet there continued to be a gap. Deshawna's teacher focused on meeting the demands of the curriculum, which hindered Deshawna's knowledge growth in grammar. She gave Deshawna worksheets instead of getting to know her as a learner and addressing her needs by including her in small-group instruction. Busy meeting the school curricular demands, Ms. Figueroa lost sight of this student's needs. In addition, I learned later from Ms. Figueroa herself that even though she was a teacher, her knowledge of grammar was limited. Therefore, moving beyond what the program outlined in order to meet Deshawna's needs was not something that she was well equipped to do.

These three stories tell of the complicated ways in which African American students like Tyree, Deshawna, and me have to negotiate challenges and develop coping mechanisms to respond to issues of vulnerability in literacy learning (Lee, 2007). Tyree, on one hand, was doing the hard work of reading, but somehow failed to receive all the knowledge that he needed to sustain him as a reader. He was willing to try, but his teacher was not able to expand his knowledge. Deshawna, in contrast, was derailed by a teacher who was focused on ensuring that her class met grade standards in order to meet the demands for accountability placed on the school. What went wrong for Deshawna was that her teacher failed to assess and then address her individual needs. Instead, she simply made her way through the curriculum mandated by her administration. I, similarly, had to learn to negotiate the differences of a dominant language pattern. Imagine if, however, all of the teachers in these examples had been fully prepared for their crucial role as educators of children facing special challenges in a world where all students need to develop complex skills; they would have been able to meet the demands of the program while also actively addressing the individual literacy needs of their students. In the end, in order to grow into this role, teachers in situations like these need strong, proactive support from teacher training programs, schools, parents, and communities. In addition, teachers may also benefit from a critical reexamination of the literacy curriculum, as sketched in the following section.

## Literacy Education and Students of Color

Traditional literacy practices and curricula arm students with literacy skills that allow them to function in society, hence the term "functional literacy." This means that students learn how to break the code of a text, but seldom do they become text users or text analyzers. Functional literacy teaches students a systematic process to read by teaching skills such as phonemic awareness, phonics, and spelling. Classrooms that embrace this functional approach to learning focus on decoding words and responding to predetermined comprehension questions. The instruction from a functional perspective uses highly specific scripts for teachers, in order to facilitate direct instruction of skills and specific assessments to monitor student success. Learning to read in this scripted and systematic way, however, often fails to develop many of the critical thinking skills required of an informed citizenry (Morgan, 2008).

In this context, and particularly where students of color are concerned, it is useful to recall Freebody and Luke's (1990) taxonomy of the key elements of the social practice of proficient and critical reading: coding competence, semantic competence, pragmatic competence, and critical competence. Students need to be educated in the full spectrum of critical literacy skills in order to enable them to be vital members of the community and of the world. Many students—particularly in high-needs urban public schools, where there may be less than the desirable amount of support for literacy learning in the home and where the resources needed to go beyond minimum standards may be scarce or lacking—may learn coding and semantic competence and yet not achieve pragmatic or, especially, critical competence. As these are the skills that can make them effective text users and text analyzers, so-called "functional" literacy may, in fact, be transforming many students of color and other learners into second-class readers—partial literates who may stand little or no chance of competing effectively in today's highly competitive, highly articulate world.

Functional literacy teaches students a systematic reading process by drilling reading skills, such as the previously mentioned phonemic awareness, phonics, and spelling. Other literacy practices may be less narrowly focused on a specific set of skills, yet they prepare students in literacy in a manner that operates under the dominating shadow of a presumption of national social harmony. In the so-called cultural literacy approach, students learn to be literate without questioning or challenging the dominant culture—hence the term "cultural literacy" (Cadiero-Kaplan & Smith, 2002; Ladson-Billings, 2005; Lee, 2007). Cultural literacy looks at the use of content in texts, often focusing on issues of the day, but the curriculum is typically limited to proscribed materials and discourses. Students in classrooms focused on cultural literacy learn to read and to fit into society, as opposed to learning to create the type of society in which all voices are embraced.

Some educators may indeed find it easier or more appealing to their personal sensibility to fit their students into the culture as they or the framers of the curriculum may perceive it to already exist than to create a discursive community that is inclusive of all groups and cultures. Yet the impact of such an uncritical approach to critical reading or basic literacy skills is that all students are educated from the perspective of the dominant cultural group. In the view of many scholars of culture and education, this amounts to students who are not of the dominant culture being implicitly taught that their experiences are irrelevant (see, for example, Hirsch, 1988, 2009). Students need literacy skills that include their home or heritage culture's literacy, as well as a sense of what can be learned from all of the cultures of the world. Such a literacy foundation enables students to look critically at their communities in order to transform them into places in which all voices are embraced.

## What Do African American Communities Need to Know about Literacy Education?

We have seen something of how literacy instruction plays out in our schools and of the impact of different kinds of literacy learning on students and teachers. But what about the impact of literacy education on the community? African American communities, like others, benefit from the presence of informed citizens who know their rights and who aim to create neighborhoods, towns, and cities that work collectively to meet residents' needs. To achieve such a community, we need schools that teach reading to learn, not just learning to read (Lee, 2007). In order to participate in a community and in society, members need to be able to speak out in ways that will allow them to be heard. Obama's school initiatives focus on high-quality education with the goal of producing good workers and good citizenry; however, it is important for these students also to think critically and to evaluate the world, in order to make decisions about their lives and the community in which they live.

The family is one important source of this community foundation. However, James Heckman of the University of Chicago reports in his article "Schools, Skills and Synapses" (2008) that the largest decline in education is neither in the area of school quality, nor in the shortage of funding, nor even in rising college tuition. There is a crisis in family environments, which have deteriorated steadily since the 1960s. This crisis can be attributed to less family interaction, with fewer knowledgeable adults who are available to read to children or to engage in conversation about social issues. Hence, children who are left alone at home to find their own interactions come to school less prepared or less aware of what is important to the community. The world of many of these children becomes that of the media or the music industry, since that is where they are engaged much of the time. This is not necessarily the fault of families that cannot afford childcare, but it is something that schools, educators, and families need to understand in order to reverse negative trends in literacy achievement. Community programs that bring families together around literacy or other disciplinary areas can help in this regard (see, for example, the list at the end of this chapter). This can be as simple as establishing an afterschool mentoring group for students in the upper elementary grades. Community groups and organizations can also be responsive to community needs by supporting grassroots groups and nonprofit organizations. The Boys and Girls Club of America, for example, offers a great place to start.

In Black America, the way that members of the community live their lives impacts the lives of others in the community. As community members, it is important to set high standards. "Strong effort and achievement" should be a cry echoed from all corners of the community so that young people will be inspired and reminded to do their best. This is what develops communities of care, connection, and power. And, as the desire to have strong leadership within the community grows, so too will the understanding of the need for literacy. The goal for all of us should be to live in such a way that it impacts others positively. This has profound implications for the world in which we live. We can start by individually adopting as our goal that we will strive for a better world in which all children of color are equipped with strong literacy tools. We can do this by paying close attention to the cultural literacy needs of African American students. Another way to do this is by insisting that qualified teachers are allowed to teach using effective literacy strategies that meet the individual learning needs of their students. We can do this also by rallying together as a community to improve literacy education.

## Next Steps in Literacy Education for Schools Serving African American Learners

What actions can schools that are striving to improve take? To start, examine current literacy programs to see how students' needs are being met—both skill and cultural identity needs. If the program lacks the potential to meet student needs, implement a book of the month program. Selected texts that support cultural identity can be read aloud in all classrooms and discussed at home with parents, guardians, and families. Examining existing literacy programs and questioning how they ensure students' ability to learn beyond the functional aspects of decoding and answering simple comprehension questions is also critical. For schools that are ready for large, school-wide initiatives, teacher inquiry and investigation into issues around literacy might be a good way to start. Schools might consider forming a focus group on effective teaching strategies that enable students to think deeply about texts and to communicate effectively, so that students' voices can be heard (see the list at the end of this chapter). To move toward growth in literacy, moreover, schools may also consider professional development in the form of on-site staff development targeted at key grade levels and spanning several weeks at a time. Teachers might participate in several full days of internal development before bringing in outside staff developers.

In this current era, schools are making a difference for students like Tyree and Deshawna. More and more, schools have taken on the challenge of developing grade-appropriate literacy tools to support student growth, encouraging teacher engagement with students, and supporting parent engagement through school and community activities, such as literacy suppers (see the list at the end of this chapter). P.S. 161 in Harlem, for example, recently created a Collegiate Information Academy (CIA) that allows students access to the school library beginning at 6:45 in the morning (Teachers College, Columbia University, 2010). Students are issued membership cards that grant them permission to enter the building before school starts. Each day, 30 to 40 students attend programs in which they read, do homework, play chess, and work on computers. The school has also reached out for grants from companies such as Target, which has supported five workshops in which parents learned about reading aloud to their children in grades K–3, and has donated books so parents and students could develop libraries at home.[9] These steps may seem like small actions, but they should be viewed as one school's attempt to help its students and their community be heard by a much larger audience.

## Conclusion

James Bernard, the great American writer (b. 1965), once wrote that "our lives, hopes, and dreams depend on our ability to be heard" (Quinn, 1996, p. 111).

Currently, African Americans who live below the poverty line in this country are not being educated in the same way as their counterparts in more affluent communities, which scarcely gives them the same chance to be heard. In fact, the truth about contemporary literacy education is that it teaches our kids to pass the test, but it is weak in ensuring that African Americans and other students of color are instructed in ways that meet their varied needs. Teachers assess and evaluate students, but they are challenged when they do not have the materials to support their students' learning. There are schools of hope in America, like P.S. 161, but there are not enough of these to meet the needs of most of America's students of color. As a result, many students opt out of the system before graduation, and the impact of early school withdrawal on their economic potential and personal growth is devastating.

To counteract this trend, we need a larger force of teachers who are better prepared to meet the needs of students like Tyree, Deshawna, and myself. Teachers can help move their students beyond functional literacy, and most do have the potential to empower their students with a level of literacy that will ensure their ability to think in critical ways, to be active, engaged citizens, and to have successful careers. To achieve this goal, we need to provide the best possible teachers and the most effective training and support for educators in all our nation's school districts. Needless to say, however, the efforts of schools and of teacher training institutions will be fruitless without the support of parents and communities.

I have presented the challenge of creating schools of hope for the Obama era by outlining the problem, sharing literacy stories from today's students and from my own life, and presenting a few steps that parents and community leaders can take to promote change (see the list that follows). I encourage readers to take these steps and to expand upon them in their own schools and communities. It is time to take back what has been put aside and to revel in the fact that being Black and literate is powerful. Literacy brings power, knowledge, and hope for individuals and communities that all things are possible, and I dream of the day when institutions of public education educate all children of color so they are capable of achieving success, like that of Barack and Michelle Obama.

## Appendix Activities to Bring Back the Power of Literacy in Your School or Community

1. Support a pajama night at your school or local library, where a parent and child spend the evening reading aloud to one another.
2. Family read-in. Sponsor a read-a-thon highlighting local authors and illustrators.

3. Plan a book swap where families can bring old books and swap them for new or slightly used ones.
4. Work with local bookstores to give away free books to children who purchase a set number of books from the establishment. Or, develop a reward point system which allows students to earn points for free books.
5. Invite local writers, poets, and artists in to speak to the students about their work.
6. Inquire about the literacy program in your schools. Are students reading enough trade books that adequately support them as readers?
7. Encourage school administrators to provide professional development for teachers rather than purchasing new programs.

## Suggestions for Educators to Bring Back the Power of Literacy

1. Provide a book swap corner in the front lobby where parents can take books or donate books to be read at home.
2. Start a "get to know your students and their community" breakfast group; invite parents and have community leaders as guest speakers.
3. Provide parents with a monthly calendar of simple suggestions for reading or writing at home to support the work in school.
4. Take your back-to-school-night presentation to your church to inform parents how to help their students at home.
5. Start a book club that is culturally relevant to your students' lives.

## Suggested Readings for Elementary Students

Grimes, Nikki. (2008). *Barack Obama: Son of Promise, Child of Hope*. New York: Simon & Schuster.
Grimes, Nikki. (2007). *Rosa*. New York: Square Fish.
Hest, Amy. (2007). *Mr. George Baker.* Somerville, MA: Candlewick Press.
Levine, Ellen. (2007). *Henry's Freedom Box*. New York: Scholastic Press.
Rappaport, Doreen. (2007). *Martin's Big Words: The Life of Dr. Martin Luther King, Jr.* New York: Hyperion Books.
Weatherford, Carole Boston. (2006). *Dear Mr. Rosenwald.* New York: Scholastic Press.
Wiles, Deborah. (2005). *Freedom Summer.* New York: Aladdin.

## Suggested Readings about African American Literacy for Adults or Young Adults

Curtis, Christopher Paul. (1998). *The Watsons Go to Birmingham*, 1963. New York: Laurel Leaf.
Hill, Lawrence. (2008). *Someone Knows My Name*. New York: W. W. Norton.
Obama, Barack. (2006). *The Audacity of Hope: Thoughts on Reclaiming the American Dream*. New York: Crown Publishers.

Paulsen, Gary. (1995). *Night John*. New York: Laurel Leaf. Paulsen, Gary. (1999). *Sarny*. New York: Laurel Leaf.

## Notes

1. For Obama's full remarks, see Jeff Zeleny (2010, p. A14).
2. For the complete document, see Common Core Standards (2010).
3. Ibid.
4. For the full position paper on No Child Left Behind, see National Council of Teachers of English (2006).
5. See, in addition, Ellin Oliver Keene (2008, p. 11) and Alfred Tatum (2005, p. 38).
6. Ibid.
7. All names of teachers and students appearing in this chapter are pseudonyms.
8. For further readings on code-switching, see John R. Rickford (2000), Alfred K. Spears (2007), and Rebecca Wheeler and Rachel Swords (2006).
9. This school has learned the lesson that private industry can be called upon to help urban schools, but schools need to be specific and professional about the help they need when addressing these sources. Schools must reach out and ask in order to make it happen!

## References

Allington, Richard. (2001). *What really matters for struggling readers: Designing research-based programs* (2d ed.). New York: Allyn and Bacon.

Allington, Richard. (2002). *Big brother and the national reading curriculum: How ideology trumped evidence*. Portsmouth, NH: Heinemann.

Baugh, John. (2000). *Beyond ebonics: Linguistic pride and racial prejudice*. New York: Oxford University Press.

———. (2003). Linguistic profiling. In Sinfree Makoni, Geneva Smitherman, Arnetha Ball & Arthur Spears (Eds.), *Black linguistics: Language, society, and politics in Africa and the Americas* (pp. 155–68). New York: Routledge.

Cadiero-Kaplan, Karen, & Smith, Karen. (2002). Literacy ideologies: Critically engaging the language arts curriculum. *Language Arts*, 79(5), pp. 372–81.

Common Core Standards. (2010). Common Core Standards, August 2010. RetrievedAugust 30, 2010 from http://www.corestandards.org

Cooper, Patricia M. (2003). Effective white teachers of black children: Teaching within a community. *Journal of Teacher Education*, 54(5), pp. 413–27.

Duncan-Andrade, Jeffrey. (2007). Gangstas, wankstas, and ridas: Defining, developing, and supporting effective teachers in urban schools. *International Journal of Qualitative Studies in Education*, 20(6), pp. 617–38.

Duncan-Andrade, Jeffrey. (2009). Note to educators: Hope required when growing roses in concrete. *Harvard Educational Review*, 79(2), pp. 181–94.

Fisher, Maisha. (2009). *Black literate lives: Historical and contemporary perspectives*. New York: Routledge.

Fountas, Irene, & Pinnell, Gay. (2002). *Leveled books for readers grades 3–6: A companion volume to guiding readers and writers*. Portsmouth, NH: Heinemann.

Freebody, Peter, & Luke, Allan. (1990). "Literacies" programs: Debates and demands in cultural contexts. Prospect: *The Australian Journal of TESOL*, 5(3), pp. 7–16.

Gere, Anne Ruggles, & Berebitsky, Daniel. (2009). Standpoints: Perspectives on highly qualified English teachers. *Research in the Teaching of English*, 43(3), pp. 247–62.

Greene, Stuart, & Abt-Perkins, Dawn (Eds.). (2003). *Making race visible: Literacy research for cultural understanding*. New York: Teachers College Press.

Heckman, James. (2008). Schools, skills, and synapses. *Economic Inquiry*, 46(3), p. 289.

Hirsch, Edward, Jr. (1988). *The dictionary of cultural literacy: What every American needs to know.* New York: Vintage.

———. (2009). *The making of Americans: Democracy and our schools.* New Haven, CT: Yale University Press.

Keene, Ellin Oliver. (2008). *To understand: New horizons in reading comprehension.* Portsmouth, NH: Heinemann.

Ladson-Billings, Gloria. (2005). Reading, writing, and race: Literacy practices of teachers in diverse classrooms. In Teresa McCarty (Ed.), *Language, literacy, and power in schooling* (pp. 133–50). Mahweh, NJ: Lawrence Erlbaum Associates.

Lee, Carol D. (2007). *Culture, literacy, and learning: Taking bloom in the midst of the whirlwind.* New York: Teachers College Press.

Morgan, Holly. (2008). Reading teachers' attitudes toward scripted reading programs: A multiple case study. ProQuest Dissertations and Theses. http://ezproxy.cul.columbia.edu/login?url=http://search.proquest.com/?url=http://search.proquest.com/docview/89248936?accountid=10226.

National Council of Teachers of English Guideline. (2006). *NCLB recommendations.* Retrieved. February 2011 from http://www.ncte.org/positions/statements/nclbrecommendation06

Newkirk, Tom. (2009). *What are you willing to fight for? Holding on to good ideas in a time of bad ones.* Portsmouth, NH: Heinemann.

Orfield, Gary, Losen, Daniel, Wald, Johanna, & Swanson, Christopher B. (2004). *Losing our future: How minority youth are being left behind by the graduation rate crisis.* Cambridge, MA: The civil rights project at Harvard University. Retrieved January 2011 from. http://www.urban.org/uploadedPDF/410936 _LosingOurFuture.pdf

Quinn, Eli. (1996). *African-American wisdom: A book of quotations and proverbs.* Philadelphia, PA: Running Press.

Rickford, John R. (2000). *Spoken soul: The story of black English.* New York: John Wiley & Sons, Inc.

Sirota, Elaine & Bailey, Lora. (2009). The impact of teachers' expectations on diverse learners' academic outcomes. *Childhood Education*, 85(4), pp. 253–56.

Spears, Alfred. K. (2007). African American communicative practices. In H. Samy Alim & John Baugh (Eds.), *Talkin black talk: Language, education, and social change* (pp. 100–11). New York: Teachers College Press.

Tatum, Alfred. (2005). *Teaching reading to Black adolescent males: Closing the achievement gap.* Portland, ME: Stenhouse.

Teachers College, Columbia University. (2010, May 5). Transformative leadership, under fire. *Press Room.* Retrieved May 22, 2010 from. http://www.tc.columbia.edu/news/article.htm?id=7479

U.S. Department of Education, Institute of Education Sciences (IES), National Center for Education Statistics (NCES), Common Core of Data (CCD). (2010, July). *NCES common core of data state dropout and completion* [data file] (school year 2006–2007, version 1a). Retrieved January 2011from. http:// nces.ed.gov/pubs2010/2010015/figures/figure_18_1.asp

Wheeler, Rebecca. S., & Swords, Rachel. (2006). *Code-switching: Teaching standard English in urban classrooms.* Urbana, IL: National Council of Teachers of English.

Zeleny, Jeff. (2010, March 1). Obama backs rewarding districts that police failing schools. *The New York Times* (late ed., East Coast), p. A14.

|| SEVENTEEN

# A Pedagogy of Wholeness

Rochelle Brock

> Trying to write beyond the assignment of language to a medium of personal expression. I have been cognizant that writing does not translate a reality outside itself but, more precisely, allows the emergence of a new reality. (Simon, 1992, p. 4)

OSHUN: Rochelle, who will help our children? Can you? Will you?

ROCHELLE: Let me tell you a story about Jake. About a year ago I awoke early to put the finishing touches on an article I was completing. It was 5:00 a.m. and I felt relaxed. I knew what was needed to tie all of the disparate pieces together, and time, for once, was on my side. I made a fresh pot of coffee and sat to read the paper before I returned to the computer. I vividly remember the instant I sat down with my coffee and looked at the first page of the morning paper my relaxation left me. I was forced to remember why I chose the topic I did, why I had so much trouble theorizing about education, why I got "emotional" whenever I thought about/discussed the miseducation of African American youth.

Staring at me from the front page of *USA Today* was Jake Williams (Johnson, 1997). He appeared to be a handsome Black man. Chocolate complexion, like the sweet-bitter coffee I was drinking, oval eyes that were staring right through me, broad nose that reminded me of the Black men in my life, sensuous lips that seemed to be in a grimace, like only they know the funny and strange secret held by Jake and if the rest of the world knew it they would also smile. As soon as I recorded the picture in my sensory register my brain and heart stepped in and told me Jake was either in trouble or an athlete/entertainer.

OSHUN: I would be willing to bet it was trouble.

ROCHELLE: And you would win. The caption under his picture read, "New prisons isolate worst inmates" and the prison was in Texas, the state that was the last to release enslaved Africans.

OSHUN: So I see they are still trying to hold us.

ROCHELLE: In mind, body, and spirit. I read the story which was filled with words/phrases like "animals," "superbad people," "inhuman," "no hope of parole." There were two smaller pictures on the next page of the article, both of Black men—Curtis Hayden and David Hawkins. Jake, Curtis, David, and all of the unnamed, unpictured Black boys/men and girls/ women are why I become angry. My anger hides my fear, showing itself when I am confronted with (as I am daily) the realities of what my young brothers and sisters are experiencing daily.

OSHUN: I know the pursuit of education for African American peoples is not simply academic; it is both a survival and personal pursuit. But I feel a struggle within you, a confusion.

ROCHELLE: I keep asking myself what does Jake have to do with the theme of this book, Black women, and theorizing away the pain. But it is all so connected. I am a Black woman and a teacher, a Black woman who teaches, a Black woman teacher, and my concern does not concentrate itself in one area, with one gender, ignoring the realities of another part of me. The sociopolitical realities of African Americans and all minorities engender pain. The economic realities of African Americans engender pain. If I can effectively help my Black female students and myself theorize away the pain that dominant structures have made synonymous with being Black, then that knowledge is also valuable to all students. I see an attack on African Americans from all sides and especially the far right, which is providing a framework of domination against African Americans. I need to operate within a Black "way of knowing," which draws a connection between learned knowledge and actual experience, either personal experience or that of the community in general. Jake is both my personal experience and the experience of my community. What happened to Jake is the manifestation of an ideology of modernist thought and action. I had to re-remember Jake to re-remember my reason and purpose for being.

OSHUN: Just keep thinking your way into an understanding. When we accept that this society cares little for its other we see it as only logical that they are putting the Jake's of society in a super maximum facility. And it is this same ideology of dehumanization of the other that constructs images of Black women. When we see Jake dehumanized and despiritualized we also know that there are countless other Black men and women who are struggling to remain human and whole.

ROCHELLE: The reality of Jake becomes fragmented, thereby mystifying the relationship between the sociopolitical and economic forces, which created the conditions that led to Jake's imprisonment. We understand that the same ideology that constructs superprisons is the ideology that controlled Jake the African American man, forcing him into prison. His guilt or innocence is not as important as what led him to commit a crime or what led the "powers of law enforcement" to accuse him of committing a crime.

Once he entered the superprison, Jake was removed from existence both in the concrete and in the abstract. We, society, are made to forget about the circumstances of Jake's life, the powers that shaped all that Jake is. He is expurgated from and discussed in terms of separation from the social context that defined him. We begin to think that Jake controlled the decisions he made and therefore deserves his punishment for making the wrong decisions. We forget, or are unaware, when we do not look at the social context of Jake's life—that he went to a bad school, had teachers who did not care, could not find a job or found a job beneath his skill level, or had no skills because of a bad school. We forget that Jake saw the front pages of any newspaper and saw African Americans doing wrong. Jake looked at television and saw the "chains and images of psychological slavery" (Akbar, 1984, p. 2). Na'im Akbar states,

> . . . [When slavery] captures the mind and incarcerates the motivation, perception, aspiration, and identity in a web of anti-self images, generating a personal and collective self-destruction, is more cruel than the shackles on the wrist and ankles. The slavery that feeds on the psychology, invading the soul of the man, destroying his loyalties to himself and establishing loyalties to forces which destroy him, is an even worse form of capture. The influences that permit an illusion of freedom, liberation, and self-determination, while tenaciously holding one's mind in subjugation, is the folly of only the sadistic. (p. 2)

Jake could be put in a superprison because the mind that developed the concept of superprison is sadistic. They are certain that Jake is not worth saving, both because of his crime and because of his color. Or maybe his crime is his color.

OSHUN: Rochelle, I know it is hard for you not to feel pain. Remember society is no longer worried about saving Jake; he is unsalvageable. The time and money that could be used to help Jake either before he went to prison or once he was in prison can be better spent ensuring his contact with real humans is limited. It is easier to lock Jake's body away than to reconstruct society into one that affords liberation, freedom, and equity to all members instead of oppression, objectification, and colonialization to select members.

ROCHELLE: But when I discuss and analyze Jake am I taking away his culpability in the making of his own reality?

OSHUN: No, I think we both accept that Jake made some bad choices and in certain ways created his situation. But at the same time I know that we live in a society that has historically set up barriers for Black folk. A modernist paradigm seeks to master nature (Kincheloe & Steinberg, 1997). Black men and women represent nature, the object that must be controlled either through force, acquisition, colonization, ideology, culture, on and on and on. The ultimate control for the uncontrollable (animal) is to not only take away every semblance of their humanity and dignity, but also do it in such a way that they have no will to fight. The superprison that encased Jake's body is a metaphor for the prison that tries to encase the souls of our children.

ROCHELLE: I know I get tired of constantly fighting. Despite my exhaustion at least I know how to fight and importantly who to fight against. For Jake control ensures the tools with which to fight have been taken away, or never provided. Although these tools are many and the tool bag is large all are necessary. Political astuteness and power, economic basis, sociological understanding, knowledge of history, etc., come together in an interlocking pattern to weave a relationship of knowing, understanding, and acting on modernist ideology. Since I am a teacher I see education as the dominant pattern that encircles all others.

OSHUN: Did the article say anything about Jakes schooling?

ROCHELLE: No, it didn't, but African Americans in educational systems throughout America are experiencing the same devastation. Looking through the lens of education I can place Jake back into the social context of his existence which modernism took him from. It is readily seen that African American education is in a crisis throughout America. From New York to California statistics on educational achievement and disparity between Black and White students fill the pages of national and local reports on schooling for African Americans (Asante, 1991; Fordham, 1988; Gordon, Piana & Keleher, 2000; Jordan-Irving, 1990; Shujja, 1994).

As a society or individual we can make one of two generalizations. First, we could surmise that the evidence of poor school achievement proves (once again) that Black students are incapable of learning and therefore deserve their failure. Moreover, because Black students are incapable of real learning ,we, as Americans, need not worry about providing educational support in the form of better schools or more effective educational programs.

In contrast, the second option assumes that society in general, as well as the school system, is failing Black students. Although we do not look at Black students as completely victimized objects we nevertheless accept that Black students partake in a colonial educational system that ensures their failure. Joan Davis Ratteray (1991) states:

> Public education wasn't designed for students of color, especially it wasn't designed for African American youngsters. It was designed to develop a consensus, a social contract where the plight of African American children has never been on top of the agenda. Some children are going to make it anyway, but that's a few. The majority of our African American youngsters have to be in a setting that's going to cater to their needs. (p. 103)

OSHUN: And of the two, which do you choose?

ROCHELLE: I choose to believe the second option and with this choice come the responsibility (self- and community-imposed) to do something about the situation of African American youth in America's public schools. The emotion I feel every time I read and hear about a Jake can never remain on a purely theoretical plane. I can never "prove" my feelings empirically. I don't have to. Because I name my reality and that of my fellow African American brothers and sisters I am forced to transform the world (Freire, 1970). I have given voice to the problems of Jake and therefore have opened the problems to be renamed.

OSHUN: The power of definition moves Jake from object to subject. You can begin to understand Jake when you place a name on his reality.

ROCHELLE: I like the phrase Freire uses—"Men are not built in silence, but in word, in work, in action-reflection" (1970, p. 76). I also like the term conscientizacao—being conscious of my consciousness. It names the pabulum I feast on in acting against the oppressive elements of society that put Jake in a superprison.

OSHUN: But in reality Jake is the reason for a curriculum, which provides struggle, and survival for Black students. Jake and the thousands (millions?) of children like him are the reason you are here, sitting up at 3:00 a.m. writing and thinking and hoping to make a difference. You see the world and education through Jake. Although you are both Black, he was not able to handle and surpass the suffering brought on by his complexion. You cannot be dispassionate about Jake or analytical regarding what you should and must do.

ROCHELLE: I read and experienced that racism works at the decomposition of the cultural integrity of Blackness (Murrell, 1997). At times I can deal with that and other times I can't find the strength. Thank goodness somewhere in my life I was taught what was needed to get through. In my arsenal of Black survival weapons, I at least had a few that I could use. But see those things have become so emic to my being, so much a part of the total makeup of Rochelle I can no longer name them, identify them. What has been taught to me so that I remain whole and in turn what do I teach my students so they become complete beings?

OSHUN: To answer, or begin to answer, both of your questions we need to remember that U.S. schools are not set up for our success. Of course all of the statistics say that Black students are failing. But more important than that knowledge is to understand the "how" of what is going on.

ROCHELLE: What I am working through and coming to understand is that education, curriculum, pedagogy, theory has to bring about a transformation of Black students into critical cultural agents of change and revolution. Education for Black students cannot afford to be benign. Instead, through education these students must realize how the system is set up for their failure. Subverting it is of the utmost importance.

OSHUN: I should get a T-shirt made that says—Subverting the Constructs of Education. Explain education for African Americans, but be brief.

ROCHELLE: To place Black students in a contextual framework, it is vital to consider the root philosophies and goals of the American education system because it is here that African American students struggle to survive. The American educational system performs three essential functions. It both provides information to students and functions as a means of social control. Importantly, schooling is structured as a socialization agency through which the dominant political, social, economic, and cultural norms are imposed and reinforced. As political instruments, schools mold future citizens, maintain and stabilize the political system, and preserve the current balance of political power (Bowles & Gintis, 1976; Nelson, Palonsky & Carlson, 2000; Watkins, 2001). The goals of public education are intrinsically linked to social, political, and economic stability (Spring, 1991). The combination of these functions or goals predetermines what is taught, how it is taught, and who gets taught what.

OSHUN: False knowledge and/or partial knowledge is forced on Black children thereby never allowing them to really understand the realities of being Black in America.

ROCHELLE: Case in point. It was not until 1991 when I started my undergraduate degree that I began to learn Black history. Remember I was 34 when I did my undergrad. It was at that time that I finally had the knowledge to understand the craziness of my parents was in part due to the crap they went through growing up in Alabama in the early 1900s. Pieces of my life or their life finally made sense.

OSHUN: And because you didn't have the information in your cognitive bank it was virtually impossible to truly understand them.

ROCHELLE: Once I gained certain knowledge, even though a part of me was still angry with them, I at least was able to rationalize that anger; it lost its impotency.

OSHUN: Clearly, for African American students, the American education system has not provided access to equality, let alone the American Dream.

ROCHELLE: The American Dream for many has been the American Nightmare. The knowledge, culture, and experience of African American students are denigrated or silenced in the public schools while those of the dominant are imposed. Likewise, short- and long-term African American goals (for example, social and economic equality, and political voice) are undermined in favor of maintaining the status quo. The "dehumanization and despiritualization," which were so much a part of what happened to Jake, is a "truth" for many Black students. Our children are not failing; they are succeeding based on the structures and systems of American society. Since public education was not designed for the achievement of Black children. . .

OSHUN: . . . it therefore attempts to ensure their failure.

ROCHELLE: And although Black and White children enter school on the same level, for Black children the longer they stay in school the farther behind they fall (Jordan-Irving, 1990). This holds true in the middle class as much as it does in the lower class. Something depresses Black children at every level of preparation, even the highest. The women in sista dialogue spoke on this point from a personal place. Like Claude Steele (1992), they talked about the devaluation they experienced in the school setting. Throughout schooling, Black students have the added fear that others will see their "full humanity fall with a poor answer or a mistaken stroke of the pen" (Jordan-Irving, 1990, p. 74). The students have the burden of constantly having to prove themselves. Furthermore, with each new class and level of schooling the acceptance must be won again. The struggle for Black students to gain acceptance is continuous throughout their schooling. They learn that if acceptance is won, it will be hard-won.

OSHUN: The negative images of Black America that you so passionately wrote about in previous chapters are pervasive—they permeate all sectors of American life. What Black youth are exposed to in the television media, newspapers, magazines, and in the lesson plans of the school they attend usually portray African Americans in a negative light. These images are often not even perceived on a conscious level. Over time, however, they are internalized. Blackness is equated with badness. Conversely, Whiteness is equated with goodness and is held up for all to emulate—acting good is equated with acting White. Black children learn to hate who they are. They learn that just as White equals good, Black equals bad. They are disempowered and one of the results is academic underachievement.

ROCHELLE: I guess my writing is passionate because writing helps me process what I am attempting to understand. I didn't enter our conversation knowing the answers for Jake, but when I leave I will have answers.

OSHUN: And additional questions.

ROCHELLE: Yes, but questions that have a purpose. Scanning the newspapers on any given day illuminates the obstacles that face Black people and other ethnic minorities. Poor housing, unequal political representation, high unemployment, lack of Black men and women in positions of power are among the myriad of obstacles that Black children know they must overcome.

OSHUN: What impact does this have on the aspirations of Black children?

ROCHELLE: It creates a contradiction, or ambivalence, in their attitude toward education and their educational achievements. A body of scholars believes that the "main" deterrent to achievement for African American students is caused by the cultural dissonance between public education and the culture of Black children (Boykin, 2000; Jagers & Carroll, 2002; Jordan-Irving, 1990). According to the cultural difference framework the failure of African American students in the public school system is a direct result of the incompatibility of the dominant curriculum and African American norms.

Children from non-European, lower socioeconomic status cultural groups are at a disadvantage in the school because the American educational system has evolved out of a European philosophical, theoretical, and pedagogical context. White children are involved in an educational experience that complements their culture, whereas Black children exist within an educational system that denies Black culture. Not only does the educational system deny Black culture it also denies Black children having talent beyond athletics. This denial is a primary reason for the academic underachievement of Black students. Janice Hale-Benson (1986) agrees that the difficulties Black children experience in school have their antecedents in the fact that the educational system exists under a "different culture than their own" (p. 84). She stresses the importance of laying the foundation for delineating and identifying those points of mismatch between Black culture and European American culture that may have educational consequences for Black children.

OSHUN: Are you placing cultures in a hierarchal relationship?

ROCHELLE: The treatment of cultural difference does not imply that one culture is superior to the other. What it does is recognize the importance of cultural differences in pedagogical practices. Jordan-Irving (1990) notes that even in instances where non-Black teachers acknowledge the cultural differences, it may result in further racial stereotyping, differential treatment, and lower teacher expectations when they are unfamiliar with Black culture.

OSHUN: Hold on. You are creating a binary between Black and White teachers and placing each within some hierarchy of understanding the essence of Blackness.

ROCHELLE: Shit, I guess I did. Let me rephrase what I just said. I realize that there can be good and dedicated White teachers and poor and clueless Black teachers. What I meant to say was that regardless of the "color" of the teacher, if they do not practice a culturally relevant pedagogy, then they are creating an environment that makes learning difficult.

OSHUN: Okay, that statement is a little better but you need to watch yourself in the future.

ROCHELLE: Well, regardless of the connection between the cultural incongruity of Black children and school, it appears relevant for minority student success. Because the culture of Black children is often ignored, misunderstood, or discounted, Black children will often experience cultural discontinuity in school. The combination of Afrocentric students and Eurocentric schools results in conflict because of a lack of cultural congruence (Jordan-Irving, 1990). This lack of cultural synchronization becomes evident in instructional situations in which teachers misinterpret, devalue, and dismiss Black students' language, nonverbal cues, physical movements, learning styles, cognitive approaches, and worldview. When teachers and students are out of synchronization, they "clash and confront each other, both consciously and unconsciously in matters concerning proxemics, the use of interpersonal distance; paralanguage, the behaviors accompanying speech, such as voice tone, pitch, speech rate, and length; and coverbal behavior, gesture, facial expression, eye gaze" (Jordan-Irving, 1990, p. xxi).

Black student empowerment and Black revolutionary thought are two dynamics that are complementary. The dynamics between the two make it possible for the world not to be someplace where we must be tolerated or that we want or have to find some quiet corner and hide away. Instead, we look at the world as something, given the right tools, we can change. Empowerment is agency. Agency is the ability to act on and change our world/environment. We must remember that while we want and strive for individual empowerment, only collective action can effectively generate lasting social transformation of political and economic institutions.

In order to reach educational parity for Black children, an educational system must recognize and integrate Black culture into the school. Clearly cultural difference negatively affects Black students, thereby causing or exacerbating underachievement. The importance of a culturally relevant curriculum and pedagogy in the academic achievement of minority students has been a prevalent theory among African American scholars (Henry, 1994; Lee, Lomety, & Shujjaa, 1990; Lomotey, 1991; Steele, 1992).

OSHUN: Okay, I understand the importance of culturally relevant curriculum for Black students. But tell me how you are using it to develop a pedagogy to theorize away the pain of Black women? Better yet, how is it helping you to understand Jake.

ROCHELLE: I am seeking greater understanding through Jake and the impact a racist society had on him. He is the foundation to my ruminations. And as the foundation I place the various theories of African American education on him to see if they afford me a greater understanding of what put his picture on the front page of *USA Today*. Clearly African American children must receive something other than what they are getting in our educational system. An effective reform of education and schooling must be concerned with all areas of a Black child's existence.

OSHUN: Existence? To me that sounds like what education is already doing—allowing us to merely exist, nothing more.

ROCHELLE: You're right. Instead of existence let's say transformation. To transform means that I don't just look at what happens in school but I attempt to understand everything that constructs a Black child's reality and then I plan accordingly. As such I can develop an educational theory, which deconstructs and then allows students to reconstruct who they are, individually and collectively. My purpose is to define and construct what is needed in a pedagogy, which reconceptualizes the realities of Black students. I have positioned myself in such a way that I am forced to accept that there are many difficult societal barriers to the self of Jake. But that understanding also tells me that ultimately as a teacher, and someone who works at teacher reform, education can and must provide to Black students a belief in self.

OSHUN: Let's return to your earlier question of what we teach students so that they become complete beings.

ROCHELLE: Schooling—as it is theorized and practiced—despiritualizes and dehumanizes Black children, or at the very least it does nothing to return what society has taken away (King, 1994). Black children enter the educational system and begin to lose their concept of self from the very first day they sit in class ignored by the curriculum, the teacher, and the system. Bit by bit, they are stripped of the seed of humanity that is part of their ontological makeup. As they grow and mature into adulthood, the struggle to regain what school and society robbed from them begins to eat away, causing anger. It's like a cancer that invades the body, destroying the inside as well as the outside.

OSHUN: Moraga, the deep sister that she is, asked, "How do we organize ourselves to survive this war? To keep our families, our bodies, our spirits intact?"

ROCHELLE: There is a war I too wonder about as I struggle to hold onto the pieces of my spirit that are under assault. Moraga and Anzuldula (1981) tell us that:

> Sometimes in the face of my own/our own limitations, in the face of such world-wide suffering, I doubt even the significance of books. Surely this is the same predicament so many people who have tried to use words as weapons have found themselves in—?Cara a cara con el enemigo de qúe valen mis palabras? Face to face with enemy, what good are my words? (Npn)

OSHUN: What good are words if they are from the language of the oppressor?—none. What we must instead do is develop a language of critique, but one in our own voice filled with anger, emotion, and caring. "Ultimately the liberation of our thought from its colonized condition will require the creation of a new language" (Ani, 1994, p. 10).

ROCHELLE: If not careful, words can be limiting or a weapon against us. Instead, we develop our own language—one filled with truth, honesty, anger, emotion, spiritualness, pride—to critique the war waged against us. We are in a war for the souls of our children and my goal as an educator is to foster a critical consciousness in my students. As such, I try to create a way of interacting, which brings students to a Black consciousness.

OSHUN: And a pedagogy of wholeness works at creating this language of critique? So how does it differ from the various pedagogical sites, which are already out there in the educational realm?

ROCHELLE: I believe that education should work at the whole person. When education targets wholeness of being and spirituality, individual and collective transformation happens. A transformative pedagogy has two distinct and related parts. First, a sociopolitical transformation must occur for the student, which allows the second part, life transformation, to happen. When I use critical pedagogy, students realize their connection to the world. They begin to understand the political and economic structures of domination and oppression and develop tools for change. And this is something I would bet Jake didn't experience in his schooling.

OSHUN: Critical pedagogy is the framing tool that provides a language of critique to question the structures of the education system in general and classroom pedagogy in particular. According to Giroux and Simon (1989), critical pedagogy

> Refers to a deliberate attempt to influence how and what knowledge and identities are produced within and among particular sets of social relations. It can be understood as a practice through which people are incited to acquire a particu-

> lar "moral character." As both a political and practical activity, it attempts to influence the occurrence and qualities of experiences. (p. 239)

Critical pedagogy can/should be transformative. I don't have patience with a teacher who professes to use critical pedagogy but doesn't want to deal with transformative thinking.

ROCHELLE: When I use Jake as the foundation to my understanding, it is clear that to effectively educate Black children, a pedagogy must frame schooling and teaching within a critical dynamic that affords students an ability to name their world, to reflect critically on self and society, and have the agency to act for change (Giroux, 1997; Kincheloe, 2004; McLaren, 2000; Pozo, 2003; Wink, 1997). This ability changes the student from an object to be constructed to a subject in the construction of his or her own knowledge. As such, critical pedagogy speaks to issues of power, how power is distributed to some and kept from others and what influence it has on schooling. Critical pedagogy forces the student and teacher to view the world critically, taking nothing for granted but instead questioning the reasons behind various systems of domination.

Two important tools Black children need, which critical pedagogy offers, are the ability to read the word and read the world. When Black children read the word they can decode and encode those words by understanding the words as they relate to their experiences, possibilities, culture, and knowledge. And I know, just like I know that I am Black, that if Jake had that tool then he could have understood negative depictions in text surrounding Blackness. Rather than accepting and internalizing as truth he would be able to place the negativity in context. Not dismiss it but understand the purposes dominant structures in society had in putting it out there. He would know the workings of hegemony.

OSHUN: I feel a problem with critical pedagogy. Are you too accepting of its "power"?

ROCHELLE: No. I understand that despite its obvious benefits it stops short of being a revolutionary force in the education of Black students. Critical pedagogy is often more concerned with the individual and their ability to critique and change their world whereas culturally relevant pedagogy concerns itself with collective action and is "grounded in cultural understandings, experiences, and ways of knowing the world" (Ladson-Billings, 1992, pp. 382–383). In her critique of critical pedagogy, Ellsworth (1992) asserts that "the goal of critical pedagogy was a critical democracy, individual freedom, social justice, and social change—a revitalized public sphere characterized by citizens capable of confronting public issues critically through ongoing forms of public debate and social action" (p. 302). She continues by saying that the language of critical pedagogy operates at a "high level of abstraction" (p. 302) offering "decontextualized criteria for choosing one position over others" (p. 303). Accordingly, the abstraction that some attribute to critical pedagogy serves to alienate its concepts from the very people it aims to help.

OSHUN: I agree. Much of what I read through your eyes discussed critical pedagogy in language that can be so inaccessible it turns folks off. Another question or problem I have with critical pedagogy is that the place of minorities is not central in its framing. I don't see us.

ROCHELLE: Which is why we, I, must take the "bits and pieces" from various other theories to create what I need. For me the term "pedagogy of wholeness" underscores the varied inadequacies of other pedagogies. It is hard as hell being Black in America and one of anything ain't gone get it. Because of that I take whatever little pieces of various pedagogies to create my own. Critical, cultural, transformative, Afrocentric, feminist, etc. For example, when we layer Afrocentric theory onto critical pedagogy we can challenge the structures of oppression in society and call for change. The problematics and hegemony of critical pedagogy utilize the voices of mostly White male scholars, giving legitimacy to their work; on the other hand, Afrocentric theory uses Black scholars in understanding Black realities. Afrocentric theory is distinct and in ways opposed to a Eurocentric worldview (Asante, 1991; Asante & Atwater, 1986). Traditional scholarship defines the worldview of Black people as "reflections of quantifiable, biological differences among humans or residual categories that emerged in response to institutionalized racism" (Collins, 1991, p. 27). In contrast, Afrocentric theory states that an Afrocentric belief system reflects a "long standing belief system among African people" and that "being Black encompasses both experiencing White domination and individual and group valuation of an independent, long-standing Afrocentric consciousness" (Collins, 1991, p. 27).

Framing pedagogy through the lens of Afrocentric theory allows Black students to be central to its development. What happens when Black children are placed at the center of a pedagogy? Lee, Lomotey, and Shujja (1990) contend that an African-centered pedagogy has the following goals:

1. legitimizes African stores of knowledge;
2. positively exploits and scaffolds productive community and cultural practices;
3. extends and builds on the indigenous language;
4. reinforces community ties and idealizes service to one's family, community, nation, race, and world;
5. promotes positive social relationship;

6. Imparts a worldview that idealizes a positive, self-sufficient future for one's people without denying the self-worth and right to self-determination of others; and
7. supports cultural continuity while promoting critical consciousness (p. 50).

OSHUN: Henry (1994) states that an African-centered pedagogy resists dominant structures that "damage Black children's spirits and self-identity" (p. 300). Yet despite the positive influences of an African-centered pedagogy, gender bias is often inherent in Afrocentric scholarship.

ROCHELLE: Which is why I need to utilize a Black womanist theory in my little mixture of understanding. Black feminist thought utilizes a structural analysis of the intersection of race, class, and gender when theorizing a Black woman's standpoint. This becomes an epistemological discussion of not only who creates knowledge but how knowledge is created.

I have discussed Black feminist thought throughout this book. I have talked about its epistemology, its understanding of various types of knowledge. I have stated that Black feminist thought is not only concerned with the intersection of race, class, and gender but also the interface of politics, history, the economy, and society.

When I think of Jake and the Black women I teach, I clearly see that growing in a critical way would allow all the ability to read the world. For Jake, his surroundings—people, places, and things—would have lost (much of) their mystification and therefore their power. See, it's all about life transformation. Afrocentric theory in education does that, in part. Students stop thinking of themselves in individualistic terms and instead as part of a community, realizing their freedom cannot come at the expense of the freedom of all Black people. Students understand the historical connections between struggle and survival and they create a self-defined standpoint.

OSHUN: Can I call it a revolution of the mind and soul?

ROCHELLE: I like the sound of that. As we try to demystify Jake's world (the visible and invisible), a mental revolution will be the vehicle. And when we move a step past critical pedagogy we create a revolutionary force. Remember earlier I said that I see and analyze my world through the lens of education. The way I see it is that education must provide the intellectual catalyst towards both revolutionary thought and action.

OSHUN: Thought and action for whom? Articulate what you mean.

ROCHELLE: It would provide thought and action for self first and then extend it to the Black community. As I think about the pedagogies and theories out there, I need to see that they foster, promote, and teach for revolution. Culturally relevant pedagogy urges collective action grounded in cultural understandings, experiences, and ways of knowing the world versus the more individualistic nature of critical pedagogy (Ladson-Billings, 1992). But don't think that I am completely dismissing critical pedagogy. It has its place in creating a public space populated by politically empowered people who are knowledgeable about how to shape the political and social agenda to critical democracy, individual freedom, social justice, and social change (Ellsworth, 1992).

OSHUN. So what you are saying is that if we take the benefits of these various pedagogical sites, then a fuller pedagogy is born.

ROCHELLE: I have been attempting to develop a purpose for an Afriwomanist pedagogy of wholeness within a variety of pedagogical sites. I find myself still thinking through questions of pedagogy given certain types of epistemological concerns. By combining critical pedagogy, Afrocentric theory, and Black feminist thought I can engage in the dialectics of micro-level and macro-level structures that are working to oppress Black women. I hope to stretch critical pedagogy by looking at the three theories that speak to me. The goal of theory is to have a description and sense of the world, which allows me to write and teach about Black women.

OSHUN: As you understand it so far, what is a pedagogy of wholeness? How is it theorized and practiced? Who really needs it? How does it differ from the various pedagogical sites, which are already out there in the educational realm?

ROCHELLE: My pedagogy must foster in Black students the knowledge of self—being in touch with the world as a Black person. King (1994) tells us that "Being free is based on knowing one's humanity from within" (p. 270). Vanzant (1995) reminds us that "Spirituality examines and reveals the truth of your being" (p. 189). She adds, "Everything happens twice, first on the inside and then on the outside" (p. 201). That is why I need to combine the three theories to create a wholeness in my pedagogy. What I feel is essential to Black students is the complete whole, the closure to the circle of existence. I want to work on the mind but I need to work on the spirit as well.

OSHUN: We can never forget to work with the spirit of a child. Recognizing the importance of the spirit, "An African centered critical pedagogy resists the dominant structures, which damage Black children's spirits and self-identity" (Henry, 1994, p. 300).

ROCHELLE: I have come to believe that working on the spirit of the individual must come before they will even accept or think important the sociopolitical information I want to impart. When in your heart you believe you are nothing, you can memorize the facts in order to pass a test, but the information really does not and cannot transform beyond that. I have had too many Black students who received and could regurgitate the information I provided but the information was not life changing. On the other hand, I have had Black students whom I have watched over the years become.

OSHUN: Do you mean become in touch with self, knowing and learning self, in touch with who they are?

ROCHELLE: All of that plus an understanding of the process of rehumanizing self. Of placing self back into the life equation. Of loving all parts of self. "The Valley of Love is designed to teach us that the only relationship we can have in this life is the relationship we are having with ourselves" (Vanzant, 1995, p. 296). When all of this is not present the "best" pedagogy on the bookshelf will mean nothing, because it cannot force the information upon Black students. They have to be ready to accept and internalize what you give. I believe that Jake's "clarity of soul was missing" (King, 1994), allowing the pain to fester in that empty space.

I'm going to backtrack for a moment. I began this process wondering what my pain and the pain of my Black female students had to do with teaching. I realized that my personal pain was allowed because my belief in self had never been fully developed. Because of my arrested development I could feel and experience the negative and the positive, always allowing the negative to win. I vividly recall making Phi Beta Kappa and immediately calling my therapist with the news. At our next visit he said he wondered who was going to walk in his office—the woman who made Phi Beta Kappa or the woman who doubted everything about her intellect. On that day, it was the latter who entered the office; my euphoria had lasted less than a day. I immediately went back to the Rochelle unsure of self.

At the same time I realized the origins of my pain, I realized that for many Black women and Black people the pain originated from the same place inside that was missing something. I can understand Jake because my "clarity of soul" was also missing (King, 1994), and as a Black teacher who cares for the spirit of Black students, I knew I had to include my journey towards that clarity in my pedagogy and philosophy of education. Education should be the means toward Black students reestablishing their connection with self and the world (Henry 1993, 1994; King, 1994; Shujja, 1994). Moreover, education should be the key to a student unlocking the mysteries of their existence and provide the road map to creating their own knowledge. For Black women education should not only afford them an understanding of the sociopolitical forces that oppress, but also ensure that the new knowledge is internalized with enough strength to uproot the old.

A vitalness of humanity is essential to the education of Black students and Black women. King (1994) gives a definition of human vitalness as:

> aliveness of the human spirit expressed with honest vigor . . . being awake; looking; seeing, tasting, and engaging in nonoppressive uses of the power of one's autonomous soul; participating in self's human rights and responsively demonstrating the Afrohumanity of caring, closeness, creating, and calling for truth. (p. 271)

She crafts her language with such love and care for Black thought and existence and at the same time it is solid language, grounded in Black cultural theory; a cultural theory which determines the trajectory of not only our (as Black people) existence but our transformation. The healthy survival of Black women is dependent on the transformative, human vitality education should provide.

OSHUN: Would "clarity of soul" have helped Jake surmount the obstacles in his way?

ROCHELLE: I think so. Wait, I know so. The most important issue to me as a teacher and as a political activist working toward social justice and equity for all students is to foster that belief in self. Okay, go with me on this. Let's say that the story attached to Jake's picture is positive. Let's pretend that his education allowed him to grow into the man his ancestors intended him to be.

OSHUN: How? Does your scenario include creating a different social reality for his life?

ROCHELLE: No, that would be a dream. My scenario, which is based in theory, is about the possibilities if we do what is within our power to do. Unfortunately, I cannot change the destructive society Jake found himself living in. What I'm doing is putting him in an educational system that provides the tools he needed to transform his world.

OSHUN: So how do we meet Jake in this new picture?

ROCHELLE: The same way. I still see Jake's picture on the front page of *USA Today* in an article about Texas and the creation of these maximum-security superprisons. But now Jake's story is not that of an inmate, but of a man fighting to have the money spent in his daughter's school system instead of the prison system. He is not a politician but a concerned parent who understands the workings of the political system. He is astute and politically and socially aware. Jake's consciousness was created when all around him allowed Blackness to become central to his being. Jake is not lost. Instead he is framed within a Black consciousness and therefore connected to himself and his community. Because Black children were placed at the center, Jake experienced a system that loved and supported his full development.

OSHUN: Damn, that's so true.

ROCHELLE: It is my job—no, my obligation—as a teacher to center the margin, in my own mind, of Black existence. Black folk exist (in the minds of others) at the margins of society. I must destroy that concept, not only in my reality, but also in the reality of my students. I must teach them how to bring their life into the center. As a Black teacher I must teach my students to rebel, fight, learn, struggle, know, believe in themselves—and that belief will then afford a wholeness of spirit. This is the only way I was able to survive and come out able to find wholeness, having a sense of struggle and commitment as a Black person. This is the best way to allow the same for my students. I do it in the spirit of Jake.

## References

Akbar, N. (1984). *Chains and images of psychological slavery*. Jersey City, NJ: New Mind Productions.

Ani, M. (1994). *Yurugu: An African-centered critique of European cultural thought and behavior.* Trenton, NJ: Africa Free World Press.

Asante, M. K. (1991). The Afrocentric idea in education. *Journal of Negro Education*, 60, 170–179.

Asante, M. K., & D. Atwater. (1986). The rhetorical condition as symbolic structure in discourse. *Communication Quarterly, 34*, 170–177.

Bowles, S., & Gintis, H. (1976). *Schooling in capitalist America: Educational reform and the contradictions of economic life*. New York: Basic Books.

Boykin, A.W. (2000). The challenges of cultural socialization in the schooling of African American elementary school children: Exposing the hidden curriculum. In W. Watkins, J. Lewis, & V. Chou (Eds.) *Race and education* (pp. 190–191). Needham, MA: Allyn & Bacon.

Collins, P. H. (1991). *Black feminist thought: Knowledge, consciousness and the politics of empowerment.* New York: Routledge.

Ellsworth, E. (1992). Why doesn't this feel empowering? Working through the repressive myths of critical pedagogy. In L. Stone (Ed.), *The education feminism reader* (pp. 300–327). New York: Routledge. (Original work published in 1989)

Fordham, S. (1988). Racelessness as an actor in black students' school success: Pragmatic strategy or pyrrhic victory? *Harvard Educational Review* 58: 54–84.

Freire, P. (1970). *Pedagogy of the oppressed.* New York: Continuum.

Giroux, H. (1997). *Pedagogy and the politics of hope: Theory, culture, and schooling.* Boulder, CO: Westview Press.

Giroux, H., & Simon, R. (1989). Popular culture and critical pedagogy: Everyday life as a basis for curriculum knowledge. In H. Giroux & P. McLaren (Eds.), *Critical pedagogy, the state and cultural struggle* (pp. 236–252). Albany: State University of New York Press.

Gordon, R., Piana, L. D., & Keleher, T. (2000). *Facing the consequences: An examination of racial discrimination in U.S. public schools.* Oakland, CA: Applied Research Center.

Hale-Benson, J. (1986). *Black children: Their roots, culture, and learning styles.* Baltimore, MD: Johns Hopkins University Press.

Henry, A. (1993). Missing: Black self-representations in Canadian educational research. *Canadian Journal of Education* 18 (3): 206–222.

Henry, A. (1994). The empty shelf and other curricular challenges of teaching for children of African descent: Implications for teacher practice. *Urban Education 29* (3): 298–319. End Press.

Jagers, R. J. & Carroll, G. (2002). Issues in the education of African American children and youth. In S. Stringfield and D. Land (Eds.), *Educating at risk students.* Washington, DC: National Society for the Study of Education.

Johnson, K. (1997, August 4). Serving superhard time: New prisons isolate worst inmates. *USA Today*, 01.A

Jordan-Irving, J. (1990). *Black students and school failure: Policies, practices, and prescriptions.* New York: Greenwood Press.
Kincheloe, J. (2004). *Critical pedagogy primer.* New York: Peter Lang.
Kincheloe, J., & Steinberg, S. (1997). *Changing multiculturalism.* Bristol, PA: Open University Press.
King, J. E. (1994). Being the soul-freeing substance: A legacy of hope and humanity. In M. J. Shujaa (Ed.), *Too much schooling too little education: A paradox of Black life in White societies* (pp. 269–294). Trenton, NJ: Africa Free World Press.
Ladson-Billings, G. (1992, Summer). Liberatory consequences of literacy: A case of culturally relevant instruction for African American students. *Journal of Negro Education, 61*(3): 378–391.
Lee, C., Lomety, K., & Shujjaa, M. (1990). How shall we sing our sacred song in a strange land? The dilemma of double consciousness and the complexities of an African centered pedagogy. *Journal of Education 172*(2): 45–61.
Lomotey, K. (Ed.). (1991). *Going to school: African-American achievements.* Albany: State University of New York Press.
McLaren, P. (2000). *Che Guevara, Paulo Freire, and the pedagogy of revolution.* Boulder, CO: Rowman & Littlefield.
Moraga, C., & Anzuldula, G. (Eds.). (1981). *This bridge called my back: Radical writings by women of color.* New York: Kitchen Table Women of Color Press.
Murrell, P. C. (1997). Digging again the family wells: A Freirean literacy framework as emancipatory pedagogy for African-American children. In P. Freire, J. W. Fraser, D. Macedo, T. Mckinnon, & W. T. Stokes (Eds.), *Mentoring the mentor: A critical dialogue with Paulo Freire* (pp.19–55). New York: Peter Lang.
Nelson, L. J. Palonsky, B. S., & Carlson, K. (2000). *Critical issues in education: Dialogues and dialectics.* (4th ed.). Boston: McGraw Hill.
Pozo, M. (2003). Towards a critical revolutionary pedagogy: An interview with Peter McLaren. *St. John's University Humanities Review. 2*(1). Retrieved April 2004, from http://facpub.stjohns.edu/~ganterg/sjureview/vol2-1/vol2-1.html
Ratteray, J. (1991). African-American achievement: A research agenda emphasizing independent schools. In K. Lomotey (Ed.), *Going to school: The African-American experience* (pp. 197–208). Albany: State University of New York Press.
Shujja, M. S. (1994). *Too much schooling too little education: A paradox of Black life in White societies.* Trenton, NJ: Africa Free World Press.
Simon, R. I. (1992). *Teaching against the grain: Text for a pedagogy of possibility.* New York: Bergen & Garvey.
Spring, J. (1991). *American education: An introduction to social & political aspect.* Oldwestbury: State College of New York.
Steele, C. M. (1992, April). Race and the schooling of black America. *The Atlantic Monthly,* 68–78.
Vanzant, I. (1995). *The value in the valley: A Black woman's guide through life's dilemmas.* New York: Simon and Schuster.
Watkins, W. (2001). *The White architects of Black education: Ideology and power in America, 1865–1954.* New York: Teachers College Press.
Wink, J. (1997). *Critical pedagogy: Notes from the real world.* New York: Longman.

|| EIGHTEEN

# A Comprehensive Evaluation of Life Space Crisis Intervention (LSCI)

Larry F. Forthun, Jeffrey W. McCombie & Caroline Payne

Crisis intervention skills are essential for all educators. However, many teachers enter the profession feeling unprepared to manage a student crisis (Lewis, Parsad, Carey, Bartfai, Farris, & Smerdon, 1999; Merrett & Wheldall, 1993), and as a result, it falls upon the local school district to provide training and support. For most classroom teachers and staff, professional development typically consists of short-term (1 day or less) in-service seminars and workshops (Parsad, Lewis, & Farris, 2001). However, there is concern that short-term training may not be enough to effectively learn crisis intervention skills and generalize the skills to the classroom (Parsad et al., 2001). Life Space Crisis Intervention (LSCI) is different. Life Space Crisis Intervention is a competency-based professional development training for educators. Unlike traditional professional development opportunities, LSCI is a highly intensive, strength-based training that teaches educators a new approach to intervention for students in crisis. It trains educators in crisis intervention skills from verbal de-escalation of a crisis to intervention strategies that help students develop better coping skills. Studies have shown that educators who implement LSCI in the classroom often experience fewer disruptive behaviors among students and are less likely to refer students for disciplinary action (Dawson, 2003; Forthun, McCombie, & Freado, 2006; Grskovic & Goetze, 2005; Naslund, 1987).

Life Space Crisis Intervention (LSCI) is a competency-based approach specifically designed to help classroom teachers, guidance counselors, administrators, and other school staff reduce the negative psychological, social, and emotional consequences of poor decision making and promote positive development among students. No longer just the purview of administrators or school counselors, classroom teachers and other school staff are being called upon to assist in addressing the social and emotional needs of students (Long, Morse, Fecser, & Newman, 2007). Many children and youth with behavioral and emotional difficulties are being integrated (mainstreamed) into the regular classroom, and more students than ever are entering the classroom with difficulties that are not severe enough for enhanced educational services but may be disruptive to the learning process (Farrell & Tsakalidou, 1999; Landrum, Katsiyannis, & Archwamety, 2004). Research suggests that the overall quality of teacher-student interactions and the academic progress of the students both suffer when disruptions are not managed effectively (Shores & Wehby, 1999). LSCI offers educators specific skills to focus their efforts to addressing the *central issue* (e.g., the underlying pattern of self-defeating behavior) rather than getting bogged down in attempts to determine who is at fault and who should be disciplined. The goal is to encourage more adaptive problem-solving behaviors among students that will lead to an improved quality of life and a reduction in disruptive behaviors at school (Long, Fecser, & Wood, 2001).

However, as a promising approach to crisis intervention, the research on LSCI has been limited to only assessing its impact on student behaviors, mostly within alternative or special education classrooms. For example, DeMagistris and Imber (1980) found that the use of LSCI significantly decreased maladaptive behavior (up to 72%) and increased academic performance among those who received the intervention within a special education classroom. A more recent study by Dawson (2003) found similar results among male junior high special education students. Compared to a similar classroom that did not use LSCI, students in the LSCI classroom experienced fewer crises, fewer suspensions, and better attendance by the end of the school year. In other research, Naslund (1987) kept daily records of the classroom use of LSCI among classroom teachers of elementary school children in an emotional support classroom. Over the course of a school year, daily reports showed that although LSCI continued to be used quite frequently, the content of the interviews changed from complaining about rules to discussing with the student new ways (skills) to be more successful in the classroom. For Naslund (1987), the change in the content of the interviews demonstrated that the students were making progress. Similarly, Grskovic and Goetze (2005) recently reported a significant decrease in challenging behaviors among learning-disabled students exposed to LSCI in the classroom.

Although LSCI results in significant changes in student behaviors, little is known about *how* LSCI is implemented within the schools and *how* training and implementation of LSCI might work in changing the attitudes and behaviors of the educators who are trained (Dawson, 2003; Forthun et al., 2006). The purpose of the study that is the subject of this chapter, then, was twofold. First, we sought to evaluate the *implementation* of LSCI by educators (see Forthun, Payne, & McCombie, 2009 for a full description). A successful LSCI requires a commitment from educators to work with the student to address their immediate and long-term needs. Yet most educators do not have the luxury of spending large amounts of time with a student in crisis. Therefore, as a goal of the implementation, or process of evaluation, it was important to understand how teachers learn to adapt the quasi-therapeutic skills of LSCI into the natural flow of the school day.

A second goal for the study was to examine the impact of LSCI on educators' responses to student misbehavior (e.g., the frequency of use of crisis intervention skills in response to crisis, referrals for disciplinary action, quality of teacher-student relationships) and on the causal beliefs, sense of self-efficacy, and emotional reactions of educators to student misbehavior (see Forthun & McCombie (unpublished) for a full description). Past research suggests that changes in the knowledge and beliefs of educators are a necessary precursor to the successful implementation of new skills or educational strategies (Adalbjarnardottir & Selman, 1997; Stein & Wang, 1988; Tillema, 1995). In fact, Hoy and Weinsten (2006) suggest that teacher's beliefs about students are a significant influence on teaching practices, which ultimately leads to improved student learning and behavior. For example, research has shown that causal beliefs that focus on child temperament or parental divorce (e.g., characteristics that are less amenable to change) often result in negative emotional reactions such as anger or resentment (Hastings & Brown, 2002; Poulou & Norwich, 2002). These negative emotional reactions can lead to a lowered sense of self-efficacy in intervening with disruptive students and a greater likelihood of using restrictive or punitive disciplinary strategies or removing students from the classroom (Hughes, Barker, Kemenoff, & Hart, 1993; Poulou & Norwich, 2002). This study was designed to assess the impact of LSCI on an educator's beliefs, emotions, and behaviors regarding student misbehavior and how this may translate into improved teacher-student relationships and reduced referrals outside of the classroom.

## Brief Overview of LSCI

During LSCI training, current conceptions of students with emotional and behavior problems as "disordered" are challenged and replaced with a "reclaiming" philosophy that views students as individuals who may be acting out as a result of developmental or psychosocial anxiety or pain (Brendtro & Shahbazian, 2004). For example, students may experience developmental anxiety as they struggle to develop a sense of identity or psychosocial pain because of a break-up in a close relationship. In addition, LSCI teaches educators that emotional and pychological *pain* can develop from a variety of sources leading to stress, anxiety, conflict, and crisis, even among well-functioning students (Long et al., 2001). As a result,

*Table 1: Steps and Interventions for Life Space Crisis Intervention (LSCI)*

| Steps | Descriptions |
|---|---|
| **Diagnostic Steps** | |
| 1. Drain Off | Student "cools down" and teacher holds back any counter aggression feelings s/he may be experiencing toward student |
| 2. Timeline | Obtain and validate the student's perception of the crisis by having the student help create a timeline of the incident |
| 3. Central Issue | Determine which one of the six patterns of student self defeating behaviors is being used by the student |
| **Reclaiming Steps** | |
| 4. Insight | Help the student develop insight and accountability for the specific self-defeating behavior the student used during the crisis |
| 5. New Skills | Teach the student new social/interpersonal skills to overcome their pattern of self-defeating behavior |
| 6. Transfer of Training | Help the student generalize the new social skills and/or behaviors to other situations |
| **Interventions** | **Descriptions** |
| Red Flag | This intervention addresses emotional problems that are "imported" from outside of the immediate context; for example, a student who "explodes" on another student in the classroom because of a personal or home issue. The emotionality of the issue is carried with the student into the classroom where the student is easily set off by another student. |
| New Tools | This intervention is designed to teach new social and interpersonal skills to students who may be "acting out" or having difficulty with their peers because of inadequate skills. Generally this intervention is with students who want to succeed socially, but lack appropriate social skills. |
| Reality Rub | This intervention is designed to address misperceptions or misattributions about the nature of the situation that triggered the crisis; for example, when a student focuses exclusively on how she/he had been wronged by another. This intervention is to help students "see" the situation in a more neutral, rational way. |
| Symptom Estrangement | This intervention is used with students who attempt to avoid blame by avoiding responsibility or shifting responsibility to someone else; for example, when a student caught fighting blames the other student for starting the fight. |
| Massaging Numb Values | This intervention is designed for students who feel anxious, guilty, or inadequate; for example, a student who was physically or sexually abused at home. The intervention is to help the student develop better self-efficacy regarding her/his ability to cope in social situations. |
| Manipulation of Body Boundaries | This intervention is used for a student who is being exploited or manipulated by their peers; for example, a student who misbehaves to gain the approval of other peers. |

*Definitions taken from Long et al. (2001)*

educators are taught specific skills to disrupt the crisis, thereby reducing negative emotional reactions. These skills are taught through an understanding of the six steps of the LSCI process and the six types of LSCI interventions.

As shown in Table 1, the first three steps of the LSCI process are the Diagnostic steps that are designed to reduce the intense feelings of the student and educator (drain off), validate the student's perceptions (timeline), and identify the underlying issue leading to the current crisis (central issue) (Long et al., 2001). Once complete, the next three steps (the Reclaiming steps) use one of six interventions to promote *insight* and encourage the development of *new skills* that can be generalized to other situations (transfer of training). The six types of interventions reflect specific intervention skills that target common crises among youth. For example, a student who becomes hostile in the classroom may receive a Red Flag intervention, while a student who is unfocused may receive a Reality Rub intervention. Overall, the goal of LSCI intervention is to use the current crisis as a learning opportunity to encourage the student to take responsibility for her/his own behavior by promoting self-awareness and encouraging behavior change (Long et al., 2001).

## Research Questions

To evaluate the process of implementing LSCI in the school setting, we designed an assessment tool that allowed us to answer the following questions: How frequently was LSCI used with students in crisis? What was the average length of an LSCI? How many steps of the LSCI process were typically completed? What type of LSCI (e.g., Red Flag, New Skills) was typically used and for what types of problems? What was the average outcome of an LSCI?

The answers to these questions would provide an important foundation for understanding how educators adapt LSCI to meet the needs of students while continuing to fulfill their educational responsibilities. Second, we asked educators to complete a comprehensive survey of their attitudes, emotional reactions, and behaviors toward students. It was expected that causal beliefs about student misbehavior that blame the family or the child would be positively related to negative emotional relations, negatively related to self-efficacy in managing student behaviors, negatively related to the use of crisis intervention skills, and positively related to disciplinary referrals. Furthermore, negative emotional reactions to student misbehavior would be negatively related to self-efficacy, negatively related to the use of crisis intervention skills, and positively related to disciplinary referrals. To measure the impact of LSCI on each of these processes, a post-test comparison was performed between LSCI-trained educators and educators who were untrained. It was expected that LSCI-trained educators would be (a) less likely to adopt child- or family-focused causal attributions of student misbehavior; (b) less

*Table 2: Demographic Characteristics of LSCI and Comparison Participants**

| Variable | Value | Frequency LSCI | Frequency Comparison |
|---|---|---|---|
| Gender | Female | 66 (58.4%) | 39 (57.4%) |
| | Male | 46 (40.7%) | 29 (42.6%) |
| Ethnic Origin | Am. Ind./AK Native | 2 (1.8%) | 1 (1.5%) |
| | Hispanic/Latino | 2 (1.8%) | |
| | White/Non-Hispanic | 108 (95.6%) | 66 (97.1%) |
| Grade Level | Elementary School | 9 (8.0%) | |
| | Middle School | 39 (34.5%) | 8 (11.8%) |
| | High School | 61 (54.0%) | 56 (82.4%) |
| | Across Schools | 1 (0.9%) | |
| Teaching Experience | No Experience | | 1 (1.5%) |
| | First year teaching | | 2 (2.9%) |
| | 1-4 yrs | 34 (30.1%) | 8 (11.8%) |
| | 5-9 yrs | 15 (13.3%) | 14 (20.6%) |
| | 10-14 yrs | 17 (15.0%) | 18 (26.5%) |
| | 15-19 yrs | 14 (12.4%) | 11 (16.2%) |
| | 20-24 yrs | 16 (14.2%) | 4 (5.9%) |
| | 25-29 yrs | 8 (7.1%) | 1 (1.5%) |
| | 30-34 years | 5 (4.4%) | 8 (11.8%) |
| | 35-39 years | | 1 (1.5%) |
| | Over 40 years | 1 (0.9%) | 0 |
| Academic Position | Principal/Administrator | 6 (5.3%) | 2 (3%) |
| | Reg. Ed. Teacher | 66 (58.4%) | 8 (13%) |
| | Sp. Ed. Teacher/Aide | 18 (15.9%) | 2 (3%) |
| | Alternative Ed./Aide | 3 (2.7%) | |
| | Guidance Counselor/ Psychologist | 15 (13.3%) | 1 (1%) |
| | Other | 4 (3.5%) | 3 (4%) |
| | Missing | | 52 (76%) |
| | Total | 112 | 68 |

* *not all percentages add up to 100% due to missing data*

likely to react negatively to student misbehavior; (c) more likely to feel obligated to help a student in crisis; (d) have a higher sense of self-efficacy in managing student crises in the classroom; (e) report using crisis intervention skills more frequently in response to student crises; and (f) be less likely to refer students out of the classroom to counselors or principals.

## Method

### Sample

The training and evaluation of LSCI was part of a long-term initiative of a rural school district in the northeastern United States. The purpose was to change the school environment from "zero-tolerance" to a reclaiming environment in which teachers and staff would promote belonging, generosity, mastery, and independence among all students (see Brendtro, Ness, & Mitchell, 2002; Brendtro & Shahbazian, 2004). However, the school district was unable to train all school personnel in the district during a single academic year. Instead, approximately 25 to 50 school personnel, primarily from the middle school and high school, were invited to participate in annual trainings. This study was conducted among those who participated in the first three annual trainings with approximately 39 school personnel trained during the first year, 51 trained in the second year, and 25 trained in the third year (see Table 2). All but three participants agreed to participate in the study (n = 112).

A comparison sample of 68 untrained teachers and staff were recruited from two demographically similar schools in the region (see Table 2). Approximately 31 were teachers at a vocational/technical school and 37 were faculty who taught in a middle school or high school. In all, participants in both groups were primarily female (58%), predominately White, non-Hispanic (97%), taught in the middle school or high school (94%), and had, on average, 10 or more years of experience (58%).

### Procedures

*Process Evaluation.* Those trained in LSCI were asked to complete a report following each interaction with students where LSCI skills were used. The report asked them to identify the type of LSCI intervention that was used, the number of steps that were completed, the length of the intervention, the intensity of the situation (on a scale from 1 [low] to 5 [high]), a brief description of the situation, and a brief description of the outcome. Although not all of the participating educators completed a report after each LSCI, approximately 702 reports were submitted over the course of the 3-year study.

*Table 3: Definition of Situations Coded from the LSCI Reports*

| Situation Codes | Definitions |
|---|---|
| Misbehavior: Non-Physical | The situation involved a behavior that was disruptive to the class, school environment, teacher, or other students but was not physical, i.e.: talking at inappropriate times, inappropriate comments or writings, harassment, or disrespect for others. |
| Misbehavior: Physical | The situation involved a behavior that was disruptive to the class, school environment, teacher, or other students and was physical, i.e.: fighting, pushing, or hitting. |
| Academic Issues | The situation took place as a direct result of an academically centered issue, i.e.: failure of a subject, difficulty with homework. |
| Family Issues | The situation was the direct result of an issue stemming from the student's home environment, i.e.: parental divorce, death of a family member, or sickness in the family. |
| Relationship Issues | The situation took place between two individuals who were experiencing difficulties in their romantic relationship or as a result of a romantic relationship. |
| Personal Issues | The situation took place as a result of a personal or emotional issue that the individual student was experiencing, i.e.: depression, eating disorder, or suicidal thoughts. |
| Peer Issues | The situation involved two or more students having social problems with one another. The problem may have escalated to become verbal or physical, but was still centered around peer difficulties, i.e.: trouble making friends, disagreements between friends, or clique status. |
| Teacher-Student Issues | The situation took place between a teacher and a student, i.e.: disagreement over grades, or miscommunication. |
| Follow-up | A meeting was scheduled in which the student-educator met to further discuss a previous situation. |

Written descriptions of the situation that precipitated the LSCI and the outcome that followed were coded using a content analysis approach. First, descriptions of the LSCI situation were compared to a list of common disciplinary infractions obtained from each school (e.g., disciplinary codes). When a description mirrored a coded infraction, the situation was coded similarly (e.g., bullying, disrespect, etc.). For those descriptions that were not disciplinary infractions, new codes were developed (e.g., parental divorce, fighting with friend, etc.). Once complete, the new codes were reanalyzed to consolidate codes that reflected similar themes (e.g., misbehavior, personal issues, etc.). This process continued until no more higher-order themes could reasonably be identified. In the end, nine situation codes were used to describe the specific events that precipitated most LSCIs (see Table 3).

Coding for outcomes proceeded similarly. Initially, each outcome description was coded using very specific categories (e.g., insight to emotions, detention, returned to class, etc.). Following the initial coding, specific codes were consolidated into higher-order categories that reflected the general theme of the outcome (e.g., discipline, peer meeting). As a result, twelve outcome codes described most of the outcome descriptions provided by the educators (see Table 4).

*Table 4: Definition of Outcomes Coded from the LSCI Reports*

| **Outcome Codes** | **Definition** |
|---|---|
| Central Issue Identified | The central issue of the problem was established. |
| Conference Requested | A meeting took place between the parents and teacher/administrator. |
| Discipline | The result of the intervention was some form of punishment, i.e.: suspension, detention, or sent home for the day. |
| Drain Off Established | The student calmed down, relaxed, and was able to discuss the incident. |
| Promoted Insight | The educator gathered enough information from the student on the specifics of the situation and was able to encourage the student to look at the situation in different ways. |
| New Skills Discussed | The educator was able to discuss new skills that could be applied to the specific situation. |
| Ongoing Discussion | The situation was not resolved and actions were taken to continue the discussion at a later time. |
| Peer Meetings | The intervention resulted in a peer meeting of some sort either between the individuals involved in the situation, or between other peers. |
| Plan Developed | A plan was developed to help the student resolve the situation and prevent the situation from reoccurring. |
| Referred Outside School | The student was referred to an individual, program, or service outside the school. |
| Referred Inside School | The student was referred to someone else within the school that was trained in LSCI, i.e.: teacher, principal, guidance counselor, or other. |
| Resolved | The educator felt that the situation had been resolved as a result of LSCI. |

### *Outcome Evaluation*

Participants in the LSCI group completed a battery of questionnaires immediately prior to training and again approximately 6 to 8 months following the start of the academic year (e.g., a pre- and post-assessment). Data were collected from trained educators during the first year following training with data from all three cohorts (first year only) combined to form the LSCI-trained group (n = 112). Comparison group participants were evaluated only once at approximately the same time as the post-assessment for the third LSCI group (e.g., 6 to 8 months from the start of the academic year). The comparison group was assessed only once to avoid pre-test sensitization. As a result, only the post-test data from the battery of questionnaires were subjected to statistical analysis.

Participants who were trained in LSCI were also asked to participate in a focus group at the end of the school year in which they were trained. Focus group questions included: What was the most important impact of LSCI on your values as an educator? What traditional beliefs about school discipline or misbehavior have been done away with? Give an example of a significant impact of LSCI on a student.

The focus groups were conducted by the LSCI trainer, and participants were allowed to interact with one another. Focus group members were asked to write their reactions/responses on note cards that were analyzed by the researchers using a similar content analytic approach as described above.

### *Measurement*

The *Attribution Inventory* was designed by Poulou and Norwich (2000) to evaluate teachers' causal attributions about student misbehavior and their subsequent cognitive, emotional, and behavioral responses. Participants are asked to read a vignette about a problem student and asked to respond to the following scales.

### *Causal Attributions*

Causal attributions for the student's misbehavior described in the vignette were evaluated in four domains: family environment, child, teacher, and school. Five to seven items were used to assess each domain. Examples of items in the family environment scale included: "poor attachment between parent and child" and "parent's inability to help their child." Reliability estimates for this scale were adequate with Cronbach's alpha estimated at 0.69 for the LSCI group and 0.79 for the comparison group. Examples of items in the child scale included: "Child cannot control his behavior" and "child's low intelligence level." Reliability estimates for this scale were also adequate with Cronbach's alpha estimated 0.65 for the LSCI group and 0.71 for the comparison group. Examples of items from the teacher scale included: "Teaching style" and "poor classroom environment." Reliability estimates for this scale were excellent with Cronbach's alpha estimated at 0.87 for the LSCI group and 0.86 for the comparison group. Finally, examples of items from the school scale included: "Irrelevant curriculum for the child's interest" and "class size too large." Reliability estimates for this scale were good with Cronbach's alpha estimated at 0.74 for the LSCI group and 0.83 for the comparison group.

### Reactions to Misbehavior

Three items were used to assess *self-directed emotional reactions* to the student in the vignette. Examples of items in this scale included: "I would feel stressed/anxious" and "I would feel helpless/depressed." Reliability estimates for this scale were adequate with Cronbach's alpha estimated at 0.63 for the LSCI group and 0.79 for the comparison group.

Three items were used to assess *child-directed emotional reactions* to the student in the vignette. Examples of items in this scale included: "I would feel angry/resentful toward the child" and "I would feel sympathy/compassion toward the child" (reverse coded). Although reliability estimates for this scale were adequate for the comparison group with Cronbach's alpha estimated at 0.74, the reliability estimate for the comparison sample was poor at 0.55. Items were examined to identify their contribution to the overall estimate of reliability; however, given the low number of items, removing a single item did not improve the estimate. Results for this scale for the LSCI group should be interpreted with caution.

Three items were used to assess the *level of felt responsibility* in helping the student in the vignette. Examples of items in this scale include: "I would feel responsible to help" and "I would feel committed to help the child." Reliability estimates for this scale were good with Cronbach's alpha estimated at 0.75 for the LSCI group and 0.86 for the comparison group.

### Self-Efficacy

Participants complete the Perceived Self-Efficacy in Classroom Management subscale of the Teacher Interpersonal Self-Efficacy Scale (Brouwers & Tomic, 2001; Brouwers, Tomic, & Stijnen, 2002). Examples of the 13 items in this scale include: "I am able to respond adequately to defiant students" and "I am always able to make my expectations clear to students." Reliability estimates for this scale were excellent with Cronbach's alpha estimated at 0.90 for the LSCI group and 0.88 for the comparison group.

### Crisis Intervention Skills and Referrals

Finally, both the LSCI and comparison group participants were asked to answer several questions on their use of, and comfort with using, skills for managing crises (see Dawson, 2003). LSCI participants were asked about their use of LSCI skills, while the comparison participants were asked about their use of general crisis management skills. Participants were asked to rate on a scale from 1 (very uncomfortable) to 5 (very comfortable) how comfortable they felt working with students in "crisis." Participants were also asked to rate how frequently they used their skills with youth in crisis from 1 (not at all) to 5 (very frequently). In a separate line of questioning, participants were asked to rate on a scale from 0 percent to 100 percent the percentage of time their interventions with students resulted in positive outcomes and the percentage of time interventions resulted in a referral to the principal or counselor.

### *Design and Analysis*

Qualitative procedures were outlined previously. To analyze the quantitative data, relationships between variables were first examined using Pearson's correlation. We expected the variables in our analysis to be related to each other in a theoretically consistent manner. Second, mean scores of the scale items were statistically compared between groups by using a 2 (LSCI group; comparison group) X 2 (male; female) ANOVA on the post-test scores only. Gender of the educator was included as an independent variable in the analyses based on previous research that suggested that outcomes may differ based upon the participant's gender (Forthun et al., 2006). Years of experience was included as a covariate. To avoid potential Type I errors (concluding a mean difference between groups is significant when it is not), the probability level was set at 0.01 for all ANOVA analyses.

## Results

### *LSCI Process Evaluation*

Data gathered from the LSCI reports are summarized in Table 5. To ease interpretation, the educators were separated into five groups: classroom teacher/aide, alternative teacher/aide (including special education, alternative education, and emotional support), principal/administrator, guidance counselor/psychologist, or other staff (e.g., school resource officer, student liaison). On average, principals and guidance counselors spent the most time with students (about 30–35 minutes), while classroom teachers spent the least amount of time (about 22–24 minutes). Likewise, on average, most educators only completed four of the six steps of the LSCI process (see Table 5). Most reported the completion of the first three steps in the order in which they occur in the model: Step 1 (Drain Off), Step 2 (Timeline), and Step 3 (Central Issue). However, Step 4 (Insight) and Step 5 (New Skills) were often completed independently when the completion of Step 5 (New Skills) occurred by skipping Step 4 (Insight) in the process. Transfer of Training, the last step in the LSCI process, was least likely to happen (22.7% of the time). The results suggest that all educators completed the first three LSCI steps relatively consistently, although the limited time with students may have led to adaptations of the last three steps.

Table 5 summarizes the three most common student difficulties by educator group. The most common student difficulty reported by principals and classroom teachers was student misbehavior. For mainstream teachers and guidance counselors, personal and peer issues also prompted an LSCI. In fact, alternative education teachers were the only educator group with academic issues as one of the top three issues addressed. This suggests that when students are experiencing personal difficulties, mainstream classroom teachers, along with guidance counselors, are

*Table 5: Summary of LSCI Implementation by Type of Educator*

| Type of Educator | # Submitted | Mean # of Stages | Most Common Incident Codes | Most Frequent LSCI | Average Intensity of Contact | Length of LSCI (Minutes) | Most Common Outcome Codes |
|---|---|---|---|---|---|---|---|
| Principal/ Administrator | 82 | 3.96 | 1 Misbehavior: Non-Physical<br>2 Misbehavior: Physical<br>3 Peer Issues | 1 Red Flag<br>2 New Tools<br>3 Reality Rub | 3.38 | 34.49 | 1 Insight<br>2 Discipline<br>3 Resolved |
| Emotional/ Special/ Alternative Ed | 247 | 3.09 | 1 Misbehavior: Non-Physical<br>2 Academic Issue<br>3 Personal Issues | 1 Red Flag<br>2 New Tools<br>3 Reality Rub | 2.95 | 22.49 | 1 Insight<br>2 Resolved<br>3 Ongoing |
| Classroom Teacher/Aide | 233 | 3.95 | 1 Misbehavior: Non-Physical<br>2 Personal Issues<br>3 Peer Issues | 1 Red Flag<br>2 New Tools<br>3 Reality Rub | 2.82 | 23.99 | 1 Insight<br>2 Ongoing<br>3 Resolved |
| Guidance/ Psychologist | 42 | 4.09 | 1 Personal Issues<br>2 Peer Issues<br>3 Family Issues | 1 New Tools<br>2 Red Flag<br>3 None | 2.90 | 30.88 | 1 Resolved<br>2 Insight<br>3 New Skills |
| Other Staff | 91 | 3.95 | 1 Peer Issues<br>2 Misbehavior: Non-Physical<br>3 Personal Issues | 1 Red Flag<br>2 New Tools<br>3 Reality Rub | 3.49 | 26.22 | 1 Insight<br>2 Referred inside school<br>3 New Skills |

the educators who are most likely to be able and available to intervene. On the other hand, given that many of the student difficulties were either for misbehavior or were personal in nature, it is not surprising that the most common LSCI interventions used were the Red Flag (35% of the time), New Tools (23% of the time), and Reality Rub (15.5% of the time) interventions (see Table 5). The only variation in the frequency of use of the three LSCI interventions was for guidance counselors who were more likely to use the New Tools intervention.

In the analysis of the outcomes of each reported LSCI, the most frequent outcomes were Promoting Insight (e.g., efforts by the educator to gather information from the student to encourage them to think or behave in a different way), Ongoing Discussion (i.e., educator to continue discussion at a later time), New

*Table 6: Correlations between Variables in the Study for All Participants Combined*

| | Child Causes | Teacher Causes | School Causes | Self Efficacy | Self Dir Emot | Child Dir Emot | Responsible | Comfort with Skill | Freq of Skill | Positive Outcome | Referral |
|---|---|---|---|---|---|---|---|---|---|---|---|
| Fam Env Causes | .15* | .03 | .18* | .07 | .19** | .22** | –.08 | –.05 | –.04 | .01 | .20* |
| Child causes | | .52** | .60** | –.03 | –.09 | –.21** | .12 | –.06 | –.02 | –.06 | –.14 |
| Teacher causes | | | .67** | –.01 | –.08 | –.18* | .16* | .08 | .00 | .01 | –.11 |
| School causes | | | | –.13 | –.05 | –.17* | .13 | .00 | –.07 | –.09 | –.12 |
| Self-efficacy | | | | | –.15* | –.07 | .05 | .17* | .15 | .16* | .03 |
| Self dir emotion | | | | | | .65** | –.14 | –.27** | –.26** | .03 | .11 |
| Child dir emotion | | | | | | | –.34** | –.22** | –.21** | –.07 | .18* |
| Responsible | | | | | | | | .23** | .16** | .14 | –.20* |
| Comfort with skills | | | | | | | | | .54** | .39** | –.15 |
| Freq of skills | | | | | | | | | | .29** | .00 |
| Positive outcome | | | | | | | | | | | –.10 |

* $p < 0.05$ **; $p < 0.01$

Skills Discussed (i.e., educator noted discussing prosocial skills), and Resolution (i.e., educator felt issue was adequately resolved). As expected, Discipline (e.g., detention, suspension, etc.) was a common outcome only for school principals.

### *Outcome Evaluation*

Using correlation analyses to evaluate the relationships among the quantitative variables (see Table 6), results showed that, consistent with expectations, attributing the cause of the student's misbehavior to the family environment was positively related to both self-directed negative emotions ($r = 0.19$) and child-directed negative emotions ($r = 0.22$) (see Table 6). These negative emotional reactions, in turn, were negatively related to both the comfort of using crisis intervention skills with students ($r = -0.27$ with self-directed emotions; $r = -0.22$ for child-directed emotions) and frequency of the use of crisis management skills with students ($r = -0.26$ with self-directed emotions; $r = -0.21$ with other-directed emotions). Additionally, child-directed emotional reactions were positively related to student referrals ($r = 0.18$). However, when attributions were focused on the child, teacher, or school as the cause of the student's misbehavior, teachers and staff were less likely to report child-directed negative emotional reactions ($r = -0.17$ to -0.21). When causal attributions were directed at themselves, teachers and staff were more likely to report feeling responsible to intervene ($r = 0.16$); and therefore, were less likely to refer students.

### *ANOVA Analyses*

*Causal Attributions.* In separate analyses comparing the LSCI group with the comparison group, the LSCI group (see Table 7) endorsed three of the four causal factors more strongly. They were more likely to identify, teacher ($F\,(1, 160) = 24.84$, $p < 0.01$), school ($F\,(1, 160) = 17.08$, $p < 0.01$), and child ($F\,(1, 160 = 17.79$, $p = 0.01$) factors as influential in explaining the student's disruptive misbehavior. On the other hand, mean scores were lower for LSCI participants on family environment factors ($F\,(1, 159) = 14.02$, $p < 0.01$). Additionally, a significant interaction emerged by group and gender for family environment causal beliefs ($F\,(1, 159) = 8.01$, $p < 0.01$). Females in the comparison group ($M = 3.72$, $SD = 0.79$) were much more likely to endorse family environment causes than those in the other groups (comparison group males ($M = 3.24$, $SD = 0.74$), LSCI group females ($M = 3.05$, $SD = 0.53$), or LSCI group males ($M = 3.15$, $SD = 0.52$)). The opposite occurred for child factor causes with males ($M = 2.94$, $SD = 0.68$), regardless of training, endorsing child factor causes significantly more often than females ($M = 2.60$, $SD = 0.70$) ($F\,(1, 160) = 5.11$, $p < 0.01$). These trends suggest that LSCI training had its greatest impact on reducing the endorsement of family environment causes among female educators.

### *Reactions to Misbehavior*

Significant main effects were found for negative emotional reactions directed toward the self ($F\,(1, 160) = 25.18$, $p < 0.01$) and toward the child ($F\,(1, 160) = 33.02$, $p < 0.01$) with mean scores significantly lower for LSCI participants. LSCI participants reported that they were much less likely to respond to the misbehav-[illegible] the student with anxiety or stress, and they were much less likely to report [illegible]ted reactions like feeling angry at the child or feeling indifferent. On [illegible]nd, a significant main effect was found for the level of felt responsibil-

*Table 7: Analysis of Variance for LSCI and Comparison Participants (Main Effects Only)*

| Variable | LSCI Mean (*SD*) | Comparison Mean (*SD*) | *F* | Adjusted $R^2$ |
|---|---|---|---|---|
| Family Environment Causes | 3.09 (.525) | 3.52 (.793) | 14.02** | .136 |
| Child Factor Causes | 2.92 (.615) | 2.47 (.757) | 17.79** | .145 |
| Sex | *Female* *2.60 (.701)* | *Male* *2.94 (.680)* | *11.87*** | |
| Teacher Factor Causes | 3.17 (.623) | 2.59 (.849) | 24.84** | .123 |
| School Factor Causes | 3.15 (.527) | 2.72 (.817) | 17.08** | .08 |
| Negative Emotions Directed at Self | 1.91 (.639) | 2.59 (1.05) | 25.18** | .143 |
| Negative Emotions Directed at Child | 1.61 (.523) | 2.31 (.969) | 33.02** | .178 |
| Felt Responsible To Help | 4.31 (.648) | 3.70 (.950) | 21.15** | .119 |
| Self-Efficacy in Classroom Management | 4.99 (.465) | 4.95 (.478) | .120 | .00 |
| Frequency of Use of Crisis Management Skills | 3.38 (1.04) | 3.09 (1.18) | 2.73 | .00 |
| Comfort Working with Students in Crisis | 4.05 (.776) | 3.53 (.915) | 15.86** | .086 |
| % Positive Outcomes in Crisis Interventions | 73.69 (22.60) | 70.52 (21.54) | 1.09 | .00 |
| % Intervention Results in Referral | 19.46 (22.18) | 40.98 (31.71) | 20.40** | .137 |

* $p < 0.05$
** $p < 0.01$

ity to help the disruptive child ($F$ (1, 159) = 21.15, $p < 0.01$). The LSCI group felt a greater sense of responsibility to respond to the misbehavior of the student.

### *Self-Efficacy*

There were no statistically significant differences between groups on the self-efficacy scale. Comparison participants were just as likely as LSCI participants to feel confident in their ability to manage student misbehavior in the classroom.

*Crisis Intervention and Referrals.* Both groups reported that they use crisis management skills relatively frequently (no statistically significant differences between groups); however, a significant main effect ($F(1, 164) = 15.86, p < 0.01$) showed that LSCI participants felt more comfortable implementing their skills in crisis situations. At the same time, while both groups reported positive outcomes as a result of interventions with students in crisis (~70% of the time), the LSCI group was much less likely, on average, to refer students outside of the classroom (only 20% of the time compared to 40% of the time for the comparison group;) $F(1, 150) = 20.40, p < 0.01$.

## Focus Group Responses

*Impact on Beliefs of Those Trained.* During focus groups, LSCI-trained personnel were asked to share how implementation of LSCI had affected them, and two themes characterized those responses. First, educators reported that they were more willing to listen and provide encouragement to students: "I believe I can make a difference." They reported that they had become more tolerant, kind, gentle, and compassionate towards students, that they were more understanding and aware of students' needs, and that they were more patient and calm when discussing issues with students, avoiding overreaction and criticism. Second, they also reported that they were more reflective and open-minded toward students. The following participant had this to say about the change in attitudes and beliefs regarding disruptive students:

> It has helped me to reframe my thoughts as I approach student problems. It helps in providing a framework from which to begin instead of blindly asking questions in order to find out who's to "blame." This approach focuses more on getting at the root of a problem in order to help a student solve it.

## Beliefs That Were Challenged

LSCI participants noted that many strongly held beliefs about student problems and effective management strategies were challenged. The strongly held beliefs that were challenged included:

1. Punishment first; lock-step discipline; send the student to the office when they misbehave.
2. Schools *must* use traditional discipline strategies (e.g., suspension, detention, and expulsion) in response to misbehavior.
3. Intimidation of student by teachers to encourage appropriate behavior.

eld beliefs were substituted with the following beliefs and practices:

ng to the student rather than sending them to the principal's office.

2. Traditional detention has been replaced with other consequences.
3. Fewer "write-ups" and more flexibility in managing disruptive behavior.

*Impact on Students*

LSCI participants related many personal stories about how their different approach to student misbehavior impacted their relationships with students. Several themes characterized these stories. First, many stories emphasized the positive relationships that were created and that previously disruptive students had become their "buddies" or would often stop by the classroom/office "just to talk." This transformation in the teacher-student relationship occurred through a series of steps beginning with the teacher stopping and listening to the student's needs followed by more self-disclosure from the students (i.e., trust). One teacher noted, "I have several students who just 'hang out' in my room before and after school. This used to annoy me. Now I know that my room is a comfortable, safe place for them. They need this."

Second, school personnel commented on the transformations they had observed in student behavior both in and out of the classroom. For example, previously disruptive students were more able to control their temper, get along better with peers, be more respectful toward others, and accept responsibility. One teacher stated: "One student who has 'issues' at home and was on the path to failure has developed some level of trust in me and is succeeding academically in my classroom."

## Discussion

The purpose of this study was to more fully evaluate the efficacy of Life Space Crisis Intervention (LSCI) as a training tool for classroom teachers and other school personnel. Our goal was to evaluate both the process of implementation and the outcomes among educators. The goal of the process evaluation was to assess how educators implemented LSCI and adapted the skills to best meet the needs of all students. The goal of the outcomes evaluation was to assess the impact of LSCI training on the attitudes, beliefs, and behaviors of educators. More specifically, the goal was to examine causal beliefs about student misbehavior, negative emotional reactions to misbehavior, self-efficacy in classroom management, intent to intervene with student misbehavior, use of crisis intervention skills, and typical outcomes of crisis intervention (i.e., referral and teacher-student relationships). The results of this study suggest that training and participation in LSCI had a significant impact on these processes.

Results from the evaluation of LSCI implementation suggest that educators throughout the school system, not only special education teachers, were able to successfully use and implement LSCI with students. Mainstream classroom teachers not only intervened with student misbehavior, but they also acted as "counselors" and discussed personal and peer issues with students. In fact, educators who used LSCI spent a great deal of time with each student discussing one situation (between 22 and 35 minutes). That is a significant investment, an indication of the educator's commitment to the process. The results also indicate that educators who used LSCI saw little need to refer students outside of the classroom, an indication that they felt confident in their abilities to intervene. On the other hand, educators reported that they rarely completed all 6 steps of the LSCI process, on average completing the first three steps (see Table 5). However, the outcomes of Promoting Insight, Ongoing Discussion, and Resolution may reflect less formal ways of addressing Step 4 (Insight), Step 5 (New Tools), and Step 6 (Transfer of Training).

Results from the outcome evaluation show that those trained in LSCI were more likely to report child, school, and teacher causes for misbehavior and were less likely to adopt family-environment causes. That scores for only family-environment causal attributions were significantly lower, and not child causal attributions as we expected, is curious. It may be that LSCI participants evaluate family-environment causal attributions as less amenable to change than child factors. This is partially supported by the correlation results that showed family-environment attributions were significantly positively related to both self- and child-directed negative emotional reactions while the relationship with child attributions was significantly negative. On the other hand, causal attributions directed at teachers and school were beneficial because they were negatively related to negative emotional reactions directed at the child. Although speculative, the results appear to confirm the hypothesis that when adults attribute causes for misbehavior to characteristics that they see as unchangeable (either in the child or in the family), they may be more likely to respond with frustration, resentment, and negative disciplinary actions (Hastings & Brown, 2002).

Additionally, differences between LSCI trained and untrained educators showed that LSCI participants were less likely to report negative emotional reactions, either directed at the self or the child. It may be that this difference in the likelihood to respond with negative emotions plays a pivotal role in shaping the teacher-student relationship (Montague & Rinaldi, 2001). Focus group responses confirm the importance of positive emotional responses on improvements in the teacher-student relationship, beginning with the simple step of stopping and listening to the student's needs. Educators reported that they had become more tolerant, patient, and compassionate towards students and were more willing to listen and less willing to criticize. These responses lead to a more positive teacher-student relationship and improved behavior within the classroom.

The results also showed that LSCI educators were more likely to feel comfortable using their crisis intervention skills with students. However, the higher level of comfort was not generalized to self-efficacy in classroom management. This may be due to differences in the measurement of each construct. Classroom management self-efficacy was measured using a questionnaire that assessed the perceived ability of educators to maintain order in the *classroom* (Brouwers & Tomic, 2001); whereas, the frequency of use of crisis intervention (or LSCI) skills was assessed with a single question that focused on implementation of specific skills with *students* in crisis.

Finally, LSCI educators were less likely to report referring a student out of the classroom (20% of the time compared to 40% of the time for untrained educators). This is important given that referrals may result in students falling behind in their classes. According to the correlation results, educators who endorsed family environment causes for a student's disruptive behavior and who experienced negative emotions directed at the student were more likely to refer the student outside of the classroom. This suggests that decisions to refer a student outside of the classroom are influenced by both the attributions and the emotions of the educator, with LSCI educators much less likely to endorse family environment causal beliefs or report experiencing negative emotions. This was mirrored in focus group responses when LSCI educators reported that their beliefs about "dealing with problem students" shifted from a focus on punishment to a focus on cooperation. Traditional disciplinary beliefs including detention, suspension, and expulsion were substituted with more cooperative beliefs that focused on prevention and natural consequences.

Based on these findings, it appears that LSCI is an effective intervention for students in crisis. However, the process evaluation results suggest a few necessary modifications. A useful model for guiding these modifications is offered by Long, Fecser and Wood (2001) in their description of an LSCI "safe and reclaiming school." Similar to the "pyramid of interventions" that is being adopted in school districts across the U.S., a safe and reclaiming school would distinguish between the needs of all students (base of pyramid), the needs of at-risk or occasionally involved students (middle of pyramid), and the needs of high-risk students (top of pyramid) (Blankstein, 2004). For Long, Fecser and Wood (2001), the three levels of student needs could be addressed by three levels of training. Primary prevention training would begin with training all school employees on the basic concepts and skills of creating a positive and predictable school environment and managing their own emotional reactions towards student misbehavior. The second level of training in early intervention skills would be taught to all classroom teachers and support staff and teach more specific skills for connecting with and supporting students who are experiencing difficulties (e.g., the first 3 steps of the LSCI process). Finally, LSCI (or advanced reclaiming strategies) would be taught to members of the *crisis reclaiming team,* composed of principals, guidance counselors, and special education teachers. The reclaiming team is called upon when initial efforts at crisis intervention are unsuccessful.

### *Limitations and Strengths*

Several limitations to this study warrant caution when interpreting the results. First, the primary measurement tool used in the process evaluation, the LSCI report, was developed for use in this study and has not been validated in other studies (however, see Naslund, 1987). Additionally, the educators who completed the LSCI reports may have been a selective group of educators who were more highly motivated to succeed with LSCI. They may have offered more socially desirable responses on the LSCI reports or only selectively submitted reports that showed positive outcomes. However, if social desirability was an issue, one would have expected a greater number of reports submitted with more LSCI steps completed and more outcomes seeking resolution.

For the outcome evaluation, the inability to randomly assign educators to groups could not guarantee that the groups were similar. It may be LSCI participants volunteered to participate in the training and research because the values/beliefs that were taught were consistent with existing beliefs (Tillema, 1995). Likewise, the participants may have differed in other ways that could not be controlled for in this study; although years of experience was included as a covariate and a post-test only design does control for testing effects within the comparision group. Finally, the child-directed emotional reactions scale demonstrated poor reliability. Given the sensitivity of estimates of internal consistency to sample size and the number of scale items, the poor estimate may reflect greater variability in responses among the LSCI group.

Appreciating these limitations, the strengths of this study included the comprehensive evaluation of both the process and outcome of LSCI training on educators including their cognitive, emotional, and behavioral responses to the disruptive behavior of students. It is clear from past research that the relationship between attributions and beliefs about the reasons for student misbehavior and emotional and behavioral responses of educators was a key component to successful implementation of LSCI (Alvarez, 2007; Hastings & Brown, 2002; Hughes et al., 1993; Poulou & Norwich, 2000). An additional strength of this study was that it was conducted on a program that was initiated within the local school district. One of the difficulties in large-scale rigorous experimental studies of intervention programs is that the program often fails to survive once the grant funding is removed (Greenberg, 2004). This study was conducted on a program that was initiated by the local school district and could be realistically sustained over time. This type of research is important because it evaluates whether programs that are implemented in "real world" settings can be effective.

## Conclusions

LSCI is an intensive strengths-based program that not only meets the needs of students in crisis, but it also offers a practical set of skills that can be used with all students (Forthun et al., 2006). Previous research has shown that experienced classroom teachers generally become more punitive in their interactions with students (Woolfolk & Hoy, 1990), and it is more difficult to change beliefs and behaviors once existing beliefs and behaviors have become established (Tillema, 1995). The results of this study are remarkable because training in LSCI appeared to change the educator's style of interacting with students. An additional implication of this study is the importance of evaluating the emotional, cognitive, and behavioral responses of educators because it is critical that professional training change the way educators think and feel about students and their role as educators if behavior change is to be successful. This knowledge could not only lead to a better understanding of how to ultimately change educators' responses to students in crisis but also how to design and implement successful crisis intervention training programs.

## Acknowledgments

The authors would like to gratefully acknowledge the financial assistance of the Pennsylvania Department of Education, Division of Student and Safe Schools Services in supporting the implementation and evaluation of Life Space Crisis Intervention. We would especially like to thank Myrna Delgado, Division Chief, for her continued encouragement in this evaluation project.

## References

Adalbjarnardottir, S., & Selman, R. L. (1997). "I feel I have received a new vision": An analysis of teachers' professional development as they work with students on interpersonal issues. *Teaching and Teacher Education, 13*(4), 409–428.

Alvarez, H. K. (2007). The impact of teacher preparation on responses to student aggression in the classroom. *Teaching and Teacher Education, 23*(7), 1113–1126.

Blankstein, A. M. (2004). *Failure is not an option: Six principles that guide student achievement in high-performing schools.* Thousand Oaks, CA: Corwin Press.

Brendtro, L. K., Ness, A., & Mitchell, M. (2002). No disposable kids. *Behavioral Disorders, 27*(4), 423–424.

Brendtro, L. K., & Shahbazian, M. (2004). *Troubled children and youth: Turning problems into opportunities* (1st ed.). Champaign, IL: Research Press.

Brouwers, A., & Tomic, W. (2001). The factorial validity of scores on the teacher interpersonal self-efficacy scale. *Educational and Psychological Measurement, 61*(3), 433–445.

Brouwers, A., Tomic, W., & Stijnen, S. (2002). A confirmatory factor analysis of scores on the teacher efficacy scale. *Swiss Journal of Psychology/Schweizerische Zeitschrift für Psychologie/Revue Suisse De Psychologie, 61*(4), 211–219.

Dawson, C. A. (2003). A study on the effectiveness of life space crisis intervention for students identified with emotional disturbances. *Reclaiming Children and Youth, 11*(4), 223–230.

DeMagistris, R. J., & Imber, S. C. (1980). The effects of life space interviewing on academic and social performance of behaviorally disordered children. *Behavioral Disorders, 6,* 12–25.
Farrell, P., & Tsakalidou, K. (1999). Recent trends in the re-integration of pupils with emotional and behavioural difficulties in the United Kingdom. *School Psychology International, 20*(4), 323–337.
Forthun, L.F., & McCombie, J.W. (unpublished). The impact of Life Space Crisis Intervention (LSCI) on educators' cognitive, emotional, and behavioral reactions to students in crisis.
Forthun, L.F., McCombie, J. W., & Freado, M. (2006). A study of LSCI in a school setting. *Reclaiming Children and Youth: The Journal of Strength-Based Interventions, 15,* 95–102.
Forthun, L.F., Payne, C., & McCombie, J.W. (2009). LSCI in a school setting: Final results. *Reclaiming Children and Youth: The Journal of Strength-Based Interventions, 18,* 51–57.
Greenberg, M. T. (2004). Current and future challenges in school-based prevention: The researcher perspective. *Prevention Science, 5*(1), 5–13.
Grskovic, J. A., & Goetze, H. (2005). An evaluation of the effects of life space crisis intervention on the challenging behavior of individual students. *Reclaiming Children and Youth: The Journal of Strength-Based Interventions, 13*(4), 231.
Hastings, R. P., & Brown, T. (2002). Behavioural knowledge, causal beliefs and self-efficacy as predictors of special educators' emotional reactions to challenging behaviours. *Journal of Intellectual Disability Research, 46*(2), 144–150.
Hoy, A.W., & Weinstein, C.S. (2006). Student and teacher perspectives on classroom management. In C.M. Evertson & C.S. Weinstein (Eds.), *Handbook of classroom management: Research, practice, and contemporary issues* (pp. 181–219). Mahwah, NJ: Lawrence Erlbaum Assoc.
Hughes, J. N., Barker, D., Kemenoff, S., & Hart, M. (1993). Problem ownership, causal attributions, and self-efficacy as predictors of teachers' referral decisions. *Journal of Educational & Psychological Consultation, 4*(4), 369–384.
Landrum, T., Katsiyannis, A., & Archwamety, T. (2004). An analysis of placement and exit patterns of students with emotional or behavioral disorders. *Behavioral Disorders, 29*(2), 140–153.
Lewis, L., Parsad, B., Carey, N., Bartfai, N., Farris, E., & Smerdon, B. (1999). *Teacher quality: A report on the preparation and qualifications of public school teachers. statistical analysis report* No. NCES-1999–080. Retrieved: http://nces.ed.gov/pubsearch/index.html
Long, N. J., Fecser, F. A., & Wood, M. M. (2001). *Life space crisis intervention: Talking with students in conflict* (2nd ed.). Austin, TX: Pro-Ed.
Long, N. J., Morse, W.C., Fecser, R.A., & Newman, R.G. (2007). *Conflict in the classroom: Positive staff support for troubled students* (6th ed.). Austin, TX: Pro-Ed.
Merrett, F., & Wheldall, K. (1993). How do teachers learn to manage classroom behaviour? A study of teachers' opinions about their initial training with special reference to classroom behavior management. *Educational Studies, 19*(1), 91–106.
Montague, M., & Rinaldi, C. (2001). Classroom dynamics and children at risk: A followup. *Learning Disability Quarterly, 24*(2), 75–83.
Naslund, S. R. (1987). Life space interviewing: A psychoeducational intervention model for teaching pupil insights and measuring program effectiveness. *Pointer, 31*(2), 12–15.
Parsad, B., Lewis, L., & Farris, E. (2001). *Teacher preparation and professional development: 2000. E.D. tabs* No. NCES2001–088. Retrieved: http://www.nces.ed.gov
Poulou, M., & Norwich, B. (2000). Teachers' causal attributions, cognitive, emotional and behavioural responses to students with emotional and behavioural difficulties. *British Journal of Educational Psychology, 70*(4), 559–581.
Poulou, M., & Norwich, B. (2002). Cognitive, emotional and behavioural responses to students with emotional and behavioural difficulties: A model of decision-making. *British Educational Research Journal, 28*(1), 111–138.
Shores, R. E., & Wehby, J. H. (1999). Analyzing the classroom social behavior of students with EBD. *Journal of Emotional and Behavioral Disorders, 7*(4), 194–199.
Stein, M. K., & Wang, M. C. (1988). Teacher development and school improvement: The process of teacher change. *Teaching and Teacher Education, 4*(2), 171–187.

Tillema, H. H. (1995). Changing the professional knowledge and beliefs of teachers: A training study. *Learning and Instruction, 5*(4), 291–318.

Woolfolk, A. E., & Hoy, W. K. (1990). Prospective teachers' sense of efficacy and beliefs about control. *Journal of Educational Psychology, 82*(1), 81–91.

|| NINETEEN

# Transformative Educational Spaces

## *Black Youth and Education in the Twenty-First Century*

Shanesha R. F. Brooks-Tatum

> Every generation confronts the task of choosing its past. Inheritances are chosen as much as they are passed on. The past depends less on 'what happened then' than on the desires and discontents of the present. Strivings and failures shape the stories we tell. What we recall has as much to do with the terrible things we hope to avoid as with the good life for which we yearn. But when does one decide to stop looking to the past and instead conceive of a new order?
>
> —Saidiya Hartman[1]

Recent study results by Brandeis University's Institute for Assets and Social Policy report that the wealth gap between White and African American families has grown more than four times over one generation, from $20,000 in 1984 to $95,000 in 2007 (Schapiro, Meschede, & Sullivan, 2010). According to this study, in 1984 the White–African American wealth gap was equivalent to less than three years' tuition for one child to attend a public university. In 2007, the wealth gap was the equivalent of four years' full tuition for two children to attend a four-year public university and for one child to attend a public medical school. While the extremity of the wealth gap is disheartening and in need of more media, research, and political engagement, it is fitting that the study's researchers utilize the cost of higher education as a financial proxy for the wealth gap. Historically and contemporarily, educational attainment has been a major avenue through which African Americans improve their socioeconomic statuses. However, this is a time when the wealth gap has been exacerbated by increased tuition costs being met with cuts in financial aid; the lack of access to competitive secondary and post-secondary institutions and subsequent enrollment in for-profit educational institutions; and the overrepresentation of Black students in underresourced schools, leading to students' underpreparation for college post-graduation. These immense challenges illuminate the ongoing imperative to create and fortify what I call *transformative educational* spaces that exist outside of traditional, institutionalized educational tracks. As students of color, and African American students in particular, face heightened crises in the public and private educational systems, the added socioeconomic burden of the wealth gap makes it increasingly difficult for African Americans to leverage monetary and social resources needed to achieve quality education.

While this chapter is concerned with these larger, troubling trends in education as it relates to Black[2] students in underserved communities, I chiefly focus on exploring the challenges and opportunities in creating and maintaining transformative educational spaces for Black youth in an era that is riddled with educational and financial crises. These transformative spaces include afterschool art programs, performance groups, Saturday academies, and other venues through which educators and youth-investors recognize and respond to the need to rethink and recenter youth education as a collective process of creating change and transformation for all who are involved. In the spirit of Paulo Freire's *Pedagogy of the Oppressed*,[3] these transformative[4] and often non-institutionalized spaces center students' intellectual interests and life experiences even while facilitators are forced to become especially resourceful during challenging economic times. Rather than deeming these often noninstitutionalized and non-mainstream educational spaces as "alternative" or "supplementary," I choose to call them *transformative* so as not to define them by their marginalization in some educational spaces, but rather by the research and experiential outcomes for the student and instructor participants in such spaces. These outcomes communicate and suggest intense social, communal, and individual transformations that are in no way alternative or supplementary for those involved.

Despite the lack of opportunities for educational attainment for Black youth, these educators are focused on imagining the world otherwise. They center youth's own subject positions and interests in educational lessons and activities, while also pushing them to enhance and further develop their critical thinking skills as they relate to their areas of study. The educators that I will discuss in this chapter see themselves as teacher-learners, implicated in the process of learning and critical engagement just as much as the students. This chapter proceeds by outlining implications of what it will mean for educating Black youth who are living and coming of age in the Obama era. I discuss the idea of a postracial America in relationship to Black youth education. Then I turn to a brief discussion of the historical imperative for transformative educational spaces in the context of Black youth and adult education in the United States, drawing on archival research and secondary sources. This section is followed by a discussion of some key transformative educational spaces (TES) serving Black youth in the United States, including BlackLight in Newark, New Jersey; Saving Our Lives, Hear Our Truths (SOLHOT) in Urbana, Illinois; and Detroit Summer in Detroit, Michigan. While I will then focus most intently on my experiences with Living the Arts, an arts-based program I cocreated in Detroit, Michigan, I discuss and reference these other programs as TES that continue in the African American educational activist tradition of creating nontraditional contexts for creative sharing and learning. These spaces often exist outside of, or alongside, institutionalized educational spaces, such as those in schools and colleges. In the age of Obama, in a purported postracial society where racial discrimination is often covert and subtle, there is a need for continual cultivation of these transformative educational spaces even while educators, parents, and community workers continue their grassroots efforts to transform mainstream educational systems and institutions.

## A Postracial America

To live in a postrace America would mean not only that race would be of no tangible consequence, but also that distinctions based on race would no longer exist. While some pundits may claim that race no longer matters and that racial distinctions are moot, authors such as Tim Wise (2010), William Jelani Cobb (2009), and Beverly Guy-Sheftall and Johnnetta Betsch Cole (2010) critique the concept of a postrace America, a concept that, at its core, relies on and utilizes Barack Obama's successful presidential election as evidence for postraciality. These and other authors illustrate that while socioeconomic and educational gains have been made for African Americans, Blacks occupy a precarious position due to their "overrepresentation in contexts of social misery" (Hill, 2010, para. 6). When compared to the larger society, while there are gains, President Obama's success is the exception to the rule.

Although race is a socially constructed paradigm, and racial distinctions are consequences of the hegemonic nature of such pervasive paradigms, race still matters for African Americans, and particularly for Black youth who often encounter obstacles to educational success and the ability to enhance their social positions in life. Because race still matters and because America continues to operate on racialized paradigms, we must continue to forge new knowledge about how these paradigms affect and influence the lives of young people. Furthermore, we must continue to create spaces that support youth in critically engaging with and advancing beyond the stigmatizations of Blackness in the twenty-first century. Historically, TES have been crucial in interrupting, interrogating, and altering if not transforming racial, class, and gender paradigms that shape societies. These transformative educational spaces not only worked toward educating Black youth and adults, but also questioned facts, histories, and protocols that worked to marginalize and, in some cases, misrepresent Black history, life, and culture. These TES illustrate the important function of educational spaces in disrupting paradigms, valuing students' and instructors' backgrounds and experiences, and fostering the development of critical thinking and critical analysis needed to unpack and challenge these paradigms.

## A Historical Imperative

As access to mainstream education continues to decrease for Black youth, educators must rethink education as being a communal effort. As educators work with community leaders, parents, and youth groups, the continual need to formulate and fortify transformative spaces of education that have historically served Black people in the United States will be realized. Nontraditional educational organizations, such as the Chautauqua Circle in Atlanta, Georgia, created spaces where Black women who did not have access to formal education systems could create and engage in lessons to teach each other.[5] The Chautauqua Circle in Atlanta, part of the Chautauqua adult education movement, met monthly in the late-nineteenth and twentieth centuries, reading key texts such as W. E. B. DuBois's *The Souls of Black Folk* (2005 [1903]) upon its release in 1903, and discussing controversial ideas surrounding Black racial uplift, the history and cultures of West Africa, and gender dynamics in Black communities. The Chautauqua Circle also met to discuss issues concerning world travel and Black diasporic communities outside of the United States.

Clubs and programs for youth in Black churches also addressed the need for educational spaces and opportunities from a religious or moral perspective. While many Black churches across several denominations are still working to provide key educational experiences for youth today, they stem from the efforts educators made in Sunday Schools, in Vacation Bible Schools, and in trade programs that provided needed educational outlets for their membership and communities.[6] During the Black civil rights and Black power movements, community theaters and community centers were key sites for education and community empowerment. They often served as the invisible forces behind the rallies, marches, and other forms of public protest and agitation. Although the politics that inform these movements diverge even as they overlap, the movements' goals coincided in their similar historical imperative to take seriously the need to educate Black youth and adults first and foremost. Education was a central component of racial uplift, not only in instances where Blacks aspired to racially assimilate or acculturate, but also in cases of Black radical, separatist thought; Black feminism; and in countless social and political movements.

While community leaders, educators, parents, youth, and so many others are working together to make formal education more accessible and relevant to Black youth, there are real factors that are decreasing the probability of Blacks gaining a quality primary and secondary education and going on to achieve a college degree. Decreased access to academia and quality education and the subtler racist tenor of a so-called postracial society confound the experiences of Black youth seeking a way out of their socioeconomic realities. At the same time that educators and youth-investors are actively working to transform the educational system for Black youth, those invested in the future *of* Black youth must simultaneously identify and cultivate transformative educational spaces *for* Black youth. This historical imperative persists today, as many scholars and community leaders have written volumes on the ruptured nature of the educational system, citing the structure as outmoded, condescending, stifling, and even crippling.[7] While some changes to the system will be long term and while some scholars and educational policy pundits believe that the change will be slow coming or perhaps not possible, youth continue to matriculate through this largely fractured and mangled system, if they do not drop out or if they are not pushed out first. The ongoing efforts toward the long-term change of the American educational system and of institutions within this system must be matched by grassroots efforts to meet youth where they are right now, working with and for them with genuine concern for their well-being and for their life chances in a society that seems to lack many of the support structures necessary to ensure their success.

## Transformative Educational Spaces Serving Black Youth

Transformative educational spaces are often born as a result of a critical juncture in one's work with a community program or organization. BlackLight is an arts-based social justice project that emerged from Aimee Cox's work in Fresh Start, a shelter and transitional living program serving primarily young women in Detroit. After a protest coordinated by the shelter's residents, the young women in Fresh Start formed a dance and creative writing group, which was the impetus for the creation of BlackLight, a performance activism group that gave the women residents a creative space for exploring their stigmatization in larger society, and the possibilities that existed for them to question and ultimately change their own realities. Now located at three sites (one co-ed) in Newark, New Jersey, BlackLight engages students' interests and offers training in music, dance, and theater to question labels often placed on youth, such as "poor," "at-risk" and "high school dropout" (Cox, 2009, p. 55). Instead of magnifying these labels for so-called "troubled" youth, BlackLight privileges students' agency and their ability to create conceptions of their own identities in performing who they are.

BlackLight developed three years after the protests as an institutionalized part of Fresh Start, and Cox, who was working at the shelter at the time, was asked by some of the young women to participate. Now as a tenure-track professor at Rutgers University, Newark, and a former dancer with Alvin Ailey II, Cox brought both theory and practice with her into the workshop space, helping to facilitate students' use of "dance, poetry, and oral history as artistic methodologies through which they could address inequities that impact the communities in which they locate themselves based on shared geography and identity politics" (Cox, 2009, p. 58).

SOLHOT, or Saving Our Lives, Hear Our Truths, is also an activist-oriented, transformative educational space "dedicated to the celebration of Black girlhood in all of its complexity," created by Ruth Nicole Brown, assistant professor of gender and women's studies and educational policy studies departments at the University of Illinois at Urbana-Champaign. In her book *Black Girlhood Celebration: Toward a Feminist Hip-Hop Pedagogy* (2008), Brown illustrates what created the possibilities and the necessity for a space such as SOLHOT: "The concept of SOLHOT was born out of disturbing research that reported that girls, particularly adolescents, were at-risk and suffering from societal pressures instrumental in the development of low self esteem, loss of voice, and self-inflicted harmful behaviors" (Brown, 2008, p. xiii). SOLHOT was also a result of Brown's direct participation in a "girl empowerment program" aimed to serve all girls, yet Brown observed that the program also worked in ways that marginalized Black girls.

SOLHOT, like BlackLight, uses performance-based methods to engage participants. The program is now active in four sites throughout central Illinois, and for the past few years its members have performed several plays or ethnodramas.[8] One was titled "The Rhythm, the Rhyme, and the Reason" and the other was "Check-In," which create audience and community dialogue around the central dichotomy that Brown takes issue with in her book—two competing discourses or schools of thought about girlhood that she calls "Reviving Ophelia" and "Girl Power." These plays or ethnodramas engage these discourses from the perspective of Black girls' lived experiences as articulated in the practice of doing SOLHOT.

Recently, SOLHOT has begun several collaborations with local middle and high schools at the request of students' parents, who actively wanted SOLHOT to be a part of their children's formal education. From its beginning, SOLHOT has existed in and outside of educational institutions as a space for young women of a variety of ages to engage and critique paradigms that stigmatize them and their identities as young Black women. Similar to BlackLight, SOLHOT's aim is to recreate narratives of Black girlhood, as it is "a space where Black women and girls come together to try and be positive, to try new things, to relate to each other in ways that challenge the status quo, to work together" (Brown, 2008, p. 8). In the cases of BlackLight and SOLHOT,[9] transformative educational spaces are nurtured and facilitated on the individual or personal level, as well as the communal and, in some cases, regional and national levels.[10] Through touring performances, showcases, weekly workshops, and conference presentations the women and girls within these projects create a space where education is personal, political, and ongoing outside of the classroom. It is a space where one transforms conceptions and misconceptions of oneself and others.

Both Cox and Brown were heavily influenced by the work of Detroit Summer, a forerunner of BlackLight, SOLHOT, and other transformative educational spaces. Detroit Summer is "a multi-racial, inter-generational collective in Detroit, working to transform ourselves and our communities by confronting the problems we face with creativity and critical thinking. We currently organize youth-led media arts projects and community-wide potlucks, speak-outs and parties" (detroitsummer.org, para. 14). Detroit Summer (DS) is a youth-led, youth-oriented organization that began in 1992 by creating murals and community gardens all over the Detroit metropolis. In 2006, DS created a hip-hop audio documentary, *Rising Up from the Ashes: Chronicles of a Drop Out*, that featured interviews that youth conducted with students, teachers, and administrators to uncover the reasons why students were dropping out at a higher rate. They have since utilized the hip-hop audio documentary CD, which also contains original poetry, hip-hop songs, and beats, to create opportunities for dialogue and problem-solving (detroitsummer.org). Detroit Summer has been instrumental in creating the coalitions and networks necessary for forging such creative spaces, especially through their 2010 Live Arts Media Project (LAMP), which showcases the transformative work being done in Detroit and is centrally concerned with the plight of youth in Detroit and with what youth are doing to transform their lived realities and to impact Detroit as part of the global economy.

## Living the Arts

In summer 2008, I had the fortunate opportunity to cocreate a transformative educational space in Detroit titled Living the Arts. As a second-year doctoral student, I had endeavored to create this program with assistance from grant funding from Arts of Citizenship.[11] As I was in the process of preparing my application for funding, I was notified that the grant program had been discontinued for the coming academic year. After a two-year hiatus, Arts of Citizenship programming and grants were reinstituted on the University of Michigan, Ann Arbor campus, but the organization no longer offered graduate student grants, only faculty grants. Therefore, I was encouraged to partner with a faculty member on campus, Professor Lori L. Brooks, musician and assistant professor at the University of Michigan, Ann Arbor; and Nandi Comer, poet and, at the time, the community projects coordinator for InsideOut Literary Arts Project, a nonprofit organization in Detroit. We codeveloped an interactive, workshop-based program for high school students that centered youth in their exploration of the historical and contemporary connections between music, poetry, and performance in Black culture.

This program ran from fall 2008 to spring 2009 and was generously funded by Arts of Citizenship, with support from the Center for Afroamerican and African Studies and the Program in American Culture at the University of Michigan, Ann Arbor. Professor Brooks and I worked with approximately 15 youth on the East Side of Detroit twice a month, while Comer participated in a few of our sessions and assisted with the planning and logistics of our meetings in her role as the community projects coordinator. Our program was embedded in the InsideOut Literary Arts Project's afterschool poetry program, Citywide Poets, which met weekly with two instructors.

The Living the Arts Program endeavored to return to the ethic of arts and literature as "tools for living."[12] Historically, the arts in Black communities have been embedded in social practice—a site of anti-racist politics as well as a space for personal intellectual growth. Our project was explicitly and intentionally connected to this Black arts tradition. Moreover, the project was invested in exploring how identities and identity categories, such as race, gender, class, and religion, are performed. We were also invested in exploring performers as public intellectuals engaging in important political and cultural work for understanding our world. Our project endeavored to do the following: (1) reinvigorate the arts as a site of politics and positive identity formation for ourselves and for high school students; (2) reinforce the historical link between cultural production and public intellectual work while bringing the university back into the public space of non-university collaborators; and, finally, (3) demonstrate the unique and fertile historical relationship[13] between the arts and leadership in Black communities.[14] Our explicit purpose was to facilitate workshops in which we focused on African American history and politics and how they manifested creatively, overtly, and subtly in music, poetry, and theatrical performance. We set out to explore the debate about art for art's sake versus art as a political, racial, uplifting tool, so that students could explore how they themselves fit into this debate, and also to look at the delimiting effects of such dichotomous views of art and politics. Ultimately, though, we endeavored to facilitate a transformative educational space that nurtured positive self-development and critical identity formation.

Throughout the year we facilitated workshops on topics such as Erykah Badu's connection to the Black blues tradition and twenty-first century Black migration; Langston Hughes's blues and jazz poetry paired with a contemporary live performance of his *Ask Your Mama: 12 Moods for Jazz* by a jazz band; an African drumming and poetry session; and Sonia Sanchez's radical, feminist poetry and its use of music and poignant performance techniques in communing with her audiences. As InsideOut's instructive focus was on honing students' poetic craft on the "page" as well as the "stage," in Living the Arts we made sure to focus on teaching writing as well as performance techniques; students often performed the pieces that they worked on during our sessions and continued working on them outside of our meeting times. Moreover, students often taught the facilitators and their peers their own techniques for preparing for a performance, which included meditation, intense practice, and entering one's "performative persona."

The outcomes of the program consisted of an end-of-the-year poetry performance showcase held at the University of Michigan Detroit Center, which brought together students from InsideOut's three other sites in Detroit. Additionally, some of the students' poetry was published in a poetry anthology released annually by InsideOut. Students from our particular site and from the other three sites all participated in a spring term visit to the University of Michigan. Lorna Goodison, University of Michigan professor and award-winning poet and novelist, performed some of her poems and gave a talk on her experiences as a poet and the importance honing one's craft. In addition, she generously sponsored a poetry contest, in which the authors of the top three poems were awarded a monetary prize. Professor Brooks's students from her lower-division African American Studies course also attended the session. Most of Brooks's students were African American, and they participated in an informal discussion about college life with the high school students from InsideOut–Living the Arts. They discussed their transition to college, as well as the contrast between what they had expected and what they experienced as students at the University of Michigan, giving opportunities for the high school students to ask questions. This was an opportunity for informal mentoring and creating connections, as many of Brooks's students were also from Detroit or the Detroit metro area.

In the qualitative survey that we conducted with the students, a majority of them stated that InsideOut–Living the Arts was their only creative and performative outlet. In some ways, the hours we shared together were sacred spaces and moments of personal and professional transformation. Our sessions offered a space where students did not have to feel like they were the only poets and performers in their schools. As one student stated, "This is a place where I don't have to feel like a nerd or 'weird.'" As a poet myself, in addition to facilitating these activities, I also reveled in the creative space that we cocreated and worked inside of. I participated in many of the poetry activities along with the students, such as writing a blues poem, and performed one of my poems at our end-of-the-year showcase at the students' request. As a graduate student coming from a music and poetry background, I was reinvigorated by a space of creativity where there were no absolutes, no all-rights and all-wrongs in responses. It was a very much welcomed space for all participants as we cherished this outlet to bring forth our creative selves.

There is no program or project, however, without its logistical and structural challenges. As we decided to implement this program in Detroit, getting to and from Detroit each late afternoon or evening for our sessions, during what was essentially rush hour traffic, proved to be a feat in itself. Working to be on the same page with the regular InsideOut instructors and with each other proved difficult at times, exacerbated by time constraints and the nearly one-hour commuting distance between us. As we were all working adults with jobs outside of the program (with the exception of Ms. Comer), we had demanding schedules that required significant planning to make sure our sessions came through. Once we were able to get into the rhythm of the program, we decided to reapply for funding, only to be faced with several obstacles. One member of our team was advised by senior advisors to immediately stop working with the program. Another member of our team was temporarily laid off, took another job, and subsequently enrolled in an M.F.A./M.A. program. Still another member of our team eventually accepted a new job outside of the state.

Considering the state of the economy at the time, it is interesting to note that all of the challenges to the continuation of the program concerned members' "day jobs." Unfortunately, these challenges were too great for the budding program to endure; given our small team and the ongoing schedule demands, there was neither the time nor the resources to connect with the larger and surrounding Detroit community on a deeper level. This, I believe, would have been necessary in order to build grassroots infrastructure so that the program could persist, even if in a new form, despite some key members' absence. In addition, due to these unforeseen challenges, two major goals—the co-authorship of a scholarly article on the students' experiences in the program by myself, Dr. Brooks, and Ms. Comer, and presenting at key conferences and events in Detroit and in other cities—have not yet come to fruition.

Community-based, transformative educational endeavors are even more susceptible to the whims of funding organizations and to other individuals' time and work demands. In addition, academics continue to struggle with justifying as legitimate their community-based teaching and scholarship to their departments and schools, when it is often seen as service work or as a distraction from one's "more important" work. Regardless of these formidable obstacles, academics, community leaders, educators, and other individuals have a historical and ongoing imperative to seek out, create, and fortify transformative spaces of education for the sake of helping to secure the futures of Black youth.

## Lessons Learned

At times, TES program facilitators are forced to do what they can with what they have. But under more ideal circumstances, I would have liked to put more planning and community engagement work into the development of the program. Brooks, Comer, and I had only a few weeks to get our proposal together during the late spring and early summer. Under ideal circumstances, I would have liked to have consulted with the students and community members first to explore what they wanted to learn, and to learn more about their backgrounds in poetry and music. I would have liked to have spent more time in Detroit to understand the needs and cultural/social dynamics in more depth. Although we learned this along the way through getting to know the students individually, it would have been profitable to have an informal focus group with interested students to gauge their level of interest and to learn what topics they would be interested in exploring.

However, because students already had a set syllabus for participating in the activities of their site during the weeks we were not there, we found ways for fitting our programmatic themes and ideas into the structure, rather than planning it all with the regular weekly instructors from the very beginning. Despite these challenges, we learned how to be resourceful, how to "make do" or work with what we had. In my work as a creator of transformative spaces for youth, I would like to have been even more resourceful in utilizing the community and community members as partners in this project, and in engaging with the students' parents as integral figures in their children's lives. Only in this way do we truly cocreate a grassroots program that stems from centering youth, their needs, and their communities.

Through keeping a journal early on in the program, I learned the value of continual reflection on and revision of one's process, and believe that TES creators and facilitators should actively reflect on their experiences by exploring some or all of the following questions:

1. Planning: To what degree are the youth and other community members involved in the planning process? How can the program be cocreated and potentially cofacilitated by the youth themselves?
2. Scholarship: For graduate students and/or faculty members at an academic institution, how might these experiences change our expectations of scholarship and the way we teach and what we teach? How might our learning experiences and those of our students be more fully integrated in and inform the books, articles, and edited volumes that we produce?
3. Youth involvement and feedback: To what degree are the students involved in the program or project? What is their feedback on the sessions thus far?
4. What we bring: What particular biases, fears, hopes, and expectations do we bring to the planning and implementation of these programs? How do we plan to deal with them productively?
5. Outcomes: What kinds of work and programmatic outcomes are realistic given the schedule constraints of team members?
6. Communities and partnership: How might we connect to other individuals doing similar work? What is the role of the community in our

work? How does each of the facilitators define "partnership," and what do we expect from a partner in action?

7. Language: What "linguistic experiments" must we undergo to find the proper language to translate our work from one social space to another (for example, from the community to the academy and vice versa, from the church to "the streets" and vice versa, and so on)?
8. Longevity: What are some of the different instantiations and "lives" that our program or project can manifest in? Given its current state, how may it best serve the communities that we are partnering with? What are the needed resources and members so as to keep the program alive and relevant?

Answering these questions for oneself and in discussion with the other key planners and facilitators is vital during the initial planning stages, during the duration of the program, and during moments where intense reflection is required, such as for grant funding applications and for activity reports sent to one's job or institution, partnering organizations, and to individual stakeholders. Exploring and isolating facilitators' expectations, needs, and desires from the students' needs is important in order to insure that the students' needs are indeed being met foremost.

## Outcomes from Living the Arts: Student Survey Responses

After the end-of-year poetry showcase, we conducted a survey of the students in the program to gauge their experiences and to see what sessions stood out the most to them. All of the students were African American high school students from the Detroit metro area. Here are some of their written responses:

> "I've actually listened to the song 'Afro' [by Erykah Badu] over and over and used it in a poem." (Myisha)[15]
>
> [I learned] "how to incorporate music into poetry." (Shayla)
>
> "Poetry and music [are] deeper than I have ever known." (Jamal)
>
> "[Living the Arts] has shown me different techniques that I can use. But I usually think too hard on these though. . . . I'm a vocal major at school, so I identified with music better." (Myisha)
>
> "I think everything was okay; no change needed!" (Patrice)
>
> "Citywide Poets (InsideOut) has given me inspiration to write more poems. And as a performer, lots of tips and suggestions that I barely use! (unfortunately)." (Patrice)

> "It has brought me out of my shell." (Alicia)
>
> "It has taught me to be a better performer since I'm more informed about what I do." (Tiffany)
>
> "The Living the Arts sessions affected me greatly. My writing is even more music oriented because of the program. . . . It has helped me astonishingly! I feel like next year I'll be near my climax as a writer as well as a performer." (Robert)

Overall, these responses indicate students' positive experiences, including artistic inspiration, new writing and performance techniques, and transformed perspectives on poetry, music, and performance and the connections between them. Since the Living the Arts program was embedded in InsideOut's Citywide Poets program, we were not able to completely isolate the unique impact of our program on the students, as in their survey responses and in evaluative conversations about the program, students often conflated their experiences with Living the Arts and their larger experiences in InsideOut.

On the one hand this is a positive outcome because it illustrates that we were largely successful in integrating our sessions into the larger structure of Citywide Poets. While we cannot say that our sessions were completely seamless integrations into the larger program, we did make a conscious and ongoing effort to facilitate sessions that were relevant to the themes and writing and performance techniques that were being explored in the program.

On the other hand, we were not able to talk specifically about the impact of the program on the youth outside of the direct quotations we were able to pull from the survey. Many of the students expressed that they did not have any poetry and performing outlets other than at Living the Arts and Citywide Poets, either in their schools or in their communities. For these students, Living the Arts functioned as a critically important and central space for them to engage with their poetic and performance crafts and to share their talents and discoveries with others. Whether Living the Arts simply buttressed the work of InsideOut, or whether it created an altogether separate yet integrated space of educational transformation, is not entirely clear; but we are buoyed by the positive responses of the students and the seeming lasting impact of our sessions on students' self-development and artistic endeavors.

## Larger Questions

As I reflect on my experiences planning, implementing, and participating in Living the Arts, I am left with two persisting questions about the intense and rewarding work done by educators in these transformative educational spaces, particularly for those engaged in arts and performance instruction.

1. What work do students do in pushing the boundaries of the fields of poetry, music, and performance?
2. How might teaching in these programs enhance or otherwise modify the scholarship that graduate students and faculty produce? How might these experiences impact our teaching?

Now let's look at some possible answers to these questions.

- In our scholarship and community work meetings, we can discuss how these different authors and concepts are interpreted and put to use in the creation of art. We can further explore what is largely a dialogic process in which new poets are constructing their work while directly mediating and revising works and techniques from the past.
- In our scholarship, we can showcase students' interpretive models and frameworks, some of which may challenge trends in academia in its common interpretations and accepted readings of certain authors, musicians, and poets, such as Langston Hughes.
- In our scholarship, we can incorporate performances of poetry, like we did with *Ask Your Mama: 12 Moods for Jazz*, as a way to explore how performances bring to life new interpretations and instantiations of poetry on the page. Live performances render a new character to the poetry and make it less static, as it is experienced on different levels by members of the audience.
- Our scholarship may not just be about our experiences in these programs, but using these experiences in our scholarly presentations and publications to inform how we read or render the works and concepts under consideration will enable reimaginings of historical and contemporary artistic works.

Taken together, these actions can function to create transformative spaces in which our experiences in these programs are not isolated or contained as an aside, but integral in our close readings, critical analyses, and critical thinking about ongoing issues in our fields and in our worlds. At the same time as we are advancing critical, dynamic, and more widely relevant scholarship by engaging in or developing transformative spaces of education, we are also creating spaces of education that youth direly need given the critical lack of quality, meaningful, and student-centered educational opportunities. These opportunities are spaces for developing and honing students' skills in these creative areas, which are life skills relevant to a variety of career tracks in their future college and work trajectories.

## Conclusion

Transformative educational spaces often emphasize the arts as creative avenues through which youth can explore their identities and their relationships and connections to the world. These spaces are needed, as current educational systems and institutions are not meeting the needs of a rapidly changing society that is fraught with heightened racial and socioeconomic politics. While committed educators and legislators, as well as parents and community leaders, work for change in the traditionally more-structured and governmentally mediated environment of the school system, nontraditional, supplementary spaces of transformative education are needed in order to decrease student learning gaps and White-Black family wealth gaps in broader society. These transformative educational spaces help change the discourse around knowledge and knowledge production as they relate to Black youth, while also increasing their life chances. As we work toward inclusivity and greater access to quality education for youth, we must not overlook or underestimate the power of educators who are working to create everyday spaces of transformative education that support and invest in youth in the current moment.

## Notes

1. Saidiya Hartman, *Lose Your Mother: A Journey Along the Atlantic Slave Route*. (New York: Farrar, Straus and Giroux, 2007): 100.
2. I define Black as students of African descent in America. In this chapter, I use "Black" and "African American" interchangeably.
3. Paulo Freire's *Pedagogy of the Oppressed*, originally published in 1970, advocates for a dialogic relationship between students, teachers, and larger society. In his Marxist analysis, he unpacks what he calls the "banking concept" of education, in which students are receptacles or sponges for teachers' ideas and curriculum. In viewing teaching as a dichotomous relationship, students' knowledge and experiences are undervalued or dismissed.
4. In the field of education, transformative education often refers to lifelong learning and adult learners' experiences re-entering the classroom. However, I am focused on youth education and educators who center students' life experiences and interests in educational programs and curriculum outside of the traditional classroom context.
5. The Chautauqua Circle in Atlanta was part of a national adult education movement in the late 19th and early 20th centuries and was founded by Methodists. For more information on the activities of the Chautauqua Circle, see Robert W. Woodruff Library Archives Research Center, Chautauqua Circle Collection. For the social, political, and religious thought behind the movement, please see Andrew Rieser (2003).
6. In Beverly J. Moss's *A Community Text Arises* (2003), an ethnographic study of literacy in three Black churches, she discusses the literary and educational functions of Black preachers' sermons. Through fieldwork, she illustrates how sermonic texts become sites of literacy development in Black churches, while simultaneously creating community.
7. See, for example, Grace Lee Boggs's earlier work (1977) as well as her more recent work published in *Living for Change News*, a newsletter produced by the Boggs Center to Nurture Community Leadership.

8. An ethnodrama is a written script that consists of dramatized narratives based on ethnographic research that includes interviews and participant observation. See, for example, Johnny Saldaña (2005).
9. Both Cox and Brown continue in the tradition of progressive "club women" of the nineteenth and twentieth centuries—Black women who were concerned with stereotypes and the stigmatization of Black women and girls, especially at the turn of the century. Anna Julia Cooper's *A Voice from the South*, and several other texts published at this time, engaged these themes as Black women actively worked to counter these constricting conceptions of Black womanhood and girlhood. For more, see Joanne Kilgour Dowdy's "In the Middle: An Artist/Researcher Experiences Urban Reform" (2006) and Evelyn Brooks Higginbotham's "Clubwomen and Electoral Politics in the 1920s" (1997), among others.
10. It is not coincidental that both Brown and Cox are Black women engaging Black feminist theory and epistemologies in their work. In "Black Women Activists, Leaders, and Educators: Transforming Urban Educational Practice" (2006), Jean-Marie, James and Bynum discuss the role that Black women have played in urban education historically through engaging the Black prophetic religious tradition, womanist and feminist writings, and communal resources. In their chapter, they address the work of African American women "who are concerned with issues of justice and equity in promoting the vision of urban education" (2006, p. 66). While these women are concerned with urban education and not exclusively with transformative spaces of education outside of school walls, they engage some of the central themes that the women facilitators in this chapter are concerned with regarding culturally relevant teaching, and assert that teachers should be aware that "they are teaching children who are heirs to a great tradition of art, music, dance, science, invention, oratory" (p. 68).
11. Arts of Citizenship was founded in 1998 at the University of Michigan to support community-university projects and partnerships in the arts and education.
12. For more on the concept of arts and literature as tools for living, see Kenneth Burke's essay, "Literature as Equipment for Living" (1973). See also Audre Lorde's "Poetry Is Not a Luxury" (1984).
13. One example of this history is the leadership tenure of the Harlem Renaissance. There were at least two factions during this era, the Du Boisian talented-tenth school of thought, and the Hugheseque, champion of the masses stance (for example, see his manifesto/essay, "The Black Artist and the Racial Mountain"), and both sought to cultivate leadership and social consciousness in Black communities. Additionally, the arts of the 1960s, including social gospel songs, had the explicit purpose of raising consciousness and community leadership in awareness of historical trends of racism and the needed actions to protest against them.
14. Some of this phrasing is taken from our project proposal, which Brooks, Comer, and I co-authored.
15. All names are pseudonyms.

## References

Boggs, Grace Lee. (1977). *Women and the movement to build a new America.* Detroit: National Organization for an American Revolution.

Brown, Ruth Nicole. (2008). *Black girlhood celebration: Toward a hip-hop feminist pedagogy.* New York: Peter Lang.

Burke, Kenneth. (1973). Literature as equipment for living. In Kenneth Burke, *The philosophy of literary form: Studies in symbolic action* (pp. 293–304). Berkeley: University of California Press.

Chautauqua Circle Collection. Atlanta University Center Robert W. Woodruff Library, Archives Research Center. Accessed July 2010.

Cobb, William Jelani. (2009). *The substance of hope: Barack Obama and the paradox of progress.* New York: Walker and Company.

Cooper, Anna Julia. (1990 [1892]). *A voice from the South.* New York: Oxford University Press.

Cox, Aimee. (2009). The BlackLight project: Young Black women in Detroit perform through and against the boundaries of anthropology. *Transforming Anthropology*, 17(1), 52–66.

Dowdy, Joanne Kilgour. (2006). In the middle: An artist/researcher experiences urban reform. In Joe L. Kincheloe, Kecia Hayes, Karel Rose, and Philip M. Anderson (Eds.), *The Praeger handbook of urban education* (pp. 487–95). Westport, CT: Greenwood Press.

Du Bois, W. E. B. (2005 [1903]). *The souls of Black folk*. New York: Simon and Schuster.

Freire, Paulo. (2000). *Pedagogy of the oppressed*. New York: Continuum.

Guy-Sheftall, Beverly, & Cole, Johnnetta Betsch (Eds.). (2010). *Who should be first? Feminists speak out on the 2008 presidential campaign*. New York: SUNY Press.

Higginbotham, Evelyn Brooks. (1997). Clubwomen and electoral politics in the 1920s. In Ann D. Gordon (Ed.), *African American women and the vote*, 1837–1965 (pp. 134–155). Amherst: University of Massachusetts Press.

Hill, Marc Lamont. (2010, June 24). The Black community is in the midst of a mental health crisis. *The Loop21*. Retrieved from http://theloop21.com/society/ron-artest-reshaping-the-conversation-Black-mental-health.

Jean-Marie, Gaetane, James, Channelle, & Bynum, Shirley. (2006). Black women activists, leaders, and educators: Transforming urban educational practice. In Joe L. Kincheloe, Kecia Hayes, Karel Rose, and Philip M. Anderson (Eds.), *The Praeger handbook of urban education* (pp. 59–70). Westport, CT: Greenwood Press.

"Live Arts Media Project 2010" (2010) Detroit Summer. www.detroitsummer.org

Lorde, Audre. (1984). Poetry is not a luxury. In Audre Lorde, *Sister outsider: Essays and speeches* (pp. 36–39). Berkeley: Crossing Press.

Moss, Beverly J. (2003). *A community text arises: A literate text and a literacy tradition in African-American churches*. Cresskill, NJ: Hampton Press.

Rieser, Andrew. (2003). *The Chautauqua moment: Protestants, progressives, and the culture of modern liberalism*. New York: Columbia University Press.

Saldaña, Johnny. (2005). *Ethnodrama: An anthology of reality theatre*. Walnut Creek, CA: AltaMira Press.

Schapiro, Thomas M., Meschede, Tatjana, & Sullivan, Laura. (2010, May). The racial wealth gap increases fourfold. *Institute on Assets and Social Policy Research Brief*. Waltham, MA: The Heller School for Social Policy and Management, Brandeis University.

Wise, Tim. (2010). Colorblind: *The rise of postracial politics and the retreat from racial equity*. San Francisco, CA: City Lights Publishing.

|| TWENTY

# Therapeutic Art, Poetry, and Personal Essay

## *Old and New Prescriptions*

Mary Hollowell & Donna Moye

Within the field of educational psychology, issues of how to motivate children to learn often discuss and deconstruct traditional dimensions such as cognitive, social, behavioral, and humanistic perspectives. Edith Kramer's *Art Therapy in a Children's Community* presents us with a fresh explication for motivating children to learn. Published over fifty years ago, her insights into troubled children, based on their artwork, are still applicable today. Post-modern technological inventions such as MP3 players, iPhones, videogames, and online social networking have not changed the universal themes found in the art of wounded children and youth, as they learn about themselves and others while they progress towards healing.

Kramer's art therapy first began in Prague during WWII, as she began to see patterns while working with refugee children. She is described in a wealth of literature as a pioneer in the field of art therapy. In fact, art therapy was not formally recognized in the United States until it was introduced by Kramer in the 1940s, following her immigration. She has been identified as a major theoretician-practitioner by Jean Keller in *Activities with Developmentally Disabled Elderly and Older Adults* (1991). When Melvin Miller and Susanne Cook-Greuter interviewed her in 1997 at the age of 82, they wrote, "Kramer's activities have bridged continents, integrated disciplines, and crossed domains of high expression" (p. 99). In contrast to her predecessors, who heavily psychoanalyzed artists, Edith Kramer focused more on artwork itself. Scholars Aubrey and Nya Fine write, "Edith Kramer, on the other hand, placed emphasis on an alternative direction, more towards a humanistic approach. Her work with children emphasized the healing properties of the creative process" (p. 263). Kramer was a brilliant and talented woman who sculpted, painted, and etched as well as taught art and wrote books.

From 1950 to 1957, Kramer worked as an art therapist at the Wiltwyck School in Esopus, New York, a rehabilitation center for emotionally disturbed boys. Her school was very similar to our own, fifty years later. We, Mary Hollowell and Donna Moye, taught at Peachtree Alternative School in Georgia, in different capacities. One of us was a regular substitute teacher, and the other was an art teacher at this school, for many years. Students at both Wiltwyck and Peachtree Alternative had mental health issues. Most of them were on probation and had been referred by judges. The schools were also similar in that they had racially diverse student populations averaging 100 students. According to Kramer, Wiltwyck had a caring and qualified staff, as did Peachtree Alternative. Wiltwyck School had a staunch supporter in the form of Eleanor Roosevelt, who served on the board of directors for the last twenty years of her life. Mrs. Roosevelt hosted an annual picnic for the whole school, every summer on the grounds of her Hyde Park home, where she regularly grilled hot dogs. Similarly, Peachtree Alternative School had strong community support in the form of a vocal child advocacy group comprised of ministers, foster parents, sheriff's deputies, social workers, and health care providers, who hosted school events. At Wiltwyck School, Edith Kramer used to tell her students Grimm's fairy tales in order to keep them from fighting, and at Peachtree Alternative School, the art teacher used to play soothing classical music.

Wiltwyck School differed from the contemporary alternative school, however, in that it was a treatment facility with beds and was entirely for boys. Peachtree Alternative School was a day school and almost a quarter of the students were girls. Wiltwyck was the setting for the academy Award-winning classic film *The Quiet One,* and Peachtree Alternative School is depicted in the book *The Forgotten Room* (Hollowell, 2009).

## Theory

In her four major books published between 1958 and 1979, Edith Kramer subscribes to the Freudian school of psychoanalysis. She writes that creating art can lead to emotional maturation and sublimation, the overcoming of basic instincts by the ego. Art is a means by which children who have been traumatized by war, poverty, crime, abuse, addiction, and other societal ills can express themselves, reach catharsis, and develop well-being. Art therapy is also a way to unearth repressions and overcome denials. Students can take pride in their work, particularly if it is displayed or published. At Wiltwyck School, art was regularly displayed in the dining hall, and at Peachtree Alternative School, art, poetry, and personal essays were published in annual anthologies.

Kramer defines sublimation as "any process in which a primitive asocial impulse is transformed into a socially productive act" (1958, p. 11). She gives an example. When a toddler who throws blocks becomes a child who stacks them, sublimation has occurred. Similarly, a baby matures from throwing and smearing food to spooning food; thus, he achieves sublimation.

As educators in a public alternative school filled with chronic disrupters, we saw many students lash out in ways that indicated they had *not* achieved sublimation. We saw tantrums with things that had been smeared (including walls smeared with blood), people shoved, work destroyed, and items thrown. Some psychologists equate smearing by teens with an anal fixation, an arrested stage of development. Punches were also thrown during fistfights. A few tantrums were violent enough to be called rampages, and they involved breaking walls, throwing furniture, self-injury, or injury to others. In response to violent tantrums, we observed that the best teachers, who had the most strength and fortitude, remained calm and stayed around to clean up and continue their efforts to establish relationships with students. They stayed for months and years afterwards.

We also watched preadolescent students regress into toddler-like thumb sucking and hiding inside closets and boxes. We later witnessed some of these students evolve into mature young adults, who managed to conquer their aggressive impulses, obtain educations, and lead productive and peaceful lives. Many pieces of art, poems, or personal essays in the anthologies were tributes to teachers, and it is relationships with caring teachers that usually helped turn alternative students around. Specifically, caring teachers role modeled respect, allowed students to be creative, boosted their self-esteem, and gave them hope. In many cases, there were no other adults in students' lives to help motivate them, certainly not immediate family members, many of whom experienced depression, domestic abuse, addiction, and/or incarceration. Peachtree Alternative students were teenagers who had to survive on their own, beginning at young ages, and they did not have the time or resources to develop hopes and dreams, not when they were struggling to take care of themselves. They did not even have much energy left for academic learning, but their trusted teachers gave them hope for the future and reasons to want to learn. In the absence of caring adults at home, it fell upon teachers to help at-risk adolescents achieve sublimation.

Kramer also identifies the need to possess as a basic instinct, while the desire to preserve is a more mature response. She equates a boy's desire to devour his mother (reflective in some raw student artwork, complete with huge teeth) with primitive headhunting and cannibalism. Interestingly, she cautions that we don't want student artists to be too sublimated or too rigorous, for relying on instinct while painting, sculpting, drawing, or using other mediums is an integral part of creating art. Master artists learn to channel their instincts.

The pioneer art therapist also writes, "Children naturally crave the adults' appreciation of their art, as they need appreciation of all accomplishments. Thus pictures are often given as presents to beloved adults" (1958, p. 20). We experienced much of this at Peachtree Alternative: poems and drawings given as gifts and anthologies with heartfelt dedications to teachers. Kramer also advises, "Success in treatment depends on teamwork, mutual respect, and unity among staff members" (1958, p. 32). With the exception of a couple of ineffective teachers, we definitely saw teamwork at Peachtree Alternative School. In order to help angry, disruptive, or disaffected youth, teachers relied on one another and supported colleagues when their spirits waned. Teamwork for successful alternative schooling cannot be overemphasized. Peachtree Alternative had a number of critical support specialists such as a media specialist, a registered nurse, and a school psychologist, although these positions were eliminated or reduced to part-time in the school's final year.

Kramer is a master of identifying dichotomies, and she asserts that in order to be successful, an art therapist must be both accepting and discriminating, accepting of the aggressive first attempts of alternative students while still maintaining an eye for quality. Her additional advice is that art teachers carefully balance leeway and structure, allowing students to be creative but not so boisterous that they can't hear directions.

In the foreword to Edith Kramer's second book, *Art as Therapy with Children,* public school psychologist Muriel Gardiner states that others "can learn from Edith Kramer's insights and methods, even if working in a quite different field" (1971, p. x). We, too, believe that Kramer's insights are keen, her advice is sound, and her compassion is inspiring to today's generation of educators.

## Literature of Learning and Wounded Students

Essential components of successful learning, which appear in James Banner and Harold Cannon's *The Elements of Learning,* are beyond alternative students without hope in their lives. To expect them to be diligent in their studies while they have so many physical and emotional needs or to persist towards an intellectual goal when they have no goal at all is to ask them to hoist themselves up by their bootstraps. When teenagers are solely and by necessity present oriented, they cannot be studious as an investment in their futures. Intellectual models may be few, and intellectual capital is a foreign concept. To alternative students seeking attachment who have been mired in isolation, the loneliness required in traditional studying in libraries and laboratories is not appealing, especially not without practice. Passion for learning is often something that is ignited by supportive parents, intriguing material, or outstanding teachers; it is not the result of spontaneous combustion. Curiosity is not easily aroused in students who are numbed in self-defense or are oppositional. In addition, aspirations towards endurable creations or discoveries require the assumption that you will survive to a certain age. Several nonfiction books set in urban landscapes such as *There Are No Children Here, Our America: Life and Death on the South Side of Chicago* and *Gang Leader for a Day* demonstrate that many inner-city males in our nation's ghettos do not expect to live very long. Therefore, they seek immediate gratification.

*The Elements of Teaching,* which preceded *The Elements of Learning,* inspired a multitude of teachers who saw themselves as the compassionate, creative, and authoritative characters described in the pages. The attributes identified as necessary for successful learning, however, only apply to a select group of highly motivated students. Teens who have been excluded from educational opportunities, housed in poor schools with no resources, or labeled failures from an early age simply cannot attain lofty criteria for successful learning without substantial assistance.

Another contemporary book, however, is particularly applicable to our study of alternative students and their art and writing. In *Reaching the Wounded Student,* Joe Hendershott (2009) shares his observation that in response to a question about their futures, wounded students "will just look at you with a strange look or a blank stare. This question is totally foreign to their thought process" (p. 22). He goes on to ask, "If a student has no hopes and dreams, how can an education make sense to them? What would be the point?" (p. 22). When it comes to working with severely traumatized teens, restoring hope takes precedence over academic learning. Hendershott also reminds readers, "true change happens for most people on the emotional level and not on the cognitive level" (p. 61). Wounded students must be guided from despair and into hope before they can focus on traditional school subject matter. One way to ease this transition is through therapeutic art and writing.

We have encountered those blank stares ourselves in our work with at-risk teenagers. We have also encountered them in films and in literature. Megan, one of the two main characters in the documentary film *Girlhood: Growing Up on the Inside,* springs to mind. When the filmmaker asks her, on camera, to name three wishes, Megan stares hopelessly around her ghetto neighborhood and then says, "I don't know. It ain't no sense in wishing for anything." In Alex Kotlowitz's book *There Are No Children Here,* a boy living in a blighted urban housing project says, "If I grow up, I'd like to be a bus driver" (p. x). He does not take growing up for granted. Such hopeless children with weary, ancient faces are all too familiar to us.

In some cases, particularly in the absence of parental figures, teachers may be the only ones who can rescue adolescents from boredom, poverty, or despair. We must help wounded students develop hope and aspirations, then channel them further towards academic achievement. This shepherding must be done in a gentle and flexible manner. Trying to sweep alternative students along through a straight and narrow channel doesn't work. Greg Goodman echoes this when he writes "in chaotic spaces, meaningful pedagogy requires nonlinear and complex processes to examine and negotiate the fractal borders that disaffected youth occupy" (2007, p. 16). For example, in art therapy, recovery might involve temporary regression into a monster phase to face fears before progressing to self-portraiture and portraits of family members.

An important caution that Hendershott gives is "understand that we cannot always understand where these students have been" (p. 13). This is very sound advice. He emphasizes that, in some cases, the damage wrought to students may be so severe and so hidden that we may never uncover it. In this event, we must just proceed with our shepherding. Hendershott is advocating an attitude of acceptance. So often, teachers struggle to try to understand the origin of a learning problem. It is a relief to be directed, to just proceed. Some pain and injustice are completely beyond our comprehension. It is all right, sometimes, to not know the full extent of student hardships.

Many school systems cannot afford an adequate number of school psychologists and counselors. Hendershott reassures us that in times of grave shortages of specialists, it is okay for teachers to take the lead. The caring teacher may become the expert. The overall tone of *Reaching the Wounded Student* is soothing, reassuring, and uplifting. It resonates within us.

## Methodology

This chapter is based on qualitative methods: document analysis of four years worth of Peachtree Alternative School anthologies, along with personal observations and interviews with former teachers. The rawest, most aggressive artwork was censored from the anthologies by adult advisors and relegated to a "Do Not Publish" pile. The rejected work included hideous monsters with serpent heads, enormous claws, and sinister smiles.

The patterns in the final, more evolved products, can be assessed and some have been reproduced, here. Young artists and writers at Peachtree Alternative often depict painful scenes. They face fears and express anxieties in order to overcome them. They draw or write about their demons as a step towards conquering them.

There is a scarcity of first-person data from alternative students. Greg Goodman also recognizes the need for "the deeply personal stories that alternative education students have to tell" (2007, p. 7). Alternative students have encased themselves in protective shells for so long that it is usually very difficult for them to open up during interviewing. Interviewing alternative students is often hampered by their communication problems, and it is ethically challenging. Their identities must be carefully safeguarded, and sometimes they reveal crimes that they have committed. Instead of interviewing, we studied alternative student annual anthologies, which proved to be very enlightening. We were also able to track down a handful of dropouts and graduates in order to obtain permission to reproduce their artwork. Student signatures have been blackened in the reproductions in order to maintain anonymity.

While we are not psychoanalysts who are able to delve deeply into the pasts of young artists and writers, we are both concerned educators who have worked with troubled teens. We can identify patterns, provide a basic overview of student work, and depict regression and progression for readers.

Peachtree Alternative School, in its tenth and final year, was so overcrowded and lacking in resources that an anthology was not produced, but the four previous anthologies brimmed with high quality work, thanks to talented student editors. While she is too modest to admit it, the anthologies are also largely due to the hard work of the English teacher. She conceived the project, sought funding for copying and equipment, inspired and guided student editors, and carefully preserved original materials.

In this chapter, we have chosen to include art and writing that is non-stereotypical. The student work that is reproduced or quoted is not bland or saccharine sweet. The images of monsters and heroes will speak to wide audiences. Edith Kramer argues that stereotypes begin to appear during the teenage years and that "younger children do not seem to be able to produce false sentiment in art" (1971, p. 122). The heroes that we display are not hollow heroes but ones with grace and energy.

## Results

In the following paragraphs, we describe the prominent patterns and symbols in the artwork of Peachtree Alternative students (many of whom were on parole for acts of violence such as assault, burglary, vandalism, weapons violations, drug dealing, and terroristic threat). The patterns in Peachtree Alternative student art over a four-year period included monsters, prisoners, and warrior/heroes. They were the very same patterns that Kramer found in Wiltwyck student art, fifty years before. At Peachtree Alternative, these patterns also crossed disciplines from art into writing. In addition, symbols in the artwork such as flaming hearts, bleeding jesters, and thorny roses depicted inner conflicts.

### *Beginning Sublimation*

Peachtree Alternative students faced fears and uncovered scars in their art and writing. In one drawing that could not be reproduced due to the ravages of time, a student drew a portrait of himself hanging from a hook. He was hanging from the hook by his collar with his feet dangling high in the air. Facing him was a dark knight in a helmet and full armor, who stood poised to stab him. The art was quite an expression of vulnerability, and to admit his fear on paper was a step in the right direction. Other fearsome monsters in the student artwork, besides the dark knight, were large vampire bats and werewolves with very sharp teeth. They were metaphoric monsters in students' lives. In contrast to alternative students, regular students in mainstream schools do not draw such fearsome monsters or draw them with such regularity.

Students also depicted realistic, as opposed to fantastical, monsters in the forms of drugs and alcohol, weapons, and crime. In Figure 1, there are bloody handprints on a burglarized house on the right side of the picture. They are depicted in red in the original color drawing.

*Figure 1: The Monsters in My Life Montage*

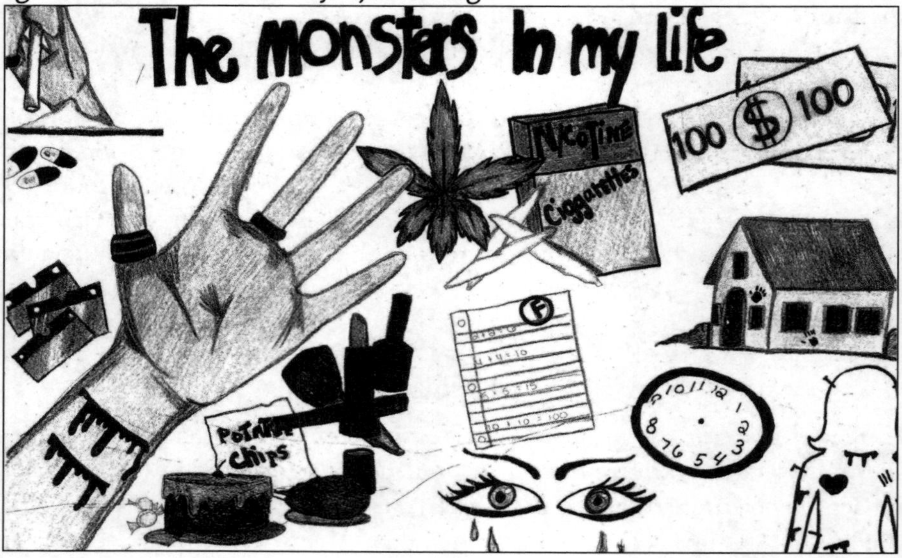


Blood was common in a number of works of art. Fangs, hearts pierced with swords, and roses with prominent thorns all dripped blood. A closer inspection of Figure 1 shows excellent use of proportions and perspectives. The marijuana leaves are in proportion. The limbs of the punctured and bleeding paper doll are also in proportion with its body. The burglarized home is set at a believable angle, with the doors and windows well spaced. The artist makes good use of shading and maximizes contrasts by boldly outlining a human figure, while leaving the inside white. The cutting seen in the sliced wrists and the realistic razor blades are two of the more vivid elements of the drawing. The artist makes excellent use of space by filling the entire page with bold elements. The weapons that she depicts include nails, drugs, razor blades and, on a smaller scale, junk food. Altogether, it is a powerful, confessional drawing by a talented artist that depicts sorrow and pain.

As audience members viewing this art, we are both disturbed and impressed. It is distressing to see such a preponderance of problems spelled out in black and white. They range from academic failure to crime to drug use to cutting behavior, but we cannot help but admire the honesty, courage, and artistry involved.

Just as Kramer indicated in 1958, Peachtree Alternative students were also quite fearful of jail. It loomed as a prominent specter in their lives. Most of them had been to jail, and quite a few had parents in prison. Students were so fearful of jail, in fact, that they refused to have their picture taken inside a paddywagon (a photographic prop discovered on a field trip). Finally, with much coaxing, we managed to have two students climb on board the paddywagon for a picture.

Peachtree Alternative students chose to use black-and-white striped prisoner graphics in the anthologies. Prisoners in Peachtree County, today, still wear black and white striped jumpsuits while working on the sides of the road. Peachtree Alternative students also began to face their fears by writing about their own experiences in jail. As Kramer says, "To delinquent children who live in a delinquent environment, prison is a serious menace. The subject, therefore, is usually avoided" (1958, p. 73). To address the topic in any form is a breakthrough.

Reflections on youth detention or prison, in the anthologies, include a very frank personal essay in which a former inmate shares her fears of being assaulted while in the shower. She escaped this, she believes, by maintaining a low profile. She avoided inmates who tried to start fights. "I ignored them so I would not get more time," she writes. To share such fears in a school-wide anthology, along with her name, is an act of courage.

Another student, who writes anonymously, shares the heavy impact of regularly visiting her sister in prison. Her sister was a crack addict who was in prison for larceny and forgery. The author concludes, "I've learned a lot of what not to do. She's really destroyed her life."

Troubled students often depersonalize their artwork and avoid painting faces. Facial features are not particularly hard to draw compared to hands and feet, yet at-risk teens avoid them by incorporating devices such as helmets, profiles, hoods, and masks. This represents their fear of emotions and was quite common in Peachtree Alternative student art.

The alternative school principal, who sanctioned the revealing anthologies, sent a strong message to students in poem format. The principal was a former English teacher and a writer herself. She also loved poetry and selected a poem about a mask for the last page of Anthology 3. The poem by Charles C. Finn is titled "Please Hear What I Am Not Saying." In the following stanza, he writes about his insecurity as a new teacher.

*My surface may seem smooth but my surface is a mask,*
*ever-varying and ever-concealing.*
*Beneath lies no complacence.*
*Beneath lies confusion, and fear, and aloneness.*
*But I hide this. I don't want anybody to know it.*
*I panic at the thought of my weakness exposed.*

In the 100-line poem, Finn makes additional references to his shield and his façade. In the end, he encourages kindness, gentleness, and sensitivity in order to scale his walls.

The principal felt strongly enough about the importance of confronting insecurities to relay this message to all of her charges. It is valuable advice for insecure and fearful adolescents, and it encapsulates what they have done in the anthologies. The English teacher included one of her very own poems in an anthology that revealed her own insecurity. Both women are avid readers and practicing writers, as well as therapeutic educators. They work alongside students and convey their humanity. It is one of Kramer's most important lessons.

On a more somber note, we were able to observe a number of young artists at Peachtree Alternative School working on spontaneous drawings that reflected great hostility. One very angry young man drew an especially violent volcano that spewed wide rivers of lava, thick plumes of black smoke, and giant boulders. While grandmothers are usually idealized in children's book illustrations as gentle and loving characters, this particular boy drew his grandmother as a troll. He also entertained himself in time out by creating monstrous paper claws, swiping the air with them, and making vicious faces. He was an overtly aggressive preadolescent in a less mature stage of emotional development. In fact, he was so disruptive that he was later transferred from the alternative school to a psychoeducational center for more intensive treatment.

Figure 2 shows an adolescent's confusion and despair over drug use. This artwork was created using a computer graphics program. The teen in the piece is isolated, for most alternative students draw single figures as opposed to multiple or interacting ones, and his hair is in wild disarray. He clutches his head in torment. A smoking joint is nearby, and he is surrounded by darkness, representing the absence of light in his life.

Former alternative teachers recall this teenager as being one of the most talented young artists that they ever taught. Sam (a pseudonym) did not make it, though, and is now in prison for murder. His tale is reminiscent of one that occurred at Wiltwyck, as conveyed in the book *All God's Children: The Bosket Family and the American Tradition of Violence.* The author, Fox Butterfield, won both a Pulitzer Prize and a National Book Award. At Wiltwyck, a boy named Walter (Kramer's pseudonym for Butch) was a master painter, but after his release, he killed a store clerk during a robbery. He stabbed the clerk once, the clerk staggered, then he stabbed him five more times. He committed two more murders before killing himself during a police shootout. Butch's son Willie attended Wiltwyck, years later, and is now serving life in prison. Violence was perpetuated from one generation to the next. Robert Coles concludes his 1995 review of *All God's Children* with the following observation. "Butch and Willie were each a living loaded gun, waiting to be triggered by anyone and anything, each with resentments difficult for those of us luckily raised in solid families to imagine, never mind comprehend" (p. 12).

*Figure 2: Drugs Make You Crazy*

At Wiltwyck, Butch revealed the depths of his despair and rage to Edith Kramer in his self-portrait of a young man holding a knife. Similarly, at Peachtree Alternative, Sam revealed the magnitude of his pain and turmoil in his "Drugs Make You Crazy" portrait. Butch and Sam were two talented artists and disturbed young men, living similar lives but separated by half a century. Their stories are eerily similar and both end tragically.

The details of Sam's last crime are horrendous. In October of 2002, he robbed a convenience store, shot the clerk, then shot him twice more. The clerk staggered away but died in the hospital. He had immigrated from India, three years before, and was described by a friend as "one of the most spiritual and courageous people I knew" (Hedge, 2008, p. 3). Sam was apprehended hours later and is now in jail, awaiting trial for murder. It is the culmination of a list of crimes including burglary and drug offenses. The agonizing art that Sam created as a teenager foreshadowed his life as a young man. Had Sam received therapy earlier and for an extended period of time, this tragedy might possibly have been prevented.

For those who subscribe to Freudian psychoanalysis, Sam also wrote a telling monster story that is published in an anthology. The short story is a classic example of the previously identified consumption fantasy (i.e., devouring something in order to possess it). Sam writes about a monster eating his dog. Later, his new dog eats his clothes and dies.

We do not wish to paint a portrait of utter doom for any of our former students, especially those who might one day read this chapter. There is indeed spiritual redemption for those who seek it. We firmly believe this.

## Advanced Sublimation

Additional patterns in the artwork were warriors, heroes, and superheroes. One student drew a fierce warrior with a mighty shield and a raised spear. The warrior was embellished with a decorative shield and armor that was aesthetic as well as functional. The artist readily identified with the heroes of Greek mythology and also drew a powerful image of Zeus in the sky amid lightning bolts.

He also demonstrated growing confidence in his writing. "Now I do all of my work without any help and I know I can do it," he writes in an essay. In fact, the student repeats this realization twice more in the same essay. He also writes that he is more adept at making friends after having attended the alternative school. The student concludes, "I've learned many things while I've been over here" and goes so far as to say that he may have learned more than any other student. He likes his teachers at the alternative school and indicates that he may become a lifelong learner. "I just keep learning," he writes. This particular student has experienced advanced sublimation, benefitted from therapeutic art and writing, and had a successful alternative school experience.

Figure 3 shows a superhero, Spiderman, with unusually large fists, making him extra powerful. In his own way, Figure 3 is a glamorous character. The Spiderman looms large on the page, with obvious muscles and bolts of energy emerging from his head. It is safe to assume that, in drawing stand-alone heroes, students were imagining themselves in heroic positions. Aspiring to be a hero is a sign of health.

One interesting assignment at Peachtree Alternative was to create a collage using construction paper, glue, and magazine clippings (Figure 4). The assignment led to the creation of honest and, in some cases, hopeful collages.

Solid values are evident in words cut from magazines. In Figure 4, the words "good" and "brave" are pasted, along with "Black!," which shows pride in one's culture. (On another boy's collage, which is not shown, the words "ready," "brave," "healthy living," and "brains" are stuck to the page.) By pasting the word "ready" to the page, the artist indicates that he is prepared to advance.

*Figure 3: Superhero*

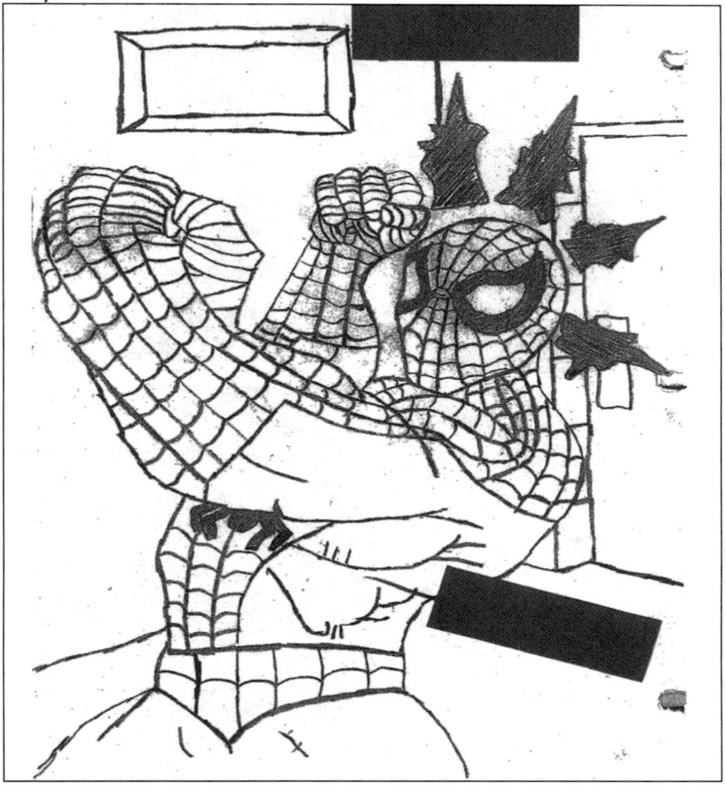

The confident artist who created the "Black!" collage also wrote a humorous and clever poem about a hero. He describes a blonde riding a horse with the wind whipping her hair. She starts to fall, her foot is caught in the stirrups, and she's in danger of a concussion. Suddenly, the hero goes over, unplugs the mechanical horse, and rescues the tot. The young poet has succeeded in startling his readers with a surprise ending.

Symbols that are repeated in the anthologies included flaming hearts (Figure 5), bleeding jesters, and thorny roses, which depicted teens' inner conflicts of broken hearts, dual identities, and troubled relationships.

Flowers were particularly common. Half of the flower drawings were unhealthy or ominous in that they had brittle leaves or big thorns, while the rest were quite lovely, sprinkled with dewdrops or surrounded by butterflies. Either way, the flowers are commendable for being honest or hopeful.

In addition to symbols, inner conflict is revealed in poetry. Nothing more clearly indicates the conflict between adolescent dual identities than the original line from a poem, "He is a creature with two faces…very few see his second face." The poem is titled "Liar." It is not hard to imagine the writer's conflict. She could be struggling with any number of opposing identities that are common to alternative students: promiscuous young man or monogamous boyfriend, absentee dad or involved adolescent father, someone in the spiral of addiction or a person in recovery, criminal or law-abiding citizen. Alternative students experience more severe internal conflicts than most mainstream students but dual identity is a universal human dilemma.

*Figure 4: A Boy's Collage*

*Figure 5: Flaming Heart*

## On Families, Friends, and Themselves

Kramer observed that students at Wiltwyck had such terribly broken homes that they never depicted their families in artwork. Only one Wiltwyck child, as he neared recovery, was able to paint his mother. Similarly, other than one grandmother troll, we never saw family members in artwork by Peachtree Alternative students. It is a heartbreaking observation.

In "A Poem to an Abusive Father," a boy reveals a history of abuse, drug addiction, homelessness, and jail. The climax of this poem is when he is shot in the leg by a police officer. The tragedy is so extreme that it is almost incomprehensible, and the most dramatic line in this ode to his dad reads, "I wanted to grow up not being like you." It is one of the most powerful poems in the entire anthology series, along with a poem about a car wreck and one about a murdered aunt.

On the other hand, another alternative student pens an ode to his mother titled "My Family." He writes, "First there is my mom; she is my world.... She is always there to pick me up when I fall." Thank goodness this young man has such a mother. It takes just one caring adult to help make a child resilient, be it a parent, a minister, a teacher, or an extended family member. The opposite of aggressiveness is tenderness, and the alternative student who can convey a tender family scene in art or writing is on his way to recovery.

According to Kramer, flattering portraits and accurate self-portraits indicate very advanced stages of development, and the artists who complete them have achieved a measure of healing. The artist who drew a warrior in decorative armor and developed self-confidence went on to draw a lovely portrait of the alternative school principal wearing a beautiful smile.

Figure 6 is an interesting self-portrait in which a teen is depicted as scowling, wearing a hood, and having baggy pants and an unlaced shoe—a very common way for teenaged boys at the alternative school to dress. The student also regularly wore a state university baseball cap. He conveyed his own early demeanor quite well and is seen in several early school photographs slouching and unsmiling.

When the face is examined in detail in Figure 6.1, a teardrop is seen under the right eye. It is unclear whether this represents an actual teardrop or a tattoo. Teardrop tattoos have signified losing a loved, one or, in gang culture, they have indicated that the wearer has committed murder. This particular student, however, had no facial tattoo.

A collection of this student's artwork is available, and he also drew hearts in flames (Figure 5), flowers, and crosses. He is a young man who has excised his demons and begun to move towards a higher level of maturation in the form of religious thinking. The superego that governs moral decision-making is taking over. Elsewhere in the anthologies, angels and poignant writing about heaven appear, additional signs of advanced sublimation and spiritual evolution. The artist who drew Figures 5 and 6 married his high school sweetheart and has gone on to become a family man and hard-working father.

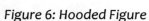

*Figure 6: Hooded Figure*

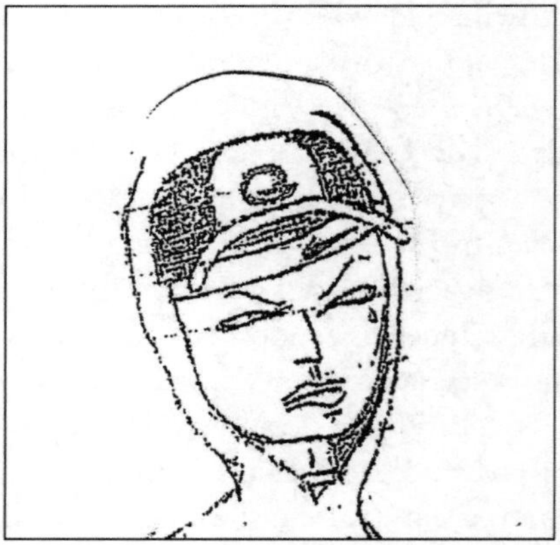

*Figure 6.1: Face in Detail*

## Discussion of Learning

As indicated in the center of Figure 1, alternative students have a history of academic failure. Many have reading problems, communication problems, and learning disabilities. Consequently, they are resistant to pencil and paper testing and other forms of traditional assessment such as oral reporting. We have witnessed entire classes of students groan in response to testing, violence in response to testing (one dangerous student threatened to stab his teacher, who dropped the testing procedure in self-preservation), and classrooms disintegrate into chaos in order to distract teachers from testing. Alternative students are more open, though, to activities perceived as nonacademic such as art, poetry, and the personal essay.

In the last year of Peachtree Alternative School, before it was replaced by a computer center for at-risk youth, dramatic staff cuts led to the elimination of high school art although poetry writing continued in the English teacher's classroom. Given its valuable therapeutic effects, eliminating art for alternative students was a grave error. Art, poetry, and personal essay all require patience, reflection, and concentration. Practicing these skills and gaining confidence in these fields can pave the way for success in other subject areas.

Edith Kramer elaborates on the value of alternative assessments, such as an art display and a published anthology. "A child who is unable to learn in the classroom needs other learning experiences. As long as learning continues in other areas, a child's development need not be seriously stunted" (1958, p. 126). According to Kramer, art, in addition to serving as a path towards more academic subjects, enables the expression of conflict and fantasies that predominate in alternative students; whereas traditional math and science have fewer fantasy outlets.

## Conclusion

Again, the very patterns of monsters, prisoners, and heroes that Edith Kramer found in the artwork of troubled children at Wiltwyck can be found in a similar population in a different region, half a century later. The maintenance of these patterns over time is impressive and well worth investigating in other regions and cultures. They are the same monsters, portraits, collages, and heart-shaped imagery found in Cathy Malchiodi's book *Breaking the Silence: Art Therapy with Children from Violent Homes,* and Malchiodi even includes a checklist to evaluate therapeutic art. Lani Gerity's *Creativity and the Dissociative Patient: Puppets, Narrative and Art in the Treatment of Survivors of Childhood Trauma* is yet another recommendation for the therapeutic arts, based on Kramerian theory, albeit for younger children.

Kramer states why art is so useful to delinquent children and youth. "Art can absorb and contain more raw affect than most other equally complex and civilized endeavors" (1971, pp. 184–185). She also asserts that it has the power "to relieve pressures or to contain what is unbearable" (1971, p. 207). We believe that writing serves the same functions, and we have provided evidence of containment and relief in both areas.

It is important to add that verbal therapy was also available to Peachtree Alternative students in the form of group counseling sessions and visits with a school psychologist, but not all alternative students could successfully discuss their feelings. Art and writing remained important alternative outlets. Finally, Kramer cautions readers that therapeutic arts are not easy, and we have learned this lesson ourselves. Therapists must "be willing to accept defeat time and again" (1971, p. 221).

In preparing this chapter, we interviewed four other former alternative teachers and a former school resource officer. All were transferred to mainstream schools, after the alternative school was closed. During interviews, we sat together, reviewed the anthologies, and discussed student outcomes.

The English teacher said she tried to structure the anthologies as loosely as possible so students could include pieces that had personal significance. If students revealed something painful, she would try to discuss it with them but they wouldn't always open up in person. She had to resolve herself to not knowing, just as Hendershott advises.

She smiled as she reread the story of the hero who saved a tot in a superstore by unplugging a mechanical horse. She remembered the author well. "He was a great kid. He had a great personality," she said. He married another former alternative student, and they had a child. Later, he was arrested for theft. "I hope he had a good reason," the English teacher said, "like he had to feed his family."

The English teacher was in the process of moving out of a portable classroom and into a main building. "About a week before you called, I was thinking of throwing these out," she said, referring to the anthology boxes. "Now, I know why I didn't." Her saving the materials was fortuitous.

"I thought about doing anthologies, here," she said about her mainstream school, "but it just wouldn't be the same. There wouldn't be the same emotion." The publishing of a loosely structured anthology at a regular school wouldn't be as emotionally cleansing and as useful to students therapeutically.

A former school resource officer remembers the final years of Peachtree Alternative School, during which these anthologies were produced, as being especially rough. It is an important observation, coming from a highly qualified Officer of the Year and a Gulf War veteran. The resource officer shakes his head in disbelief, recalling some of the students. He vividly remembers having to drag thrashing teenagers down the hall past four-year-olds, who attended preschool in an adjacent building. He also thought that the Central Office put the principal in water over her head by putting her in charge of four programs under one roof: an alternative high school, a preschool, an alternative special education program, and a state-funded psychoeductional center for severely emotionally disturbed students. He was genuinely touched by the goodbye poster he received when he was transferred. It was signed by many of the students. "That meant a lot to me," he says, "considering it was kids I had to lock up." He remembers that they wrote "Keep your head down," advising him to stay safe.

Prior to our interview with the former alternative school academic counselor (now also a high school English teacher), she was distributing candy in her classroom. She had a big candy box in her lap and was rolling up and down the aisles in an office chair, passing it out, which made for a funny image. "You see what I've resorted to," she said, "bribing them." She was rather sheepish about it but we've done it ourselves.

During our meeting, a student dropped by, asking her advice. "I love you," she told him, afterwards. "I love you, too," the boy said, without hesitation. The exchange was testimony to the strength of her relationships.

We left her classroom with sad stories and fistfuls of chocolate. The author of the poem about an abusive father had a stroke following a drug overdose and is permanently impaired. He had to learn to walk all over again. One artist now resides in a mental health facility, while another joined a gang and is lost to the streets. One student did receive his GED, however.

Our favorite phrase from Kramer's first book *Art Therapy in a Children's Community*, is "every teacher remains something of a witch or wizard to the student" (1958, p. 128). This is a positive metaphor that we haven't heard before. By this, Kramer means that the best and most gifted alternative educators appear to have almost magical powers. They have the power to transform something mundane into something relevant and engaging, and the talent to help bring the empty canvas or page to life. We have been privileged to see many such alternative educators in action, and their work does seem miraculous, at times. The trusted teachers who manage to instill hope in formerly hopeless students are truly miracle workers. Perhaps, "fairy godmothers" or "fairy godfathers" would be a more apt, given the historically negative connotation of witches.

Hendershott's prescription to school administrators struggling with growing numbers of wounded students is to focus on emotional well-being *before* focusing on academics. Starting points include art and reading/writing therapy, yet art and libraries are often cut in times of financial hardship. They (along with music and physical education) are programs which should take precedence for emotionally disturbed children and youth in public schools.

While some aspects of alternative schooling have not changed in over fifty years, the vocabulary of alternative schooling has begun to evolve. New terms are being applied, and there is a great need for these terms. Hendershott describes the overwhelming response to one of his early wounded student presentations. While he anticipated twenty-five people in the audience, the crowd swelled to a thousand. Clearly, a great many educators are concerned about the futures of disruptive and disaffected youth and are seeking answers. The calls for grace, mercy, serenity, and soul in education coming from Joe Hendershott and Greg Goodman are steps beyond the professionalism, forgiveness, peace, and caring traditionally espoused in colleges of education. They are calls for human spirit strong enough to address the dire needs of deeply troubled students. Beyond simply being decent, alternative educators must be noble. We are thankful to have encountered these new terms in the literature of education, and we know educators who embody them. They are powerful words which definitely apply to alternative schooling. They have enriched the language of education and our own aspirations.

## References

Banner, J., & Cannon, H. (1999). *The Elements of Learning*. New Haven, CT: Yale University Press.
Banner, J., & Cannon, H. (1997). *The Elements of Teaching*. New Haven, CT: Yale University Press.

Butterfield, F. (1995). *All God's Children: The Bosket Family and the American Tradition of Violence.* New York: Vintage Books.
Coles, R. (1995). "Blood Ties: Fox Butterfield's History of Willie Bosket's Family Is also a history of American Violence." New York: *The New York Times Review of Books:* 12.
Fine, A., & Nya. (1997). *Therapeutic Recreation for Exceptional Children: Let Me In, I Want to Play.* Springfield, IL: Charles C. Thomas.
Finn, C. C. (2002). "Please Hear What I Am Not Saying." Available at http://www.poetrybycharlescfinn.com
Garbus, L. (2003). *Girlhood: Growing Up on the Inside.* Santa Monica, CA: Genius Entertainment.
Gerity, L. A. (1999). *Creativity and the Dissociative Patient: Puppets, Narrative and Art in the Treatment of Survivors of Childhood Trauma.* Philadelphia: Jessica Kingsley.
Goodman, G. (2007). *Reducing Hate Crimes and Violence Among American Youth: Creating Transformational Agency Through Critical Praxis.* New York: Peter Lang.
Hedge, J. (November 20, 2008). "Convenience Store Clerk Shot to Death." Atlanta: *NRI Pulse: The South's Premier South Asian Newspaper.*
Hendershott, J. (2009). *Reaching the Wounded Student.* Larchmont, NY: Eye on Education.
Hollowell, M. (2009). *The Forgotten Room: Inside a Public Alternative School for At-Risk Youth.* Lanham, MD: Lexington Books.
Jones, L., Isay, D., & Newman, L. (1998). *Our America: Life and Death on the South Side of Chicago.* New York: Simon and Schuster.
Keller, M. J. (1991). *Activities with Developmentally Disabled Elderly and Older Adults.* New York: Taylor and Francis.
Kotlowitz, A. (1992). *There Are No Children Here.* New York: Knopf.
Kramer, E. (1958). *Art Therapy in a Children's Community.* Springfield, IL: Charles C. Thomas.
Kramer, E. (1971). *Art As Therapy with Children.* New York: Schocken Books.
Malchiodi, C. (1997). *Breaking the Silence: Art Therapy with Children from Violent Homes.* Levittown, PA: Brunner/Mazel.
Meyers, S. (1949). *The Quiet One.* Narbeth, PA: Alpha Home Entertainment.
Miller, M., & Cook-Greuter, S. (Eds.) (1999). *Creativity, Spirituality, and Transcendence: Paths to Integrity and the Wisdom of the Mature Self.* New York: Ablex.
Venkatesh, S. (2008). *Gang Leader for a Day: A Rogue Sociologist Takes to the Streets.* New York: Penguin.

# Afterword

Rochelle Brock

School Sucks! *was born out of a conversation I had with my co-editor, Greg Goodman. After not having seen each other for a year, we spent several hours discussing life and our respective jobs. As with most academics in the education field, it did not take long for the conversation to turn to schools, schooling, and what we saw was happening to students. Greg is an education psychologist, and I am a teacher educator. But we share a commitment to critical pedagogy, social justice education and, of course, shedding light on what we see as the problems with schooling. We each address the problem in different ways that we hope will lead to the same outcome—schools and schooling that will truly educate for transformation.*

*I am a teacher educator. I work to foster the development of teachers who can positively affect the education of underserved populations—Black and Brown children. I have been doing this work for almost two decades, and it is where my passion lies. I know that every child has the capacity to succeed in school and in life. Yet, far too many children, especially those from low-income backgrounds, are placed at risk by school practices that are based on a sorting paradigm in which some students receive high-expectations instruction while the rest are relegated to lower-quality education and a significantly diminished future.*

*I understand that something must be done, and the change needs to be made much sooner than later. I understand that the issues are big and all-encompassing. I know the statistics on drop-out rates of urban students, the much too high turnover of urban superintendents, the lack of adequate funding of urban schools, the systemic racism that is ingrained in our society and educational system, unfair and unequal discipline prob-*

*lems, disparities of African American and Latino(a) students in Special and Gifted Education courses and the prison pipeline that schooling has become for some students.*

*Yes, I know the research, and I know that the preceding pages have given you at least a small part of a great body of educational research written from a critical educators' perspective. So in these last few pages I just want to share with you my hope for a better tomorrow; a hope I have to give to teachers. It will take a revolution to change much of what is happening in education, and I see signs of revolution in pockets throughout U.S. society. But for now, we must place our hope in transforming the teaching force even if it has to be one teacher at a time. So I present this letter to you—the men and women on the front line of the war to save our children by giving them the education they deserve.*

## Become the Safe Space for your Students

Dear Teacher:
What words and thoughts can I give you in this letter that will keep you strong in the face of the struggles and stresses you find yourself faced with as a classroom teacher? How can I turn a phrase that you can hold close to your heart as you attempt daily to unravel the intricacies of teaching, as you try to maintain the excitement you felt on your first day as a teacher, as you remember the pleasure you experienced as your deepest passions about education were confirmed? What advice can I offer to help you re-remember all you hoped to accomplish for and with your students? These feelings are so very easy to lose when you are faced with the political venom thrown at teachers from every side. I truly understand the strength needed just to remain hopeful. Nevertheless, hope is what you must find and hold tightly, for it is hope that will lead you and your students to wholeness. If nothing else, I want to help you realize the power you possess. You inspire! Understand the human vitality of your chosen profession is the gift you can share with your students, colleagues, and community.

> *The mediocre teacher tells. The good teacher explains. The superior teacher demonstrates. The great teacher inspires* —William Arthur Ward http://www.nea.org/grants/17417.htm

Imagine what you can do in the classroom when you inspire your students to dream of a different world. Imagine who you can become when you allow yourself to believe in a different type of education. When you shift the paradigm away from test, prescribed text, boring curriculum, which leaves out teacher and student creativity, imagine what your classroom can look like. Students are more likely to be engaged because they know and can feel the love you have for them. You must infuse Freire's concept of radical love into your teaching. Read carefully the words of Freire when he says "it is not possible to be a teacher without loving one's students, even realizing that love is not enough. It is not possible to be a teacher without loving teaching" (Freire, 1998, p. 15). Run to the nearest library or bookstore and get yourself a copy of *Pedagogy of the Oppressed* by Paulo Freire. Do not just read but allow yourself to embody his words so that you become the transformative teacher. Inspiration is where teaching must live.

> *One looks back with appreciation to the brilliant teachers, but with gratitude to those who touched our human feelings. The curriculum is so much necessary raw material, but warmth is the vital element for the growing plant and for the soul of the child.*—Carl Jung http://www.nea.org/grants/17417.htm

When you constantly strive to enrich your knowledge of pedagogy, sharpen your research skills and stretch the possibilities that exist for the acquisition and dissemination of learning for both you and your students, the possibilities are endless. Life experience has taught me that education can and, in fact, should positively affect the quality of life. Professional experience has taught me that teachers function as gatekeepers or as harbingers of the good news that education and empowerment bring to society. You must work to empower yourself as teachers and the students in your classroom. The power you possess cannot be taken lightly. My *Warrior Goddess*, otherwise known as Patricia Hill Collins (1990) says that empowerment, "involves the dimensions of knowledge, whether personal, cultural, or inquisitional, that perpetuate objectification and dehumanization...[and] individuals in subordinate groups become empowered when we understand and use those dimensions of our individual, group, and disciplinary ways of knowing that foster our humanity as fully human subjects" (p. 230).

I know that the eradication of institutionalized racism is dependent on the continuation of the struggle that grows out of education. Minoritized* students who are empowered are not only equipped to struggle, they also realize that resistance is paramount to their survival. If education does not generate struggle, survival becomes difficult. And I ask you: shouldn't we teach more than survival?

> *When discourse begins among people who have recently freed their souls, the language feels fragile—the fragility that comes when we talk about dreams in a society obsessed with practicality or about community in a society obsessed with competition or about risk taking in a society obsessed with playing it safe.*—Parker, 2007, p. 182

I believe that education provides care for students' being when teachers develop a pedagogy that teaches love of self and others, inner strength, humanity and

* The definition of minoritized discusses the power relations within a given social situation. According to Dei (2006) the term refers to the ways "groups are denied access to power and their agency is structurally constrained by local and national politics" (p. 94). The term is more empowering and less subjective than minority, which can denote powerless.

humanness, survival and struggle, and hope and knowledge. Joyce King (1994) declares that "the potential—to exist fully in alignment with one's human spirit—is already present in each of us" (p. 270) and a task of education is "to help us learn hopeful principles of human existence" (p. 273). Teaching can afford both you as the teacher and your students a soul-freeing liberatory education that nourishes well-being in the individual and helps persons reconnect with their humanity. When education does not provide persons with the right tools to tap into their humanity, it is impossible for hope to survive. A "freeing legacy" in a curriculum of hope affords the acceptance of the humanity of everyone without being entangled in the web of proving legitimacy of any individual or group. Teach your students to dream and then help them make those dreams come true. Remember that *"the art of teaching is the art of assisting discovery"* —Mark Van Doren http://www.nea.org/grants/17417.htm

> *And those who recognize, or begin to recognize, themselves as oppressed must be among the developers of this pedagogy. No pedagogy which is truly liberating can remain distant from the oppressed by treating them as unfortunates and by presenting for their emulation models from among the oppressors. The oppressed must be their own example in the struggle for their redemption.*—Freire, 1970, p. 39

You must become a revolutionary in the classroom and fight to teach your students more than the prescribed curriculum. Instead you must equip them with knowledge about the world, about life, about themselves. Teach them to think critically, to see and understand the obstacles unequal power relations have placed in front of them. We do not live in a meritocratic society, and students must understand the structural inequality of the American educational systems. The myth of equal opportunity serves as a smoke screen through which the losers will be led to blame themselves and be seen by others as getting what they deserve. When people believe they are worthless, that they are the problem, their actions will be futile. Those same people will be powerhouses of action when given something to believe in, when provided the knowledge to deconstruct and then to reconstruct their world. Students will continue to believe in their own biological and cultural inferiority if their teachers perpetuate the false knowledge of race, class and gender inequalities found in American society. Truth begets power and power begets freedom of mind.

> *The problem of holding the Negro down, therefore, is easily solved. When you control a man's thinking you do not have to worry about his actions. You do not have to tell him not to stand here or go yonder. He will find his "proper place" and will stay in it. You do not need to send him to the back door. He will go without being told. In fact, if there is no back door, he will cut one for his special benefit. His education makes it necessary.* —Woodson, 1933, p. xiii

Although Carter G. Woodson wrote those words in 1933, they are still true today. We can replace the word Negro with African American, Latino, poor white, etc., and the meaning of the passage remains. When we change in a radical way how we as teachers think about what we do in the class, then we can begin to change the words of Woodson. Teach your students with passion and truthfulness. Teach them to think and act in critical ways. Instill in them love of learning and importantly love of self. Go outside of the curriculum and embrace a pedagogy of life. Bring the world and the lives of your students into the classroom and allow them to transform you, the students and the educational environment. Talk to your students and listen to them when they talk to you. Trust that they are the ones who can lead us to develop a new paradigm in education. And remember that in order for education to be liberating to any oppressed people, the people must be central to the design and implementation of their own educational policy.

> *A dedicated and well-informed teacher [brings] a group of students to life with her knowledge, passion for learning and her ability to engage them in the process of teaching themselves and others.*—Kincheloe, 2004, p. 4

Our profession is under attack. Some of those attacks we deserve but many we do not. I say let knowledge be your shield. Do not let your last methods class be the end of your own learning. Go beyond the often superficial professional development classes given by your school and district. Stay informed, read, learn, and expand your thinking while you teach the students in your care. You must commit to going beyond what is expected of you as a teacher by constantly working to enhance your pedagogical knowledge. When we carry our shields we can fend off many of the attacks, because we know we are on top of our game. We know our classrooms and what we are giving our students. Earlier I said you had power as teachers but remember with power comes responsibility. You have accepted the responsibility of educating children and being a significant part of building a better society.

> *Nothing is impossible when we work in solidarity with love, respect, and justice as our guiding lights."*—J. Kincheloe, 2004, p. 3

Yes, teaching is hard and stressful and aggravating and thankless. Yes, at times you have to deal with inept administrators, a standards craze that borders on fanaticism, students that don't care, and parents that should never have been allowed to have or raise children. I know the problems that make you come home at night and question your career choice. Stay far away from that negative place; run like hell until you can see or remember the good. Think about those administrators that care. The folks that in spite of what they are given to do by the state still try to find ways to have an invigorating environment for the students and the teachers. I want you to think about how you can subvert the standards craze imposed on you and students. Remember and feel again the joy you felt when you finally got through to that one student who made your life miserable. The quote above is what I try to live by and what I teach my students. Allow yourself to love who you are, what you do and the children you teach. Respect who you are as a teacher and respect the children you teach. Let justice for all become the purpose through which you do everything, and I believe change will happen. Many years ago one of my students told me I was teaching them to be ripples in a pond. She said that when she made a change in her classroom with her students the effect was not always big, but like a ripple it may start off small but it continuously becomes larger. Stand tall and be proud!

## References

Dei, G. (2006). Racism in Canadian contexts: Exploring public & private issues in the educational system. In Wisdom Tettey and Korbla P. Puplampu (eds.) *African diaspora in Canada: Negotiating identity and belonging.* (Africa: Missing Voices) (pp. 94–110) Calgary: University of Calgary Press.

Freire, P. (1998). *Teachers as cultural workers:Letters to those who dare teach.* Translated by Donaldo Macedo, Dale Koike, and Alexandre Oliveira. Boulder, CO: Westview Press.

Freire, P. (1970). *Pedagogy of the oppressed.* New York: Continuum.

Hale-Benson, J. (1986). *Black children: Their roots, culture, and learning styles.* Baltimore: The Johns Hopkins University Press.

Hill Collins, P. (1990). *Black feminist thought: Knowledge, consciousness and the politics of empowerment.* New York: Routledge.

Kincheloe, J. (2004). *Critical pedagogy primer.* New York: Peter Lang.

———. (2008). The Freire Project. www.freireproject.org/content-61. (accessed February 19, 2011)

King, J. E. (1994). Being the soul-freeing substance: A legacy of hope and humanity. In M. J. Shujaa (Ed.), *Too much schooling, too little education: A paradox of Black life in White societies* (pp. 269–294). Trenton, NJ: Africa Free World Press.

Ladson-Billings, B. (1992). Reading between the lines and beyond the pages: A culturally relevant approach to literacy teaching. *Theory into Practice, 31*(4), 312–320.

Palmer, P. J. (2007). *The courage to teach: Exploring the inner landscape of a teacher's life. 10th Anniversary Edition.* San Francisco: Jossey-Bass.

Woodson, C. G. (1933). *The mis-education of the Negro.* New York: Associated Publishers.

# Contributors

**Floyd Beachum** is the Bennett Professor of Urban School Leadership at Lehigh University. He is also an associate professor and program director for the Educational Leadership program in the College of Education. He has authored several peer-reviewed articles on social justice, urban education, and moral and ethical leadership in the *Journal of School Leadership, Multicultural Learning and Teaching, Urban Education,* and *The Journal of Cases in Educational Leadership*. With Carlos McCray, he has published *Cultural Collision and Collusion: Reflections on Hip-hop Culture, Values and Schools* (Peter Lang, 2011).

**Jane Bean-Folkes** is a researcher and practitioner in the department of Language, Literacy & Special Education at Rowan University. She spends her days working in K-8 classrooms with students, teachers, and administrators from diverse backgrounds in high-poverty areas of New York City and across the United States. Her other publications include "The Why Behind Teacher Research" (*Childhood Education*, 2011) and "Culturally Diverse Children's Books for Your Classroom Library" (*NCTE*, School Talk, 2011).

**Rochelle Brock** is an associate professor of Urban Education and executive director of the Urban Teacher Education Program at Indiana University Northwest in Gary, Indiana. She is also editor of *The International Journal of Critical Pedagogy* and series editor of the Black Studies and Critical Thinking series (Peter Lang Publishing). She has written books and articles on white privilege, teacher identity, critical pedagogy, African American popular culture, and Black feminist theory.

**Shanesha R. F. Brooks-Tatum** is a postdoctoral research and instruction fellow at the Atlantic University Center Robert W. Woodruff Library. "The Holy Hip-Hop Movement: Negotiating Religious and Secular Politics in Atlanta and Detroit," her manuscript-in-progress, examines sacred-secular tensions and artistic techniques in Christian hip-hop and spoken-word performance poetry. Her teaching and research interests include Black popular culture, women's and gender studies, U.S. and Black literature, Black religion and spirituality, and performance studies. She has published works on Christian hip-hop, spoken-word poetry, and Black popular culture, and is an alumna of the University of California, Berkeley and the University of Michigan Ann Arbor.

**Bettie Ray Butler** is an assistant professor of urban education in the Department of Middle, Secondary, and K-12 Education at the University of North Carolina, Charlotte. Dr. Butler's research interests focus primarily on education policy with specific attention to issues of equity, representation, and achievement among underrepresented student populations.

**Terah Venzant Chambers** received her Ph.D. in educational policy studies from the University of Illinois at Urbana-Champaign. At the current time, Dr. Chambers is an assistant professor in the Department of Educational Administration and Human Resource Development at Texas A&M University. Her research interest includes the influence of African American students' experiences in tracked schools. Specifically, she asks what are the benefits and what are the costs of high academic achievement and school engagement for students of color?

**Alfred W. DeFreece Jr** is an assistant professor of sociology at Roosevelt University in Chicago. He holds a B.A. from Hunter College, City University of New York, and earned his Ph.D. in sociology from the University of Michigan, Ann Arbor in spring 2011. Specializing in race, youth cultural production, and urban education, he teaches courses on race and ethnicity, research methods, sociology of education, and urban sociology. His research interests include youth development, qualitative methods, racial ideology, and philosophy and practice of place-based education. He is on the advisory board for the Mansfield Institute for Social Justice and Transformation at Roosevelt and serves as a co-founding member of the Boggs Educational Center in Detroit, Michigan.

**Julia Ellis** is a professor in the Department of Elementary Education at the University of Alberta and the anglophone editor for the *Canadian Journal of Education*. Her books include: *Caring for kids in communities: Using mentorship, peer support, and student leadership in schools* and *Teaching from understanding:*

*Teacher as interpretive inquirer*. She leads a website for mentorship programs for children and youth: http://www.mentorship.ualberta.ca/

**Susan Fitzsimmons** is an associate professor in the Education Department at the University of Winnipeg, in Manitoba, Canada. Her research interests include interpretive inquiry focused on understanding the nature of aesthetic experience through exploring the perspectives of adolescent girls' poetry. Current interests include aesthetic learning spaces, engaging in teacher research, and exploring arts-based approaches to research.

**Larry F. Forthun** is an assistant professor of human development in the Department of Family, Youth, and Community Sciences at the University of Florida, Gainesville. His teaching and research interests include the examination of parent-adolescent relationships and their impact on healthy psycho-social development and risky/delinquent behaviors. He is a Certified Family Life Educator (CFLE).

**Susan Fuhrman** is the $10^{th}$ president of Teachers College, Columbia University, and president of the National Academy of Education. Prior to this, she served for 11 years as dean of the University of Pennsylvania's Graduate School of Education, where she was also the George and Diane Weiss Professor of Education. She was at Rutgers' Eagleton Institute of Politics and a professor of education policy before joining the University of Pennsylvania. In addition to her deanship and teaching, she has been chair and director of the management committee of the consortium for Policy Research in Education (CPRE) since 1985. Dr. Fuhrman is a former vice president of the American Education Research Association, a member of the National Coalition on Asia and International Studies in the Schools, and she serves on the board of The Fund for New Jersey. She has a B.A. and M.A. in History from Northwestern University and a Ph.D. in Political Economy from Columbia University.

**Greg S. Goodman** is an associate professor of education at Clarion University of Pennsylvania. He is the co-editor of Pennsylvania's State System of Higher Education and Frederick Douglass Collaborative's *Making Connections* journal and Peter Lang Publishing's Educational Psychology: Critical Pedagogical Perspectives series. His recent books include *The Educational Psychology Reader* (2010) and *The Outdoor Classroom* (2008).

**Howard P. Hanson** was born in Jamaica. He currently teaches World Languages at McCaskey High School in Lancaster, PA. He has worked as a consultant to the Massachusetts Department of Education—Chapter 636 Voluntary Desegregation Programs, and he has taught as a lecturer at the University of Zimbabwe. A graduate of Earlham College, he has been a mover, construction worker, artist, designer, zoo keeper, business manager, and poet. He has two grandsons, and he resides in Lancaster, PA.

**Adriel A. Hilton** is the executive assistant to the president and assistant secretary of the Board of Directors at Upper Iowa University. He has worked as a public policy fellow at the Greater Baltimore Chamber of Commerce. Dr. Hilton is a graduate of the Higher Education Ph.D. program at Morgan State University.

**Mary Hollowell** is associate professor of education at Clayton State University. She is a former science teacher and a museum director of education. She has worked in a zoo for endangered species, for the National Park Service, and in a marine biology lab.

**Christopher Knaus** studies and teaches in urban schools, working with African American and Latino youth to understand the silencing impact of racially biased curriculum and pedagogy. He earned his doctorate in multicultural education and policy from the University of Washington and has published numerous articles as well as poetry about the role of racism in shaping urban education. Dr. Knaus is currently Associate Professor in the College of Education at California State University East Bay where he works to develop educator pipelines that identify and nurture culturally responsive urban educators of color.

**Chance W. Lewis** (Ph.D. in educational leadership/teacher education from Colorado State University) is the Carol Grotnes Belk Distinguished Professor and Endowed Chair of Urban Education at the University of North Carolina at Charlotte, where he also serves as Executive Director of the Urban Education Collaborative. Dr. Lewis is the author or editor of six books, most recently *Yes We Can!: Improving Urban Schools through Innovative Educational Reform* (2011). For his distinguished work, he has earned numerous awards and honors.

**Jeff McCombie** is a certified school psychologist with extensive experience in education including gifted education, special education, and alternative education. Jeff has served schools and institutions as a senior trainer of Response Ability Pathways (RAP) and Life Space Crisis Intervention (LSCI). His current interests include bridge, golf, children, and grandchildren.

**Carlos R. McCray** is an associate professor at Fordham University in the Graduate School of Education. He has published in both the *Journal of School Leadership* and the *International Journal of Urban Educational Leadership*. With Floyd Beachum, he has recently published *Cultural Collision and Collusion: Reflections on Hip-Hop Culture, Values and Schools* (Peter Lang, 2011).

**Luis F. Mirón** is a well-known speaker and writer. Dr. Mirón is the author of *Resisting Discrimination: Affirmative Strategies for Principals and Teachers*, and with Mickey Lauria, *Urban Schools: The New Social Spaces of Resistance*.

**Donna Moye** is an art teacher with over thirty years of experience. She has taught in both mainstream and alternative public schools. In retirement she plans to weave, make pots, and design jewelry.

**Caroline Payne** is currently completing her Ph.D. thesis on the impact of sex education programs on contraceptive use among sexually active emerging adults. Her other research interests include youth policy and eating disorders.

**Christine Sleeter** is professor emerita at California State University Monterey Bay, where she was a founding faculty member. She has been a visiting professor at San Francisco State University, Victoria University in New Zealand, San Jose State University , and the University of Washington, Seattle. She serves as president of the national Association of Multicultural Education. Dr. Sleeter has published over 100 journal articles and book chapters, Her recent books include *Doing Multicultural Education for Achievement and Equity* (with Carl Grant, 2007) and *Critical Multiculturalism: Theory and Praxis* (with Stephen May, 2010).

**Jan Small-McGinley** is a consultant with the Edmonton Public Schools in the area of Special Education. Her work involves assessment, consultation, and providing educational and behavioral programming for students with severe developmental disabilities. Jan has presented at numerous conferences on the following topics: transition planning, curricular modification, proactive behavior programming, social interaction skills, and advocacy.

**Ebony Elizabeth Thomas** is an assistant professor of reading, language, and literature in the division of Teacher Education at Wayne State University. A former Detroit public school teacher, her research and critical interests include the teaching of African American literatures in the Obama era, English language arts classroom interaction, adolescent literatures and literacies, and classroom discourse analysis. She has previously published her work in *English Journal*, *The ALAN Review*, and *Sankofa: A Journal of African Children's and Young Adult Literature* as well as the books *A Narrative Compass: Stories That Guide Women's Lives* (University of Illinois Press, 2009) and *The Pressures of Teaching* (Kaplan, 2010). She is an alumna of Florida A&M University, Wayne State University, and the University of Michigan, Ann Arbor.

**Rasheedah S Woodard** is a graduate of UC Berkeley and has been a part of the Third Root production team since 2007. She is currently a student in the pre-health postbaccalaureate program at SFSU in preparation for medical school. As a Black feminist healer, activist, and educator, her social science and physical science backgrounds converge to inform her radical activism around the ways the intersectionality of race, class, gender, and sexuality oppressions impact the health of Black and Brown women. She firmly believes that we cannot improve the health of Black and Brown communities without collectively fighting for their liberation and decolonization.

# Index

Educational
PSYCHOLOGY

## Critical Pedagogical Perspectives

Greg S. Goodman, *General Editor*

*Educational Psychology: Critical Pedagogical Perspectives* is a series of relevant and dynamic works by scholars and practitioners of critical pedagogy, critical constructivism, and educational psychology. Reflecting a multitude of social, political, and intellectual developments prompted by the mentor Paulo Freire, books in the series enliven the educator's process with theory and practice that promote personal agency, social justice, and academic achievement. Often countering the dominant discourse with provocative and yet practical alternatives, *Educational Psychology: Critical Pedagogical Perspectives* speaks to educators on the forefront of social change and those who champion social justice.

For further information about the series and submitting manuscripts, please contact:

Dr. Greg S. Goodman
Department of Education
Clarion University
Clarion, Pennsylvania
*ggoodman@clarion.edu*